A CONTEMPLATIVE ANGLER

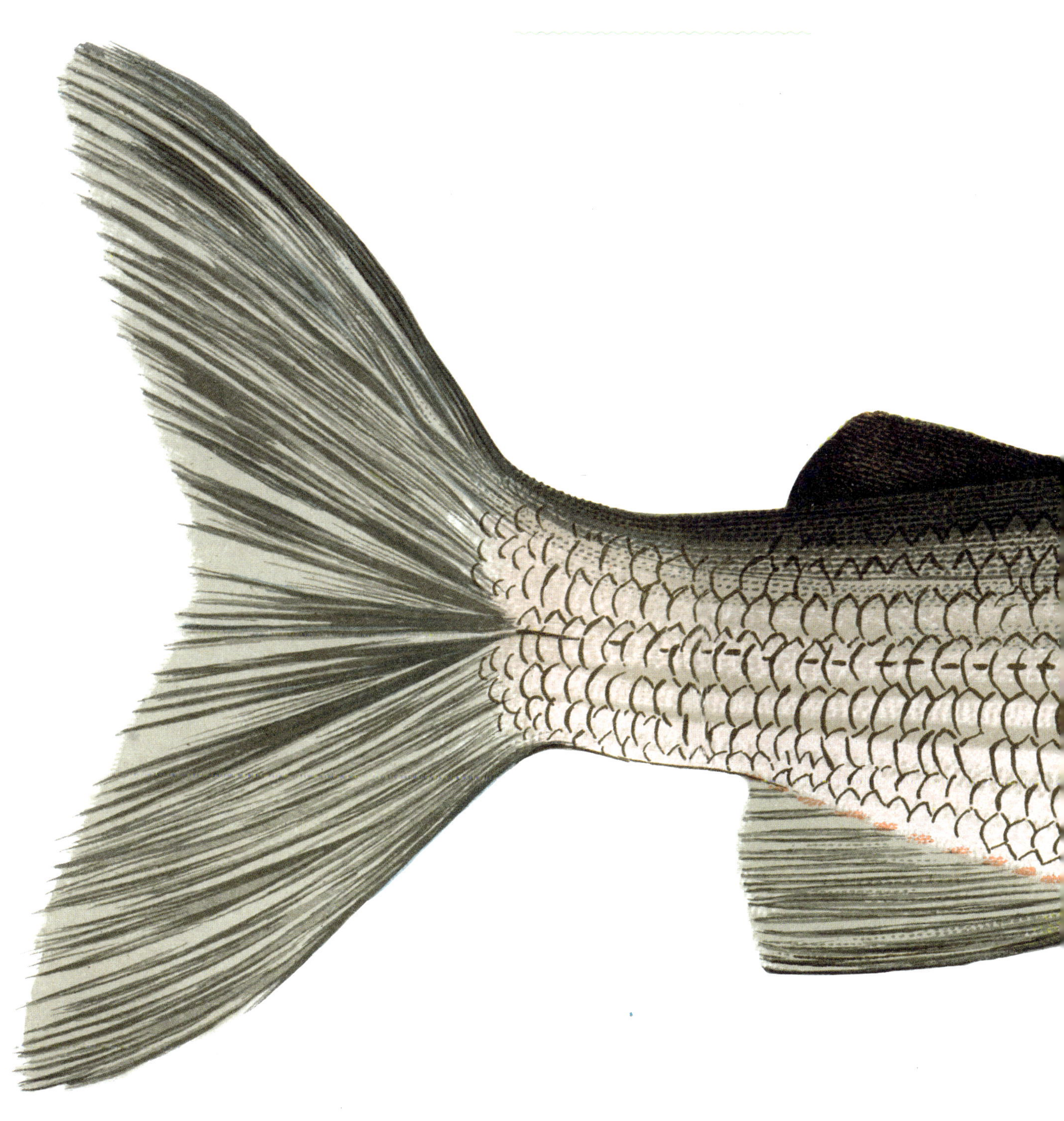

A CONTEMPLATIVE

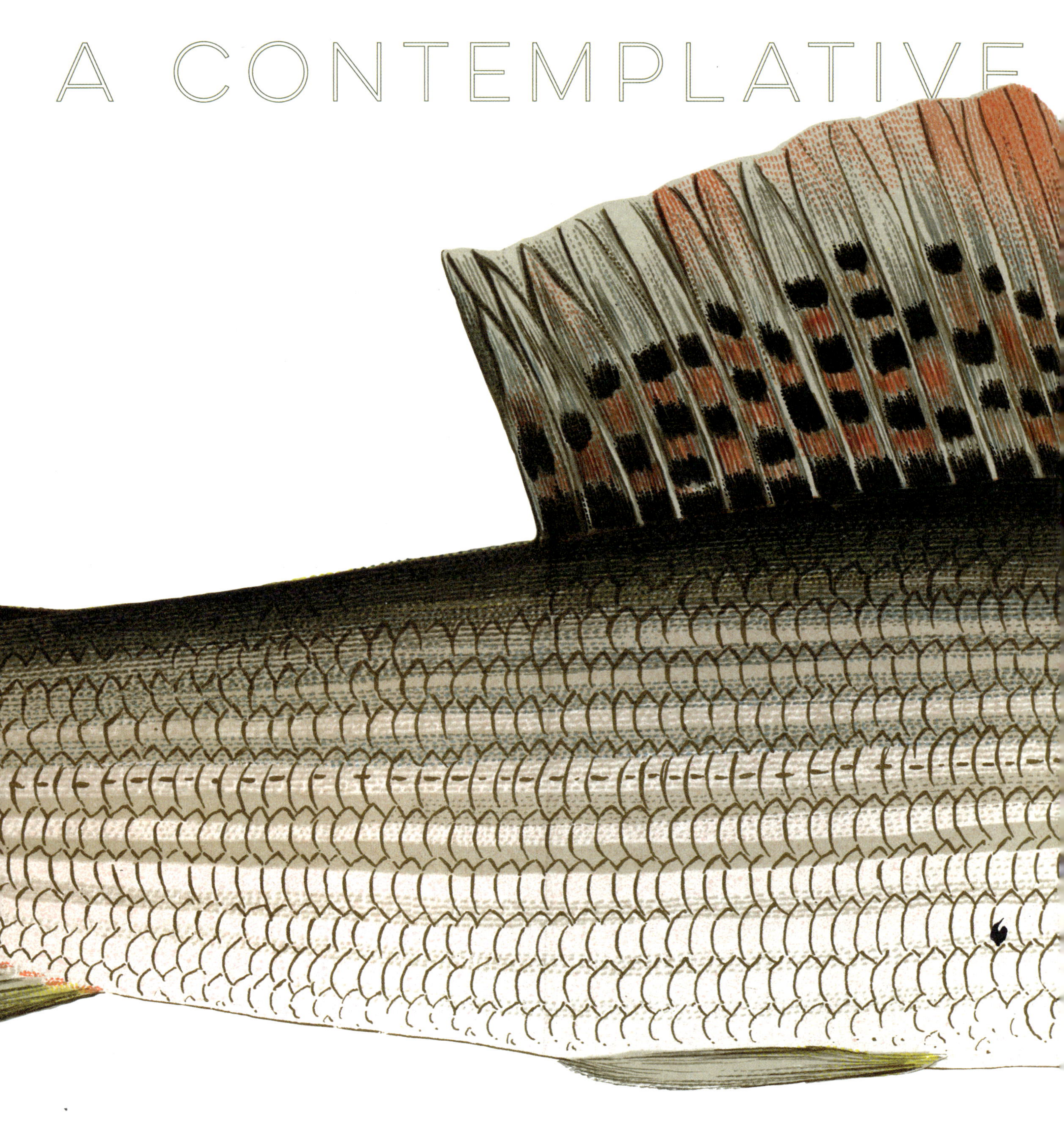

ANGLER

Selections from the BRUCE P. DANCIK COLLECTION *of Angling Books*

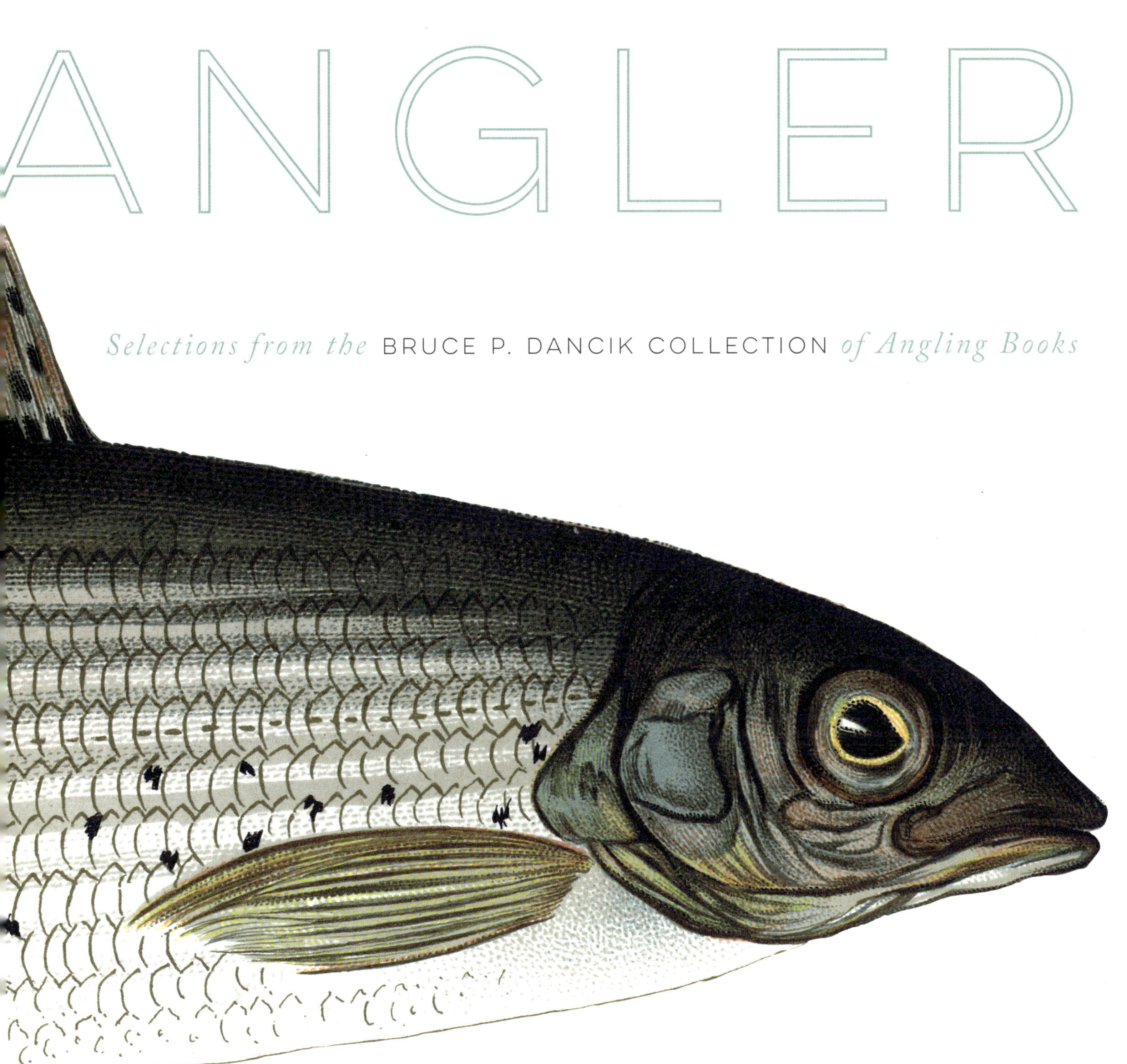

JUSTIN HANISCH

Bruce Peel Special Collections, University of Alberta

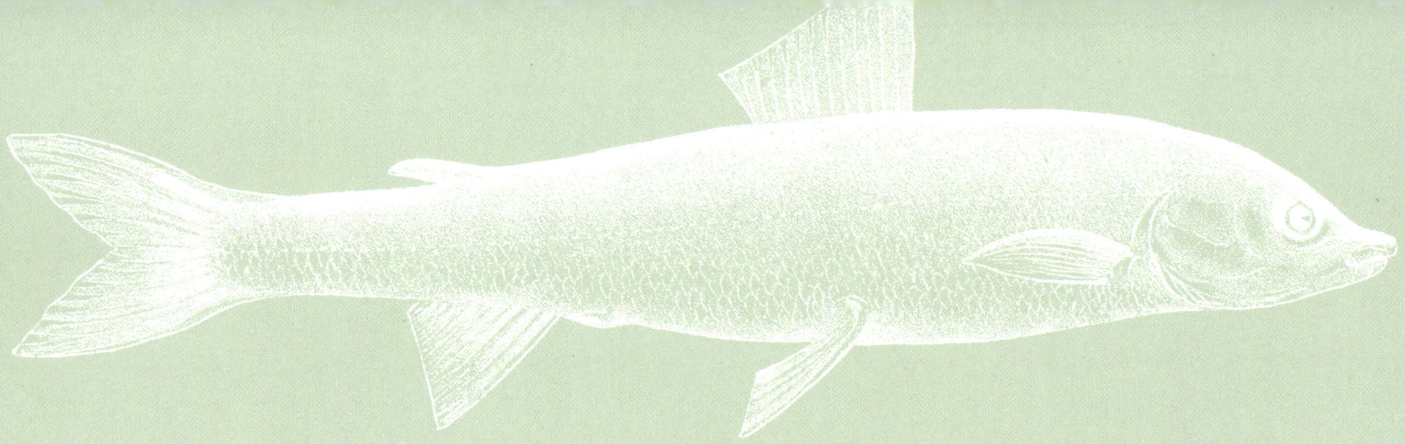

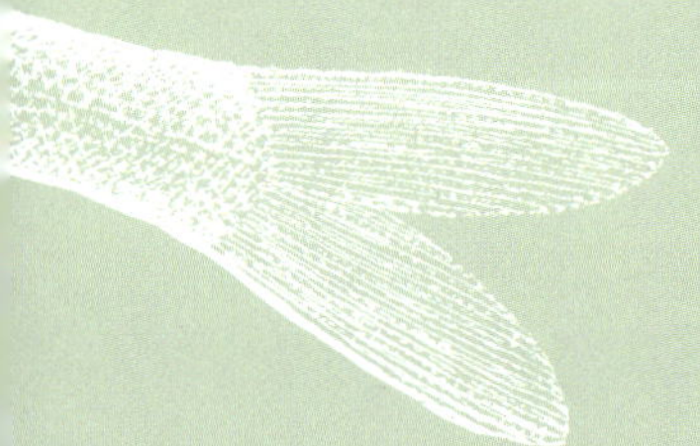

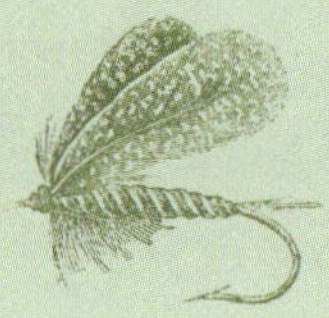

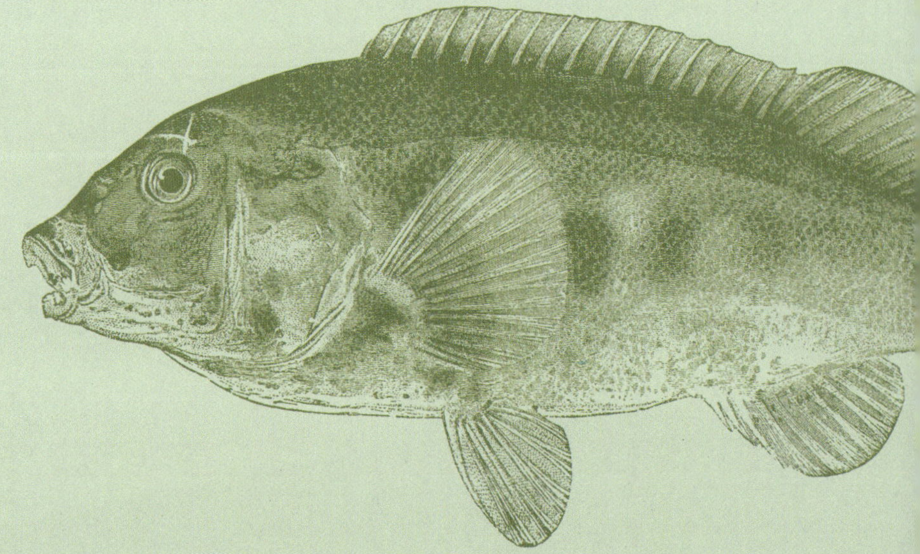

Bruce Peel Special Collections
B7 Rutherford South, University of Alberta
Edmonton, Alberta, Canada T6G 2J4

LIBRARY AND ARCHIVES CANADA CATALOGUING IN PUBLICATION

Bruce Peel Special Collections, issuing body, host institution
A contemplative angler: selections from the Bruce P. Dancik collection of angling books / by Justin Hanisch; foreword by Bruce Dancik.

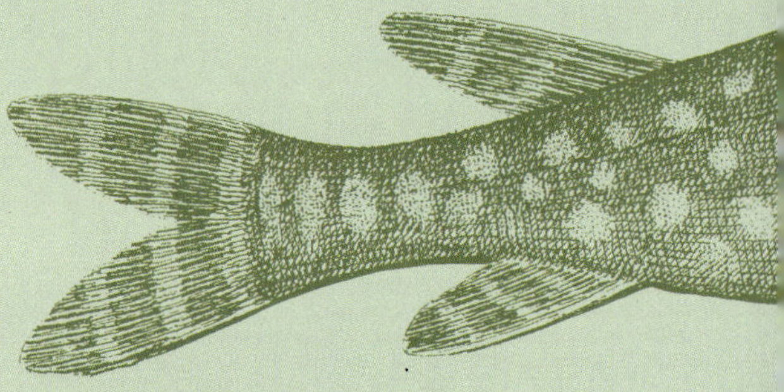

Catalogue of an exhibition held at the Bruce Peel Special Collections from October 15, 2018 to January 31, 2019.
Includes bibliographical references.
ISBN 978-1-55195-405-9 (hardcover)

1. Dancik, Bruce P.—Library—Exhibitions. 2. Bruce Peel Special Collections—Exhibitions. 3. Fishing—Bibliography—Exhibitions. 4. Rare books—Alberta—Edmonton—Bibliography—Exhibitions. 5. Exhibition catalogs. I. Hanisch, Justin, 1984-, author II. Title.

Z5971.A1B78 2018   016.79912   C2018-903794-6

Printed in Canada

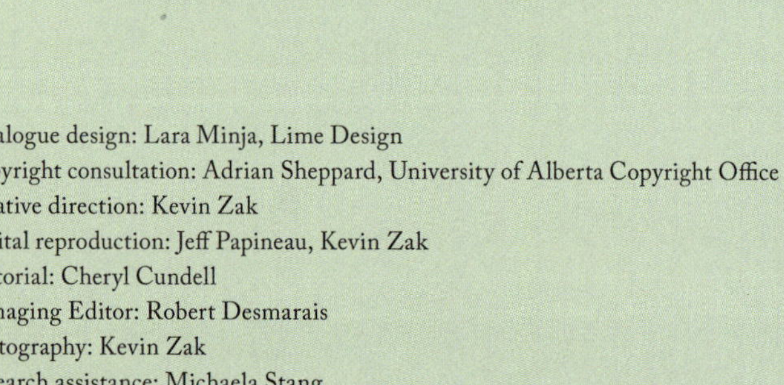

Catalogue design: Lara Minja, Lime Design
Copyright consultation: Adrian Sheppard, University of Alberta Copyright Office
Creative direction: Kevin Zak
Digital reproduction: Jeff Papineau, Kevin Zak
Editorial: Cheryl Cundell
Managing Editor: Robert Desmarais
Photography: Kevin Zak
Research assistance: Michaela Stang
Special assistance: Linda Quirk, Cori Sanderson, Carolyn Morgan

First edition, first printing, 2018
Printed by Friesens

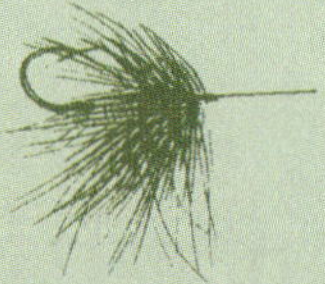

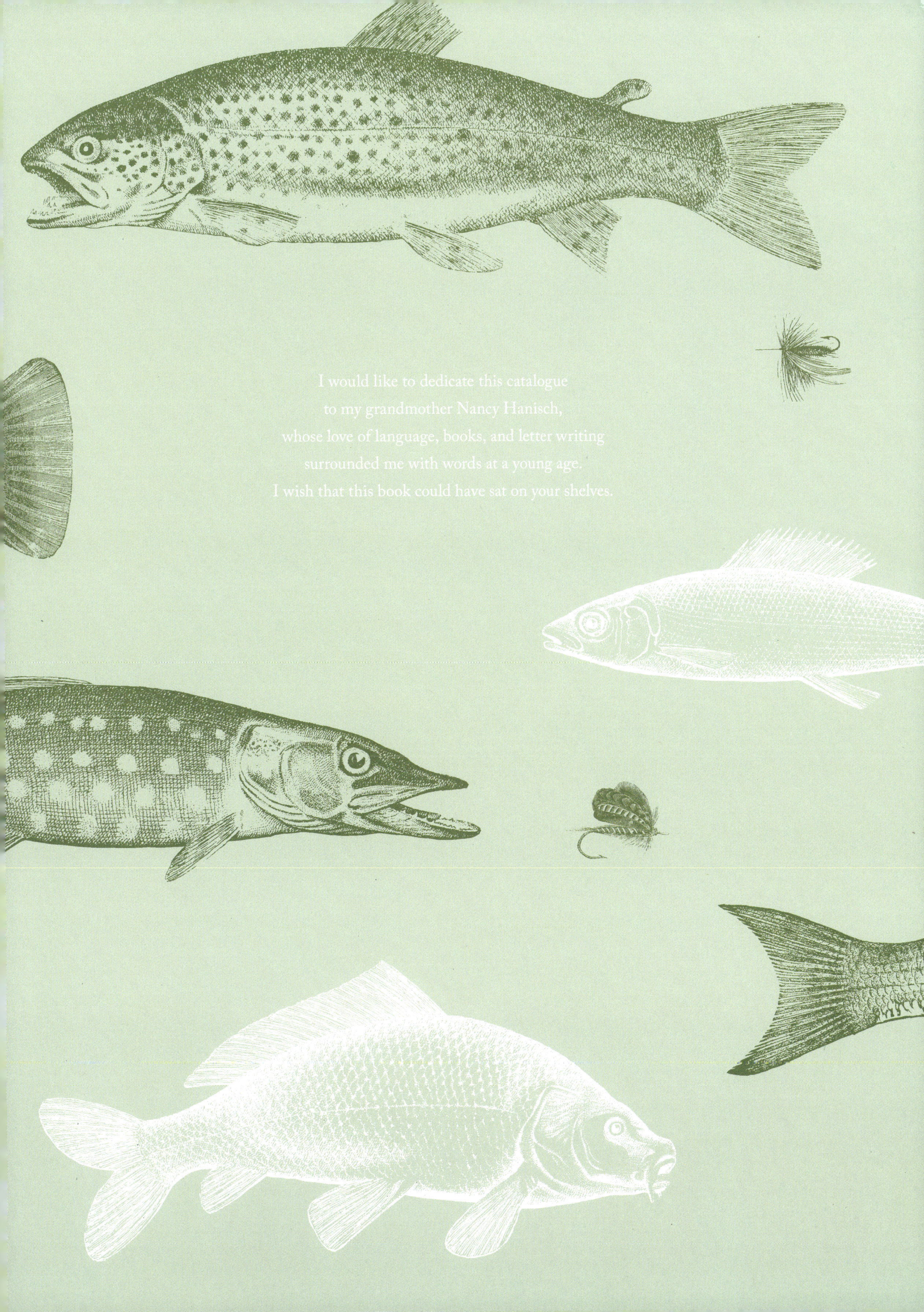

I would like to dedicate this catalogue
to my grandmother Nancy Hanisch,
whose love of language, books, and letter writing
surrounded me with words at a young age.
I wish that this book could have sat on your shelves.

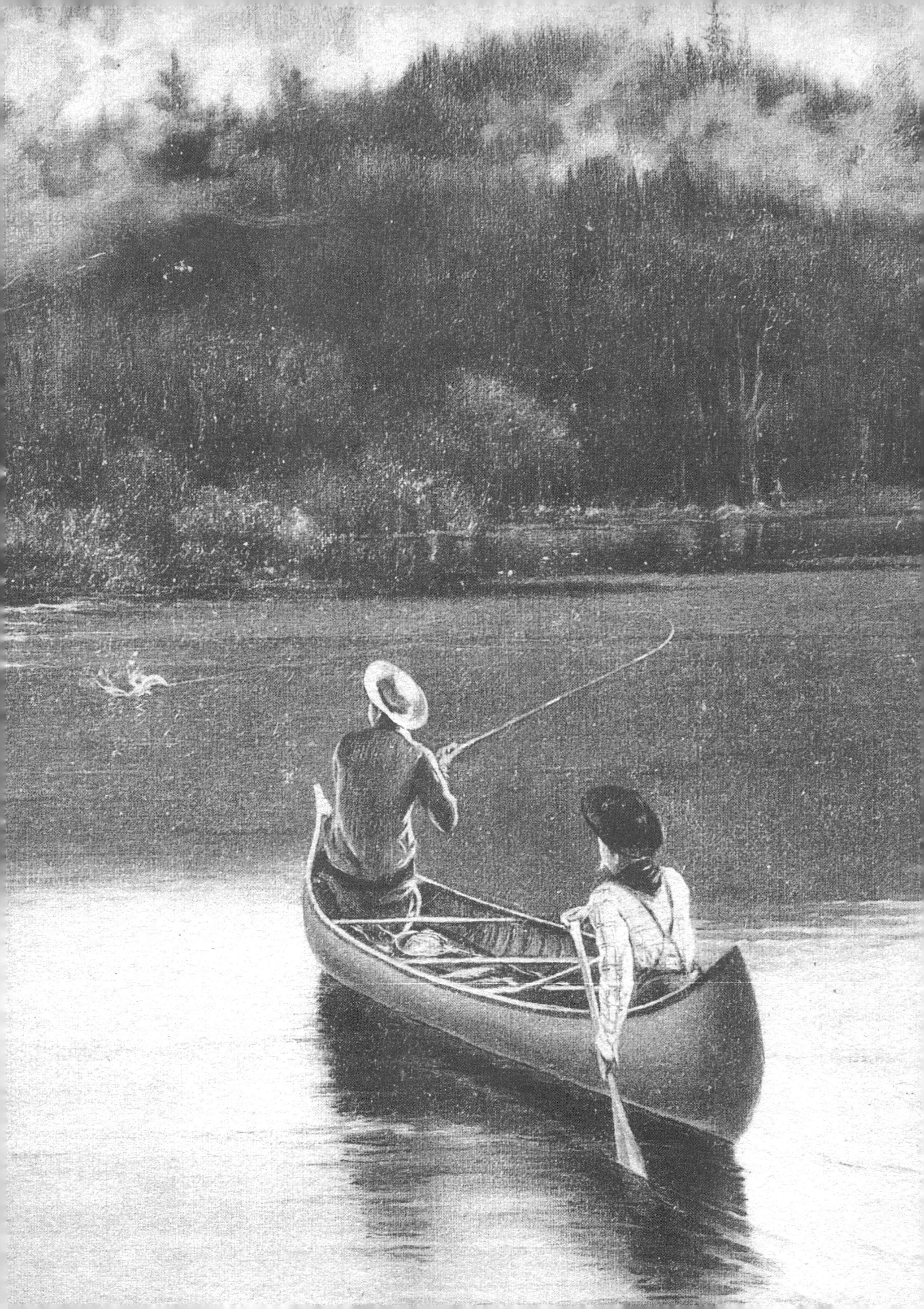

CONTENTS

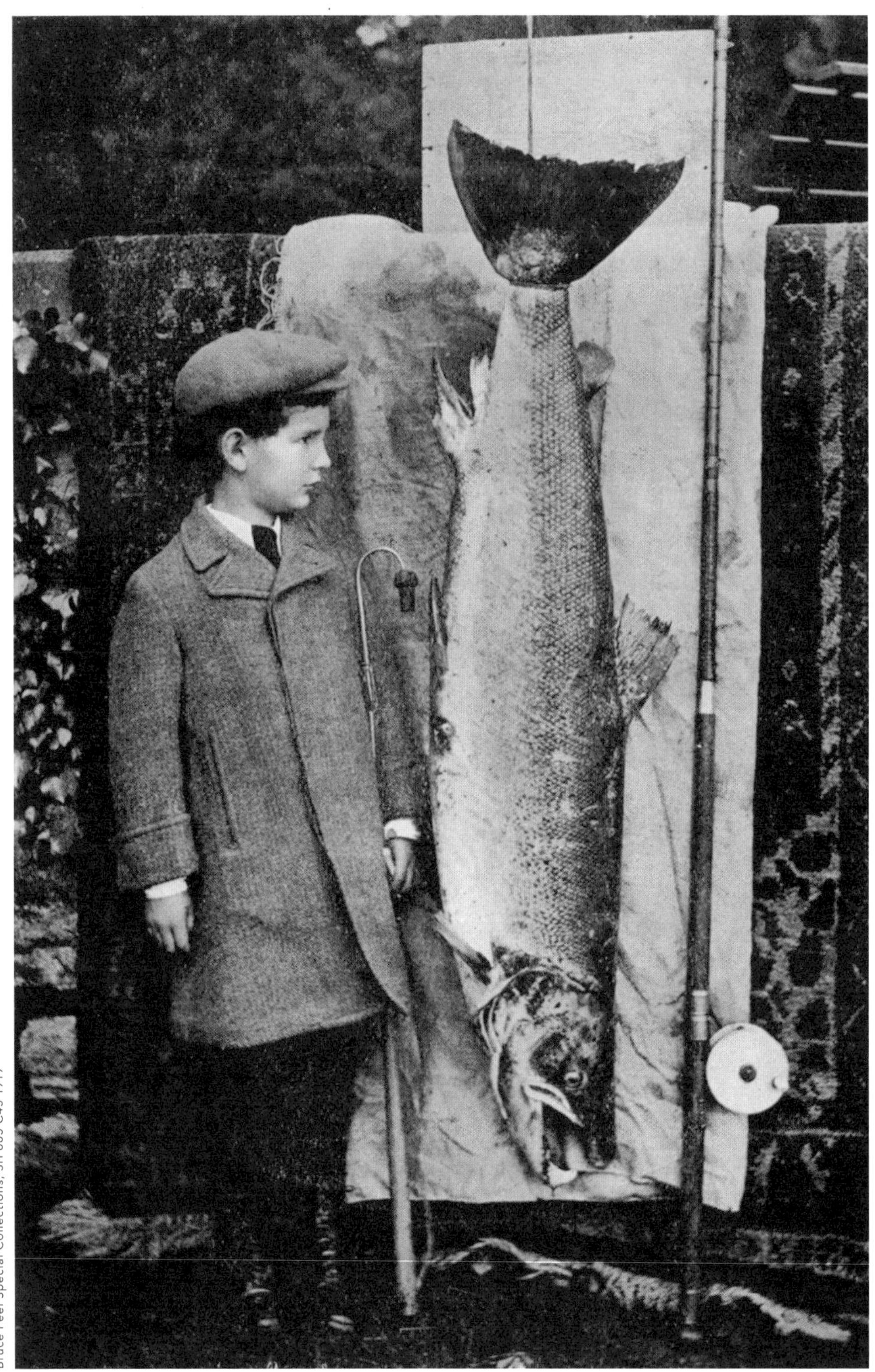

Bruce Peel Special Collections, SH 685 C45 1919

FOREWORD

BRUCE P. DANCIK

GROWING UP WITH BOOKS AND FISHING

MY LIFE IN CANADA and my academic career were shaped by my early experiences. I was raised in suburban Chicago and northern Wisconsin by a mother who, among other things, was a voracious reader, and a father whose favourite pastimes were gardening, being outdoors, and angling.

My mother was a loyal user of the public library near our home in Berwyn, Illinois, and the library near our summer home about 15 miles from the town of Crivitz in northeastern Wisconsin. She borrowed and read so many books that she would look at the list of library card numbers recorded in a particular book to see if she had already borrowed and read it. She read many books in various subject areas, especially fiction, and particularly mysteries. I was an avid reader even before entering school and tagged along with her to the library to look over the books, carefully select some, and borrow them to read. In my early years, there were children's books, then books for boys, and gradually a more focused shift to outdoor, natural history, and angling books.

EARLY DAYS ON THE PESHTIGO RIVER

MY FAVOURITE PASTIMES in the summers were wandering around the forests and fishing, usually with my father and grandfather, along with other adult friends, in the area of our summer home outside of Crivitz. My grandparents, mother, sister, and brother, and I spent the entire summer at our summer home, while my father would spend a few weeks there, then go back to running his real estate business in the Chicago suburbs for a couple of weeks, come back to the summer home, and so on for the entire summer and into early autumn. In addition to wandering around the forests and fishing, I had planted 1000 trees, mostly eastern white pine (*Pinus strobus*) and some balsam fir (*Abies balsamea*), in the openings on the property, which otherwise had been a scattered woodland of mostly northern pin oak (*Quercus ellipsoidalis*) and jack pine (*Pinus banksiana*) on very sandy soil. We never made it back to school for the first week in September, as there would be pleas to not return to Chicago—"Oh, can't we stay for just a few more days?"

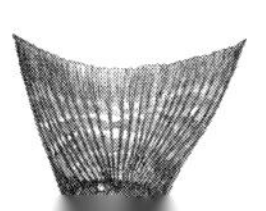

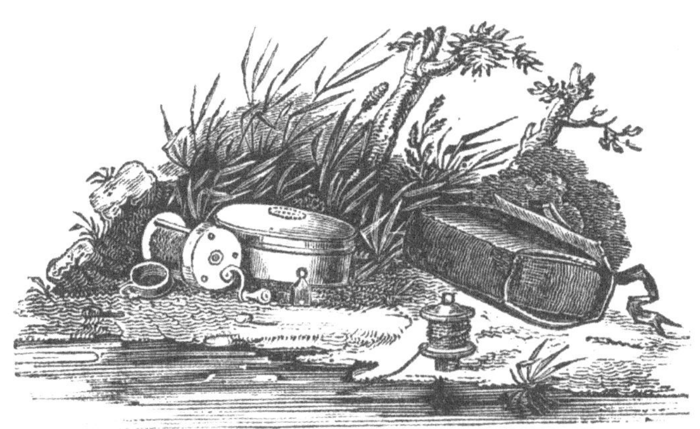

During the long summers, we often walked just five minutes to our boats, which we had moored on a small bay of High Falls Flowage on the Peshtigo River. This was a reservoir adjacent to our family property, where we would fish for bass, walleye, pike, perch, bluegills, and crappies. We also fished slightly more distant waters: the Peshtigo River itself, Thunder River, Rat River, and Otter Creek for brook, brown, and rainbow trout. There were many other streams, rivers, and lakes in the area—and we fished them all! Streams like the Thunder River had a mix of pools and rapids, and all drained off the upland area of north-central Wisconsin to Green Bay and Lake Michigan.

When my father was away in Illinois, my grandfather and I either fished the flowage within walking and rowing distance or accepted the invitations of Ray Engle, the proprietor of the nearby tavern, to come with him, and we drove to another lake or reservoir. Ray's wife or mother would handle the business, while my grandfather and I went fishing with Ray. Neither my father nor my grandfather was a serious fly-fisher, so I learned how to cast and fly-fish from books and magazines. I had observed fish taking insects off or above the surface of the water, I hadn't had much success fishing for such fish with other tackle, and the photos of fly casting looked graceful. Fly fishing was enjoyable and effective. That effectiveness turned me into a catch-and-release advocate rather early on.

My mother had the rule that those who caught the fish had to clean them, which we found quite fair and reasonable. Then she came up with a new rule (probably while rummaging in the freezer to find something): those who caught the fish had to eat them. I liked fish, so that seemed reasonable and fair, too—until I looked in the freezer one day and realized that I'd have to eat fish every day for the next year, and that problem would continue to get worse. What could the solution be? Don't bring the fish home! Thus began a practice that became reinforced with observation and learning that we couldn't just keep harvesting fish like we had been if we wanted to have fish species survive and thrive. It became easy for me to accept the philosophy and practice of Lee Wulff and others who had preached that the life of a trout or salmon was too valuable to future generations of fishers and to ecosystems to allow unrestricted harvest.

During those years before university, I wanted to fish whenever I could, especially after I discovered trout fishing and fly fishing. I even

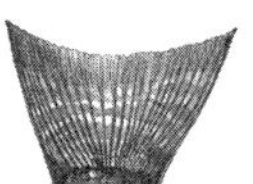

"WHAT AN IDYLLIC EXISTENCE FOR A BOY WHO LIKED THE OUT-OF-DOORS"

avoided the periodic ride into the town of Crivitz, unless I absolutely needed a haircut. My folks would typically drop me off at a favourite stretch of the nearby North Branch of the Thunder River, and pick me up later after they had done their shopping and gone to a favourite supper club, Shaffer's, for chicken dinner. They would bring me back a carefully packaged "take-out" dinner, long before take-out was an established practice. The North Branch had a long stretch of "pocket water," which I called "bust-ass rapids" because of the slippery granite rocks and boulders; these were in the midst of a series of pools and riffles, which offered an excellent variety of habitat for trout.

THE BUSINESS OF FLY-TYING

I HAD LEARNED TO TIE FLIES by then and eagerly awaited the mail order packages of fly-tying materials and supplies that would arrive periodically. My older brother was a printer and graphic designer. He designed and painted a sign that hung at the entrance to our summer home advertising my "Perfection Fly Company," and he printed cards, which were used to display the flies that I tied. I sold the flies on these cards at nearby Engel's Tavern. After watching the fisherman at the tavern for some time, I decided I'd tie fancy fly earrings for the fishermen's wives and girlfriends. ("Bring *her* a souvenir of your fishing trip.") These were the best sellers!

I also would ride my bike down to a nearby bridge, Twin Bridge, that spanned a narrow stretch of High Falls Reservoir, and proceed to fish from the bridge, catching panfish that would cruise through the channel, feeding on insects and small minnows. I would sell a lot of "Rooster's Regrets" streamer flies from the cards of flies I set up behind me, as I cast, caught, and landed fish. More than once, when I retrieved a hooked fish by hoisting it out of the water below, I inadvertently hit a passing car on the windshield with the fish, surprising everyone. Sometimes I ran out of flies to sell, and passing anglers would stop and insist on buying the bedraggled, well-used fly that still was on the end of my line. What an idyllic existence for a boy who liked the out-of-doors; I'm sure it was what prompted my pursuit of an undergraduate degree in forestry at the University of Michigan, followed by graduate work in forest genetics and ecology there.

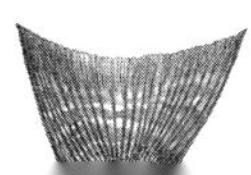

“THE ACADEMIC LIFE, ESPECIALLY IN A FIELD LIKE FOREST BIOLOGY, WAS ALSO CONDUCIVE TO CONTINUING MY FISHING HOBBY.”

UNIVERSITY ANGLING

DURING MY UNDERGRADUATE SUMMERS, I spent some time at our summer home in Wisconsin. During graduate school, I would take off a week in May to fish the Au Sable River and other waters near Grayling, Michigan with a fellow grad student friend, Terry Sharik, and a professor, John Bassett, who also fly-fished. For a modest fee, we rented a cabin right on the river and could literally walk off the porch into the river and start fishing. John Bassett's parents had a cabin on a small lake in the nearby Viking Club, and they would invite us over on the weekend for some more peaceful fishing, since the popular Au Sable also attracted a lot of canoeists, often resulting in an “aluminum hatch” on the weekends. His parents also joined us during the week on the Au Sable, where John's mother would prepare meals for us. (“No, don't bother taking off your waders, boys—just come on in and get lunch—so you can get back fishing.”) John's father would have spent the winter tying flies, and he would look over our fly-boxes and proceed to dole out handfuls of flies from his stockpile and stuff them into our boxes, saying, “Terry and Bruce, I think you need some more of these flies.” It was an intense fishing week, and we were thoroughly spoiled. This was a very special time, since we were usually too busy doing our research to enjoy many other opportunities to fish.

After finishing my PhD, I taught briefly in the Biology Department at Saginaw Valley College in Michigan. However, I was drawn by previous conservationists, fishers, and scientists—like Aldo Leopold, the Craighead brothers, and Gifford Pinchot—and kept looking for a position in the West. I finally pursued my dream and came to a position in the new Department of Forest Science at the University of Alberta in 1973. I continued selling a few flies to earn pin money even after I began teaching at the University of Alberta. My biggest customer was a former U of A grad, Brian Dunsworth. I was introduced to Brian by his son (and my former grad student) Glen Dunsworth. Brian was a former football player and was also my dentist. Brian would buy dozens of Tom Thumb and humpy flies, among others.

The academic life, especially in a field like forest biology, was also conducive to continuing my fishing hobby. The ability to take occasional days off on the spur of the moment allowed for periods of thoughtful, contemplative time when I could solve the problems of the day, whether they

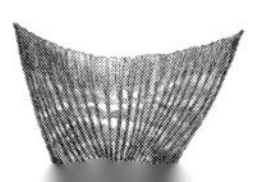

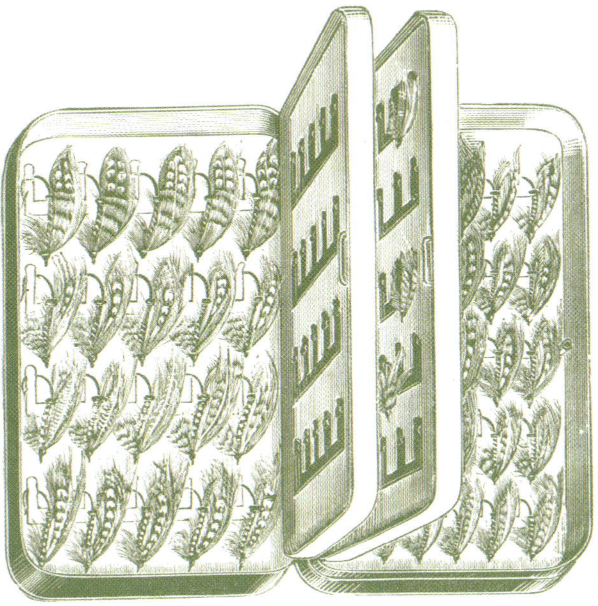

involved getting across some complex explanation or analysis in class, coming up with new approaches for research studies, or dealing with administrators and their rules. Since I often didn't plan on taking a particular day off, but decided on the morning of a nice spring day to go fishing, Linda Ehrler, the secretary in my department and I worked out a method to take care of these occasional days. She didn't want to fib to callers and say something like I was not in the office, since I was working on a research study, so when someone called asking for me, she would say I was in the field making collections, thereby not fibbing, and I would come in the next day feeling refreshed and renewed.

SIXTY YEARS ON THE BOOK TRAIL

WHY DID I BEGIN COLLECTING BOOKS?

I liked having books around, and I think reading and collecting books were natural extensions of trying to preserve memories, add to them, and relate to past experiences. Books allowed me to make a connection to nature even when I was indoors. They brought joy and comfort when I read them—and when I was surrounded by them.

The books in my collection were acquired over the almost sixty years that I was in pursuit—sometimes casually, often doggedly—of angling books. I acquired my first angling book in 1961 when I was in Downers Grove Community High School in suburban Chicago. The book was a 1959 reprint of the second revised and enlarged edition (1952) of Ray Bergman's classic work *Trout,* first published by Alfred A. Knopf, Inc., in 1938 and reprinted 13 times. When I was at the University of Michigan in 1962, I stopped by a table of books being sold by the University Women's Club and found a copy of the Canadian natural history and angling writer Roderick Haig-Brown's *Return to the River,* which I purchased, and thus began my nearly sixty-year collecting adventure. This purchase also may have been a subtle premonition of where I would later live, since I immigrated to Canada, specifically Edmonton, in 1973. Many other Haig-Brown works would end up in my collection; nearly 60 have been donated to University of Alberta Libraries. I never had the opportunity to meet Haig-Brown, but I happened to be in Campbell River in 1977 or 1978 and to have stopped by the little community museum there.

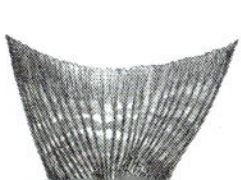

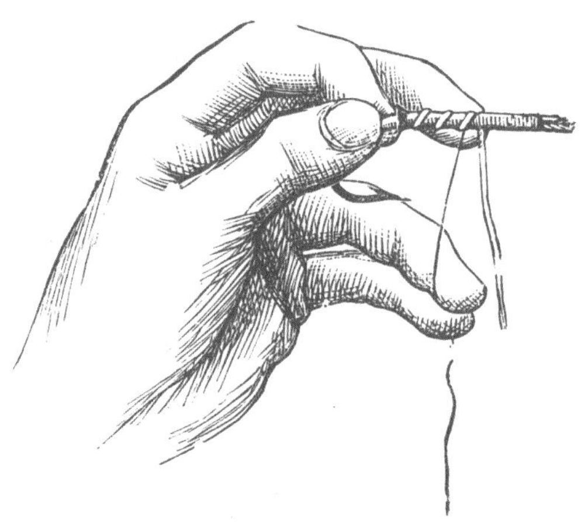

I was admiring the Haig-Brown display when a docent noticed and overheard me and asked if I'd like to meet Anne Haig-Brown, Roderick Haig-Brown's widow. She called Anne, and I was invited to drop by the Haig-Brown home, where Anne let me visit Haig-Brown's library and we talked about him and books. I cherish this memory and the connection to the author as well as his fine library.

Another early acquisition was *Trout Madness* by Robert Traver (the pen name of Justice John D. Voelker of the Michigan Supreme Court), published in 1960; I later acquired his several novels, which also have been donated to UAlberta Libraries. My first acquisition of an anthology, Raymond Camp's 1959 *The Fireside Book of Fishing,* exposed me to many authors and sent me searching for many other books. Arnold Gingrich, another University of Michigan alumnus and founding editor and long-time publisher of *Esquire*, wrote a book, *The Well-Tempered Angler* (1965), that had a great influence on me and my book collecting. In the chapter "The Angling Heritage," he reviewed some of the classic angling books and authors, focussing on thirty books (ten each in the categories of classic, vintage, and modern) that he felt were indispensable for the literary education of an angler.

Over the years, I frequented many bookstores, from little mom-and-pop used bookstores to the finest rare book emporiums. My visits to bookstores around the continent and abroad were facilitated by my frequent travels over 40 years. In addition to my university duties, I was on several boards and volunteered with agencies and the largest science publisher in Canada, the NRC Research Press (later, Canadian Science Publishing), all of which involved regular travel to various cities in Canada and the U.S., and occasionally to Europe. Friends who knew of my interests and were familiar with certain cities would suggest or take me to bookstores in those cities. Some of the dealers became long-time friends: Gary Estabrook (first in Palo Alto, California, and later in Vancouver, Washington), Paul Pursell (in Albion, Michigan), John Moldenhauer (in Elmira, and later Hanover, Ontario), Bjarne Tokerud (first in Edmonton and then Victoria), Patrick and Liam McGahern (Ottawa), and Ken Callahan (in Peterborough, New Hampshire). Up until recent years, most of my book hunts and purchases came from visits to bookstores and from the catalogues of specialty dealers. But sadly, many of those bookstores have fallen by the wayside or at least out of storefronts

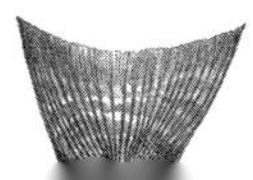

in towns and cities around the world. Today rare book collections are often found in a dealer's home, and the online site AbeBooks has now become the principal mechanism for finding elusive titles.

BEAUTY AND THE BOOK

MOST OF THE BOOKS, I selected to read, of course, but I was drawn to many because they had other noteworthy characteristics: elaborate bindings, gorgeous and fine illustrations, exquisite typography, and beautiful paper. Because of their writing, many of the authors became my favourites, and I would search for their previous titles and eagerly await their new books. Some I met and even fished with, and their inscriptions made particular books even more treasured. I would also scan publishers' advertisements and book reviews (*Gray's Sporting Journal*, in particular, had and continues to have an excellent book review column, which I still read for possible titles to buy and enjoy).

One of the authors whom I met and fished with was Norman Marsh of Motueka, New Zealand. I came to know Norman after I'd purchased his first book, *Trout Stream Insects of New Zealand*, while I was on a study leave in New Zealand in 1988. The book served as a practical reference for my recreational time while I was there. Norman was a well-known author, fisher, and guide on the South Island. I was able to meet Norman because of a long-time angling friend from Edmonton, Justice Sam Lieberman, and his wife, Nancy. They were on their way to a legal conference in Australia and stayed with me in Christchurch for several days; Sam and I fished some of my favourite rivers on the South Island. On their way down to Christchurch, Sam had fished for a few days on the North Island and had arranged to fish with Norman Marsh near Motueka, but Norman had phoned Sam and advised him not to make the journey because some stormy and rainy weather had blown out all of the streams in the area. Sam was impressed with Norman's integrity, and they had a long chat, during which Sam mentioned that he would be staying with me in Christchurch. Norman told Sam that I should call him and come to fish with him before my study leave ended.

I did contact Norman and ultimately went up to his place, Streamside, before I returned to Edmonton. When I arrived at Streamside,

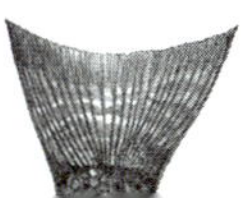

"I WAS ATTRACTED TO MANY OF THE BOOKS BECAUSE OF THEIR BINDINGS, ILLUSTRATIONS, OR OTHER FEATURES OF THE PUBLISHING PRODUCTION PROCESS."

Norman's wife Jean, looking somewhat ashen and shaken, greeted me with the news that Norman had been taken to the hospital in Nelson that day. He had been out doing some reconnaissance from his motorbike for our fishing trip, slipped on some gravel on the road, and fallen and broken his back. Fortunately, he did not injure his spinal cord, but he was laid up in the hospital for several days. While there, he had arranged with friends of his to take me fishing, and then he talked to me every evening by telephone to see how I'd been doing. For one visit to the hospital, Jean had taken my copy of his book, and I have my first inscription from Norman in that book. I returned over the next couple of years and fished with Norman, and he inscribed a few of his other books for me. These books are personal treasures and reminders of warm friendships and fond memories.

On another occasion, I had shared a dinner table with Lee and Joan Wulff, at the banquet for the Cold Water Anglers' Conference held in Edmonton in September 1984. Lee had spoken at the conference and Joan had given casting demonstrations for attendees out at Hastings Lake, west of the city. In the collection, the copy of Lee's 1980 book, *Lee Wulff on Flies,* is inscribed from him on that occasion and includes a tucked-in thank-you note from Joan for my contribution to the Atlantic Salmon Federation in honour of Lee, who passed away a few years later.

The collection includes a few groupings of books and other items. Among these are about 30 editions of Izaak Walton and Charles Cotton's *The Complete* (or *Compleat*) *Angler*, including the 1766 second Hawkins edition, the 1822 *Illustrations to the Complete Angler* by Thomas Gosden, the 1848 second Bethune edition, the 1906 first Canadian edition, the 1911 first Thorpe edition (with coloured plates mounted on thick green paper), the 1930 Adams edition (with watercolours and pen and ink drawings), and the 1929 *Songs from the Compleat Angler.* Among the more than 60 items by or related to Roderick Haig-Brown are many of the first Canadian, first American, and first UK editions of his titles, several of which are signed. One of the more notable Haig-Brown works is the very rare 1938 German version *Der gottliche Strom, Ein Roman* of the classic *Pool and Rapid*; only two copies are known to be in public libraries (The Library of Congress and The UBC Special Collections Library).

I was attracted to many of the books because of their bindings, illustrations, or other features of the publishing production process. For instance, Eugene Connett's 1939 first edition of *Random Casts* has a

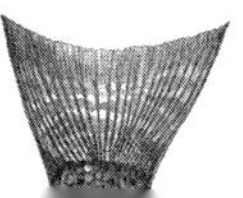

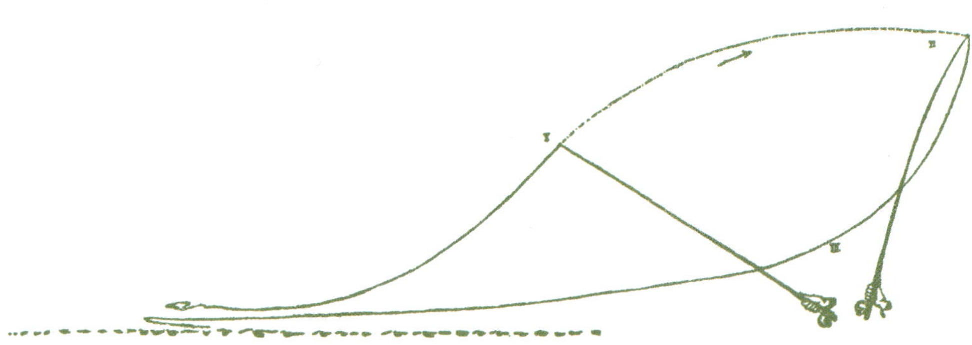

Proper position to take.

binding that looks like the surface of a lake or stream in sunlight; it creates an image and tells a story that, like a stream, draws the angler in. Similarly, Preston Jennings's 1935 edition of *A Book of Trout Flies*, a treasure with exceptional cover and binding, has gilt drawings of mayflies floating on waves of water on the cover. One with a spectacular binding is the magnificent 1836 edition of Izaak Walton and Charles Cotton's *The Complete Angler*, the first Nicolas edition by publisher William Pickering in two volumes. These are bound in a sumptuous dark green Moroccan leather gilt binding by Riviere, the premier binder of the time. They were owned by Lord Keith Rollo, whose bookplate is found inside. At the time of publication, it was stated that "... no finer edition will ever be published" (attributed to Robert W. Henderson by Peter Oliver, who produced a bibliography of *The Compleat Angler* in 1936). Since the original first edition in 1653, more than 500 editions of *The Compleat Angler* have been published in English alone; I only collected about three dozen of them, most of which are now in Bruce Peel Special Collections.

One of the first books I donated to the Peel library was the 1924 edition of John Waller Hills's *A Summer on the Test*, a beautiful folio edition of which only 25 copies were produced and which included a dozen signed, drypoint etchings by Norman Wilkinson. These exquisite etchings speak to me of my time spent on the water, the many experiences over the years that connect any angler with nature and the natural world. As soon as I saw this copy at Gary Estabrook's in 1990, I knew I had to acquire it. The 1934 *Salmon Tactics* was purchased because it had beautiful drawings and etchings (and was written) by Percy Nobbs, who was the first architect and planner for the University of Alberta campus. When Ellen Schoeck and others in the President's office asked for my suggestion of a book to be added to the UAlberta Libraries in honour of Justice Sam Lieberman when he was to receive an honorary doctorate degree, this was the title I suggested and located for them. Nobbs also provided the sketches in T.B. Fraser's *100 Years on the Godbout River* (1959). Several other special titles were selected because of the beautiful specimen flies that were included with the book. Among these are the titles by Frederic M. Halford—*Dry Fly Entomology* (1897), *Floating Flies and How to Dress Them* (1886), and *Modern Development of the Dry Fly* (1910)—as well as Harfield H. Edmonds and Norman N. Lee's *Brook and River Trouting*

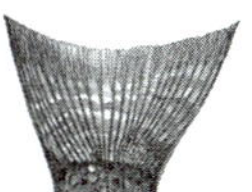

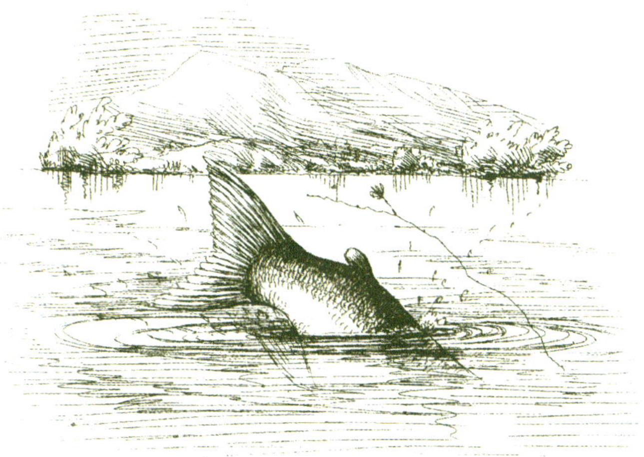

(1916, with flies and fly-dressing materials) and T. Donald Overfield's 1977 *G.E.M. Skues: The Way of a Man with a Trout*, with its separate volume of fold-out sunken mounts with 20 expertly hand-tied nymphs.

A NOTE IN TIME

MANY OF THE BOOKS WERE COLLECTED in part because of their inscriptions by the author or their previous owners or other meaningful associations. These include the 1880 edition of Dame Juliana Berners's *A Treatyse of Fysshyng wyth an Angle*, which includes the bookplate of W.E.D. Shaw, noted British angling author of the 1930s, who was editor of *The Field* and *Fly Fishers' Journal.* The 1855 edition of William Blacker's *Blacker's Art of Fly Makings, &c.: Comprising Angling and Dyeing of Colours, with Engravings of Salmon and Trout Flies, Shewing the Process of the Gentle Craft as Taught in the Pages: With Descriptions of Flies for the Season of the Year, as They Come out on the Water* includes the signatures of noted authors Arthur Oglesby and Alf Walker, the latter a well-known Canadian fly fisher and author.

Thomas Westwood and Thomas Satchell's *Bibliotheca Piscatoria* (1883) contains the bookplate of Charles Home, Earl of Home, and is inscribed on 25 November 1883 to him by Alfred Dennison, the leading British angling collector of the late nineteenth century, whose collection was crucial to *Bibliotheca Piscatoria*. I was surprised and delighted to learn that my close friend and angling buddy Bruce Goodall is the great-great-nephew of Thomas Westwood. The connections are part of the joy of the sport and of collecting. William B. Mershon's 1923 *Recollections of My Fifty Years Hunting and Fishing* is a signed presentation copy, and it includes a letter tipped in to noted author F. Gray Griswold and Griswold's bookplate with the colourful salmon fly drawing. Lawrence Pringle's 1972 *Wild River* contains the bookplate of Mark Kerridge, noted collector and author. Kerridge donated his angling collection to the library at California State College at Fullerton, and his address about his angling book collection is contained in his book *Angling Literature*, by Philip Markham Kerridge.

William Radcliffe's *Fishing from the Earliest Times* (1921) has the signature of noted author (of *Origins of Angling*) and former editor of *Fortune Magazine*, John McDonald. E.H. "Polly"

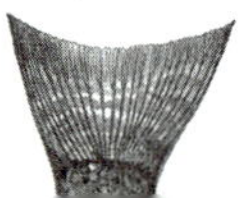

Rosborough's *Tying and Fishing the Fuzzy Nymphs* (1965) is inscribed by the author to Mike Kennedy, prominent Pacific Northwest flyfisher. Many years ago, I acquired several beautiful flies expertly tied by Polly. These flies inspire me to tie more flies of my own. H.T. Sheringham's *Fishing: Its Cause, Treatment and Cure* (1925) and John Davy's *The Angler in the Lake District* (1857) each contain a simple and distinctive bookplate with two opposing "C"s (almost like an "X"), the owner of which I and dealers I know have not been able to identify. This is an ongoing mystery to me and something I will continue to pursue—unfinished book business!

W. Agar Adamson's *Salmon Fishing in Canada by a Resident* (1860), contains the bookplate of noted American angling book collector Henry A. Sherwin. James Bloomfield's *Gun, Rod and Palette in the High Rockies* (1914) contains the bookplate of Henry A. Bruns (author of the definitive *Angling Books of the Americas*). John Colquhoun's *Salmon-casts and Stray Shots* (1858) came from the collection of David Beazley (author of *Images of Angling: Three Centuries of British Angling Prints*). I had been introduced to David by bookseller John Moldenhauer, and David invited me to lunch at the Flyfishers' Club in London on one occasion. Among other memorabilia, the Club had on display Izaak Walton's ancient (over 350 years old) leather creel. Emlyn Gill's *Practical Dry-fly Fishing* (1912) and the Rev. Richard Durnford's *The Diary of a Test Fisherman 1809–1819* (1911) both contain the bookplate of Joseph Deleplaine Bates, Jr., the author of many salmon and fly books. Both *Catalogue of an Ancient Collection of Angling Books Formed by J. C. Lynn, Esq. of Compton Down, Winchester* (1959) and Susan B. Starkman and Stanley E. Read's *The Contemplative Man's Recreation* (1970) contain the beautiful, illustrated (with a salmon fly by Charles DeFeo) bookplate of Colonel Henry A. Siegel, noted book dealer and author.

E. Marshall-Hardy's *Angling Yarns* (1936), N.K. Roberson's *Farther Thrifty Fishing* (1948), H.S. Joyce's *A Trout Angler's Notebook* [1848], J.D. Kenworthy's *A Fisherman's Philosophy* (1933), Leander McCormick's *Fishing Round the World* (1937), Arthur Sharp's *Rod and Stream* (1928), and P.D. Mallock's *Life-history and Habits of the Salmon, Sea-trout, Trout and Other Freshwater Fish* all have the blind (embossed) library stamp of Gary H. Howells, the late and famous California cane rod builder.

Both the very rare first edition of Alfred Ronalds's *The Fly-fisher's Entomology* (1836) and

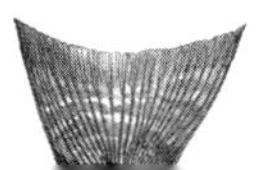

William Scrope's *Days and Nights of Salmon Fishing in the Tweed* (1843) contain the bookplate of Dermot, Earl of Mayo, while George Agar Hansard's *Trout and Salmon Fishing in Wales* (1834) has the magnificent miniature bookplate of Dermot, Earl of Mayo (dated 1888). Former U.S. President Grover Cleveland's *Fishing and Shooting Sketches* (1906) has the signature of Sparse Grey Hackle/Alfred W. Miller, noted author of *Fishless Days, Angling Nights* (1971) and member of the Anglers' Club of New York. Another item associated with Sparse Grey Hackle is a gift I received from my late publishing friend, Bill Kaufmann: a slim, dark blue-green men's tie, which, of course, is decorated with flies. Bob Elliot's *The Eastern Brook Trout* (1950) has the signature of Martin Bovey, an early Trout Unlimited activist and board member. Charles Phair's *Atlantic Salmon Fishing* (Derrydale Press, 1937) was a presentation copy from Phair to his boss, Alan Rutherford Stuyvesant. Louis V. Pirsson's *Fly-fishing Days* (1946) bears an inscription to Stan Bitchell from Ted Rogowski, Senior Water Council for the Environmental Protection Agency during the Nixon administration and one of the authors of *The Clean Water Act*. Rogowski also was president (the second one) of the famous Theodore Gordon Flyfishers Club and Executive Vice-President of the Federation of Fly Fishers.

Frank Mackie Johnson's *Reminiscent Tales of a Humble Angler* (1921) is a presentation copy to Will H. Dilg, author and famed humourist, and first President of the Izaak Walton League. *The Vade-mecum of Fly-fishing for Trout* (1851) by G.P.R. Pulman contains the bookplate of noted angling book collector, Henry A. Portang. *Fly-rods and Fly Tackle* (1885) by Henry P. Wells contains the bookplate of Charles E. Goodspeed, famous author of the definitive reference book *Angling in America* (1939) and owner of long-time iconic Boston bookstore, Goodspeed's Bookshop. The Canadian Pacific Railway brochure, *Fishing and Shooting* (ca. 1907) contains the bookplate of Jeffrey Norton, noted angling book collector and publisher. The Norton bookplate features a design by noted woodcut artist Joseph Crawhall. John Oliver La Gorce's *The Book of Fishes* (1958) contains the bookplate of Antonio Barrette, short-term premier (1960) of Quebec. W.H. Blake's *A Fisherman's Creed* (1923) is inscribed, "In memory of Canadian trout from William Lang, Gregory Clark and Tom Jull. All good wishes, Mary Pickford 1934."

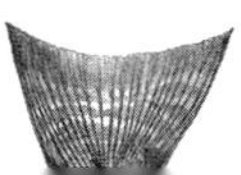

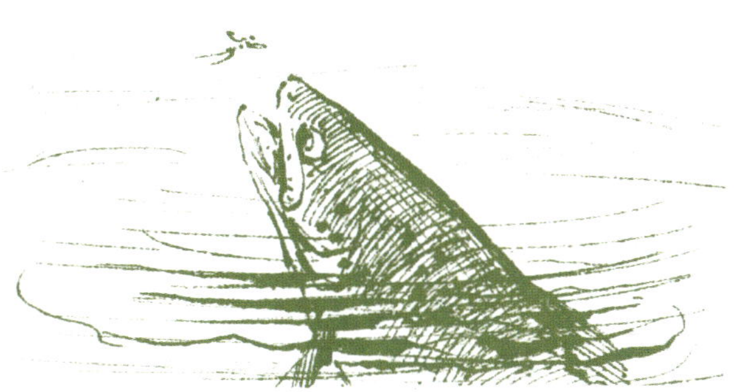

Pickford was, of course, the famous Canadian-born Hollywood actress.

The London Angler's Book (1834) by John Baddeley contains the bookplate of Dean Sage, noted angler, collector, and author of the beautiful and very rare *The Ristigouche and Its Salmon Fishing* (1888). George A.B. Dewar's *The Book of the Dry Fly* is an inscribed presentation copy from R.B. Marston, noted British angler and author. *Family Circle's Guide to Trout Flies and How to Tie Them* contains the bookplate of Hank Bruns, noted bibliographer of fishing literature, and is inscribed to him from G. Don Roy, famous photographer and illustrator.

Several books—such as John J. Brown's *The American Angler's Guide* (1846) and D. MacFarlane's *A Few Thoughts on Fly-fishing* (1819)—contain the miniature bookplate of C.R. Morphy of Ottawa, who probably had the most extensive collection of angling books in Canada in the latter part of the last century. *Always in the Way: A Little Story* (1868) contains the piscatorial bookplate of the great angling book collector, John Gerard Heckscher. Several books—J. Hughes-Perry's photo album (ca. 1935), A.R.B. Haldane's *By Many Waters; a Record of Fishing and Walking* (1940), Fraser Sandeman's *Angling Travels in Norway* (1895), and Ernest C. Pain's *Fifty Years on the Test* (1934)—contain the inked initials (C.V.H.) of Charles V. Hancock, long-time Literary Editor of the Birmingham Post. Hancock also wrote *Rod in Hand* (1958). *The Coquet-dale Fishing Songs* (1852) by A North Country Angler [Thomas Doubleday] contains the armorial bookplate of Joseph Crawhall, Newcastle-on-Tyne, the famous author, angler, and wood-cut maker.

Ernest Schwiebert's *Salmon of the World* (1970) contains a long presentation inscription from the author to Gene Hill, noted outdoors writer. It also has the publisher's plate, "presented to Gene A. Hill 'the salmon king' from Winchester Press," and is signed by Jim Rikhoff, 17 July 1974. Walter F. Silverton's *Sports-fisherman's Paradise* (1972) contains the signature of Lee Straight, long-time columnist for the Vancouver Sun, and a slipped-in letter to Straight from the publisher. *Allcock's Anglers' Guide* (1953) also has Straight's signature. Justin W. and Fannie A. Leonard's *Mayflies of Michigan Trout Streams* (1962) was inscribed to me by the authors, professors at the University of Michigan when I was a student. Justin Leonard was the admired Chair of the Conservation Department in the School of Natural Resources at Michigan.

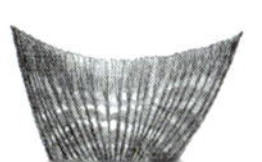

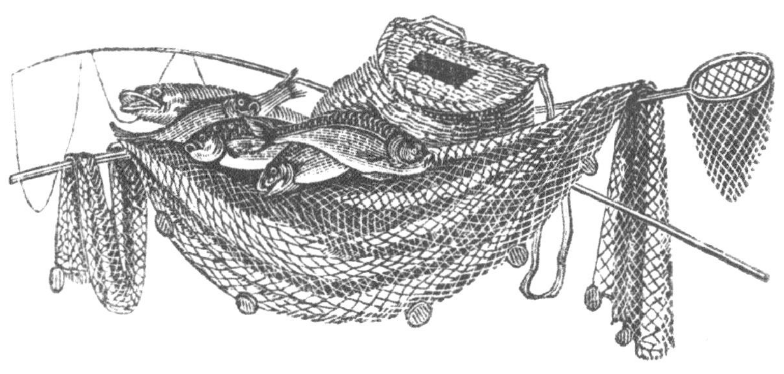

THE WIDE, WIDE WORLD OF ANGLING BOOKS

OTHER BOOKS WERE COLLECTED because of particular content. The second edition (1940) of W.H. Blake's *Brown Waters* is illustrated with the colour reproductions of eight Clarence A. Gagnon paintings and, thus, is much more desirable for collectors than the un-illustrated first edition. Frederic Tolfrey's *The Sportsman in France* (1841) contains a chapter on salmon fishing in Canada, the first real mention of sport in Canada. James Wilson's *The Rod and Gun* (1840) contains the first printed description of a Canadian fly pattern (the Sam Slick, possibly by T.C. Haliburton of Nova Scotia).

On a more humorous note, the author of *I Go a-Fishing* and *Among the Northern Hills,* W.C.L. Prime, was also known for exposing the problem of doughnut addiction in New England! Douglas McCraith's *By Dancing Streams* (1929) contains the charming dedication, "to my wife who once thought all anglers were mad." The very rare 1897 *Camp and Lamp: Rambles in Realms of Sport, Story, Song,* by Samuel Mathewson Baylis, includes stories of fishing for brook trout in Canada, fly fishing for salmon on rivers of the North Shore of the St. Lawrence River, fishing for grayling on the Au Sable River in Michigan, and making a greenheart fly rod, as well as two angling poems—although most of the book consists of non-angling stories and poetry.

Gifford Pinchot, the author of *Just Fishing Talk* (1936), was Governor of Pennsylvania but better known as a conservationist and Head of the U.S. Forest Service under Teddy Roosevelt. He and Roosevelt were responsible for the protection of much of the wildland in the western U.S. in national parks and national forests. He was a hero of mine in my undergraduate years. Alexander Mackintosh's *The Modern Fisher; or Driffield Angler* (ca. 1815) contains the first real mention of the dry fly.

Over the years, there have been several books about Atlantic salmon fishing at various private clubs or isolated places in the Maritime provinces and Quebec. Of considerable note is *A Week on the Jupiter River, Anticosti Island* by "Baldemec" (1904). The book is inscribed to J.S. O'Meara by Lord Bessborough (Governor General at the time). The letters in the pseudonym "Baldemec" refer to the following: B is Lord Bessborough; AL is A.F. Lascelles, Secretary to the Governor

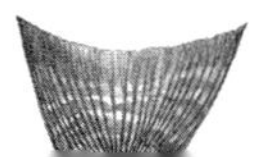

"THERE ARE STRONG LINKS BETWEEN ANGLING BOOKS AND ANGLING AND CONSERVATION—NOT ONLY WATER AND FISH CONSERVATION, BUT ALSO CONSERVATION OF ALL SORTS OF WILDLANDS AND ECOSYSTEMS."

General; D is Lord Duncannon (the Governor General's son); EM is Major Eric Mackenzie (Office of the Comptroller); and EC is Captain Eddy C. Colville. Tipped in is an invitation to an event in Vancouver honouring Lord Bessborough. The very rare *Tight Lines and a Happy Landing: Anticosti – July 1937* (1937) by Alexander E. Duncan and John E. Senmes is the account of a month-long salmon fishing trip to Anticosti Island by five anglers. The very rare *Anticosti Expeditionary Force* (1955) by Edward B. Leisenring, Alberta C. Pew, Joseph N. Pew, Jr., Margaret R. Leisenring, and Jay Cooke, is another. Edwin C. Kent's *The Isle of Long Ago* (1933) contains a chapter on salmon, including a long account of fishing on New Brunswick's Upsalquitch River with Ambrose Monell, President of Inco. This is one of several stories that claim the first use of the dry fly in angling for Atlantic salmon. I have been fortunate to fish the Upsalquitch for the last several years at Camp Watiqua with my good friend Canon Stephen Booth and other friends. Stephen was President of Trout Unlimited Canada in the 1980s, at the time I was Western Vice-President, and we became friends and have often fished together.

CONSERVATION

OVER THE YEARS, I have been a member of and/or supported several conservation organizations, ranging from the Alberta Wilderness Association to the Nature Conservancy of Canada. I have been most active in Trout Unlimited Canada, where I have served on several fund-raising dinner committees and on its executive as the Canadian representative on the Board of Trout Unlimited (USA), and where I currently chair its National Resource Advisory Committee. As a result of contacts while I was on the Trout Unlimited (USA) Board, my partner Brenda Laishley and I have been travelling to northern Patagonia to the area around San Martin de los Andes, Argentina, fishing with Andes Drifters for the past 15 years, often with friends we have encouraged to accompany us there. There also are books to be found there and in the many bookshops in Buenos Aires. A bridge between angling and books is the Harry Hawthorne Foundation for the Inculcation and Propagation of the Principles and Ethics of Fly Fishing (HHF), which supports an angling library at UBC, and whose members participate in annual trips to the Pennask Lake Fishing & Game Club

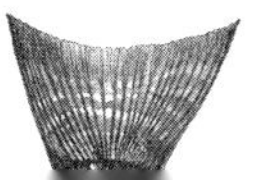

"THE BOOKS IN THIS COLLECTION WERE DONATED TO BRUCE PEEL SPECIAL COLLECTIONS BECAUSE I WANTED THEM TO BE WELL CARED FOR AND AVAILABLE TO READERS AND SCHOLARS IN THE FUTURE."

on Pennask Lake in British Columbia. Brenda and I have been members for several years and enjoy the fishing and camaraderie with the other HHF members and friends. Brenda has been a great supporter and resource in the collection of these books over the past 25 years.

There are strong links between angling books and angling and conservation—not only water and fish conservation, but also conservation of all sorts of wildlands and ecosystems. It is not just the topics but sharing knowledge of those topics to make a better place for generations to come that is important. This is especially true for books involving angling and natural history. The books in this collection were donated to Bruce Peel Special Collections because I wanted them to be well cared for and available to readers and scholars in the future. I have been donating these books over several years and will continue until pretty much my entire collection of angling books is at the Peel library. It was a little difficult to make the initial donation, because it felt a bit like losing some old friends, but then I realized they were moving nearby, I could visit them easily, and they were being cared for better than I could care for them. I hope you enjoy this exhibition and the books on display and that the exhibition encourages you to read about or participate in fly fishing and the conservation of our valuable natural environments and ecosystems.

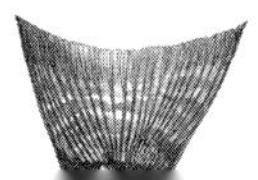

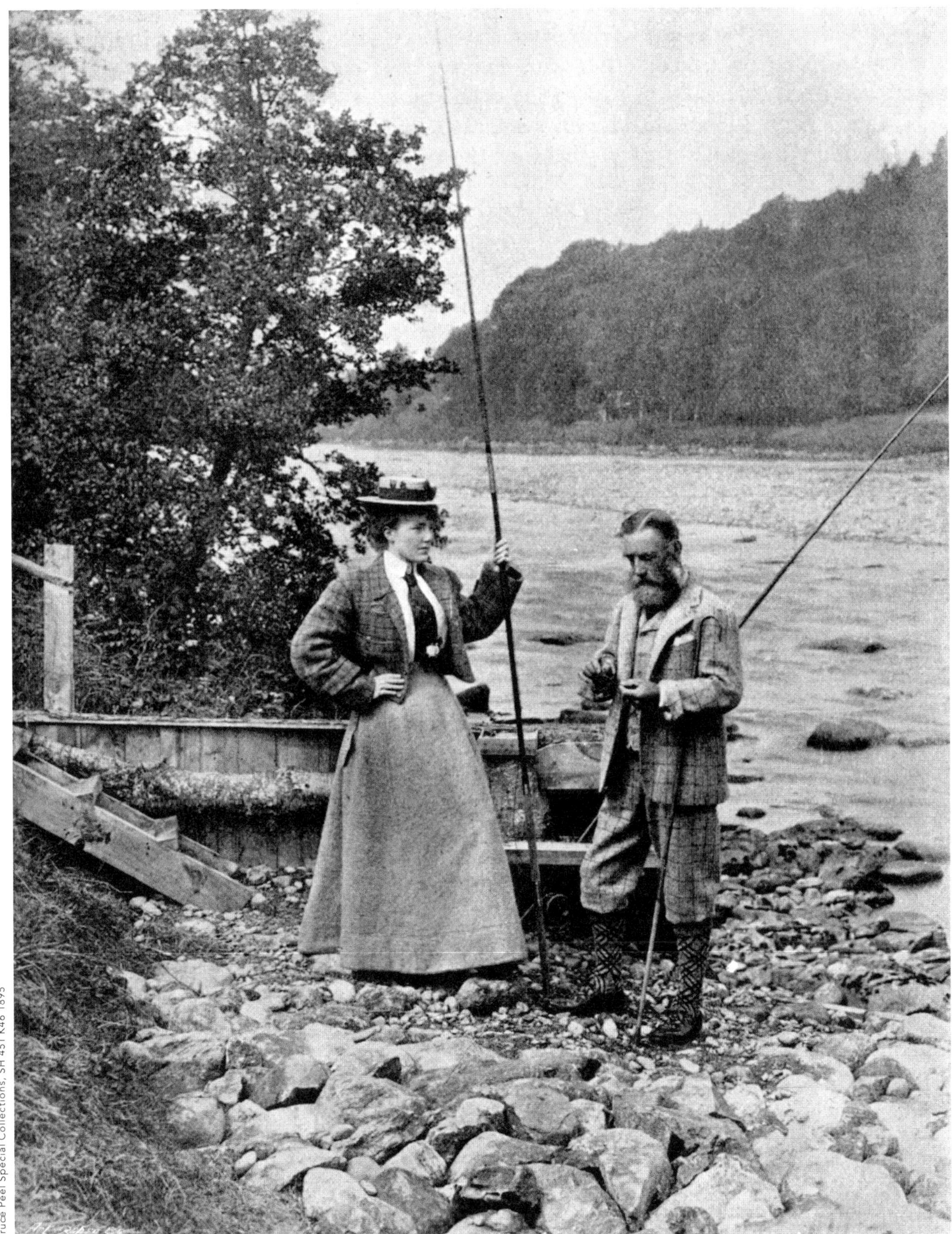

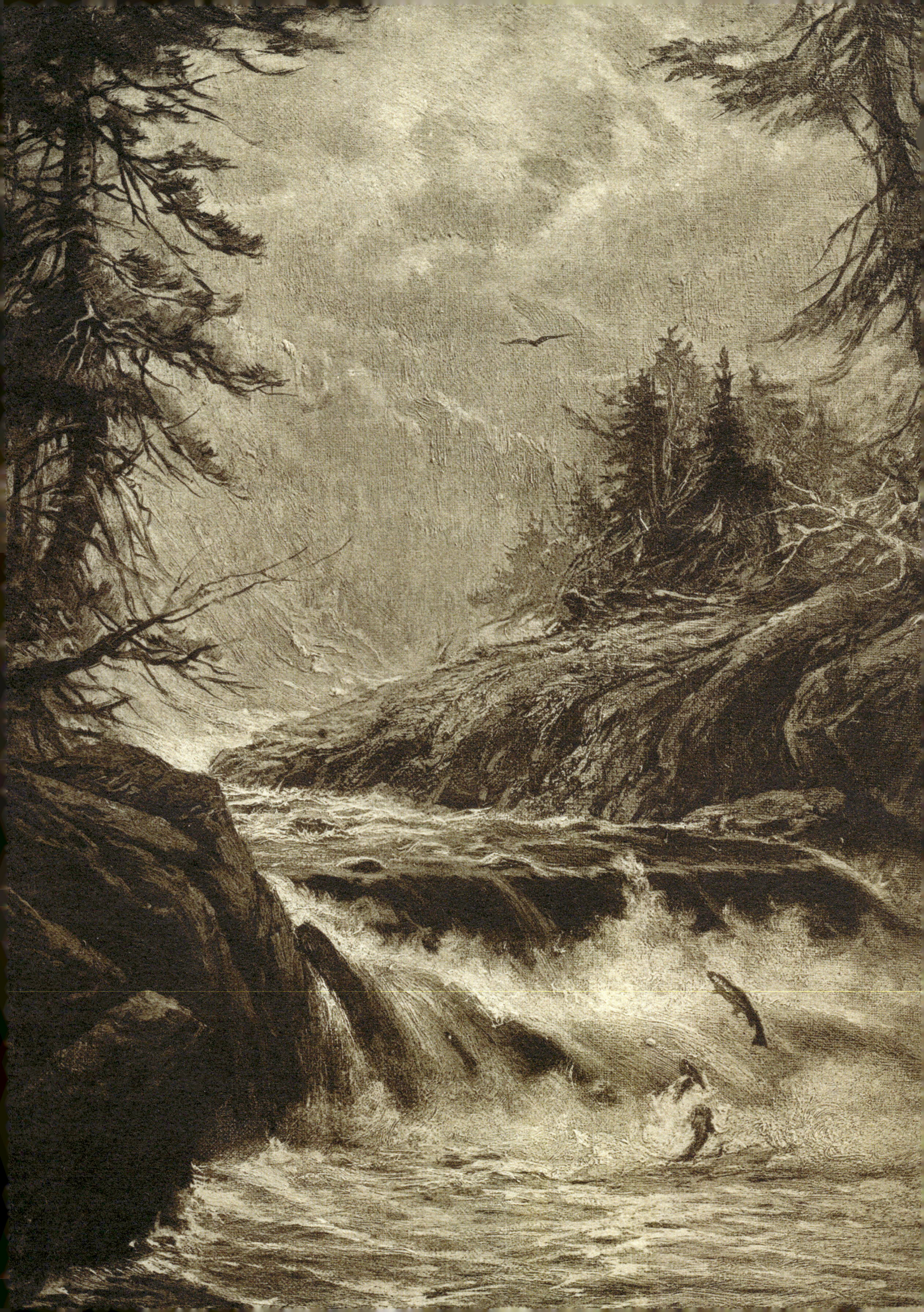

INTRODUCTION

JUSTIN HANISCH

It's about the fish. And it's not.
It's about the river. And it's not.
It's about the flies, and the rods, and the tackle.
And it's not.

ANGLING CAN BE MANY THINGS to many people, but at its core, it is a creative activity. Much of the pleasure of angling is experienced in the imagination: planning the next cast, scanning for the next rise, and playing the fish not yet caught. At first, the angler's prize exists only in the angler's mind. The fish inhabits a separate world, a world that is hidden and mysterious.

With the first cast, the angler begins building a bridge between these two worlds—between air and water, between fantasy and reality. Cast after cast, the angler's fly lands gently on the water and floats by, only to be retrieved and offered again. Suddenly, a weight is felt on the end of the line! Slowly and carefully, the angler plays the fish. Foot by foot, the angler retrieves the line and feels the space between his or her world and the fish's decrease. The angler feels the fish tiring; the angler's legs shake with anticipation; and the fish comes closer. What monster—what beauty—has been hooked? The event horizon is near; the two worlds are united by a violent splash on the surface. The mystery begins to resolve before the angler's eyes. A brief glimpse! A flash of dark green, black, white, and crimson. A brook trout has emerged through the looking glass; the grateful angler unhooks the fish, carefully releases it back into the river, and primps a fly to cast again. The next fish is a Schrödinger's animal. It could be *anything* until the moment it too slides into the angler's net. And if the angler is lucky once or twice during a lifetime, one fish or one moment on the water will surpasses everything the angler has imagined. It will be a perfect fish, a perfect moment that will remain significant for the rest of the angler's life.

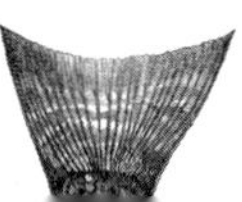

"THE HISTORY OF EARLY PRINTED BOOKS IS ALSO THE HISTORY OF ANGLING LITERATURE."

The quest for such a perfect moment has inspired a rich body of angling literature from the time of the ancient Greeks and Romans through the advent of the printing press and to the present. Oppian of Anazarbus, the second-century Greco-Roman poet, described the first few moments after hooking a fish:

> A bite, hurrah! The length'ning line extends
> Above the tugging fish the arch'd reed bends;
> He struggles hard, and noble sport will yield,
> My liege, ere wearied out he quits the field.
> See how he swims up, down, and now athwart
> The rapid stream—now pausing as in thought;
> And now you force him from the azure deep:
> He mounts, he bends, and with resilient leap
> Bounds into air! (qtd. in Badham 3)

Although written nearly 2000 years ago, Oppian's excitement at hooking and playing a jumping fish is immediately familiar to the modern angler.

The history of early printed books is also the history of angling literature. One of the first books printed in English that included angling content is attributed to Dame Juliana Berners. *The Treatyse of Fysshynge wyth an Angle* (sometimes *A Treatyse*) appeared in the 1496 edition of *Book of Saint Albans*, printed by Wynken de Worde. De Worde was assistant and successor to William Caxton, the first person to print books in English with moveable type. *Treatyse* is represented in this exhibition and catalogue in a fine 1827 reprint (item 1). Just over 150 years after the publication of Berner's foundational contribution to angling literature, the most significant book on fishing, Izaak Walton's *The Compleat Angler, or the Contemplative Man's Recreation* (1653), was published in London. Although several books on fishing were published before 1653, Walton's *Compleat Angler* is of such importance to angling literature that books are typically separated into two categories: those that came before Walton and those that came after.

After Walton, contributions to angling literature in the eighteenth and early nineteenth centuries were primarily manuals and handbooks. Although these books provide valuable insight into angling practices during this period, novel contributions to angling techniques were scarce. However, the mid-nineteenth and early twentieth centuries saw a renaissance in the fly-fishing community. Several canonical works on dry-fly fishing were published that would sow controversy in the angling world and modernize some of

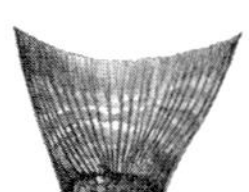

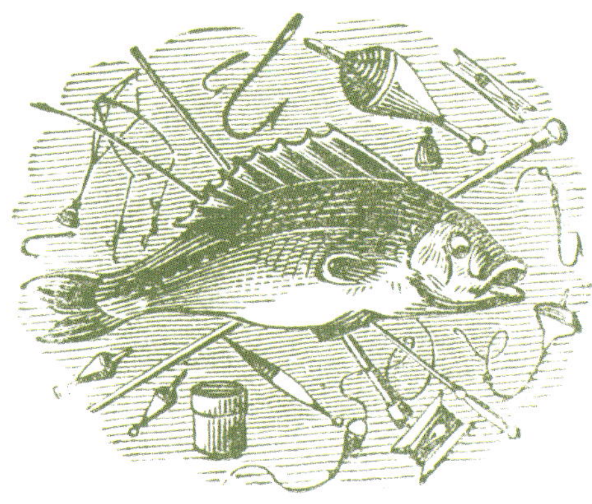

its practices and nomenclature. Books in the mid-nineteenth century also started to include actual examples of fly-tying materials, and in the late nineteenth and early twentieth centuries, publishers began to issue spectacular, heavily-illustrated limited edition volumes with numerous examples of hand-tied flies marketed directly to collectors.

In many ways, angling and book collecting are kindred pastimes. Like angling, book collecting can be pursued casually on the occasional weekend or passionately whenever and wherever opportunities can be found. Both angling and book collecting can occur at the highest level, in exotic locations, and at great expense—or simply at the local pond or neighbourhood used bookstore. Indeed, the same sense of anticipation and discovery is felt both at the threshold of the antiquarian bookstore and the bank of a storied river. Angling and book collecting even share idioms: "the one that got away," "trophy," "a great catch." It is not surprising, then, that many angling authors are also book collectors. In his essay, *On Making a Library*, Roderick Haig-Brown observes that "books are a pleasure, wisdom, experience, emotion, and civilization, and no collection of books that is not rigidly and narrowly specialized can be much less than this." But like many collectors, Haig-Brown is also drawn to books as objects in addition to their content:

> I have said that a library is many things. It is the beauty of books as well as their substance. When I have been away from home I have remembered many times, without knowing exactly why, the warm red backs of a set of Fielding, the spaced and lovely text of the Nonesuch *Plutarch*, the delicate plates of Ronalds's *Flyfisher's Entomology*, the crowded pages of an eighteenth-century Aphra Behn.

It is not difficult to image Haig-Brown's mind wandering to a favourite river after pausing on the delicate plates of *The Fly-fisher's Entomology* (item 74).

This exhibition includes books of a single collector, Dr Bruce Dancik, who is an angler-collector in the mould of Mr Haig-Brown. Dr Dancik has been a fisherman only slightly longer than he has been a book collector. His collection includes titles that have contributed significantly to the development of angling as a sport and as a philosophy—and it also includes some of the most beautiful books one could

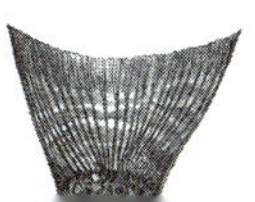

hope to find in an angling library. His collection has found a permanent home in Bruce Peel Special Collections and continues to grow with subsequent donations from Dr Dancik (for what book collector ever *stops* collecting?) and additions by the Peel library. It was a pleasure to view this collection and assemble but a small selection of highlights for this exhibition and catalogue.

The exhibition and catalogue are broadly organized into five sections: Manuals and Handbooks, Limited Editions, Angling as Adventure, Canadian Angling, and Scientific Angling. These sections are often closely related—for example, an early book on Canadian angling can also be read as an adventure narrative, and some of the lavish limited editions also include scientific content. These sections can be viewed as braided channels in a great river, flowing separately for a time but connected to the main channel by a continuity of flow and the promise of reuniting for a time downstream. Like many histories, the history of angling builds upon the accomplishments of previous authors and generations. For this reason, the exhibition and catalogue are generally organized chronologically. Exceptions are occasionally made to group related items.

Before you wade into the catalogue or tour the exhibition, please take a moment and imagine yourself on a lake or river in the tranquil hour before sunset. Feel the gentle breeze and hear a loon cry in the distance. Imagine the dimple and ring from a rising trout, a spent mayfly settling on the surface. Feel the cork of a rod in your hand and the weight of your line as you begin your first cast. Imagine what fish, and what stories, are waiting for you beneath the water's surface …

Keep this feeling close as you tour the centuries of angling literature, fine engravings, hand-tied flies, colour prints, and spectacular limited editions that you are about to enjoy, for it is this very feeling that has inspired many of these works. And don't be afraid to stare a little too long into a riffle, be distracted by the flight of a dragonfly, or get lost in a back channel. The flow will bring you back to where you need to be.

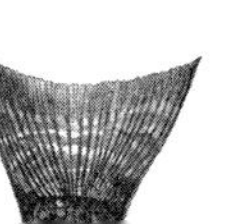

Facing page: Bruce Peel Special Collections, SH 439 H338 1866

MANUALS AND HANDBOOKS

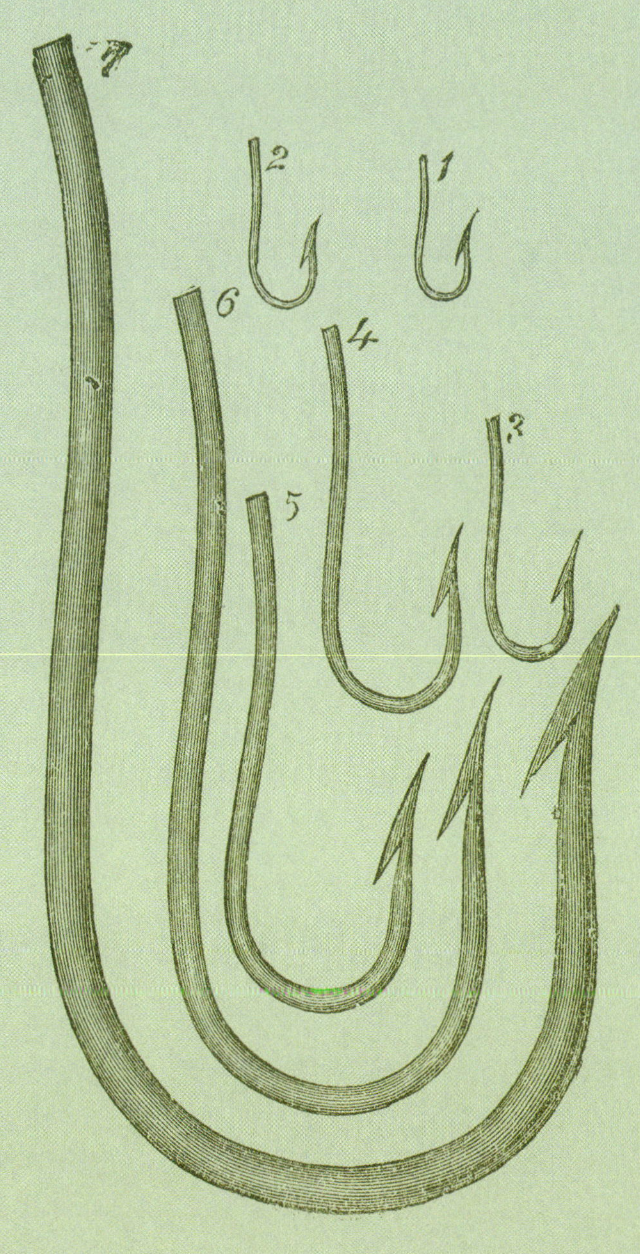

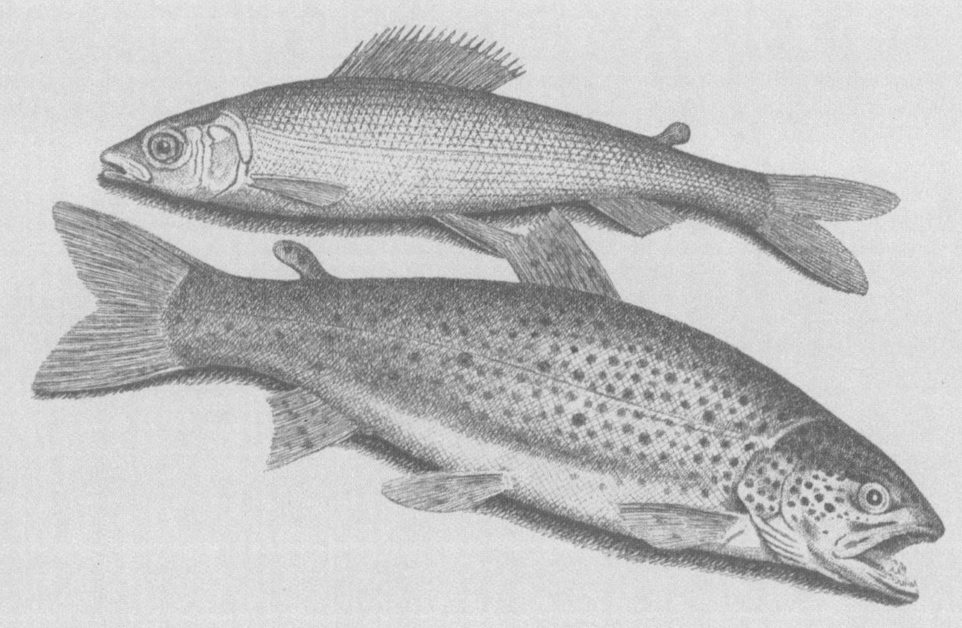

MANUALS AND HANDBOOKS

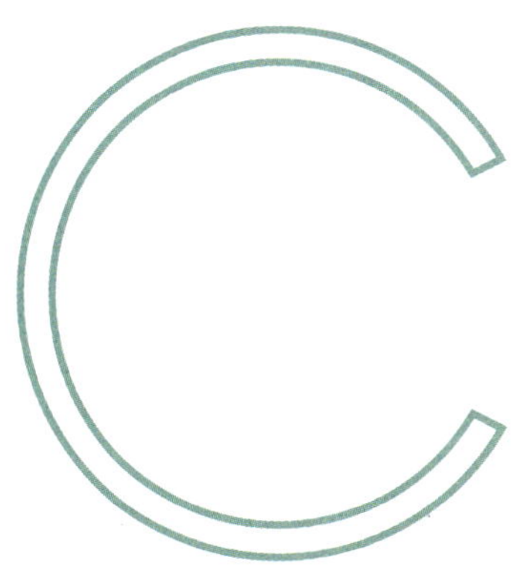

CATCHING FISH ISN'T EASY, and catching fish consistently can be downright difficult. To catch fish consistently requires skill, finesse, practice, a lot of time on the water, and a good deal of study. Anglers through the centuries have written books offering their lifetimes of experience to the eager student of fishing. This section of the catalogue includes manuals and handbooks published over nearly 150 years and containing over 400 years of angling knowledge.

The history of "modern" angling books begins with Dame Juliana Berners's *The Treatyse of Fysshynge wyth an Angle*. First appearing in 1496, *Treatyse* has had a lasting impact on angling literature. Arnold Gingrich devotes eight pages to *Treatyse* in his *The Fishing in Print* (5–13), and the book has been admired for its "delightful and inseparable connection with all that is sweetest in country life and natural scenery . . ." (Marston 26). As a manual, *Treatyse* also influenced the practice of angling for centuries. Berners's instructions for constructing a rod and line were quoted verbatim by Izaak Walton in his *Compleat Angler*, which was first published in 1653, and the instructions were still considered useful in the late nineteenth century (Marston 15–16). The book also provided the first printed description of artificial flies and included instruction on which flies should be tied and fished during each month of the year from March to August (Marston 22–24). *Treatyse* is included in this exhibition in a fine edition printed in 1827.

While *Treatyse* is the first printed book in English on angling, Izaak Walton's *The Compleat Angler, or the Contemplative Man's Recreation* (1653) is both the heart and backbone of angling literature. Walton's influence is felt heavily throughout every subsequent century of fishing writing, and there are *at least* 500 editions of *Compleat Angler*. This exhibition contains 19 editions of the book spanning nearly 175 years.

After Walton, the exhibition includes several manuals from the late eighteenth and early nineteenth centuries that preceded the landmark publications by William Blacker (items 10a–c) featuring hand-coloured engravings and actual examples of tied flies. *Blacker's Catechism of Fly-making, Angling, and Dye-making* (1843) is an early, if not the earliest, example of a book issued with actual examples of fly-tying materials. This section of the exhibition also features the first book published in the United States dedicated to American angling, manuals dedicated to specific species and techniques, and the first book on American dry-fly fishing.

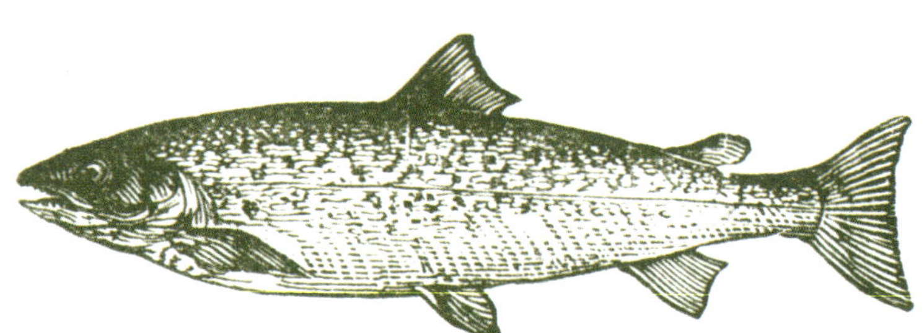

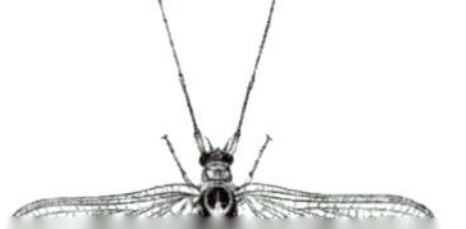

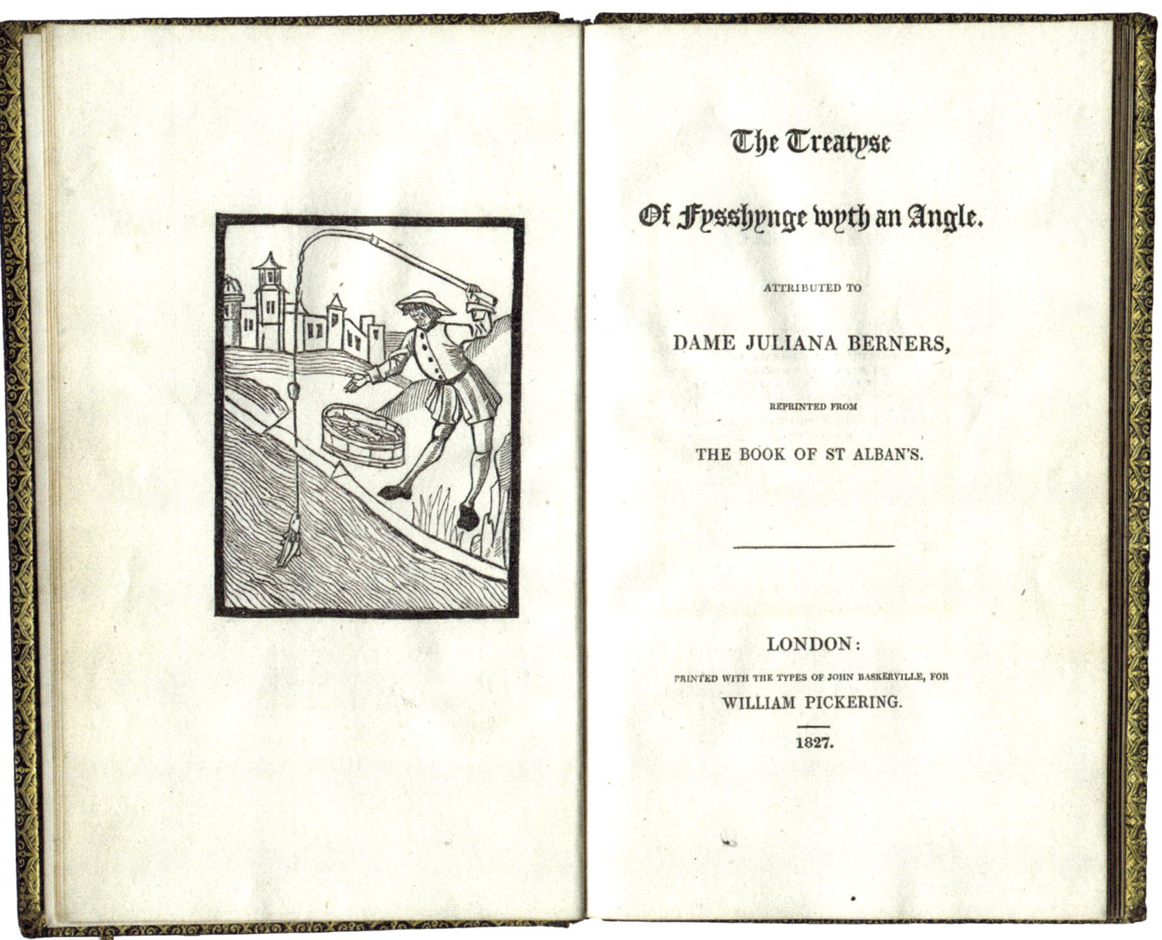

The Treatyse

Of Fysshynge wyth an Angle.

ATTRIBUTED TO

DAME JULIANA BERNERS,

REPRINTED FROM

THE BOOK OF ST ALBAN'S.

LONDON:

PRINTED WITH THE TYPES OF JOHN BASKERVILLE, FOR

WILLIAM PICKERING.

1827.

1

BERNERS, JULIANA. *The Treatyse of Fysshynge wyth an Angle*. 1496. LONDON: WILLIAM PICKERING, 1827. [SH 431 B6 1827] 18.7 CM X 11.9 CM

This edition is an 1827 reprint of the first printed book in English on fishing and one of the limited number of incunabula printed in English. The illustration reproduced in this edition was added

to the work by the printer, Wynkyn de Worde, and has since become one of the most-recognizable woodcuts of an angling scene.

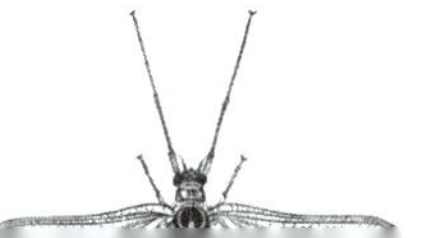

2

NINETEEN EDITIONS OF IZAAK WALTON'S *The Compleat Angler, or the Contemplative Man's Recreation*

Details of Izaak Walton's early life are scant, but he was born in Stafford, England circa 1593. Walton was initially an ironmonger by trade, but around the age of twenty-five, he moved to London, where he entered the Church as an examiner and vestryman (Marston 109–112). The first edition of *Compleat Angler* was published in 1653, just two short years after the Third English Civil War, and the book's peacefulness, tranquility, and pastoral nature provided welcome escapism for English men and women who had just endured political and religious upheaval and three civil wars (Westwood 1–2). Walton continued to add material to *Compleat Angler*, with the fifth edition (1676) being the last to be published during his lifetime and the first to contain the treatise on fly-fishing, contributed by his friend Charles Cotton.

Compleat Angler, perhaps surprisingly, has become the second-most reprinted book in English, second only after The Bible (Schurr). The precise reason for the book's longevity is somewhat difficult to isolate. Simply stated, Walton's book is a compilation of angling instruction, songs, recipes, and pastoral observations.

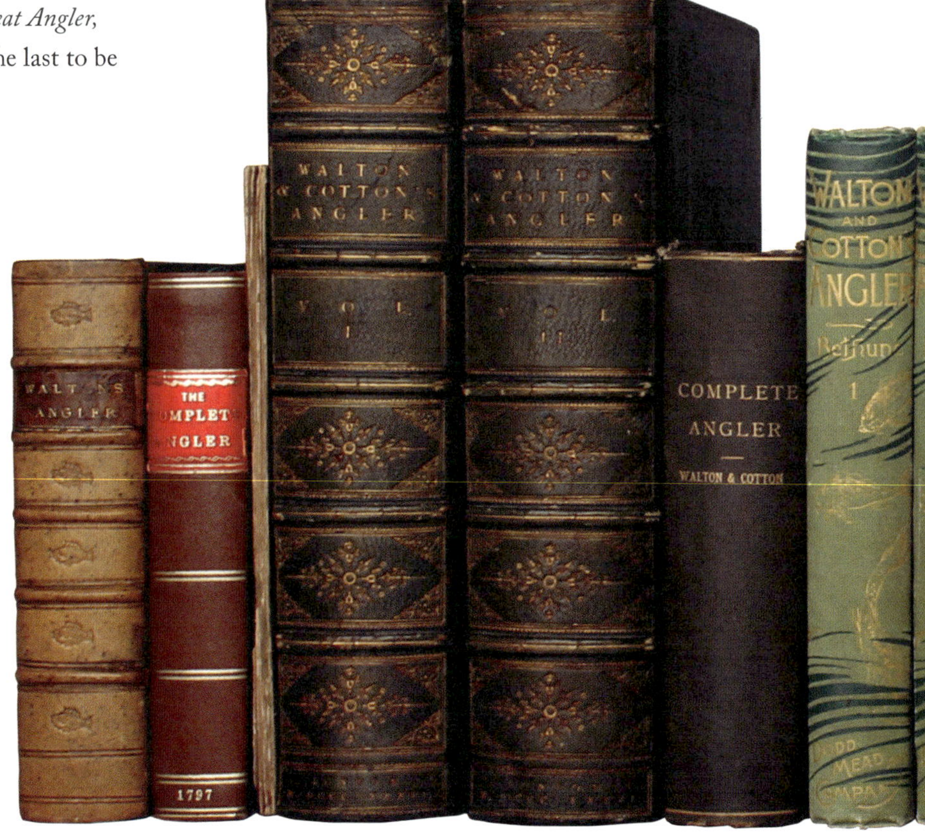

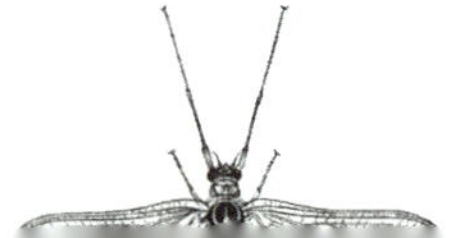

However, Walton's ability to capture the serenity and restorative aspects of angling and the outdoors is timeless. Arnold Gingrich explains the book's enduring appeal thusly: "The mood is idyllic, the setting pastoral, and to me the magic is always instant. I can be down in the dumps, or worried sick about something, and reaching for Walton is at least as soothing, and a little more lasting, than the momentary surcease found by the more routine means of reaching for a cigarette" (29).

The following 19 examples of Walton's classic include eighteenth-century editions, early American (item 2e) and Canadian (item 2j) editions, reading copies, and deluxe and limited editions, such as the first edition to be illustrated by Arthur Rackham (item 2q) and the fine Nonesuch Press edition (item 2n), which also includes biographies and other writings by Walton. William Pickering's 1836 edition of *Compleat Angler* (item 2d) is a lavish production with engravings on copper and steel. Charles Westwood, in his new edition of *Chronicle of the Complete Angler*, calls Pickering's 1836 edition "one of the handsomest publications of modern times, an ornament to the angler's library" (26). Some of the editions have their own unique stories independent of their content. For example, the engraver of the first book in the list (item 2a), William Wynne Ryland, was hanged for forgery. To the fly fisherman, *Compleat Angler* remained incomplete until Charles Cotton's treatise on fly-fishing was added to the 1676 edition. Cotton's contribution is present in many of the editions below.

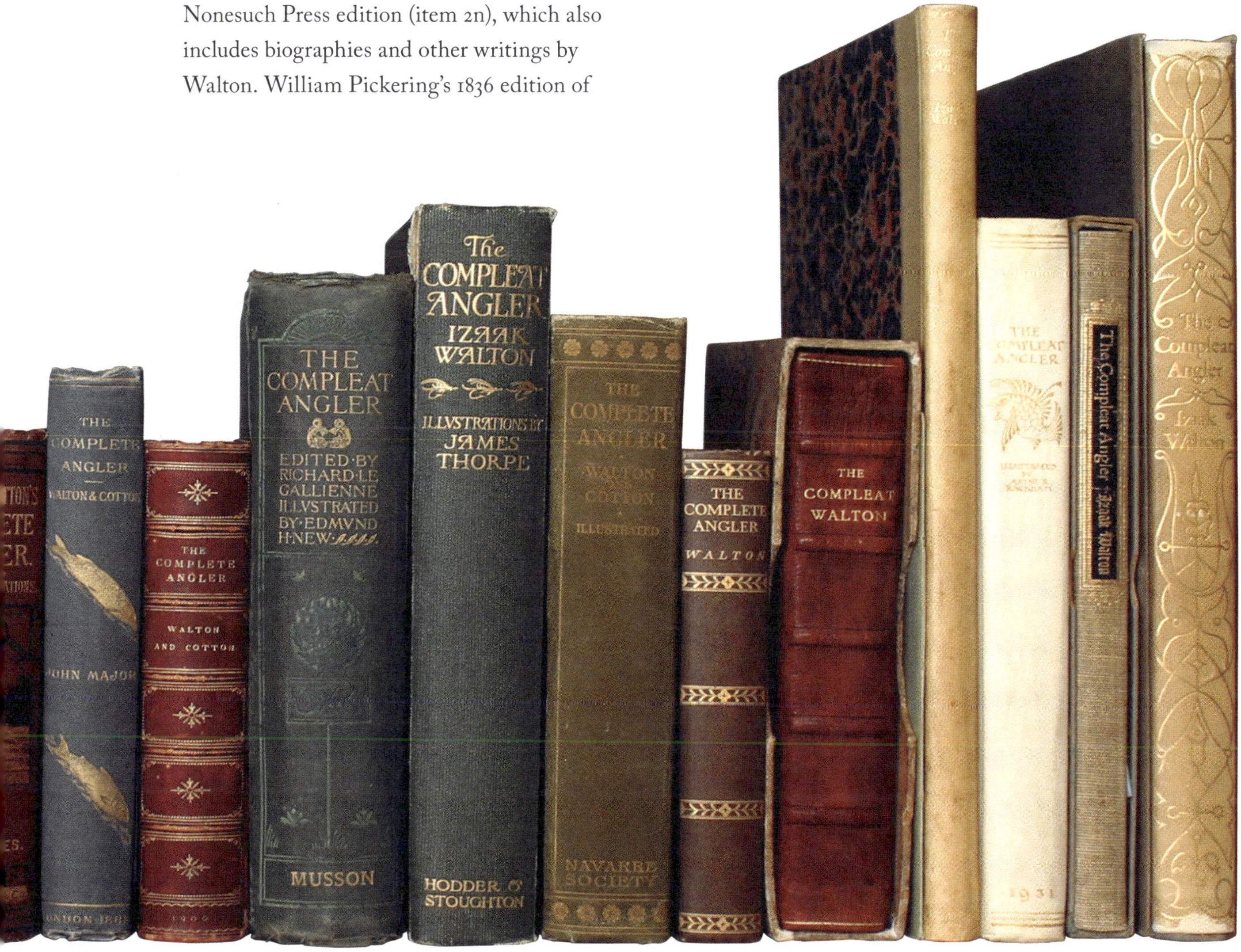

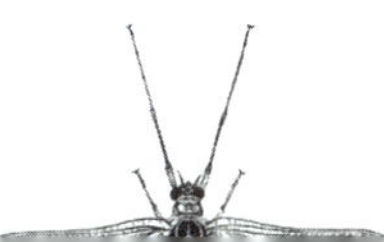

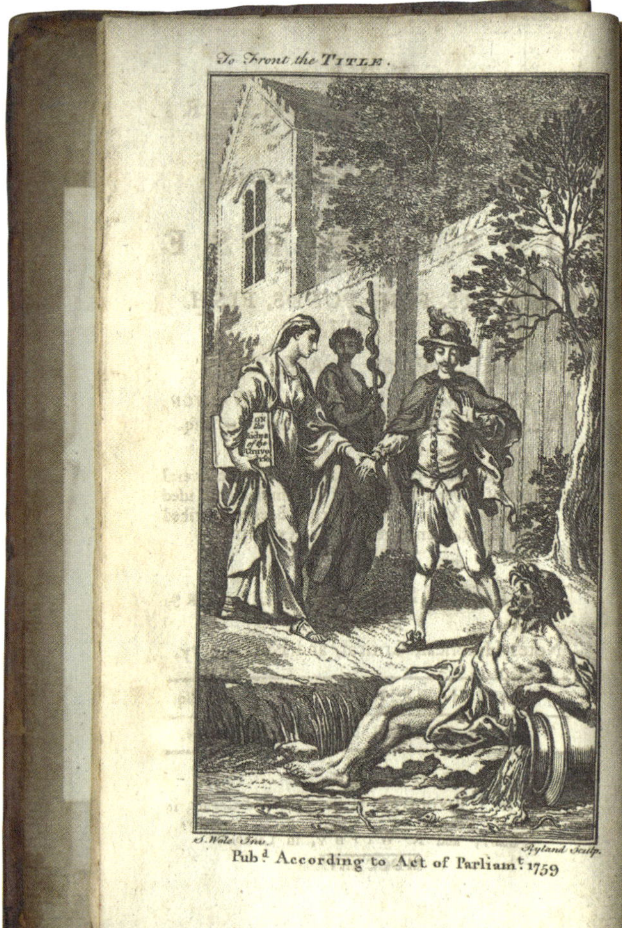

To Front the TITLE.

S. Wale Inv. Ryland Sculp.

Pub.d According to Act of Parliam.t 1759

THE
COMPLETE ANGLER:
OR,
Contemplative Man's Recreation.
BEING A
DISCOURSE
ON
RIVERS, FISH-PONDS, FISH,
and FISHING.
IN TWO PARTS.
The FIRST written by Mr. IZAAK WALTON,
The SECOND by CHARLES COTTON, Esq.
Illustrated with upwards of
Thirty COPPER-PLATE CUTS of the several Kinds of River-Fish, and of the Implements used in Angling, Views of the principal Scenes described in the Book. Engraved by Mr. RYLAND.
To which is now prefixed,
The LIVES of the AUTHORS.
AND
Notes Historical, Critical, and Explanatory.

By JOHN HAWKINS, of TWICKENHAM, Esq.

THE SECOND EDITION.

LONDON:
Printed for J. RIVINGTON, at the *Bible* and *Crown*, in *St. Paul's Church-Yard*; T. CASLON, in *Stationers Court*; and R. WITHY, in *Cornhill*.
MDCCLXVI.

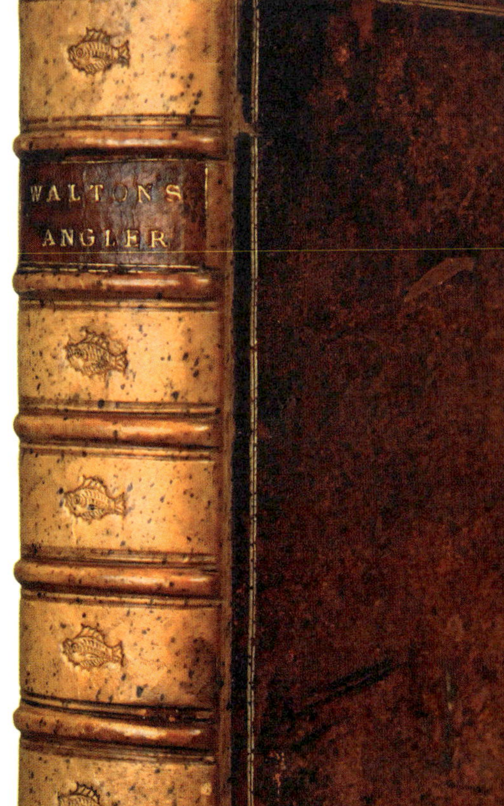

2 (a)

WALTON, IZAAK. *The Complete Angler, or, Contemplative Man's Recreation: Being a Discourse on Rivers, Fish-ponds, Fish, and Fishing: In Two Parts.* LONDON: J. RIVINGTON, ET AL., 1766. [PR 3757 W6 C7 1766] 18.1 CM X 12.1 CM

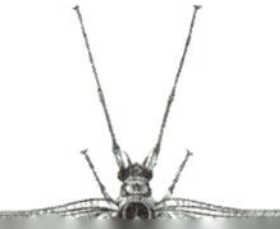

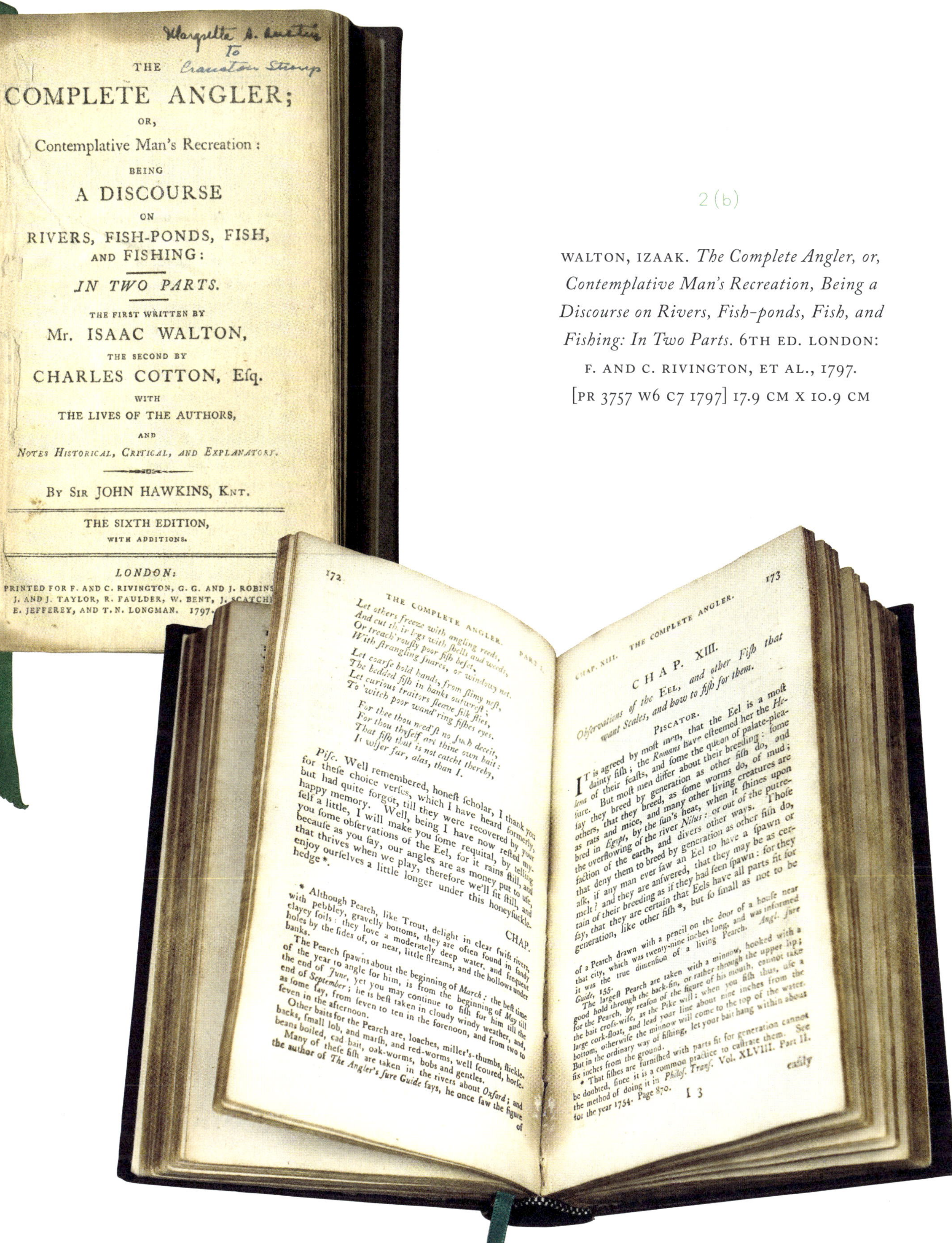

2 (b)

WALTON, IZAAK. *The Complete Angler, or, Contemplative Man's Recreation, Being a Discourse on Rivers, Fish-ponds, Fish, and Fishing: In Two Parts.* 6TH ED. LONDON: F. AND C. RIVINGTON, ET AL., 1797. [PR 3757 W6 C7 1797] 17.9 CM X 10.9 CM

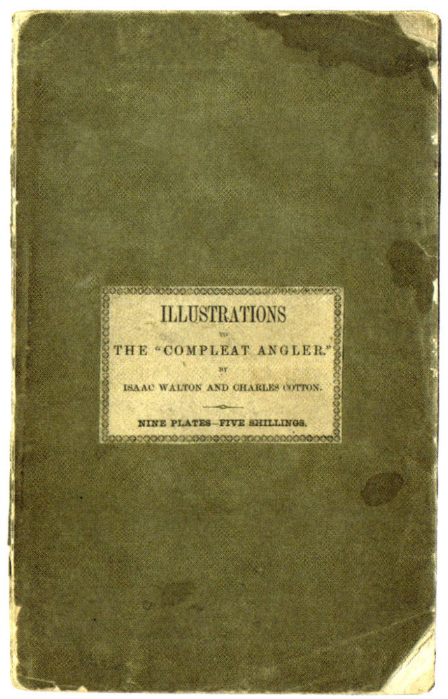

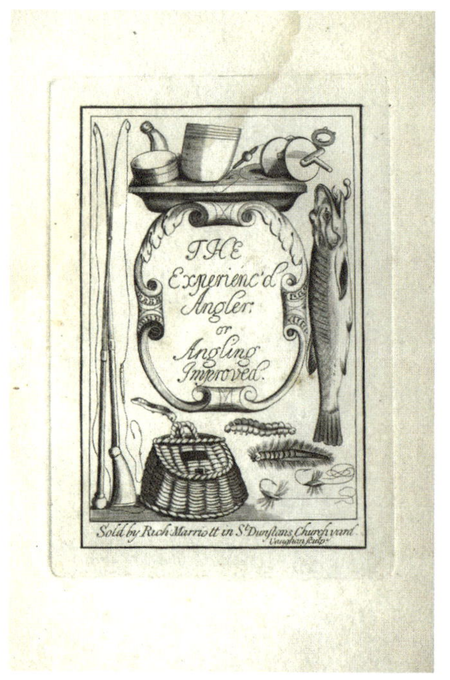

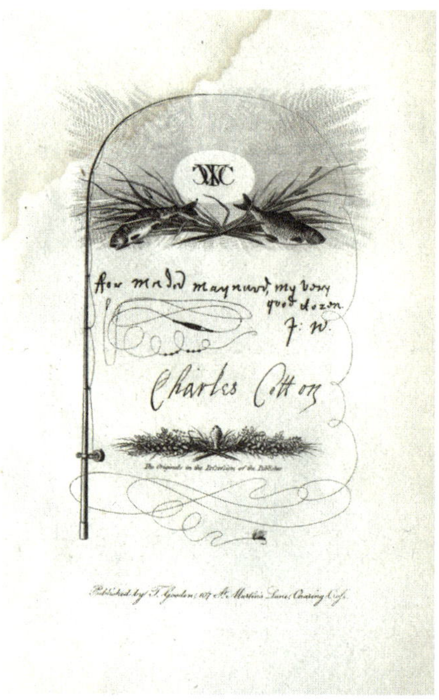

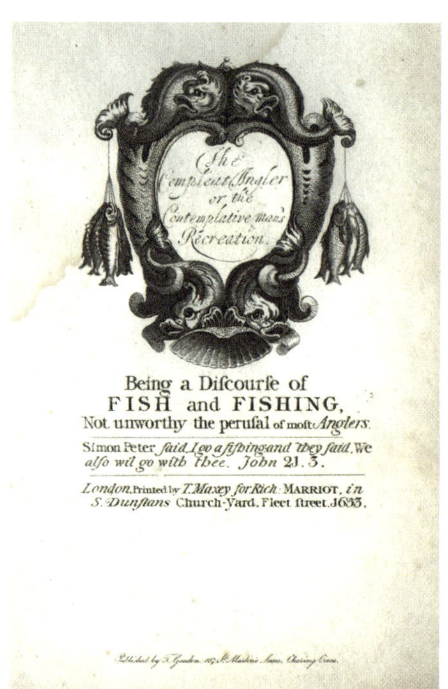

2(c)

Illustrations to the "Compleat Angler" by Isaac Walton and Charles Cotton.
CHARING CROSS: T. GOSDEN, [1823?]. [SH 435 145 1823] 21.5 CM X 13.8 CM

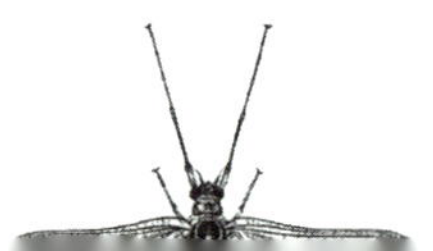

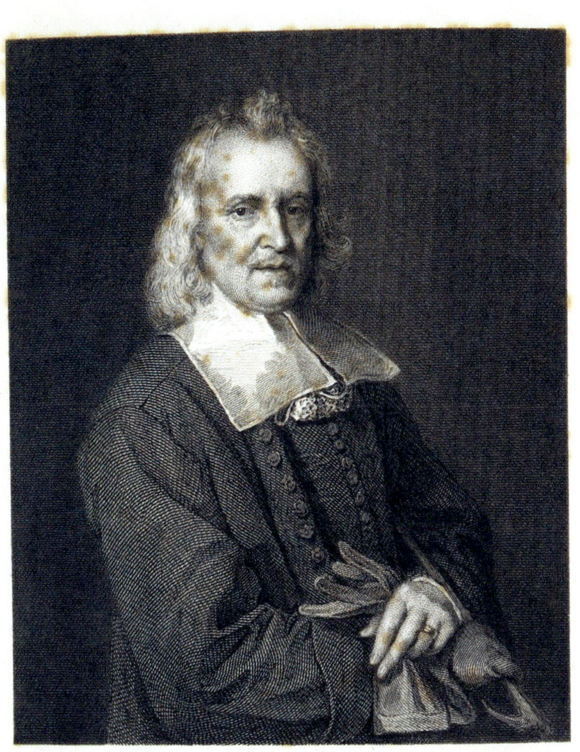

Copied by Derby from an original picture by Housman in the poſseſsion of the Rev.d Dr. Hawes.
Engraved by W. Humphrys

"A good name is better then a pretious oyntment":

Iz: Wa

Published by William Pickering, Chancery Lane London, Oct 1 1836

2(d)

WALTON, IZAAK. *The Complete Angler; or the Contemplative Man's Recreation, Being a Discourse of Rivers Fish-ponds Fish and Fishing.* 2 VOLS. LONDON: WILLIAM PICKERING, 1836. [PR 3757 W6 1836 V.1–2] 27.2 CM X 19.8 CM

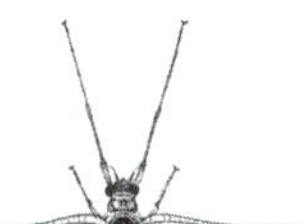

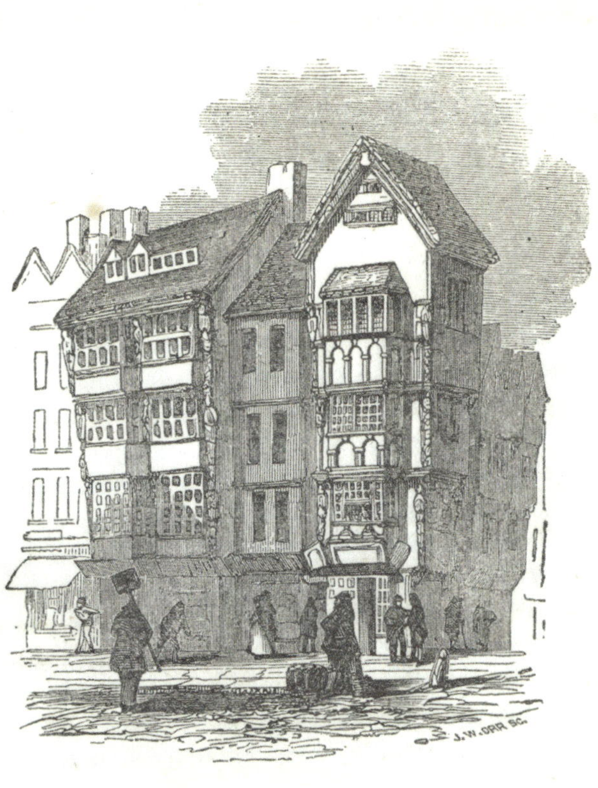

WALTON'S RESIDENCE IN FLEET STREET.

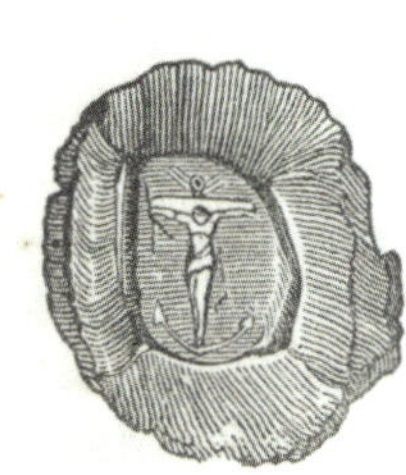

Seal presented to Walton by Dr. Donne.

Autograph.

2(e)

WALTON, IZAAK. *The Complete Angler, or, the Contemplative Man's Recreation.* NEW YORK: JOHN WILEY, 1848. [PR 3757 W6 C7 1848] 19.0 CM X 13.4 CM

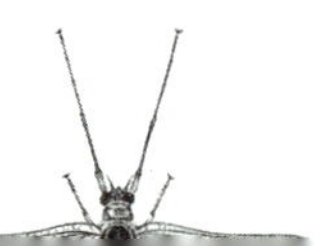

2 (f)

WALTON, IZAAK. *The Complete Angler, or the Contemplative Man's Recreation*. 2 VOLS. NEW YORK: DODD, MEAD & CO., 1880. [PR 3757 W6 C7 1880 V.1–2] 22.7 CM X 15.2 CM

2 (g)

WALTON, IZAAK. *The Complete Angler.* LONDON: FREDERICK WARNE & CO., 1888. [PR 3757 W6 C7 1888] 18.9 CM X 13.4 CM

2 (h)

WALTON, IZAAK. *The Complete Angler: to Which is Added a Treatise on Flies and Fly-hooks: With Ten Plates, Coloured by Hand, Representing 120 Flies, Natural and Artificial.* LONDON: JOHN C. NIMMO, 1889. [PR 3757 W6 C7 1889] 21.2 CM X 14.2 CM

2 (i)

WALTON, IZAAK. *The Complete Angler, or, the Contemplative Man's Recreation: Of Izaak Walton and Charles Cotton.* LONDON: GEORGE BELL AND SONS, 1900. [PR 3757 W6 C7 1900] 18.4 CM X 12.5 CM

2 (j)

WALTON, IZAAK. *The Compleat Angler.* TORONTO: MUSSON BOOK CO., LTD., 1906. [PR 3757 W6 C7 1906B] 24.8 CM X 18.1 CM

2 (k)

WALTON, IZAAK. *The Compleat Angler; or the Contemplative Man's Recreation: Being a Discourse of Fish & Fishing Not Unworthy of the Perusal of Most Anglers.* LONDON: HODDER & STOUGHTON, [1911]. [PR 3757 W6 C7 1911] 27.2 CM X 21.0 CM

2 (l)

WALTON, IZAAK. *The Complete Angler, or, the Contemplative Man's Recreation, of Izaak Walton and Charles Cotton.* LONDON: NAVARRE SOCIETY LTD., 1925. [PR 3757 W6 C7 1925] 23.1 CM X 15.8 CM

2 (m)

WALTON, IZAAK. *The Complete Angler, or the Contemplative Man's Recreation.* BOSTON: C.E. GOODSPEED & CO., 1928. [PR 3757 W6 C7 1928] 18.2 CM X 12.6 CM
EDITION OF 600 COPIES

2 (n)

WALTON, IZAAK. *The Compleat Angler, the Lives of Donne, Wotton, Hooker, Herbert & Sanderson, with Love and Truth & Miscellaneous Writings.* BLOOMSBURY: NONESUCH PRESS, 1929. [PR 3757 W6 C7 1929] 21.6 CM X 13.4 CM

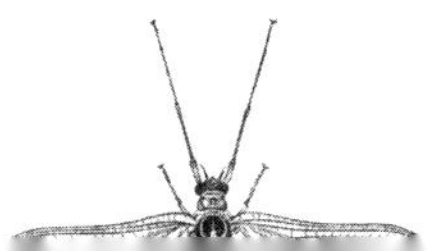

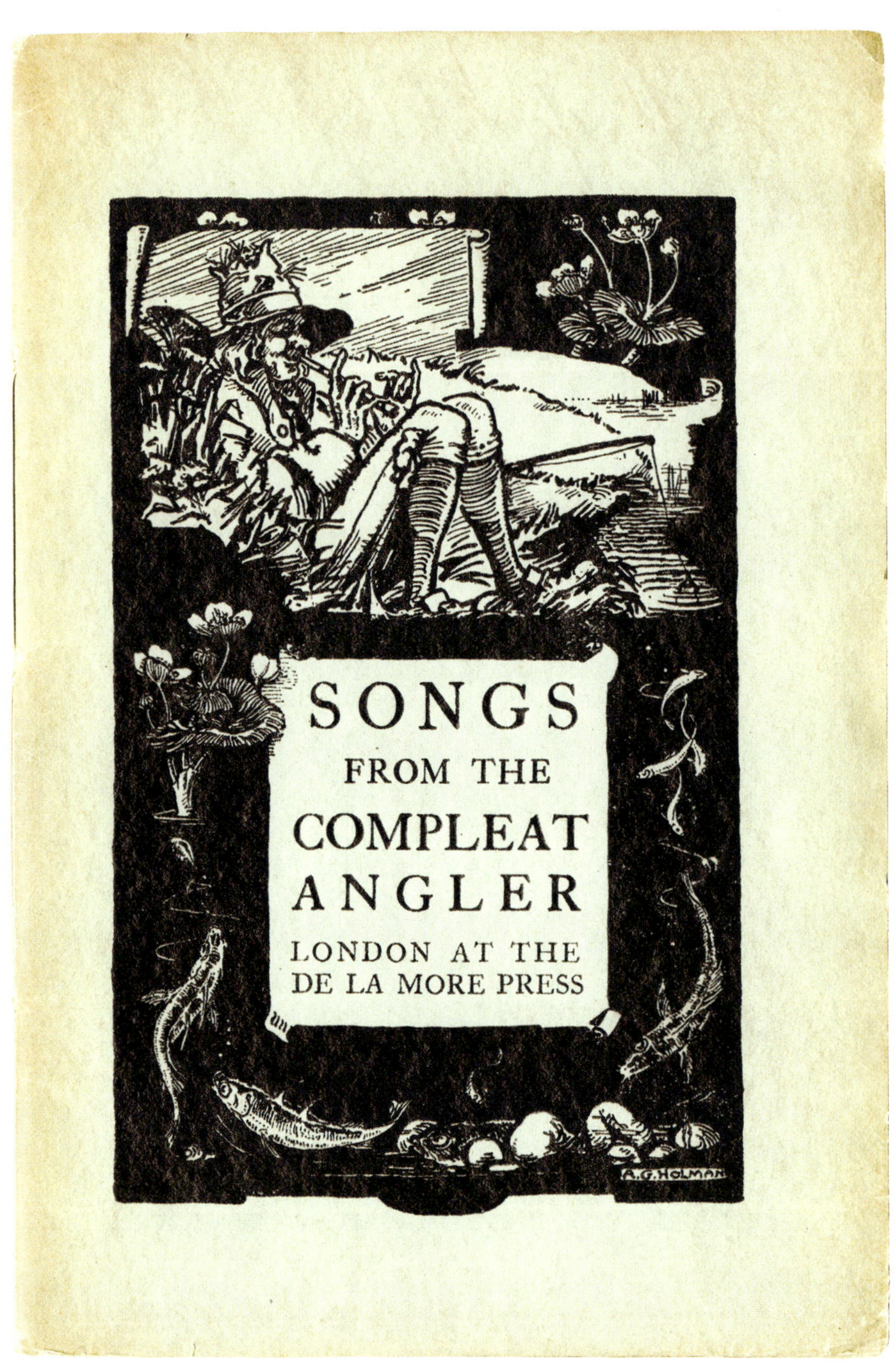

2(o)

WALTON, IZAAK. *Songs from the Compleat Angler.*
LONDON: DE LA MORE PRESS, [1929].
[PR 3757 W6 C72 1929] 19.8 CM X 13.4 CM

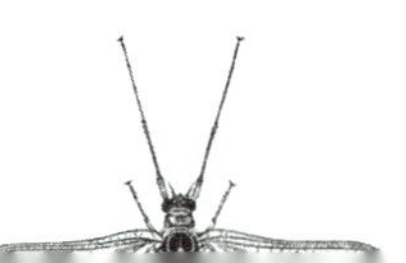

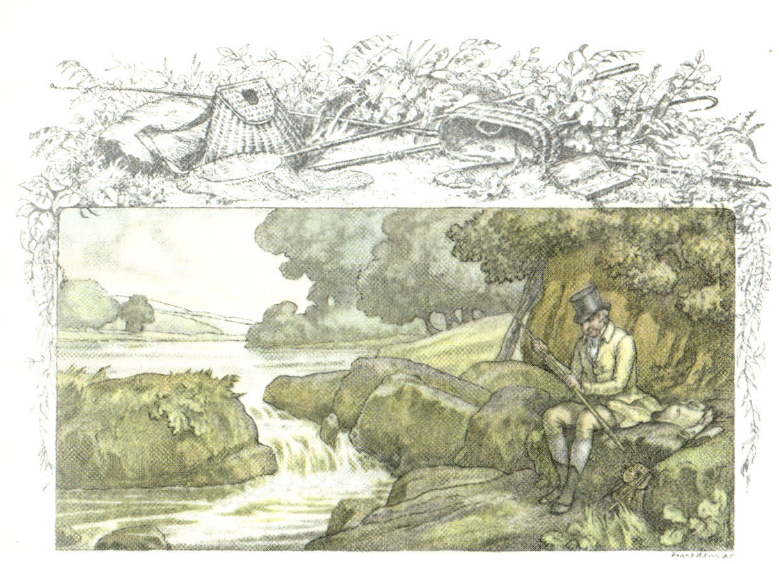

The Compleat

ANGLER

or,

The contemplative Mans

RECREATION.

Piſcator. PISCATOR. VIATOR.

YOu are wel overtaken Sir; a good morning to you; I have ſtretch'd my legs up *Totnam Hil* to overtake you, hoping your buſineſſe may occaſion you towards *Ware,* this fine pleaſant freſh *May day* in the Morning.

Viator. Sir, I ſhall almoſt anſwer your hopes: for my purpoſe is to be at *Hodſden* (three miles ſhort of that Town) I wil not ſay, before I drink; but before I break my faſt: for I have appointed a friend or two to meet me there at the *thatcht houſe,* about nine of the clock this morning; and that made me ſo early up, and indeed, to walk ſo faſt.

Piſc. Sir, I know the *thatcht houſe* very well: I often make it my reſting place, and taſte a cup of Ale there, for which liquor that place is very

2(p)

WALTON, IZAAK. *The Compleat Angler; or the Contemplative Man's Recreation, Being a Discourse of Fish and Fishing Not Unworthy the Perusal of Most Anglers.* LONDON: EYRE & SPOTTISWOODE, 1930. [PR 3757 W6 C7 1930 FOLIO] 35.0 CM X 22.3 CM | NO. 61 OF 250 COPIES

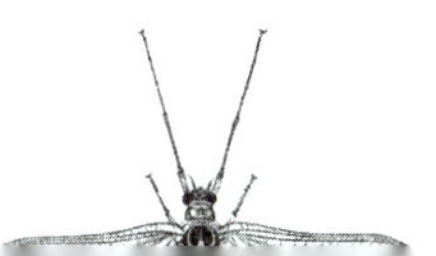

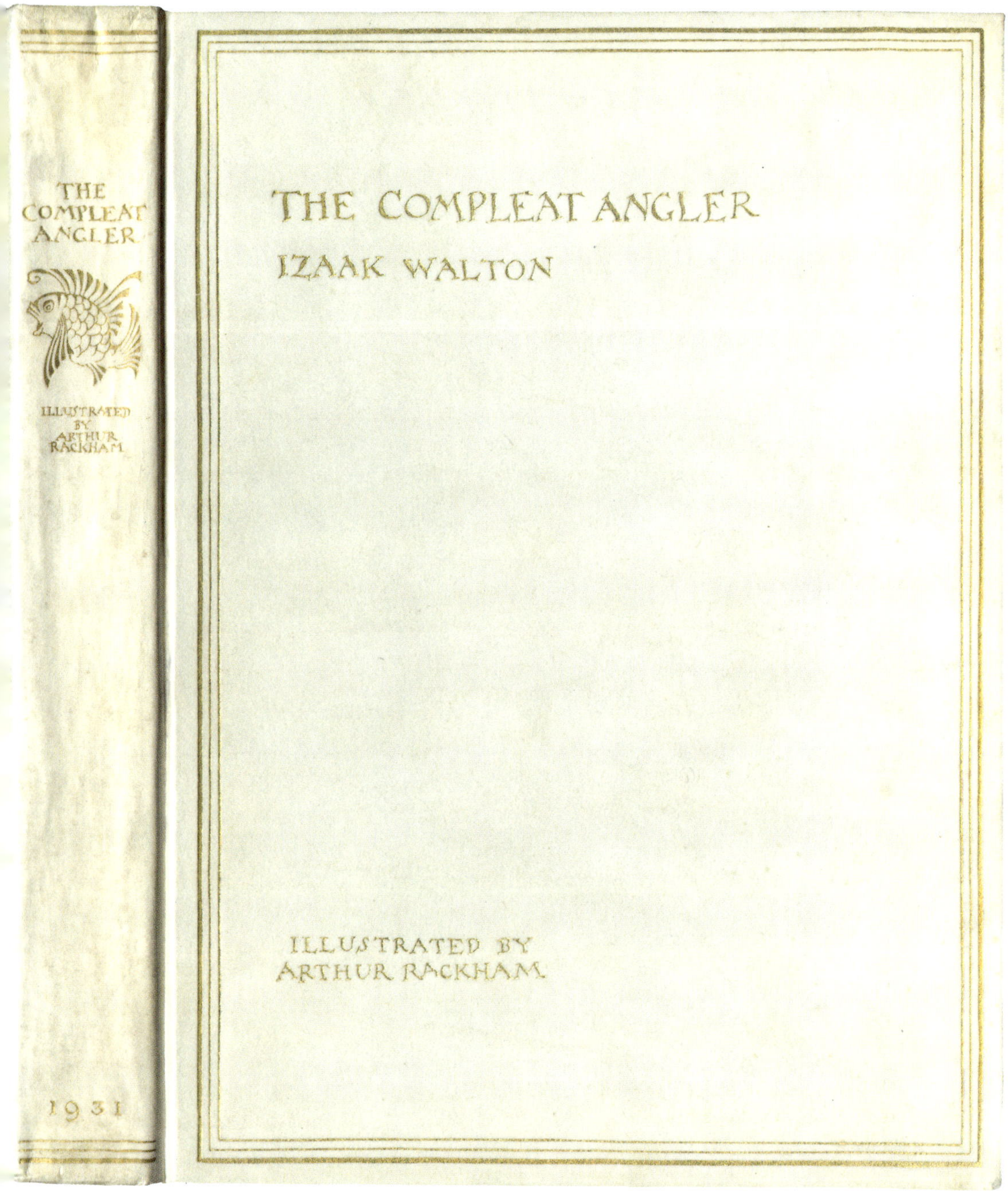

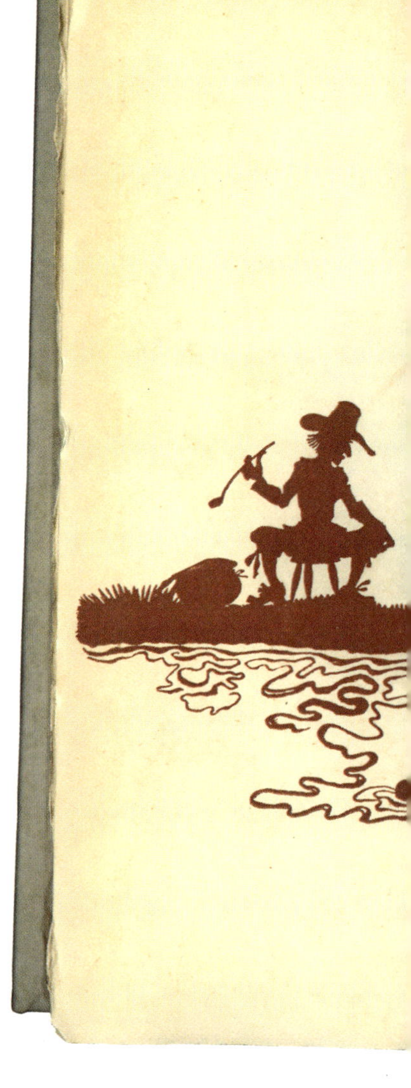

2 (q)

WALTON, IZAAK. *The Compleat Angler, or the Contemplative Man's Recreation: Being a Discourse of Rivers, Fishponds, Fish, and Fishing Not Unworthy the Perusal of Most Anglers.* LONDON: GEORGE G. HARRAP & CO. LTD., 1931. [PR 3757 W6 C7 1931]
26.9 CM X 20.6 CM | NO. 288 OF 775 COPIES

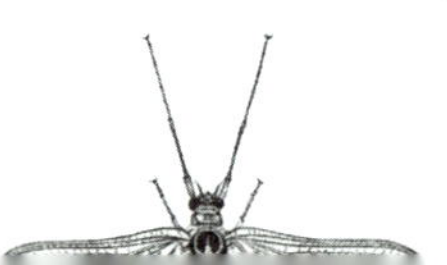

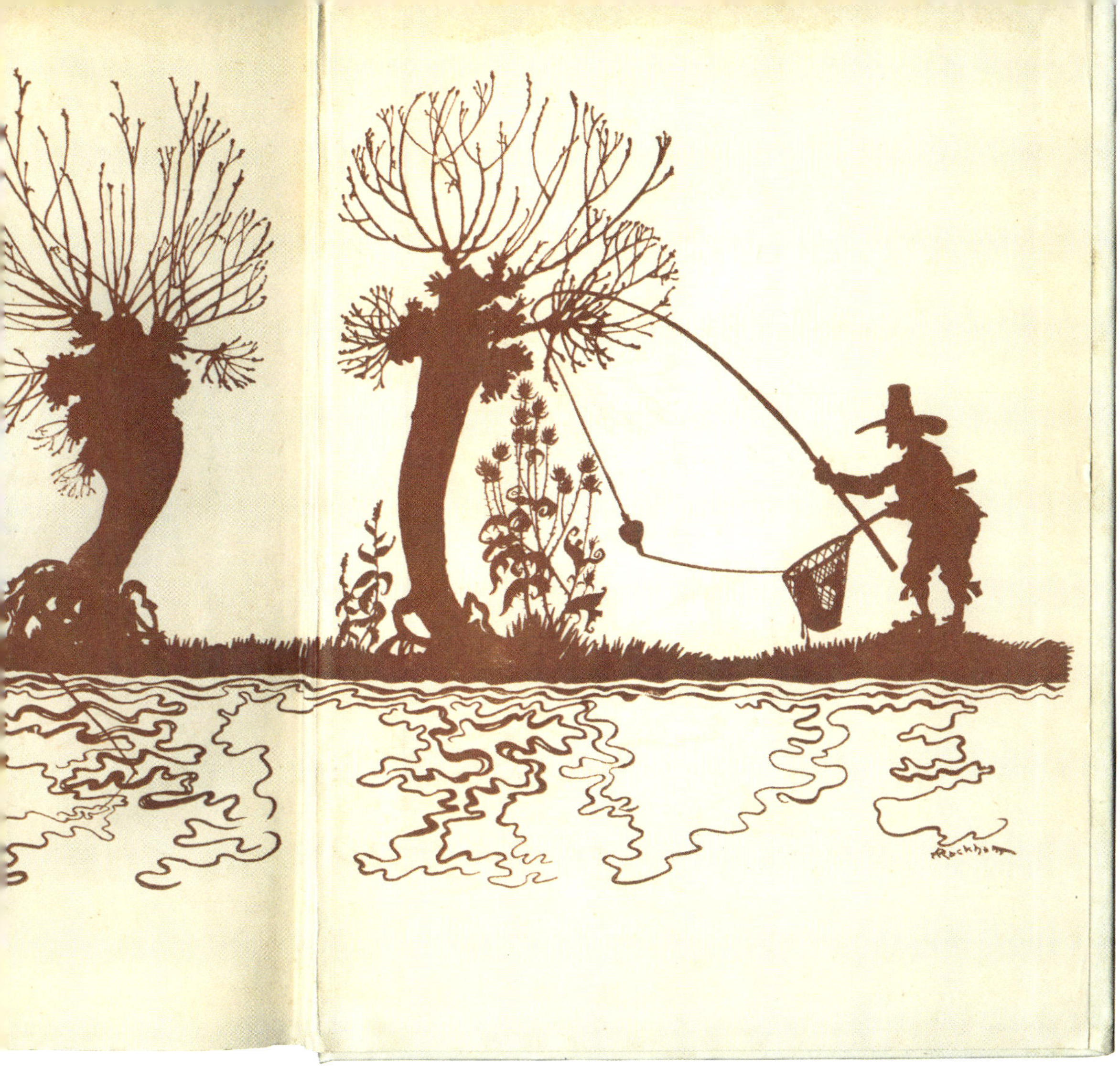

THE COMPLEAT ANGLER

OR

THE·CONTEMPLATIVE·MAN'S RECREATION

Being a Discourse of Rivers Fishponds Fish and Fishing not unworthy the Perusal of most Anglers

BY · IZAAK·WALTON

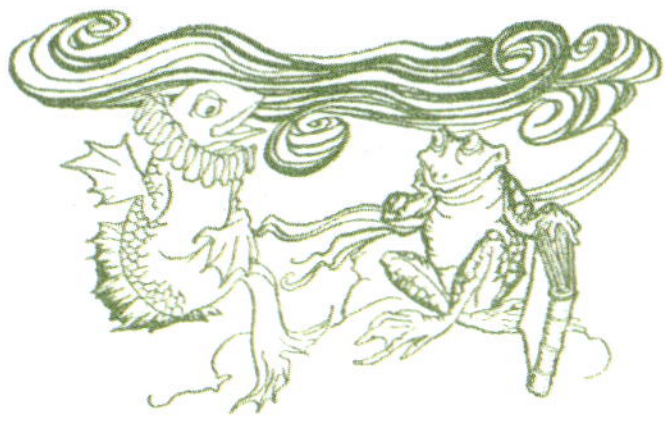

ILLUSTRATED BY·ARTHUR·RACKHAM

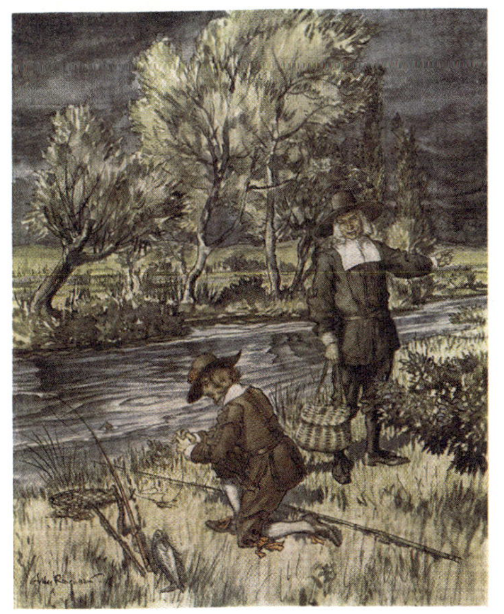

LONDON: GEORGE G. HARRAP & C°. L^TD

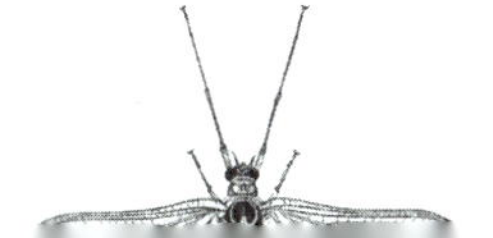

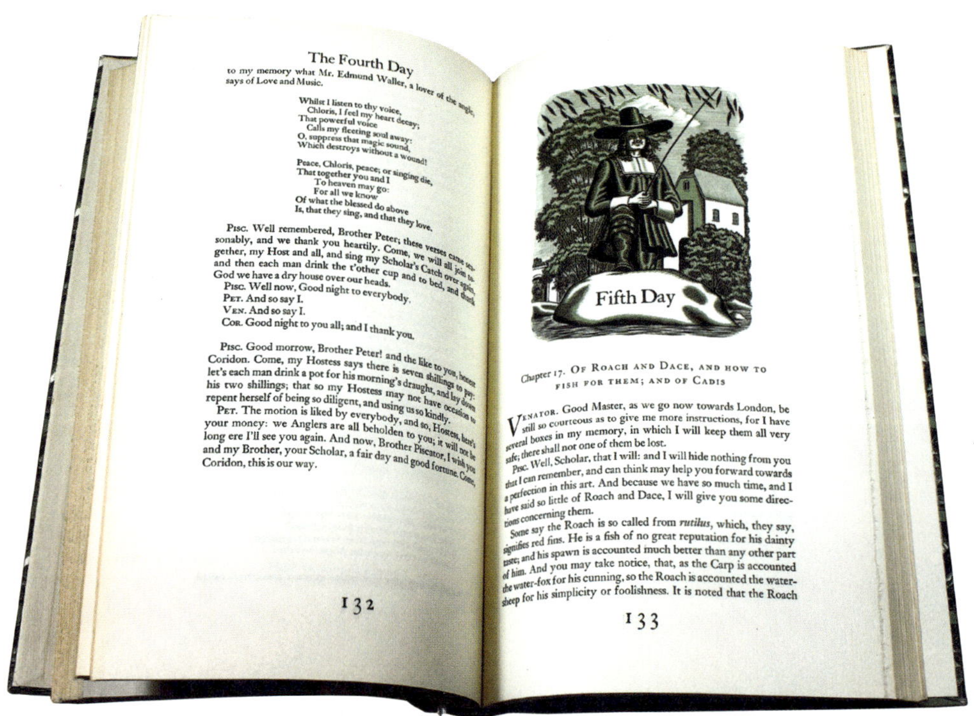

2(r)

WALTON, IZAAK. *The Compleat Angler, or, the Contemplative Man's Recreation.* MOUNT VERNON: PETER PAUPER PRESS, [1947]. [PR 3757 W6 C7 1947] 26.2 CM X 16.1 CM.

2(s)

WALTON, IZAAK. *The Compleat Angler; or, the Contemplative Man's Recreation, Being a Discourse of Fish and Fishing for the Perusal of Anglers.* NEW YORK: THE LIMITED EDITIONS CLUB, 1948. [PR 3757 W6 C7 1948 FOLIO] 33.3 CM X 22.5 CM | NO. 187 OF 1500 COPIES

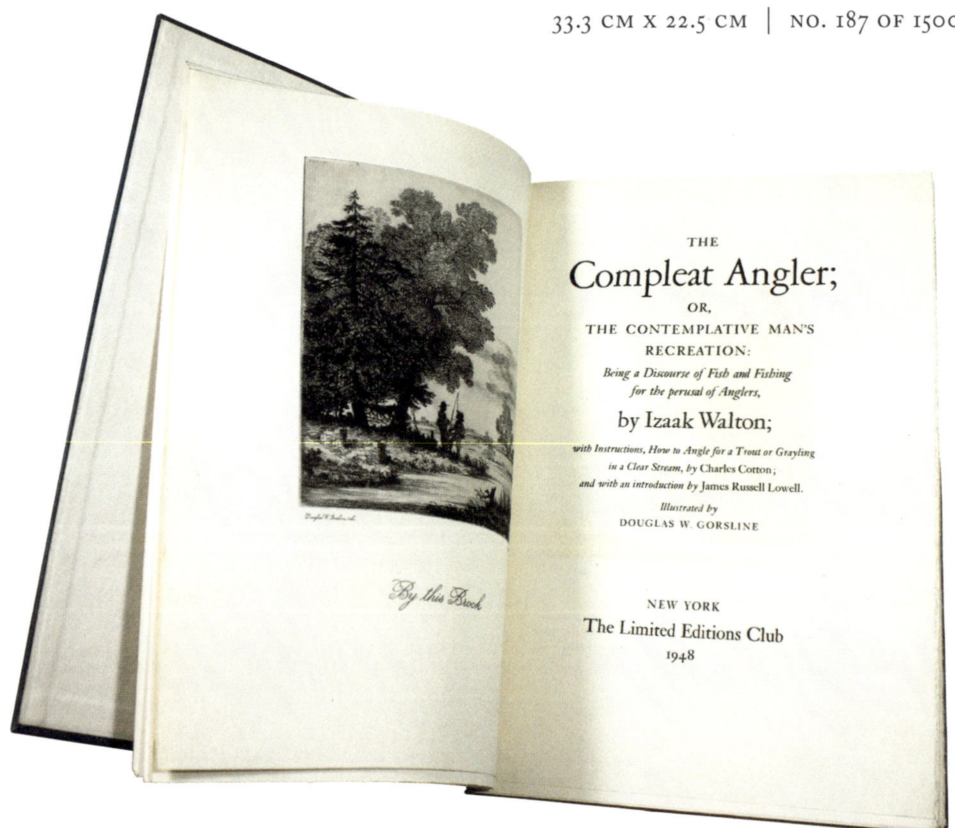

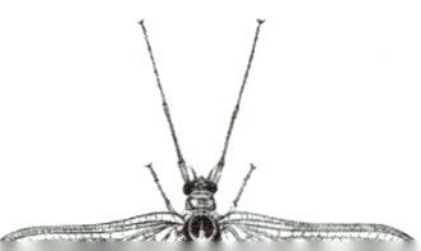

3

BROWNE, MOSES. *Angling Sports: In Nine Piscatory Eclogues: A New Attempt to Introduce a More Pleasing Variety and Mixture of Subjects and Characters into Pastoral, on the Plan of Its Primitive Rules and Manners: Suited to the Entertainment of Retirement, and the Lovers of Nature in Rural Scenes: With an Essay in Defence of This Undertaking.* LONDON: EDWARD AND CHARLES DILLY, 1773. [PR 3326 B986 P5 1773] 17.3 CM X 11.4 CM

This third edition of the manual by Moses Browne is in the form of piscatorial conversations among anglers about angling seasons, night fishing, angler's songs, and other topics. This edition contains an attractive engraved frontispiece of an angling scene.

Browne was a friend of Dr Samuel Johnson, who encouraged Browne to edit and reissue Walton's *Compleat Angler.* The Browne editions of *Compleat Angler* were the first to be published after Walton's death in 1683 (Gingrich 29).

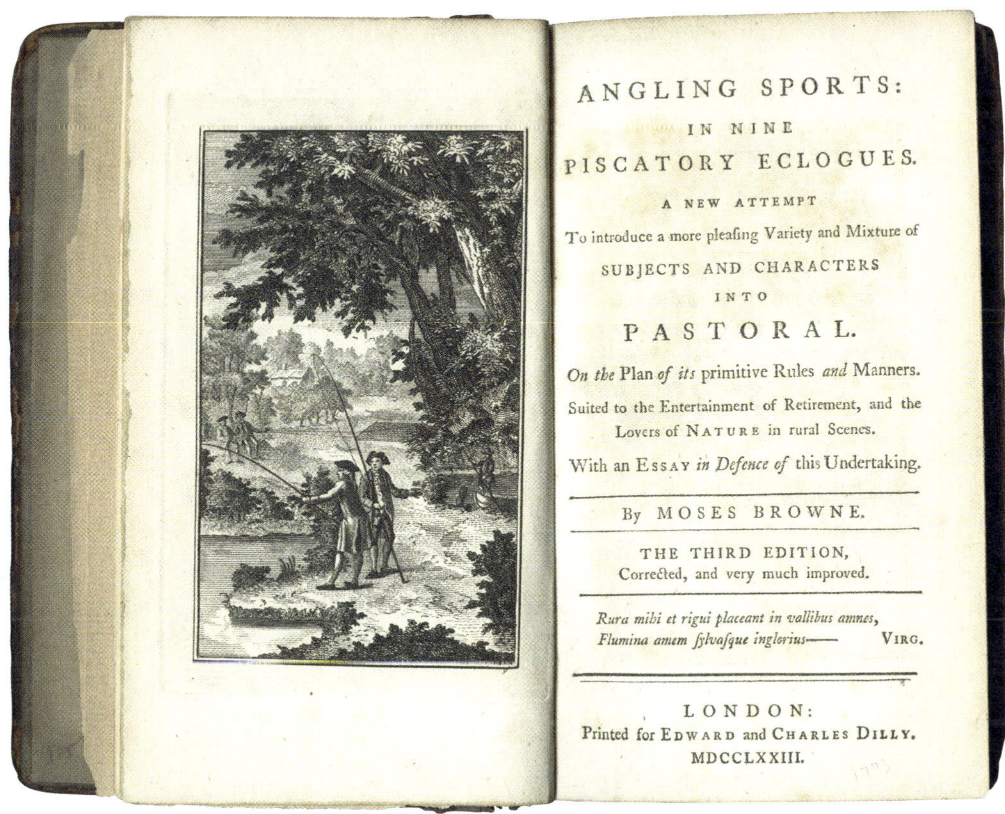

ANGLING SPORTS:

IN NINE

PISCATORY ECLOGUES.

A NEW ATTEMPT

To introduce a more pleasing Variety and Mixture of

SUBJECTS AND CHARACTERS

INTO

PASTORAL.

On the Plan *of its* primitive Rules *and* Manners.

Suited to the Entertainment of Retirement, and the Lovers of NATURE in rural Scenes.

With an ESSAY *in Defence of* this Undertaking.

By MOSES BROWNE.

THE THIRD EDITION,
Corrected, and very much improved.

Rura mihi et rigui placeant in vallibus amnes,
Flumina amem sylvasque inglorius—— VIRG.

LONDON:
Printed for EDWARD and CHARLES DILLY.
MDCCLXXIII.

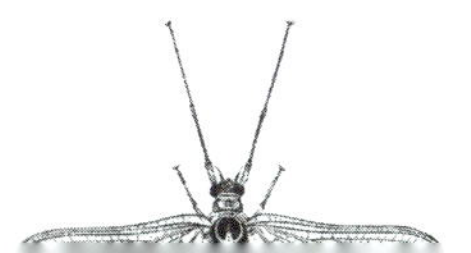

4

BROOKES, R[ICHARD]. *The Art of Angling*.
5TH ED. LONDON: T. LOWNDES, 1781.
[SH 411 B87 1781] 17.8 CM X 10.8 CM

This is the fifth edition of one of the primary eighteenth-century manuals. Although contents were borrowed liberally from other authors (Westwood et al. 42), the book, with its numerous editions, is an important compilation of eighteenth-century fishing knowledge. It contains 135 woodcuts of fish and fishing equipment.

36 CHA

Difpofition may affift them in Leaps, by whi
they and their Genus take their Prey.
CATERPILLAR, or PALMER-FLY,
WORM, is a good Bait for a Trout.

CHARS.

1. *The* GILT-CHAR.

The Latin Writers call this *Carpio Lacûs*
naci, becaufe they imagined it was only to be m
with in that particular Lake; but it has fince a
peared to be the fame Fifh with our Gilt-Ch
which is bred in *Winander-Meer*, in the Cour
of *Weftmoreland*. It is proportionably broader th
a Trout, and the Belly is more prominent, b
its Length, when greateft, never exceeds twel
Inches. The Scales are fmall, the Colour of the Ba
is more lively than in a Trout, and is beautifi
with black Spots; the Belly and Sides beneath t
lateral Line, are of a bright Silver Colour; the Sc
is tranfparent, and the Snout blueifh. It has Tee
in the lower Jaw, on the Palate and the Tongu
the Swimming-Bladder is extended the wh
Length of the Back, and the Gall-Bladder is larg
The Flefh of the Gilt-Char is red, and is a
counted fo very delicious among the *Italians*, th
they fay it excells all other Pond or Sea-Fifh wha
ever, and they efteem the Nature of it to be
wholefome, that they allow fick Perfons to eat
Winander-Meer is a Lake, according to *Ca*

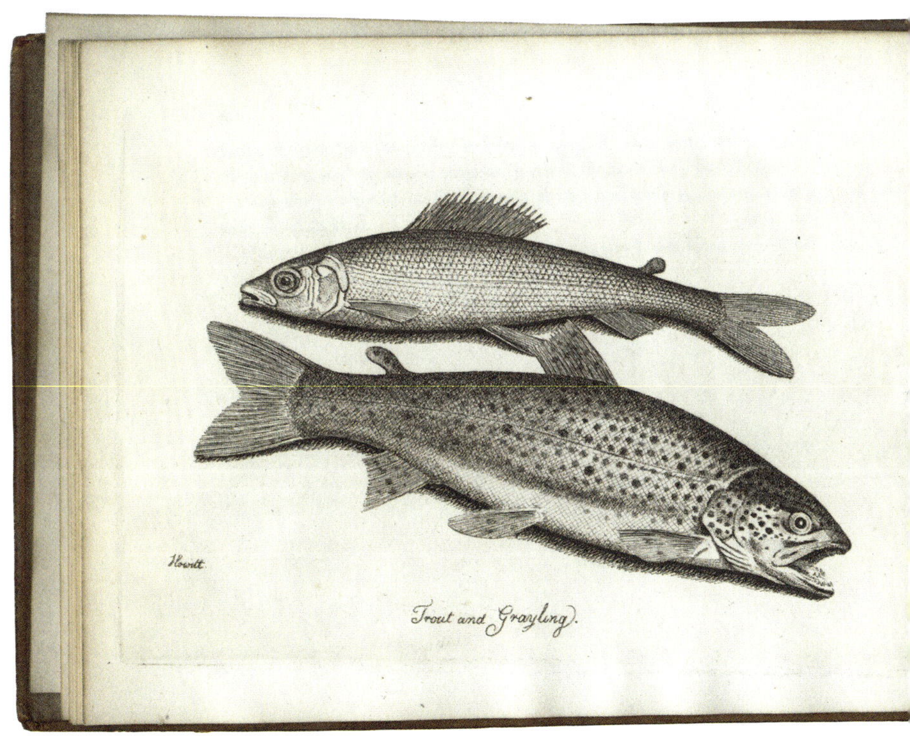

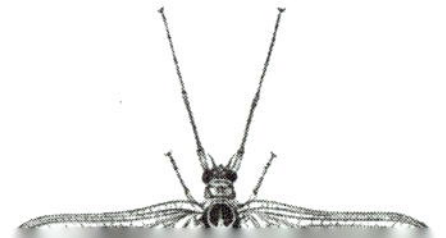

C H A 37

n, ten Miles in Length, and in ſome Places ex-
ding deep, therefore they are only taken in the
inter-time, when they go into the Shallows to
awn.

2. *The* Red Char, *or* Torgach.

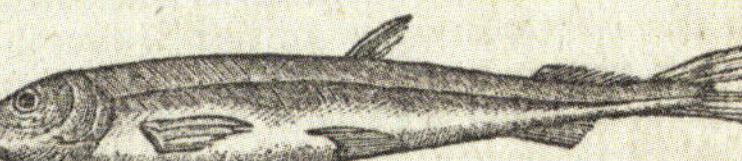

The Red Char is the *Umbla Minor* of *Geſner*
d other Authors, and is known in *Wales* by the
ame of *Torgoch*. The Body of this Fiſh is of a
nger and more ſlender Make than that of a
rout, for one of about eight Inches long was no
ore than an Inch and an half broad. The Back
of a greeniſh olive, ſpotted with white. The
elly, about the Breadth of half an Inch, is paint-
d with red, in ſome of a more lively, in others of
paler Colour, and in ſome, eſpecially the Female,
is quite white. The Scales are ſmall, and the
teral Lines ſtraight. The Mouth is wide, the
aws pretty equal, unleſs the lower be a little
arper and more protuberant than the upper; the
wer Part of the Fins are of a vermilion Dye.
he Gills are quadruple, and it has Teeth both
the Jaws and on the Tongue; in the upper
aw there is a double Row of them. The Swim-
ing-Bladder is like that of a Trout; the Liver is
ot divided into Lobes; the Gall-Bladder is large,
e Spleen ſmall and blackiſh, the Heart triangu-
r, and the Eggs of the Spawn large and round.
The Fleſh is more ſoft and tender than that of
Trout, and when boiled can ſcarcely be allowed
be red. It is in the higheſt Eſteem where known,
and

5

5

HOWITT, S[AMUEL]. *The Angler's Manual; or, Concise Lessons of Experience, Which the Proficient in the Delightful Recreation of Angling Will Not Despise, and the Learner Will Find the Advantage of Practising: Containing Useful Instruction of Every Approved Method of Angling, and Particularly on the Management of the Hand and Rod in Each Method.* LIVERPOOL: SAMUEL BAGSTER, 1808. [SH 439 A65 1808] 14.5 CM X 20.2 CM

An attractively-printed, oblong book with full-page engravings of fish delicately and accurately rendered, the manual is known more for its plates and less for the value of its text (Westwood et al. 10).

THE

ANGLER'S MANUAL.

TROUT.

TROUT-FISHING is divided into these four very different modes, viz. Worm, Minnow, Cad-bait, and Fly-fishing.

WORM-FISHING.

Rod. A bottom or trolling-rod, about fourteen feet in length, strong, but handy, top, smart in the spring, yet not too stiff.

Wheel. A multiplier, with length of line according to the breadth of the stream: in a general way, about thirty or forty yards.

B

Hook. In thick water, No. 3 or 4; if the fish run small, No. 5; a good weed or two, or a yard of gut above, with some large shots, or even a bullet, if the stream or eddy is strong enough to keep it in motion. You may then fish clumsily with success, as neither your line nor yourself can be seen.

But as Trout are to be taken in bright water and weather, with the worm, when they will not touch

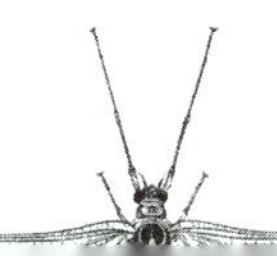

6

[LATHY, THOMAS PIKE]. *The Angler: A Poem, in Ten Cantos: With Proper Instructions in the Art, Rules to Choose Fishing Rods, Lines, Hooks, Floats, Baits, and to Make Artificial Flies: Receipts for Pastes, &c.: And in Short, Every Article Relating to the Sport.* LONDON: WRIGHT AND ILEY, 1819.
[PR 4878 L18 A6 1819] 19.1 CM X 11.7 CM

This is one in a line of eighteenth- and early-nineteenth-century pastoral angling books to present angling instruction and descriptions via poems and conversations. This edition includes attractive head- and tail-piece decorations of flies and angling scenes. However, Westwood et al. describe it as "one of the worst instances of literary appropriation on record" (131) and accuse the author of copying directly from other authors.

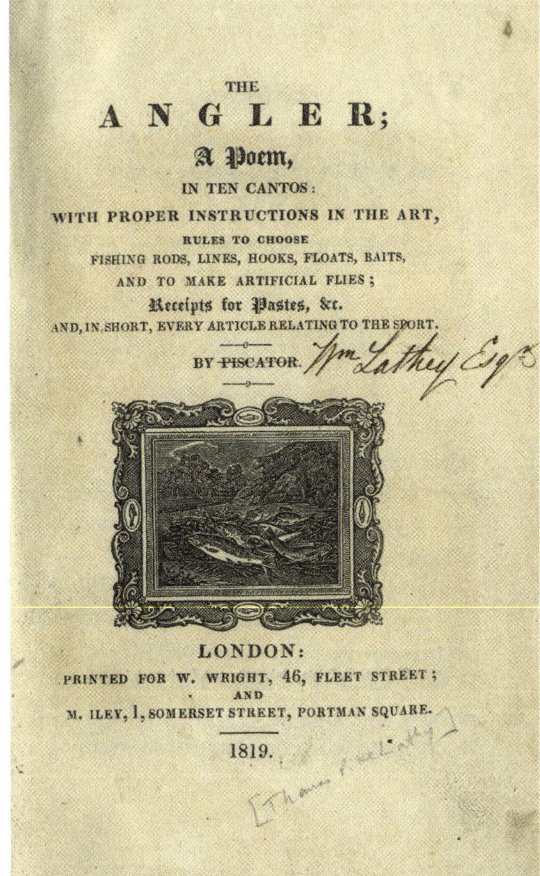

THE
ANGLER;
A Poem,
IN TEN CANTOS:
WITH PROPER INSTRUCTIONS IN THE ART,
RULES TO CHOOSE
FISHING RODS, LINES, HOOKS, FLOATS, BAITS,
AND TO MAKE ARTIFICIAL FLIES;
Receipts for Pastes, &c.
AND, IN SHORT, EVERY ARTICLE RELATING TO THE SPORT.
BY PISCATOR.

LONDON:
PRINTED FOR W. WRIGHT, 46, FLEET STREET;
AND
M. ILEY, 1, SOMERSET STREET, PORTMAN SQUARE.
1819.

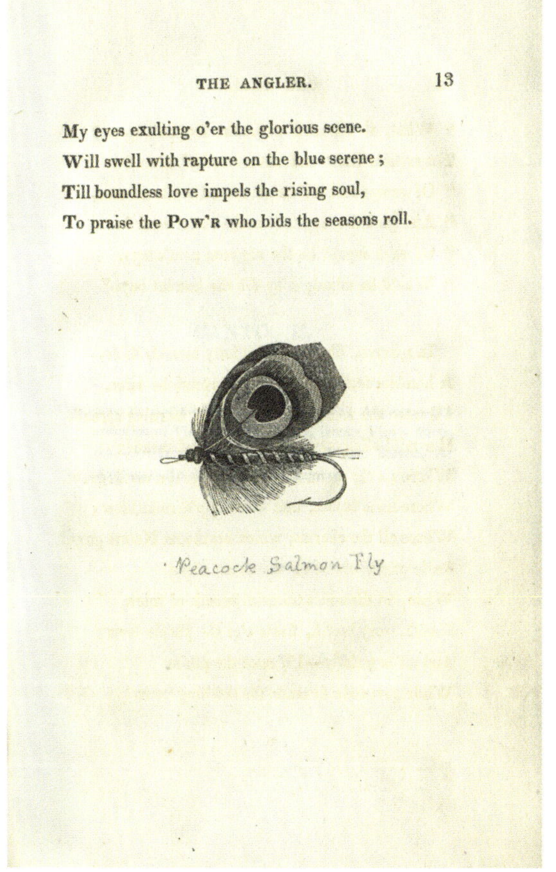

THE ANGLER. 13

My eyes exulting o'er the glorious scene.
Will swell with rapture on the blue serene;
Till boundless love impels the rising soul,
To praise the Pow'r who bids the seasons roll.

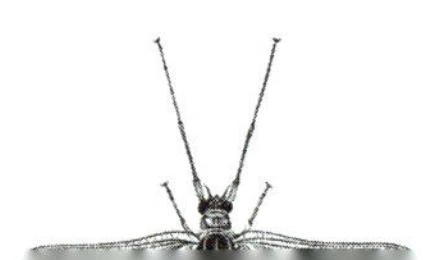

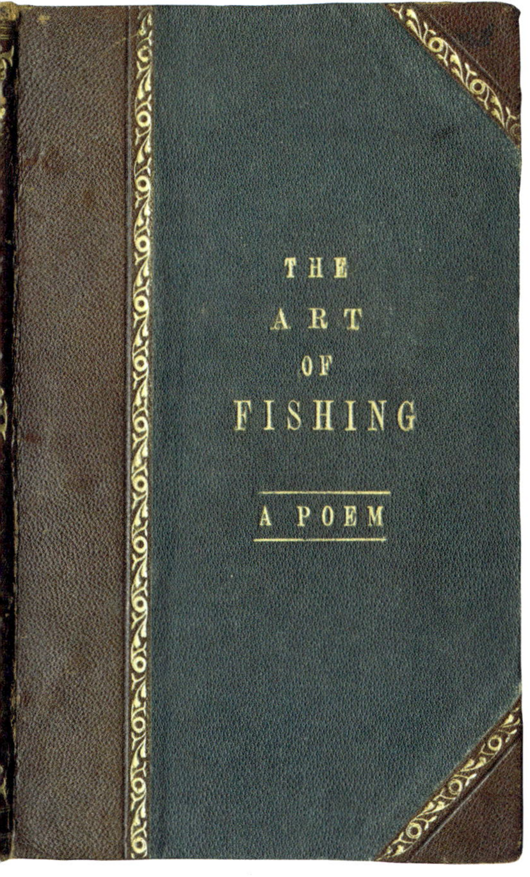

56

When at the lure the salmon rise,
Their plunge imprints a dread surprize,
And strikes an awful fear;
Into a bulge the waters swell,
And with a grumbling noise foretell,
Th' approaching salmon near.

They take their prey, then downwards turn,
Just shew their tails, which lashing spurn
The deep, as they descend:
Such was the grumbling noise through air,
When Pluto came to seize his fair,
Bade earth in chasms rend.

So Thetis rose to see her son,
Before beleaguer'd Troy was won;
The waves in rising curls,
The swelling surge bespoke her near,
And when retiring clos'd the rear,
With gulping eddying whirls.

When the strong salmon e'er you raise,
If you'd for dext'rous skill win praise,
Start not when he is near:

57

But let him take your fly and turn,
Then sideways strike, in vain he'll spurn,
But upwards strike not e'er.

In pleasant Eden you'll ne'er find,
Good salmon fishing, but in wind,
For here no streams are found:
Unless when in the Weir is made,
A breach by torrents level laid,
And even with the ground.

Then in its rapid streams you try,
With trolling or the bumbee fly,
Adapted to the stream:
And as in Tweed use all your skill,
Trying the likeliest parts at will,
As right to you shall seem.

Near Eden's mouth, where his streams join,
And with the salt wave close combine,
By the tide's boundless sway,
In April, salmon will resort;
When the tide ebbs afford much sport,
By late or early day.

7

CHARLETON, T.W. *The Art of Fishing: A Poem*. NORTH SHIELDS: J.K. POLLOCK, 1819.
[SH 439 C47 1819] 21.2 CM X 13.4 CM

Charleton's *The Art of Fishing* provides angling instructions in a long poem, including the following section on "setting the hook," which is as helpful today as it was in 1819:

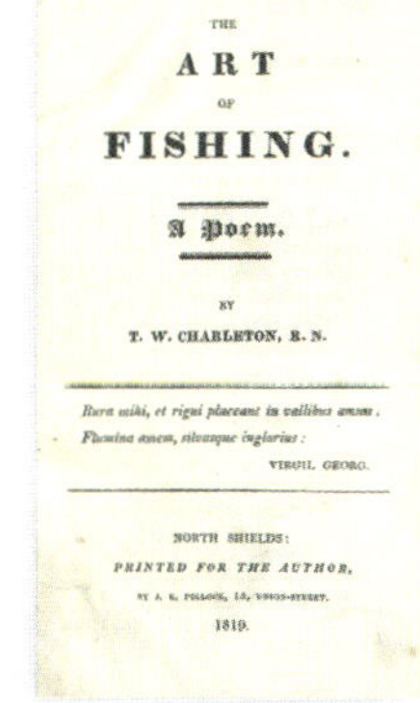
THE
ART
OF
FISHING.

A Poem.

BY
T. W. CHARLETON, R. N.

VIRGIL. GEORG.

NORTH SHIELDS:
PRINTED FOR THE AUTHOR,
1819.

When the strong salmon e'er you raise,
If you'd for dext'rous skill win praise,
Start not when he is near:
But let him take your fly and turn,
Then sideways strike, in vain he'll spurn,
But upwards strike not e'er. (56)

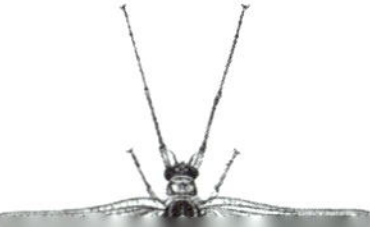

8

KIRKBRIDE, JOHN. *The Northern Angler; or, Fly-fisher's Companion.* CARLISLE: C. THURNAM, 1837. [SH 456 K4 1837] 17.9 CM X 11.5 CM

Kirkbride's *The Northern Angler* is a guidebook for Northern England that went through four editions, this being the first (Westwood et al. 127). The author provides descriptions of scores of flies, with instructions on fly-tying and fly-making for river flies, "night flies," and flies for lake fishing. The introduction has a charming description

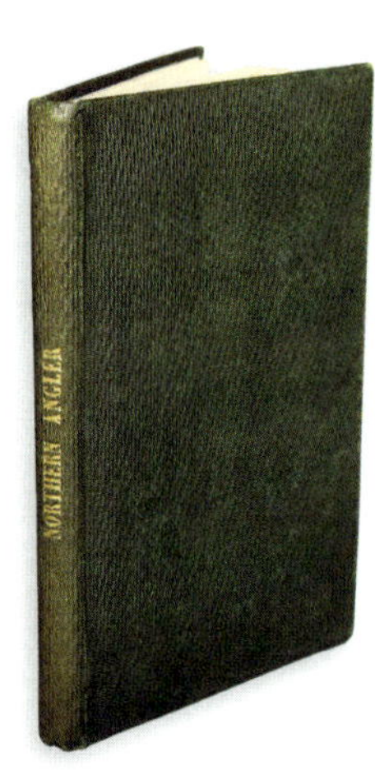

of the health benefits of angling: "How soon do the wan checks of the valetudinarian assume a healthy bloom when he is induced to snuff the morning air, perfumed by the sweets of spring, and follow the meanders of some delightful mountain stream!" (ix–x).

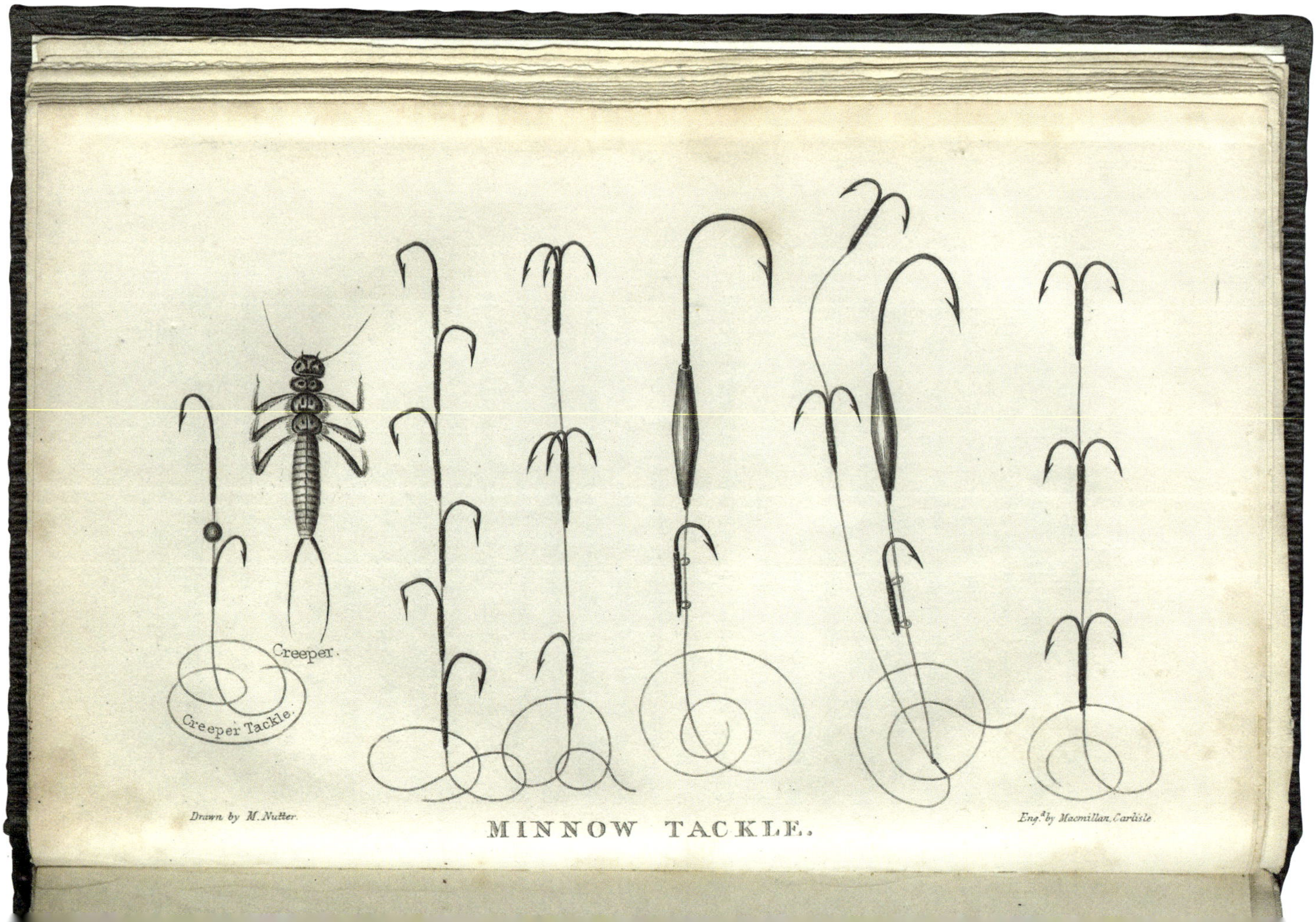

Creeper.

Creeper Tackle.

Drawn by M. Nutter.

MINNOW TACKLE.

Engd by Macmillan, Carlisle

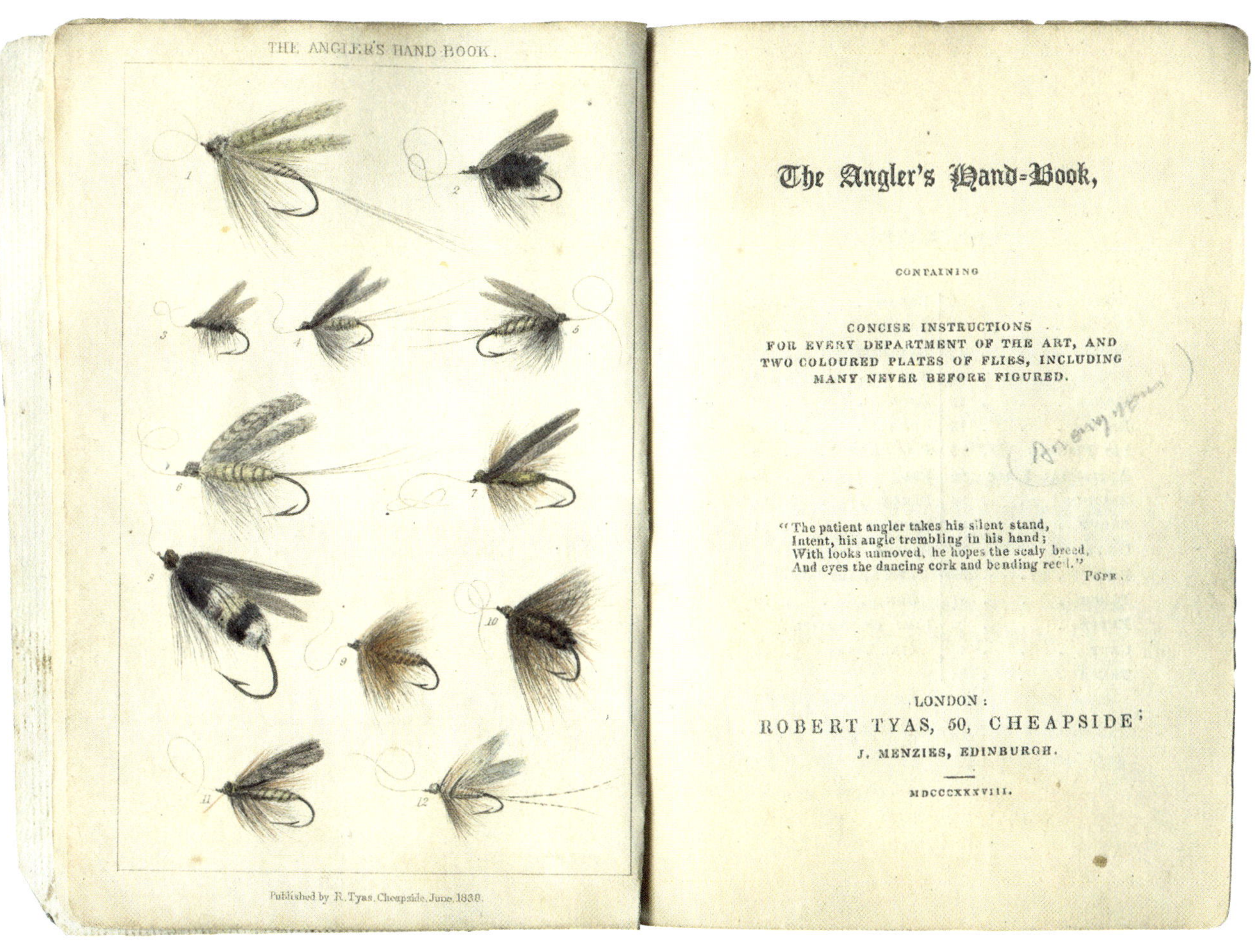

THE ANGLER'S HAND BOOK.

The Angler's Hand-Book,

CONTAINING

CONCISE INSTRUCTIONS
FOR EVERY DEPARTMENT OF THE ART, AND
TWO COLOURED PLATES OF FLIES, INCLUDING
MANY NEVER BEFORE FIGURED.

"The patient angler takes his silent stand,
Intent, his angle trembling in his hand;
With looks unmoved, he hopes the scaly breed,
And eyes the dancing cork and bending reed."
POPE.

LONDON:
ROBERT TYAS, 50, CHEAPSIDE;
J. MENZIES, EDINBURGH.

MDCCCXXXVIII.

9

The Angler's Hand-book; Containing Concise Instructions for Every Department of the Art, and Two Coloured Plates of Flies, Including Many Never before Figured.
LONDON: ROBERT TYAS, 1838. [SH 439 A62 1838] 11.6 CM X 8.1 CM

This scarce, diminutive guidebook features two colour plates of flies, including, as the title indicates, "many never before figured." It is a true pocketbook that could be slipped into the angler's vest to accompany him or her on the stream. The title went through three editions, this being the first (Westwood et al. 9).

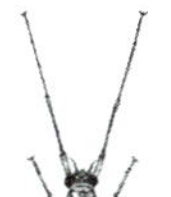

10

WORKS BY WILLIAM BLACKER

Items 10a and 10b/10c represent the second and third editions, respectively, of William Blacker's landmark work on fly tying. *Blacker's Catechism* includes actual examples of flies and fly-tying material mounted with paper seals to the pages. It is the first printing under this title, issued one year after the first appearance of the book as *Art of Angling, and Complete System of Fly-making and Dyeing of Colours* in 1842. The book is an early, if the not the earliest, example of a book issued with actual examples of fly-tying materials—a distinction often given to W.H. Aldam's *A Quaint Treatise on "Flees, and the Art a' Artyfichall Flee Making"* (1876).

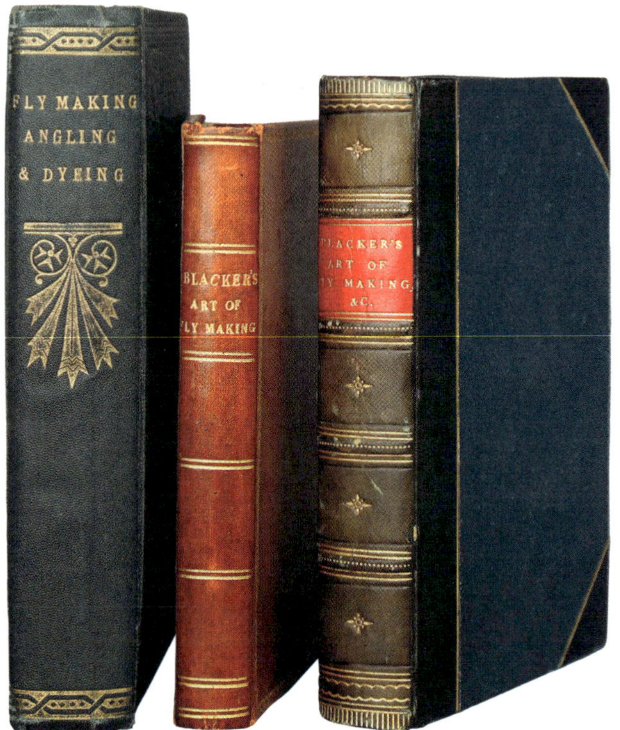

Blacker was a skilled fly tier, and his instructions and the quality of the engravings were a marked improvement over previous books (Martin 46). Although the 1855 edition did not contain examples of flies, it was significantly expanded to include spectacular hand-coloured engravings of flies. In the preface of this edition, Blacker states,

> To bring the Engravings of the flies to the greatest perfection, I have stood at the elbow of the artist who executed this part of the work, that they might be turned out exact to my own models, which renders them and the descriptions more intelligible, as the shade in the fibre of each feather is shown in the plate, in the clearest and finest manner imaginable, that it may be properly seen how these artificial flies are constructed,—the resemblance of those beautiful ones, the productions of the Great Author of Nature, that Trout and Salmon do love to feed upon (x).

The exhibition includes two copies of the 1855 edition—one with hand-coloured plates and one without. An extra-illustrated edition of the *Catechism of Fly Making* with numerous examples of hand-tied flies sold for an astounding £187,250 at Bonhams' 2012 auction of The Angling Library of Alan Jarvis.

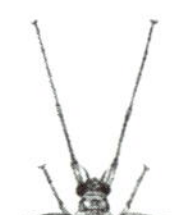

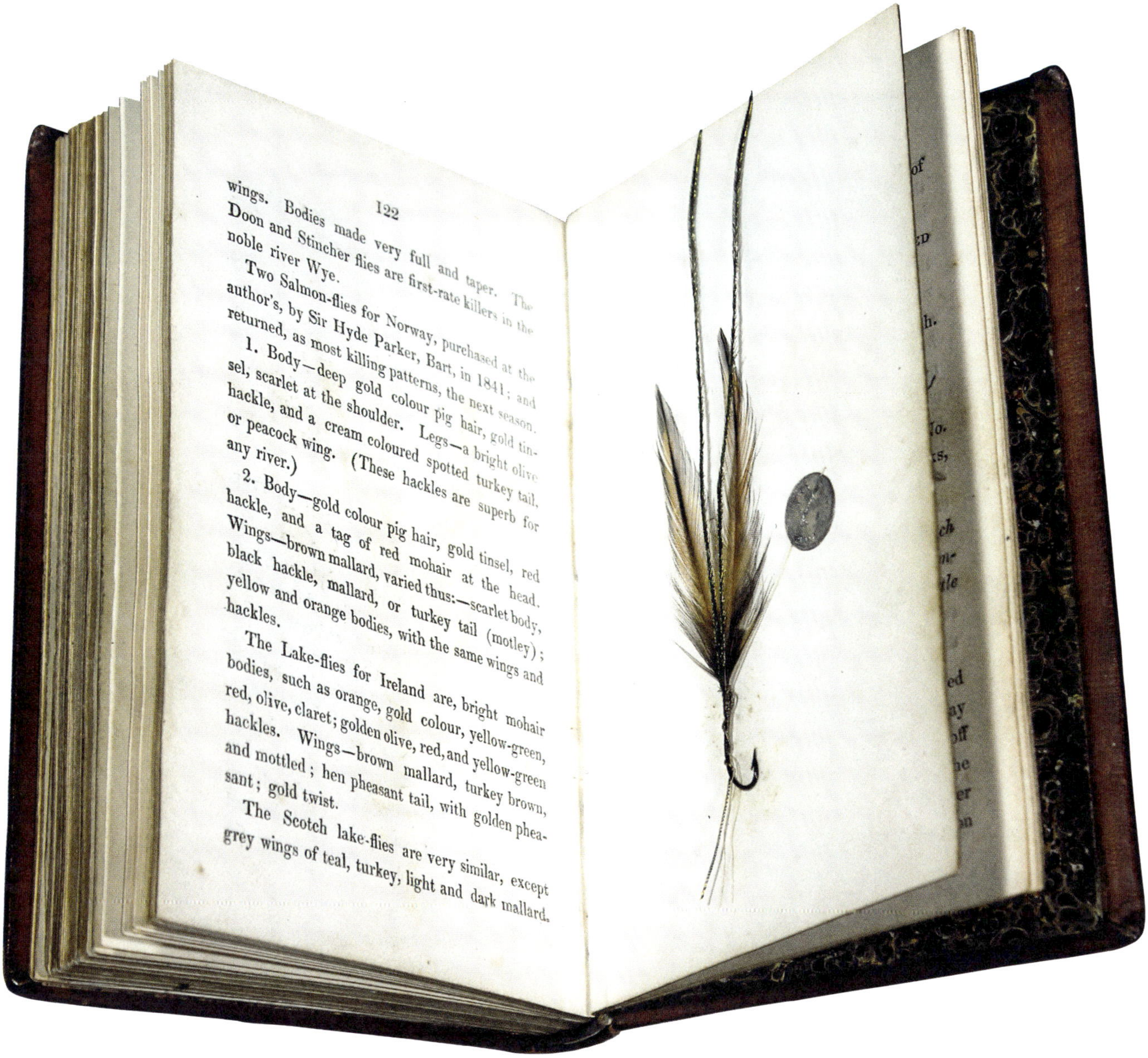

122

wings. Bodies made very full and taper. The Doon and Stincher flies are first-rate killers in the noble river Wye.

Two Salmon-flies for Norway, purchased at the author's, by Sir Hyde Parker, Bart, in 1841; and returned, as most killing patterns, the next season.

1. Body—deep gold colour pig hair, gold tinsel, scarlet at the shoulder. Legs—a bright olive hackle, and a cream coloured spotted turkey tail, or peacock wing. (These hackles are superb for any river.)

2. Body—gold colour pig hair, gold tinsel, red hackle, and a tag of red mohair at the head. Wings—brown mallard, varied thus:—scarlet body, black hackle, mallard, or turkey tail (motley); yellow and orange bodies, with the same wings and hackles.

The Lake-flies for Ireland are, bright mohair bodies, such as orange, gold colour, yellow-green, red, olive, claret; golden olive, red, and yellow-green hackles. Wings—brown mallard, turkey brown, and mottled; hen pheasant tail, with golden pheasant; gold twist.

The Scotch lake-flies are very similar, except grey wings of teal, turkey, light and dark mallard.

10 (a)

BLACKER, WILLIAM. *Blacker's Catechism of Fly-making, Angling, and Dye-making. Comprising Most Essential Information.* LONDON: WILLIAM BLACKER, 1843. [SH 451 B53 1843] 14.6 CM X 9.7 CM

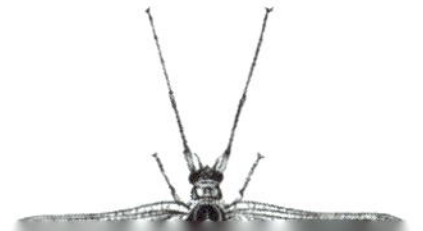

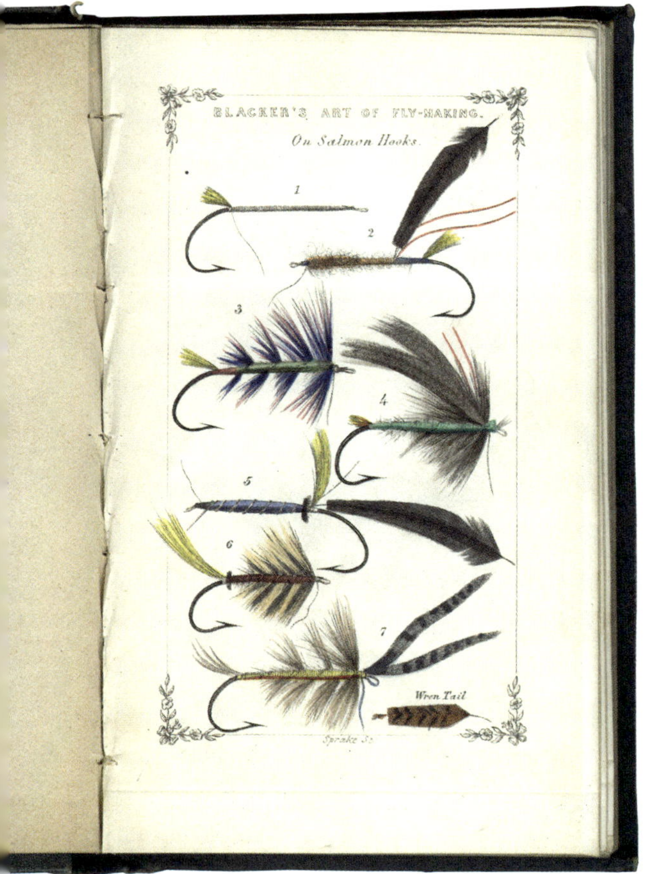

10 (b)

BLACKER, WILLIAM. *Blacker's Art of Fly Makings, &c.: Comprising Angling and Dyeing of Colours, with Engravings of Salmon and Trout Flies, Shewing the Process of the Gentle Craft as Taught in the Pages: With Descriptions of Flies for the Season of the Year, as They Come out on the Water.* LONDON: WILLIAM BLACKER, 1855. [SH 451 B53 B53 1855] [COLOURED COPY]

10 (c)

BLACKER, WILLIAM. *Blacker's Art of Fly Makings, &c.: Comprising Angling and Dyeing of Colours with Engravings of Salmon and Trout Flies, Shewing the Process of the Gentle Craft as Taught in the Pages: With Descriptions of Flies for the Season of the Year, as They Come out on the Water.* LONDON: WILLIAM BLACKER, 1855. [SH 451 B53 B53 1855 C.2] 15.9 CM X 10.8 CM [UNCOLOURED COPY]

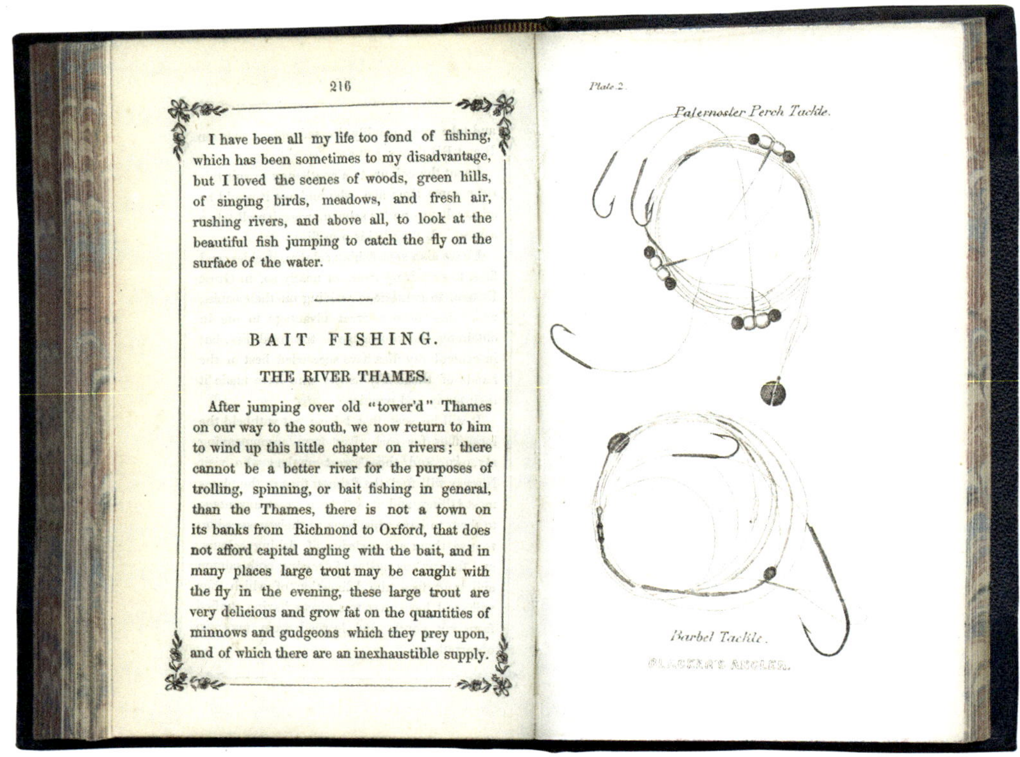

216

I have been all my life too fond of fishing, which has been sometimes to my disadvantage, but I loved the scenes of woods, green hills, of singing birds, meadows, and fresh air, rushing rivers, and above all, to look at the beautiful fish jumping to catch the fly on the surface of the water.

BAIT FISHING.

THE RIVER THAMES.

After jumping over old "tower'd" Thames on our way to the south, we now return to him to wind up this little chapter on rivers; there cannot be a better river for the purposes of trolling, spinning, or bait fishing in general, than the Thames, there is not a town on its banks from Richmond to Oxford, that does not afford capital angling with the bait, and in many places large trout may be caught with the fly in the evening, these large trout are very delicious and grow fat on the quantities of minnows and gudgeons which they prey upon, and of which there are an inexhaustible supply.

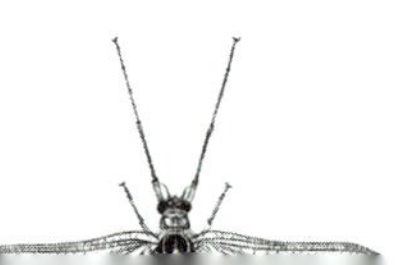

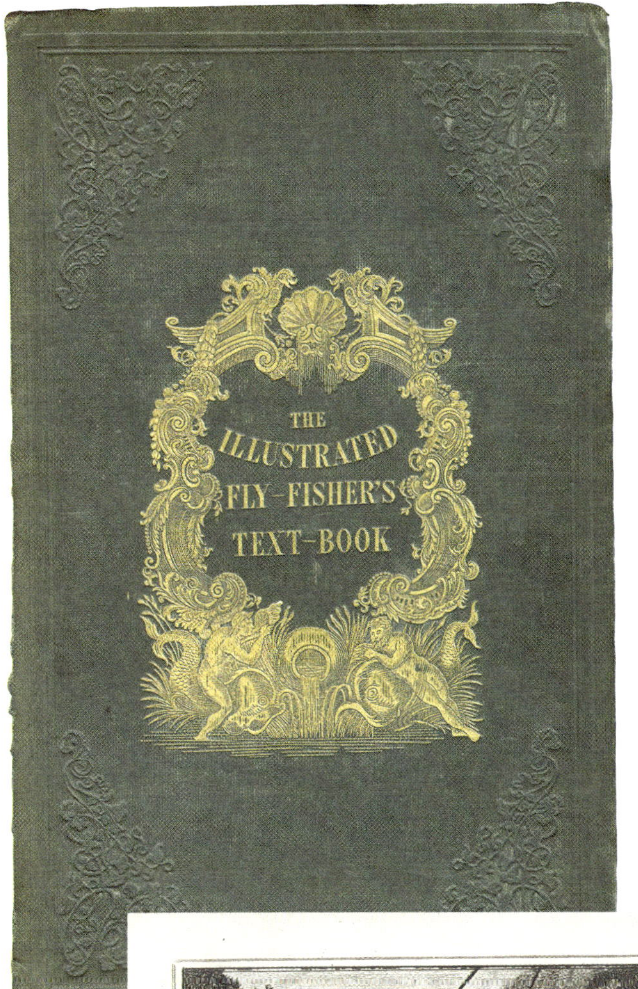

11

[BOHN, HENRY G.]. *The Illustrated Fly-fisher's Text-book: A Complete Guide to the Science of Fly-fishing for Salmon, Trout, Grayling, &c. by Theophilus South.* LONDON: HENRY G. BOHN, 1845. [SH 456 S68 1845] 23.2 CM X 15.0 CM

This title is a general fly-fishing manual that includes fine engravings of fishing scenes and fish. Westwood et al. considered the book "one of the best of its class" (198)

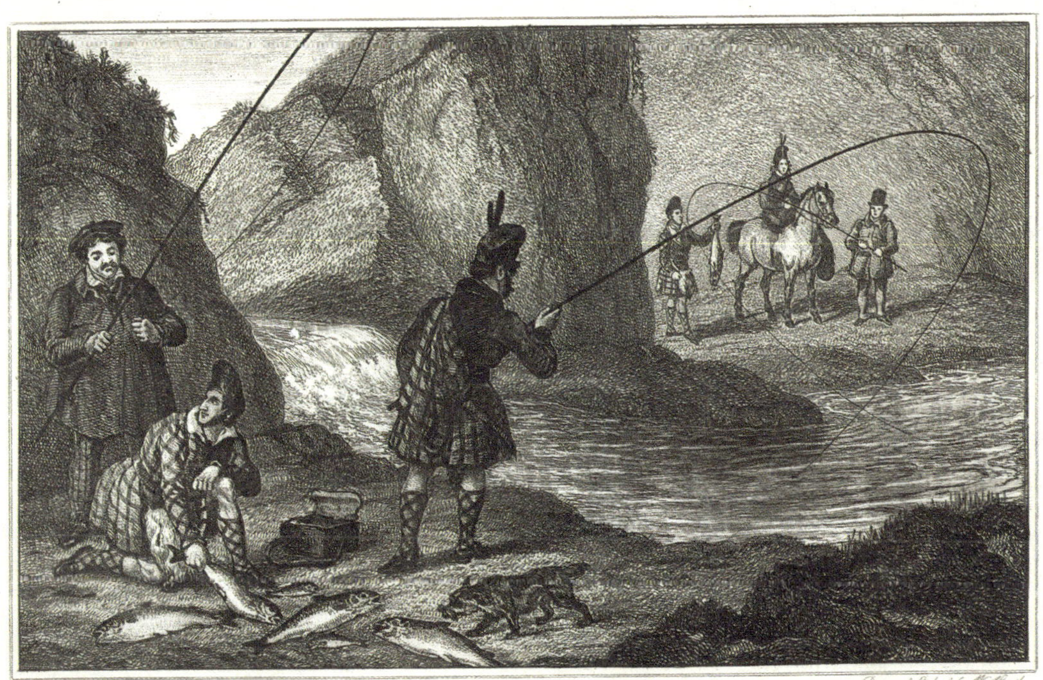

SALMON FISHING.

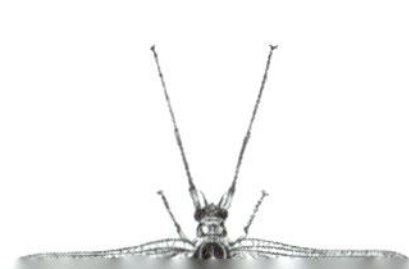

12

BROWN, JOHN J. *The American Angler's Guide: Being a Compilation from the Works of Popular English Authors, from Walton to the Present Time; Together with the Opinions and Practices of the Best American Anglers: Containing Every Variety of Mode Accepted in Ocean, River, Lake and Pond Fishing; the Necessary Tackle and Baits Required; Manner of Making Artificial Flies, &c., &c., &c.: With Engravings on Wood by an American Angler.*
2ND ED. NEW YORK: BURGESS, STRINGER & CO., 1846. [SH 441 B76 1846] 15.6 CM X 10.6 CM

This is the second edition of the first substantial book on American angling written and published in the United States. Brown was a New York tackle dealer during the early development of American recreational fishing. Prior to the 1830s, fishing in America occurred primarily for sustenance and not for sport (Gingrich 209), and the title is significant for documenting American attitudes on sport fishing during the first half of the nineteenth century. For example, Brown notes that fly-fishing was of little interest to American anglers and that most flies were purchased from England; however, American anglers were known to "examine the waters and shake the boughs of the trees, to procure the latest insect ... and imitate nature's handiwork on the spot" (Gingrich 156). Brown also takes a moment to praise the more metaphysical benefits of his sport in the book's conclusion:

> There is no recreation so admirably adapted to recruit the body and mind of the toiling citizen, as angling. Breaking away from the confining and exhausting toil in the counting-house, office, or workshop, leaving all care behind, the angler sallies forth to the river, the bay, or some more distant water; and there, amid the most beautiful scenery of nature, plies his art. The absence from the scene of toil and care, for a short season; the breathing the fresh and healthful air of the country; the transit to and from the place of amusement, and the exciting and delightful exercise of the art; all combine to give this recreating a high place in my estimation (222).

The book bears the bookplate of noted Canadian collector of angling books, C.R. Morphy.

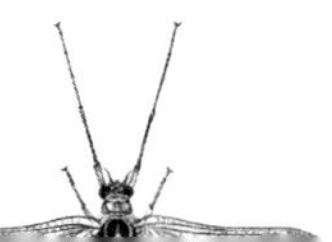

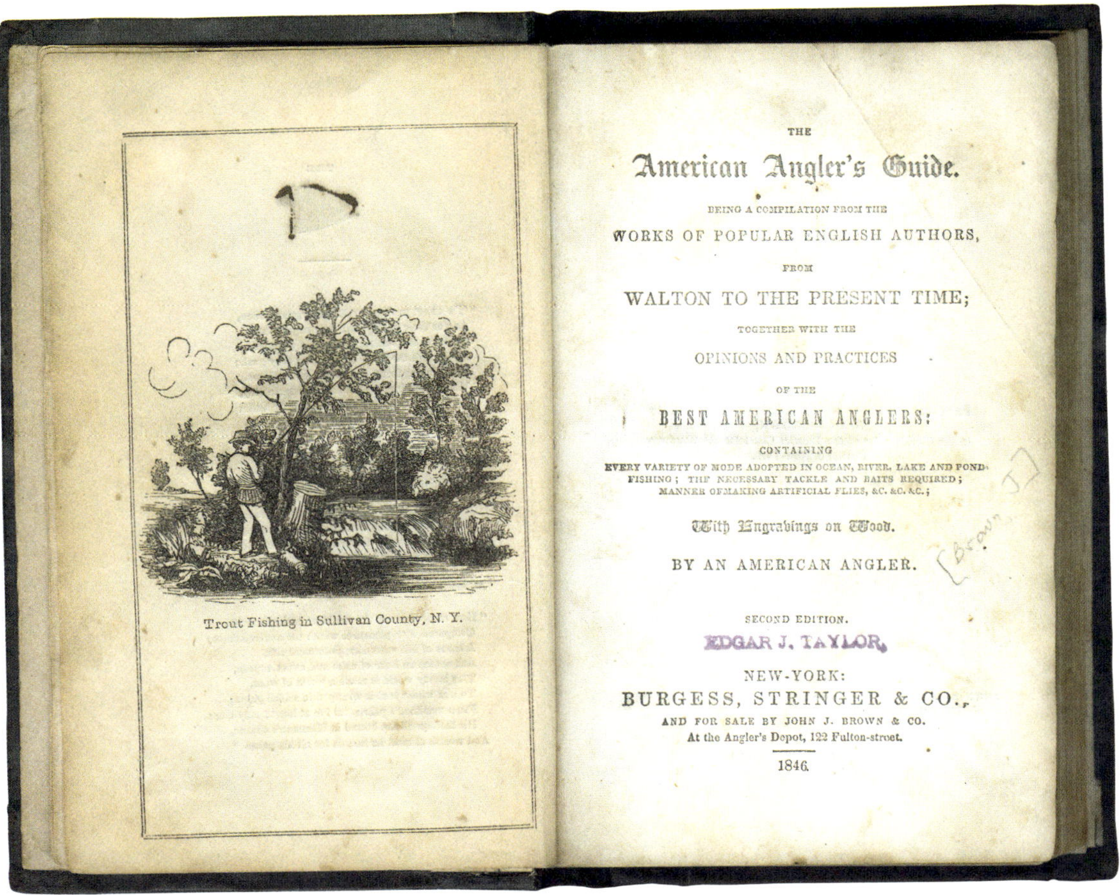

Trout Fishing in Sullivan County, N. Y.

THE

American Angler's Guide.

BEING A COMPILATION FROM THE

WORKS OF POPULAR ENGLISH AUTHORS,

FROM

WALTON TO THE PRESENT TIME;

TOGETHER WITH THE

OPINIONS AND PRACTICES

OF THE

BEST AMERICAN ANGLERS:

CONTAINING

EVERY VARIETY OF MODE ADOPTED IN OCEAN, RIVER, LAKE AND POND-FISHING; THE NECESSARY TACKLE AND BAITS REQUIRED; MANNER OF MAKING ARTIFICIAL FLIES, &C. &C. &C.;

With Engravings on Wood.

BY AN AMERICAN ANGLER.

[Brown, J.]

SECOND EDITION.

EDGAR J. TAYLOR.

NEW-YORK:

BURGESS, STRINGER & CO.,

AND FOR SALE BY JOHN J. BROWN & CO.

At the Angler's Depot, 122 Fulton-street.

1846.

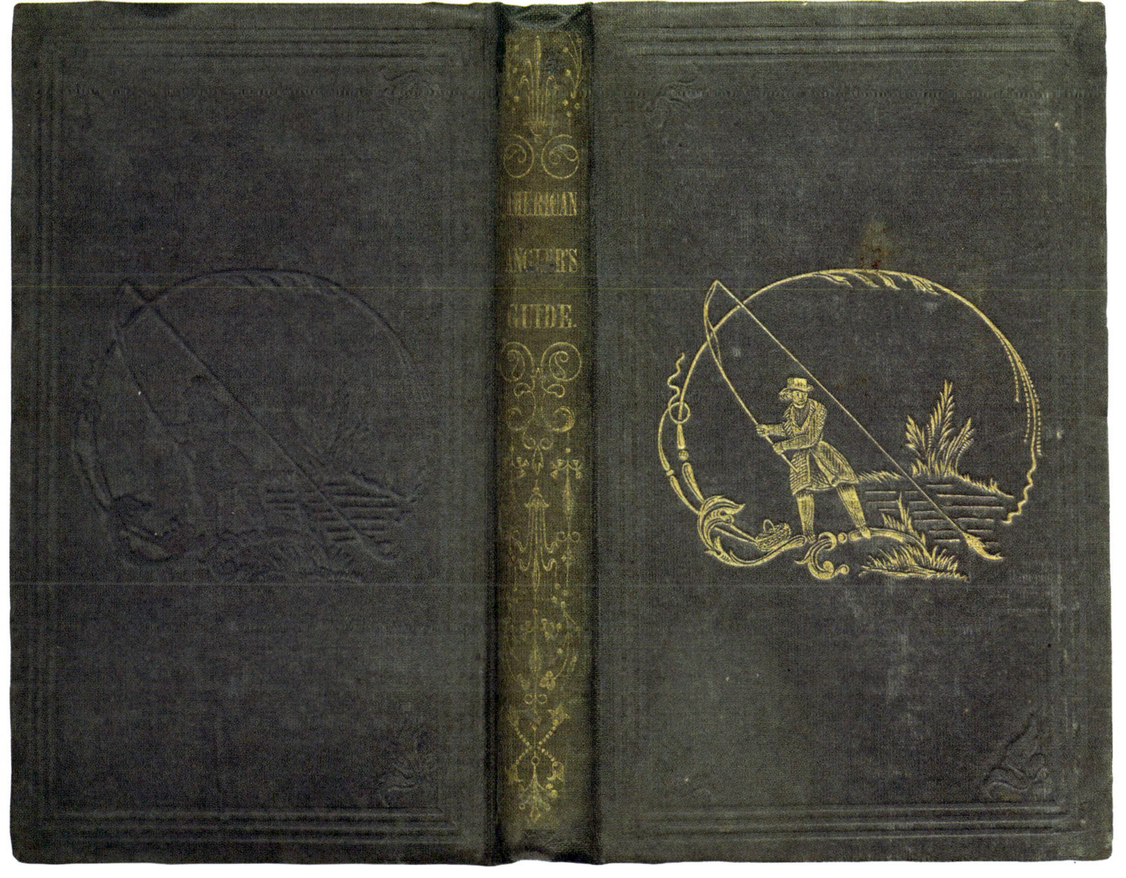

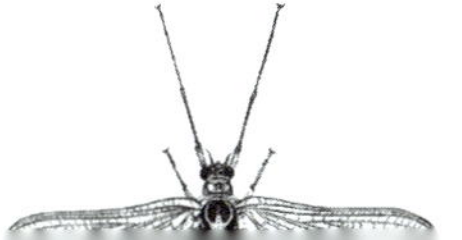

13

[FITZGIBBON, EDWARD]. *The Book of the Salmon: In Two Parts by Ephemera.* LONDON: LONGMAN, BROWN, GREEN, AND LONGMANS, 1850. [SH 685 F57 1850] 17.9 CM X 11.6 CM

One of the foundational nineteenth-century angling texts, this book is praised by Westwood et al. as being "highly esteemed" (86). It includes a section on the natural history of salmon and several fine hand-coloured engraved plates of salmon flies.

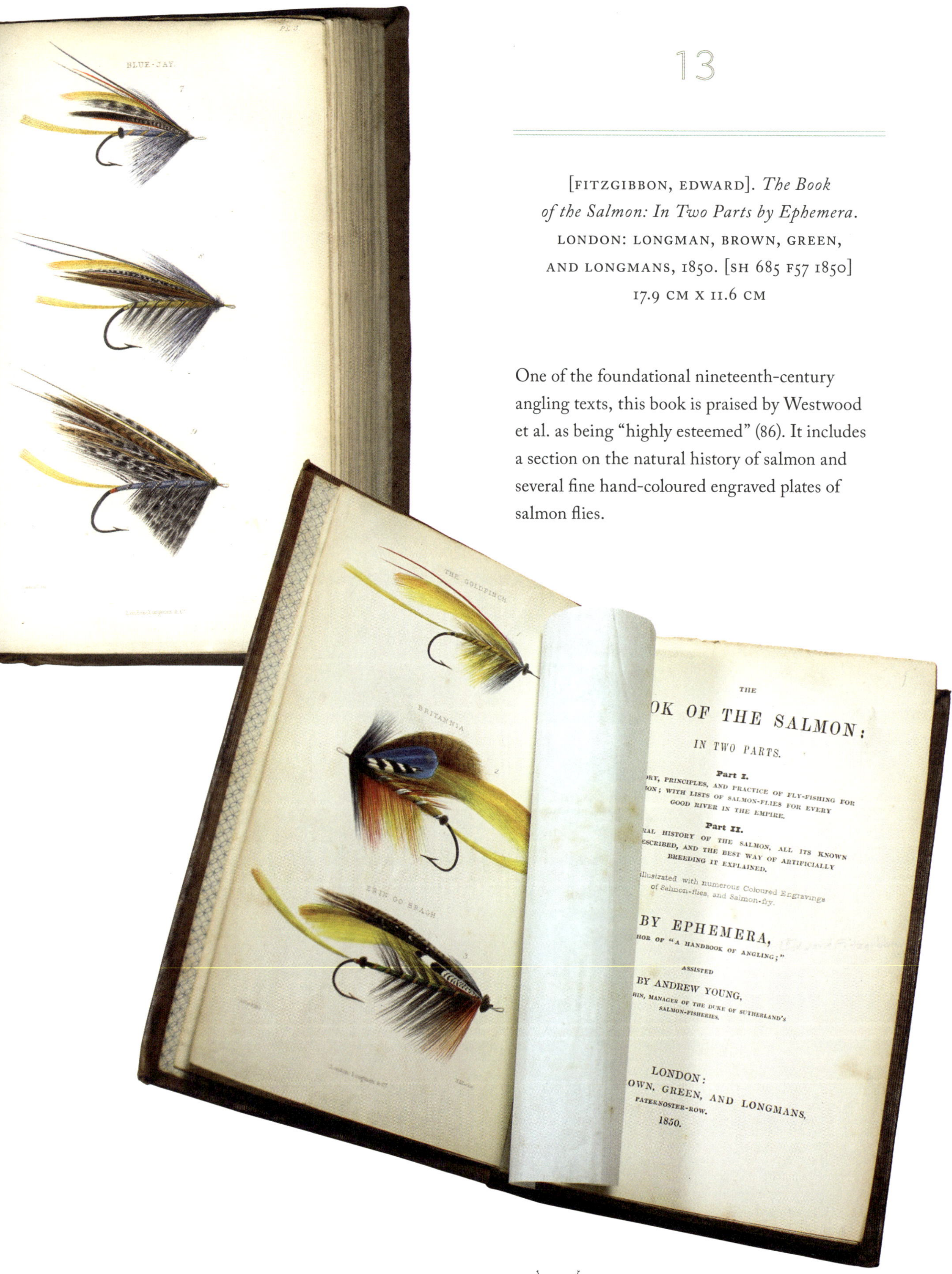

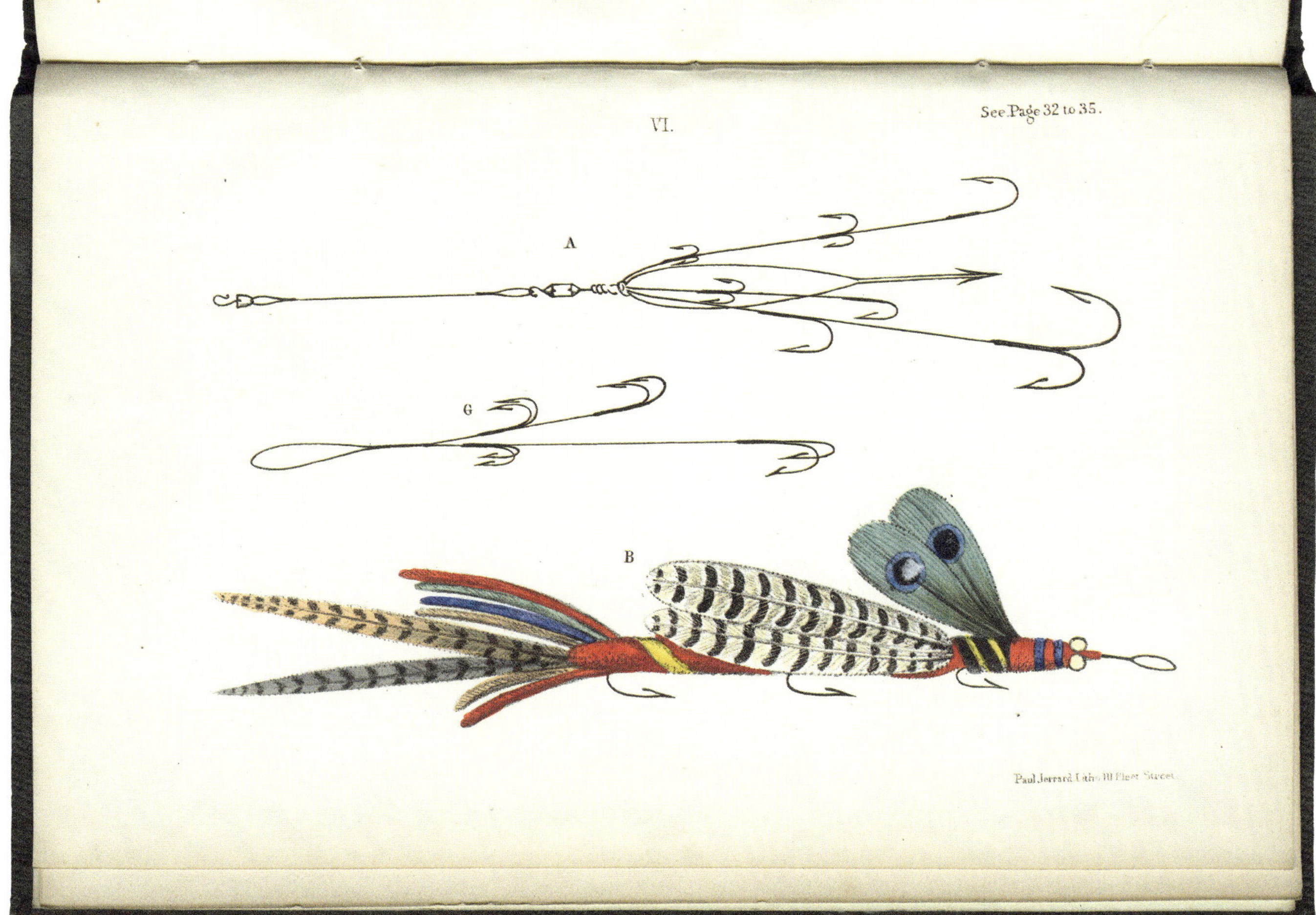

14

Fly-Fishing in Salt and Fresh Water: With Six Plates, Representing Artificial Flies, etc.
LONDON: JOHN VAN VOORST, 1851. [SH 456 F6 1851] 23.0 CM X 14.6 CM

This is a scarce title dedicated to fly fishing in fresh and salt water with vibrant, hand-coloured plates of flies. The author states he has "derived such extraordinary good sport from sea fly-fishing, that he hopes the account which he has given in this book, will be novel to most readers ..." (v–vi). The author also admonishes non-fly fisherman in his dedication: "This work is dedicated to all *true* Fly-fisherman; —that is, to all those who fish for salmon, trout, and grayling, as every gentleman ought to do, with the artificial fly only. The author looks with horror on those gentlemen who, professing to be fisherman, will coolly avow, that so they can take fish, they care not how it may be accomplished ..." (vii). This attitude will reach its apex with the "dry-fly fishing elitism" espoused later in the nineteenth century and into the early twentieth century.

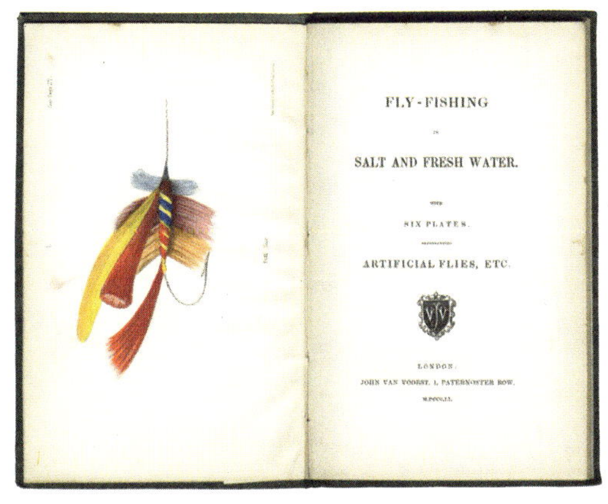

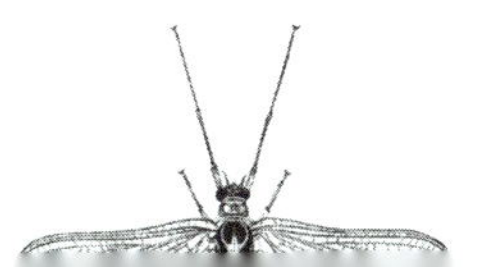

15

RECEIPT FOR GOODS SOLD BY JAMES EDMONDSON. 24 MAY 1861. MS. BRUCE P. DANCIK COLLECTION OF ANGLING BOOKS. BRUCE PEEL SPECIAL COLLECTIONS, EDMONTON. [HD 9993 T333 G736 1800Z FOLIO] 33.2 CM X 20.6 CM

This is a long, hand-written receipt on engraved letterhead for James Edmondson, Fishing Rod, Tackle, and Fly Maker on Basnett Street, Liverpool, England. The receipt lists a full kit of equipment for a grand angling trip, including salmon, sea trout, and pike rods; reels; fishing line; a gaff hook; landing nets; fly books; spoon baits; and a travelling rod case, purchased by a "Mr. Brown" and a "Mr. Rathborne." The items are grouped and labeled in the receipt's margin for their purpose (e.g., "sea trout and loch fishing," "trout rod for trolling in lochs," "for trolling"), indicating that the purchasers may have been relative novices. Curiously, flies or fly tying materials are not included in the purchase. The bill totalled 17 pounds and 14 pence, a handsome sum.

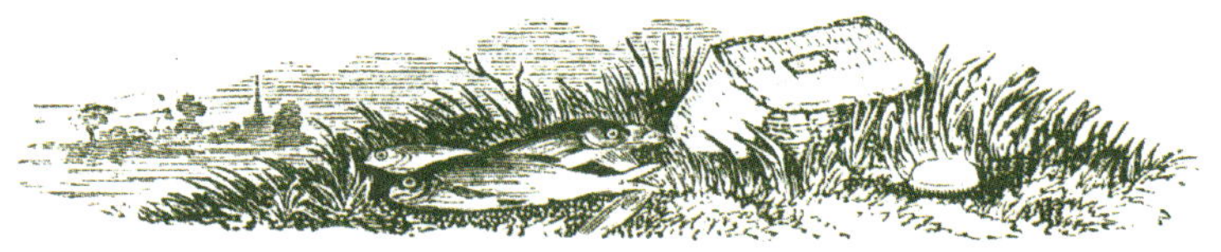

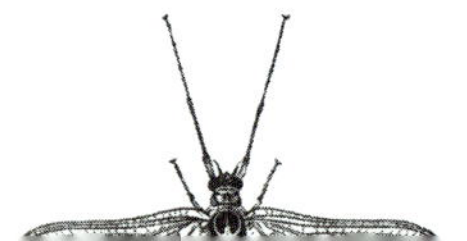

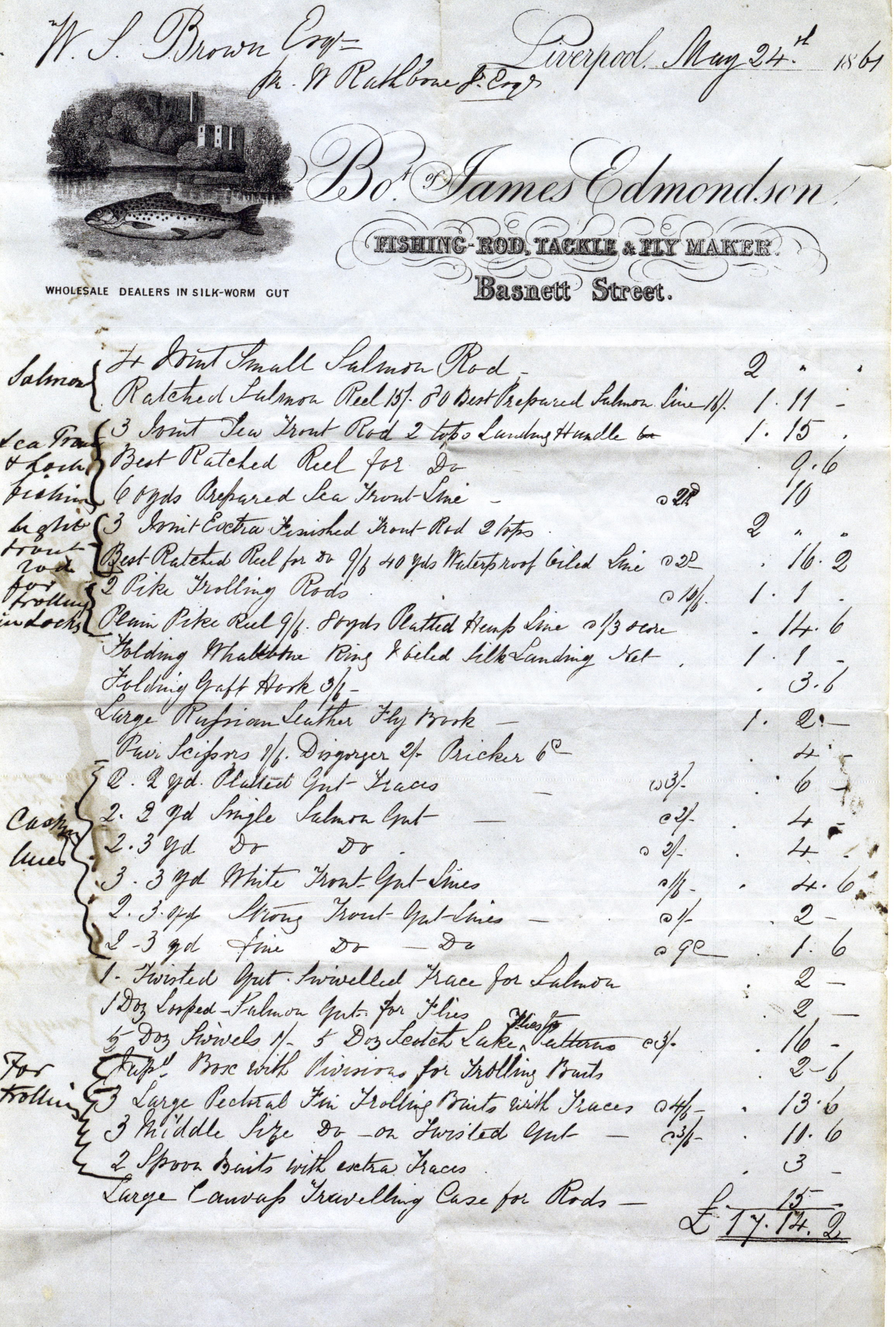

W. S. Brown Esq —
pr. W Rathbone Jr Esq.

Liverpool. May 24th 1861

Bot. of James Edmondson

FISHING-ROD, TACKLE & FLY MAKER.

Basnett Street.

WHOLESALE DEALERS IN SILK-WORM GUT

	Item	Rate	£	s	d
Salmon	4 Joint Small Salmon Rod —		2		
	Ratched Salmon Reel 15/- 80 Best Prepared Salmon Line 16/-		1	11	–
Sea Trout & Loch fishing	3 Joint Sea Trout Rod 2 tops Landing Handle &c		1	15	
	Best Ratched Reel for Do			9	6
	60 yds Prepared Sea Trout Line —	@2d		10	
Light trout rod	3 Joint Extra Finished Trout Rod 2 tops		2		
	Best Ratched Reel for do 9/6 40 yds Waterproof Oiled Line	@2d		16	2
for trolling in Lochs	2 Pike Trolling Rods	@10/6	1	1	
	Plain Pike Reel 9/6 80 yds Platted Hemp Line @1/3 score			14	6
	Folding Whalebone Ring & Oiled Silk Landing Net		1	1	
	Folding Gaff Hook 3/6			3	6
	Large Russian Leather Fly Book —		1	2	–
	Pair Scissors 1/6 Disgorger 2/- Pricker 6d			4	
Casting lines	2. 2 yd Platted Gut Traces —	@3/-		6	–
	2. 2 yd Single Salmon Gut —	@2/-		4	–
	2. 3 yd Do Do	@2/-		4	–
	3. 3 yd White Trout Gut Lines	@1/6		4	6
	2. 3 yd Strong Trout Gut Lines —	@1/-		2	–
	2. 3 yd Fine Do — Do	@9d		1	6
	1 Twisted Gut Swivelled Trace for Salmon			2	–
	1 Doz Looped Salmon Gut for Flies			2	–
	5 Doz Swivels 1/- 5 Doz Scotch Lake Flies of Patterns	@3/-		16	–
For trolling	Japd. Box with Divisions for Trolling Baits			2	6
	3 Large Pectoral Fin Trolling Baits with Traces	@4/6		13	6
	3 Middle Size Do on Twisted Gut —	@3/6		10	6
	2 Spoon Baits with extra Traces			3	–
	Large Canvass Travelling Case for Rods —			15	–
			£17	14	2

16

Hand-book of Fishing. LONDON: CASSELL, PETTER, AND GALPIN, [1866]. [SH 439 H338 1866] 13.9 CM X 9.4 CM

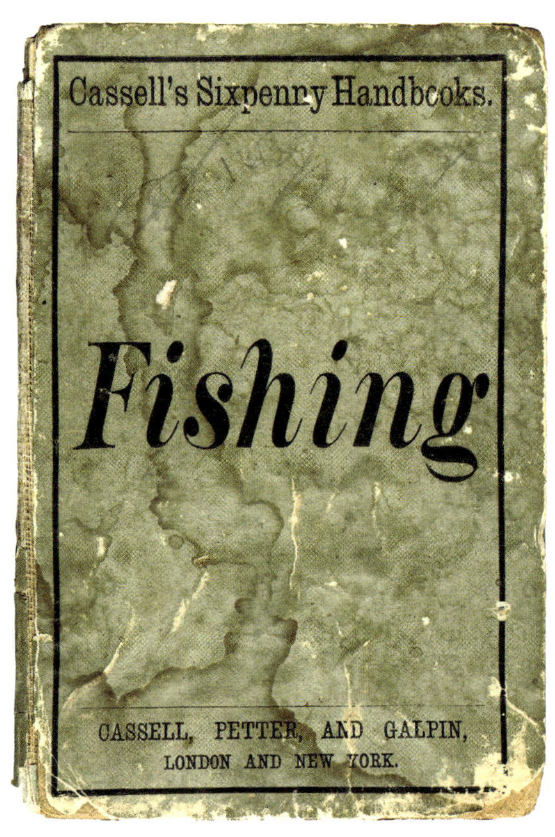

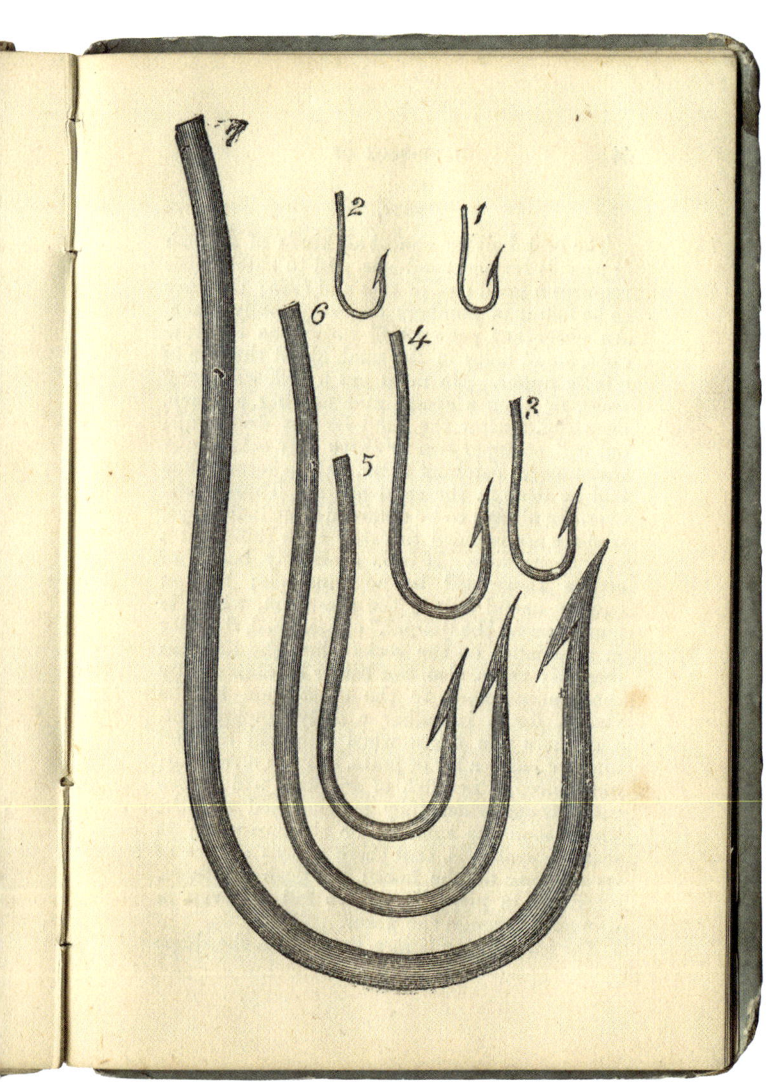

This is a true "waterside" handbook with an encyclopaedic list of angling techniques and equipment. The water damage and rough condition of this volume are intriguing potential evidence of its use. One can imagine a Victorian angler, rod in one hand and book in the other, accidently dropping the book into a river when following the guide's instructions.

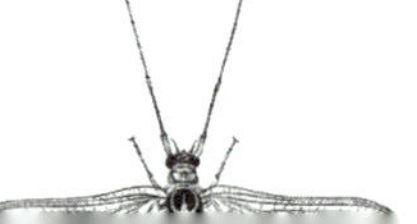

17

KNOX, A[RTHUR] E[DWARD]. *Autumns on the Spey*. LONDON: JOHN VAN VOORST, 1872. [SK 189 K72 1872] 19.8 CM X 13.5 CM

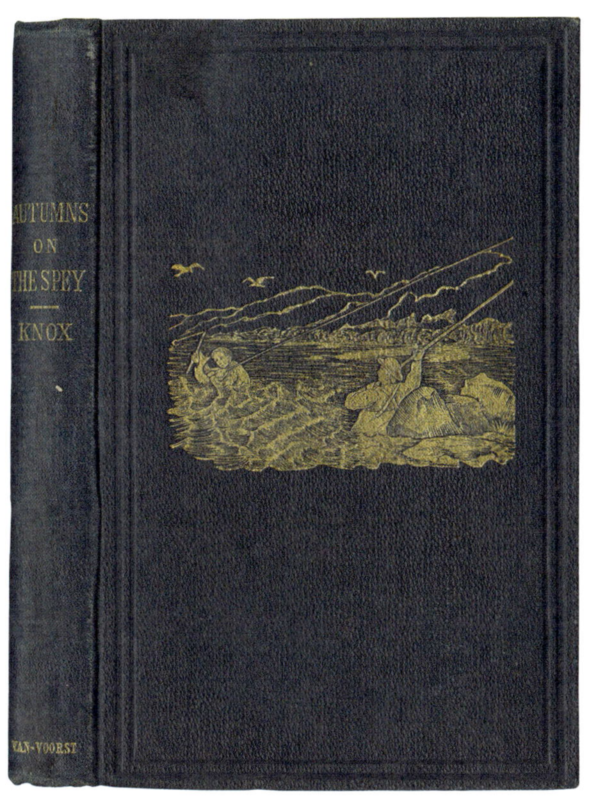

This is an early title to feature the technique of "Spey casting" developed on the river of that name and now used around the world to cast long distances on big waters. The publisher's pictorial cloth and a dramatic plate depict this style of casting with a rod up to 20 feet long. The incident depicted on the book's front board is described in the book. The author's friend must dive into the river to land a 22-pound salmon with a "fond but firm embrace" (47) after the gaff used to land the fish snaps in two.

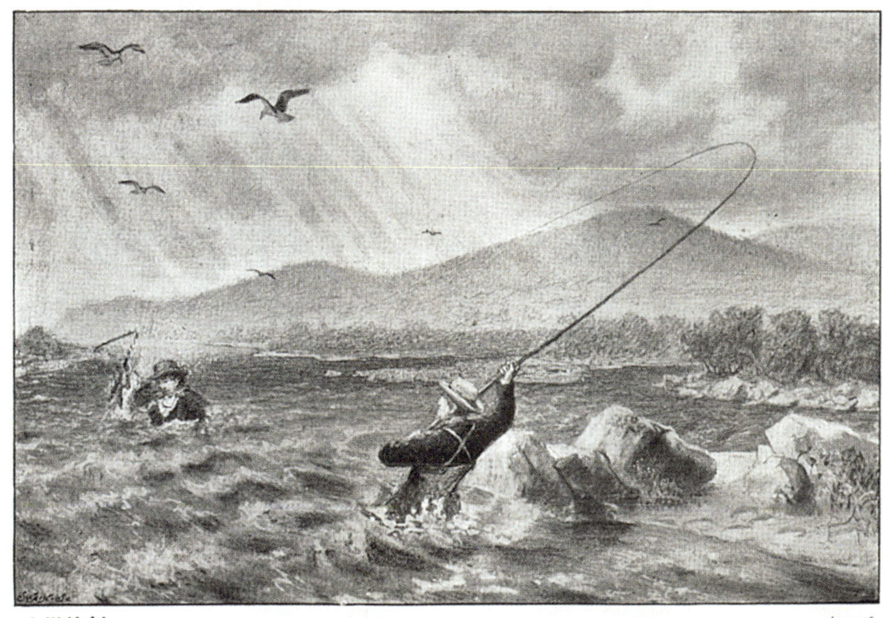

J. Wolf, del.  *page 46.*

THE LAST CHANCE.

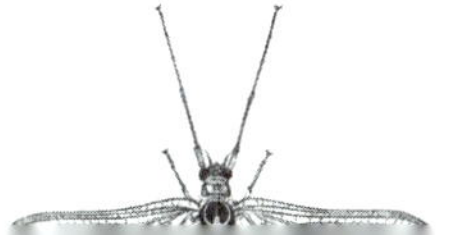

18

ORVIS, CHARLES F. AND A. NELSON CHENEY, COMPS. *Fishing with the Fly: Sketches by Lovers of the Art, with Illustrations of Standard Flies.* BOSTON: HOUGHTON, MIFFLIN & CO., 1883. [SH 441 078 1883] 19.7 CM X 15.1 CM

This is the first edition of this fly-fishing compendium, edited by the founder of the world-famous Orvis fly-fishing company. The book documents the rapid expansion of fly-fishing in North American waters. Salmon and trout fishing were the primary subjects of much of the early writing on North American fishing, and this title does include attractive colour plates of salmon and trout flies. However, flies for other fish species, such as bass, are also featured in full colour, indicating that recreational fly-fisheries for species beyond salmon and trout were well-established in 1883.

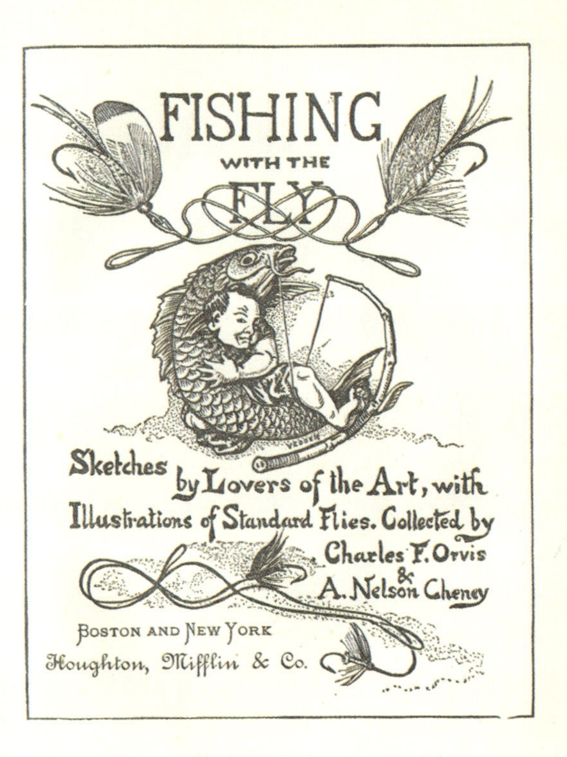

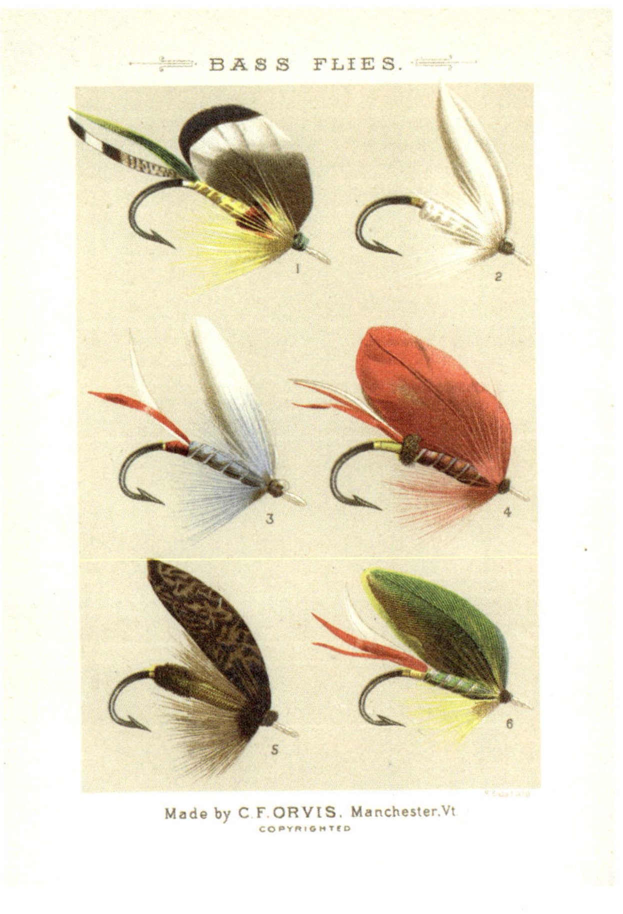

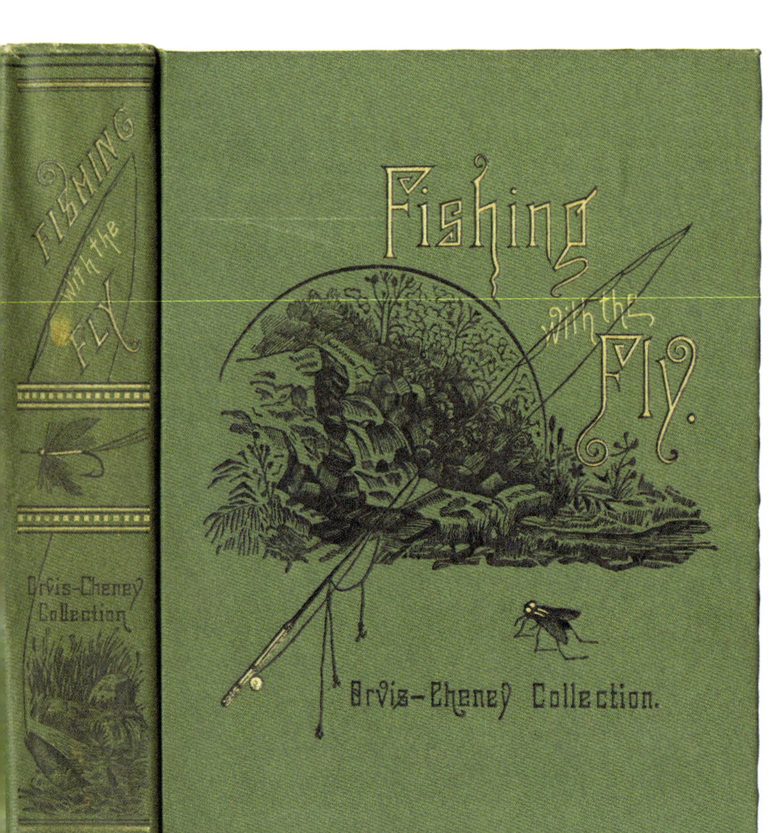

19

NINETEENTH-CENTURY RETAIL CATALOGUES

These are two attractive examples of nineteenth-century retail catalogues of fishing tackle and equipment, one English and one American. Samuel Allcock & Co was an English manufacturer and retailer of angling equipment, and the catalogue contains several colour plates of flies. The Thomas Chubb Company was a manufacturer and retailer of fishing equipment located in Vermont. Chubb's factory was destroyed by natural disasters on three separate occasions (flood, 1869; fire, 1875; and fire, 1891). Chubb rebuilt after the first two disasters but sold the business after the 1891 fire (Ford Historical Society). Mail-order catalogues were first issued in 1886; this copy illustrates items for sale and also includes a series of articles on angling.

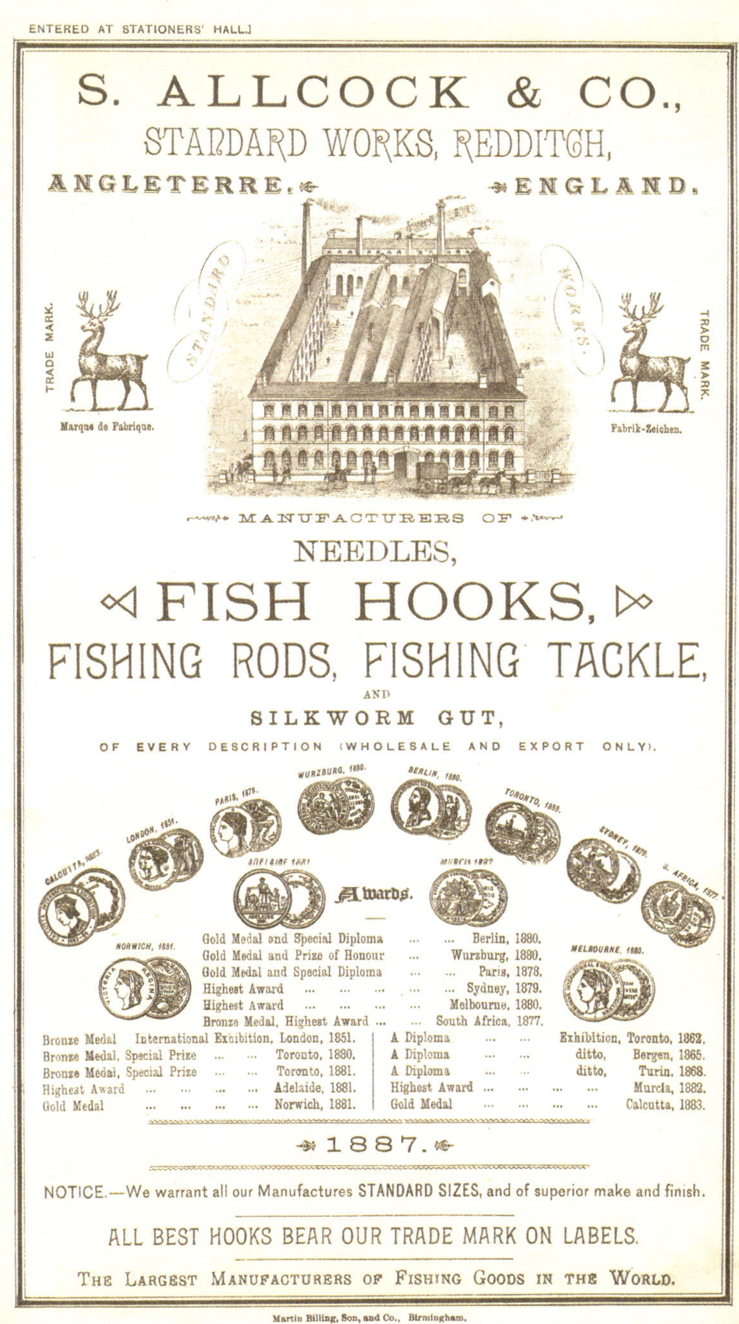

ENTERED AT STATIONERS' HALL.]

S. ALLCOCK & CO.,
STANDARD WORKS, REDDITCH,
ANGLETERRE. ENGLAND.

MANUFACTURERS OF
NEEDLES,
FISH HOOKS,
FISHING RODS, FISHING TACKLE,
AND
SILKWORM GUT,
OF EVERY DESCRIPTION (WHOLESALE AND EXPORT ONLY).

Awards.

Gold Medal and Special Diploma ... ... Berlin, 1880.
Gold Medal and Prize of Honour ... Wurzburg, 1880.
Gold Medal and Special Diploma ... ... Paris, 1878.
Highest Award ... ... Sydney, 1879.
Highest Award ... ... Melbourne, 1880.
Bronze Medal, Highest Award ... ... South Africa, 1877.

Bronze Medal International Exhibition, London, 1851.	A Diploma ... ... Exhibition, Toronto, 1862.
Bronze Medal, Special Prize ... ... Toronto, 1880.	A Diploma ... ... ditto, Bergen, 1865.
Bronze Medal, Special Prize ... ... Toronto, 1881.	A Diploma ... ... ditto, Turin, 1868.
Highest Award ... ... Adelaide, 1881.	Highest Award ... ... Murcia, 1882.
Gold Medal ... ... Norwich, 1881.	Gold Medal ... ... Calcutta, 1883.

1887.

NOTICE.—We warrant all our Manufactures STANDARD SIZES, and of superior make and finish.

ALL BEST HOOKS BEAR OUR TRADE MARK ON LABELS.

THE LARGEST MANUFACTURERS OF FISHING GOODS IN THE WORLD.

Martin Billing, Son, and Co., Birmingham.

19(a)

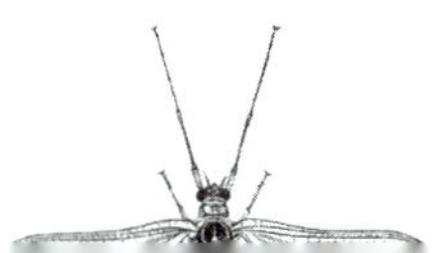

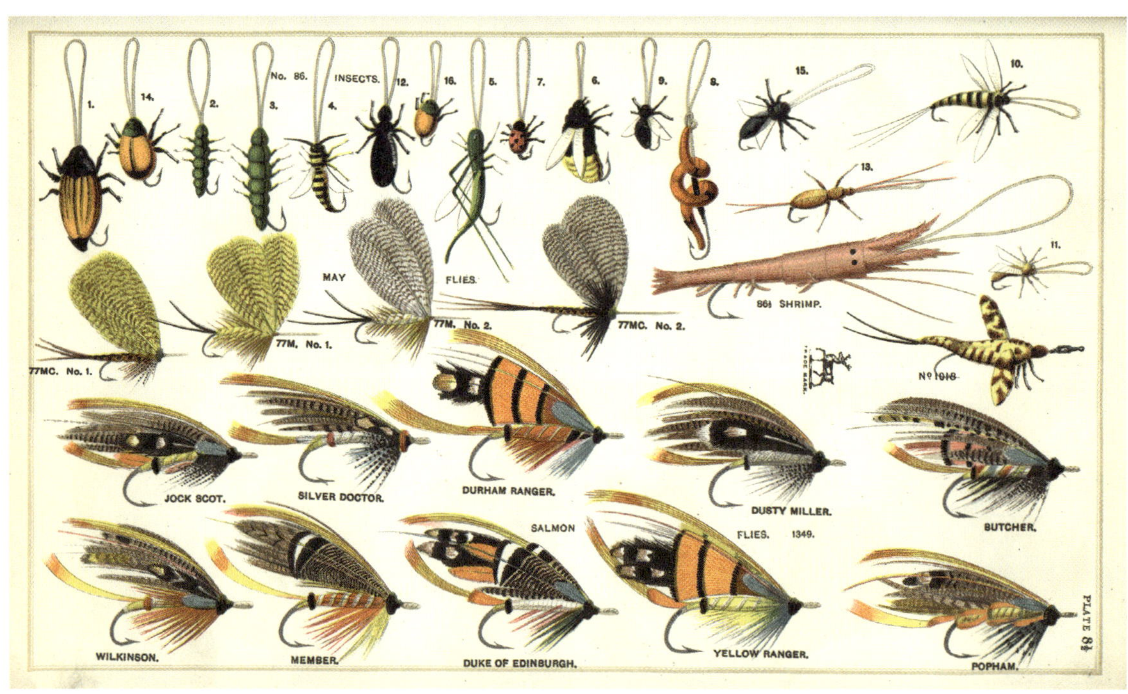

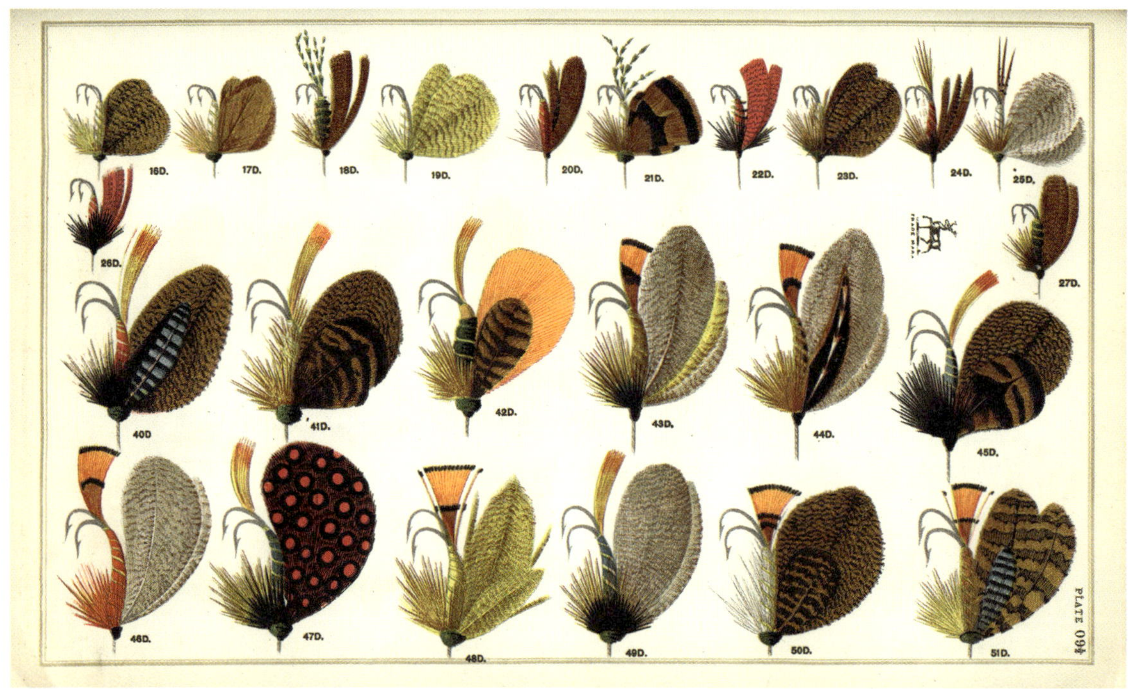

19 (a)

S. Allcock & Co., Standard Works, Redditch, Angleterre England: Manufacturers of Needles, Fish Hooks, Fishing Rods, Fishing Tackle and Silkworm Gut, of Every Description (Wholesale and Export Only). CATALOGUE. REDDITCH: ALLCOCK, 1887. [SH 453 S23 1887 FOLIO] 33.3 CM X 21.2 CM

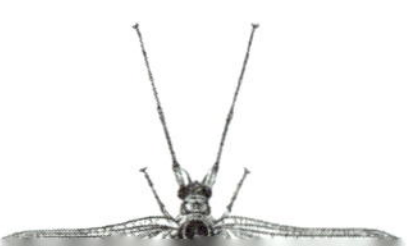

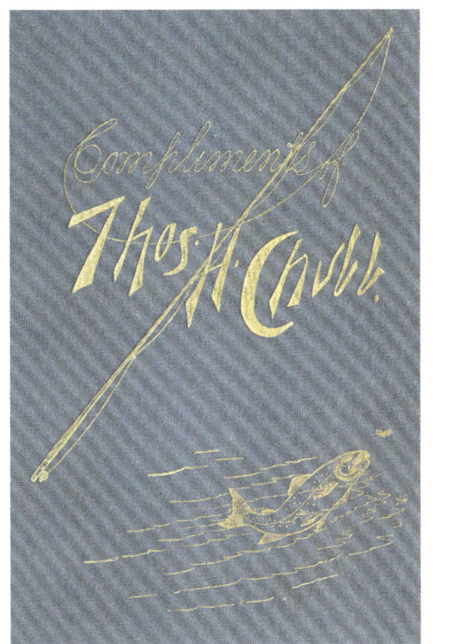

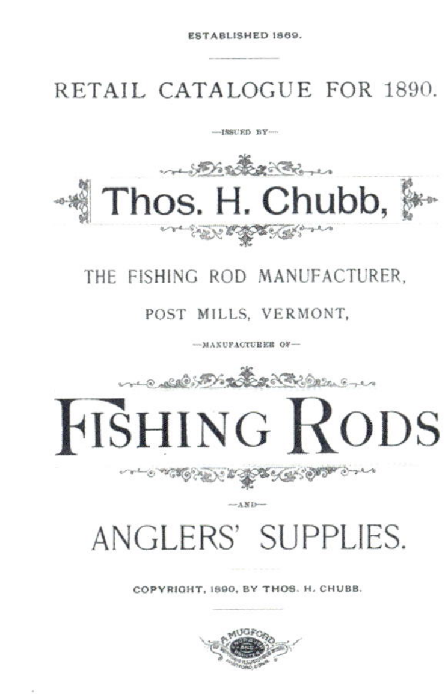

ESTABLISHED 1869.

RETAIL CATALOGUE FOR 1890.

—ISSUED BY—

Thos. H. Chubb,

THE FISHING ROD MANUFACTURER,

POST MILLS, VERMONT,

—MANUFACTURER OF—

FISHING RODS

—AND—

ANGLERS' SUPPLIES.

COPYRIGHT, 1890, BY THOS. H. CHUBB.

19(b)

Thos. H. Chubb, The Fishing Rod Manufacturer, Post Mills, Vermont, Manufacturer of Fishing Rods and Anglers' Supplies. CATALOGUE. POST MILLS, VT: CHUBB, 1890. [SH 453 C48 1890] 23.4 CM X 15.5 CM

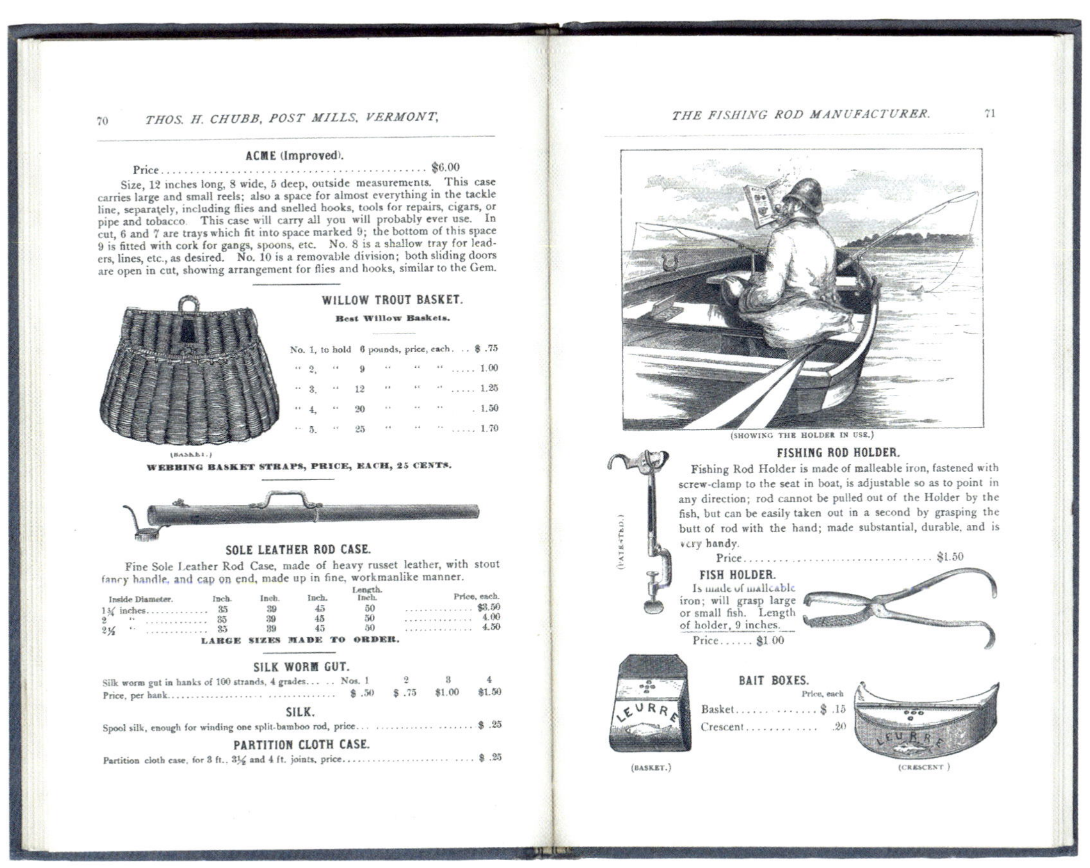

70 *THOS. H. CHUBB, POST MILLS, VERMONT,*

ACME (Improved).

Price $6.00

Size, 12 inches long, 8 wide, 5 deep, outside measurements. This case carries large and small reels; also a space for almost everything in the tackle line, separately, including flies and snelled hooks, tools for repairs, cigars, or pipe and tobacco. This case will carry all you will probably ever use. In cut, 6 and 7 are trays which fit into space marked 9; the bottom of this space 9 is fitted with cork for gangs, spoons, etc. No. 8 is a shallow tray for leaders, lines, etc., as desired. No. 10 is a removable division; both sliding doors are open in cut, showing arrangement for flies and hooks, similar to the Gem.

WILLOW TROUT BASKET.

Best Willow Baskets.

No. 1, to hold	6	pounds, price, each	$ .75
" 2, "	9	" " "	1.00
" 3, "	12	" " "	1.25
" 4, "	20	" " "	1.50
" 5, "	25	" " "	1.70

(BASKET.)

WEBBING BASKET STRAPS, PRICE, EACH, 25 CENTS.

SOLE LEATHER ROD CASE.

Fine Sole Leather Rod Case, made of heavy russet leather, with stout fancy handle, and cap on end, made up in fine, workmanlike manner.

Inside Diameter.	Inch.	Inch.	Inch.	Length. Inch.	Price, each.
1¾ inches	35	39	45	50	$3.50
2 "	35	39	45	50	4.00
2½ "	35	39	45	50	4.50

LARGE SIZES MADE TO ORDER.

SILK WORM GUT.

Silk worm gut in hanks of 100 strands, 4 grades ... Nos.	1	2	3	4
Price, per hank	$ .50	$ .75	$1.00	$1.50

SILK.

Spool silk, enough for winding one split-bamboo rod, price .... $ .25

PARTITION CLOTH CASE.

Partition cloth case, for 3 ft., 3½ and 4 ft. joints, price .... $ .25

THE FISHING ROD MANUFACTURER. 71

(SHOWING THE HOLDER IN USE.)

FISHING ROD HOLDER.

(PATENTED.)

Fishing Rod Holder is made of malleable iron, fastened with screw-clamp to the seat in boat, is adjustable so as to point in any direction; rod cannot be pulled out of the Holder by the fish, but can be easily taken out in a second by grasping the butt of rod with the hand; made substantial, durable, and is very handy.

Price $1.50

FISH HOLDER.

Is made of malleable iron; will grasp large or small fish. Length of holder, 9 inches.

Price...... $1.00

BAIT BOXES.

	Price, each
Basket	$ .15
Crescent	.20

(BASKET.) (CRESCENT.)

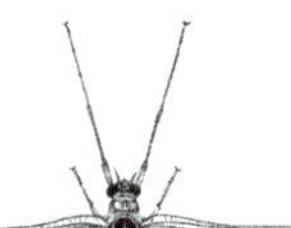

THE "CHUBB" FLY BOOKS.

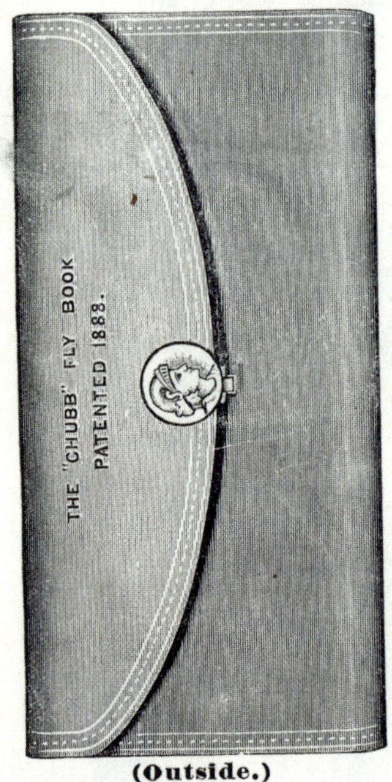

(Outside.)

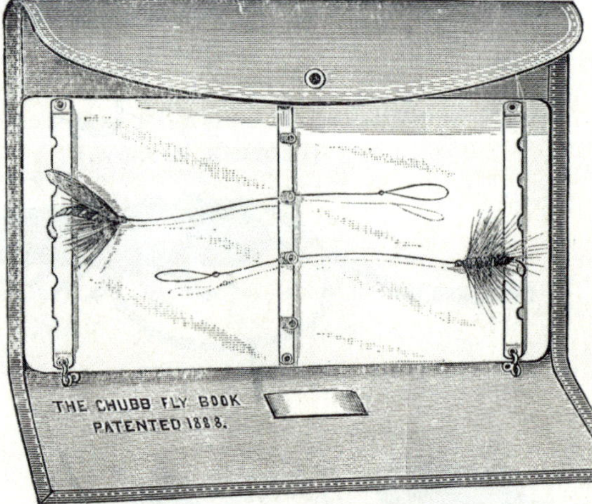

(Nos. 1 and 2.)

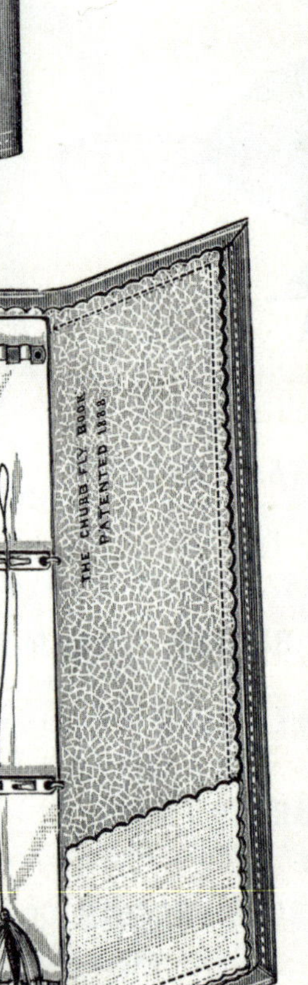

(Nos. 5, 5¼, 5½, 5¾, 6, 7 and 8.)

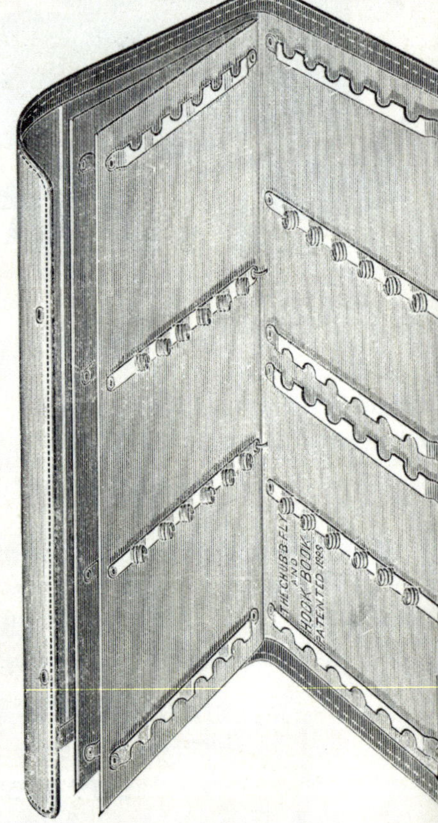

(FLY and HOOK BOOK, Nos. 11 and 1

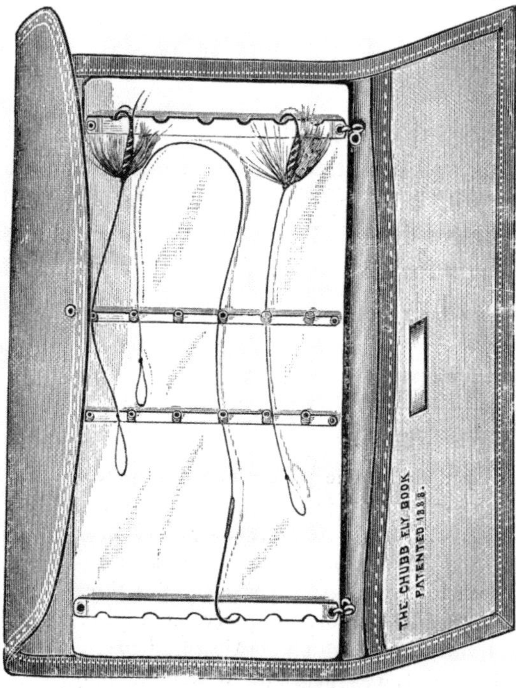

(**Nos. 3 and 4.**)

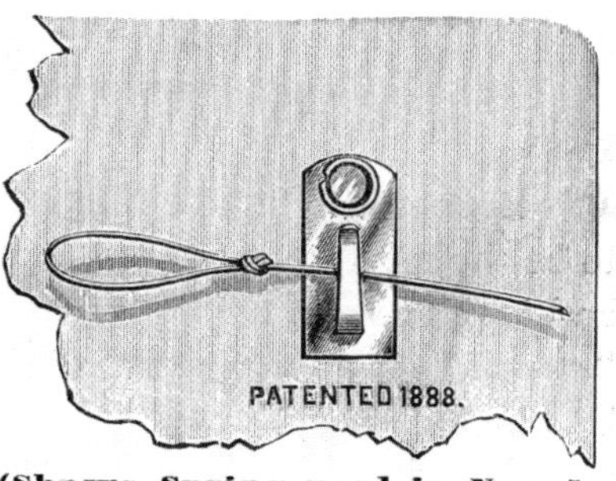

(**Shows Spring used in Nos. 5, 5¼, 5½, 5¾, 6, 7 and 8.**)

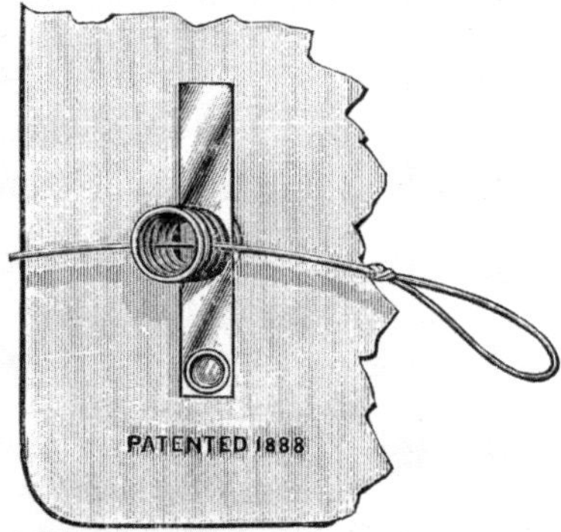

(**Shows Spring used in Nos. 1, 2 , 3, 4, 9, 10, 11 and 12.**)

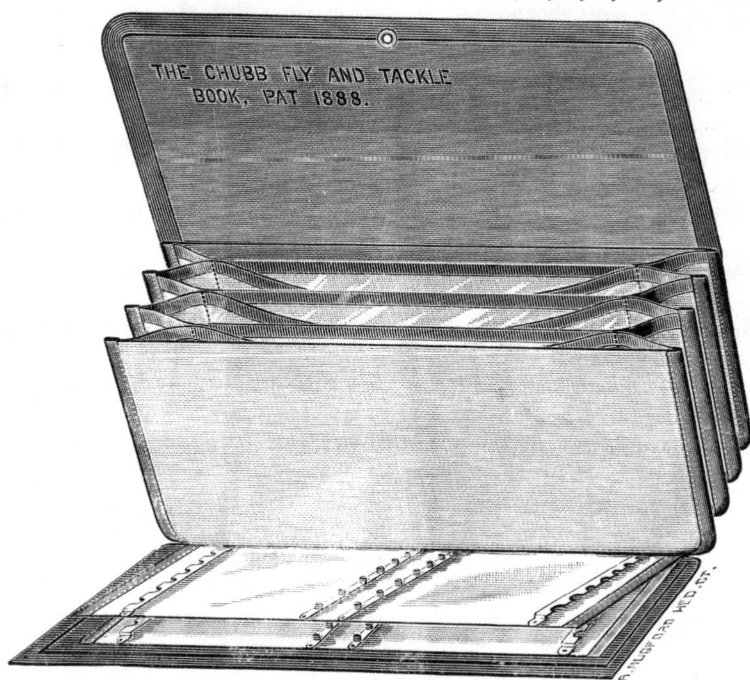

(**FLY and TACKLE BOOK, Nos. 9 and 10.**)

(***FOR DESCRIPTION AND PRICES, SEE NEXT PAGE.***)

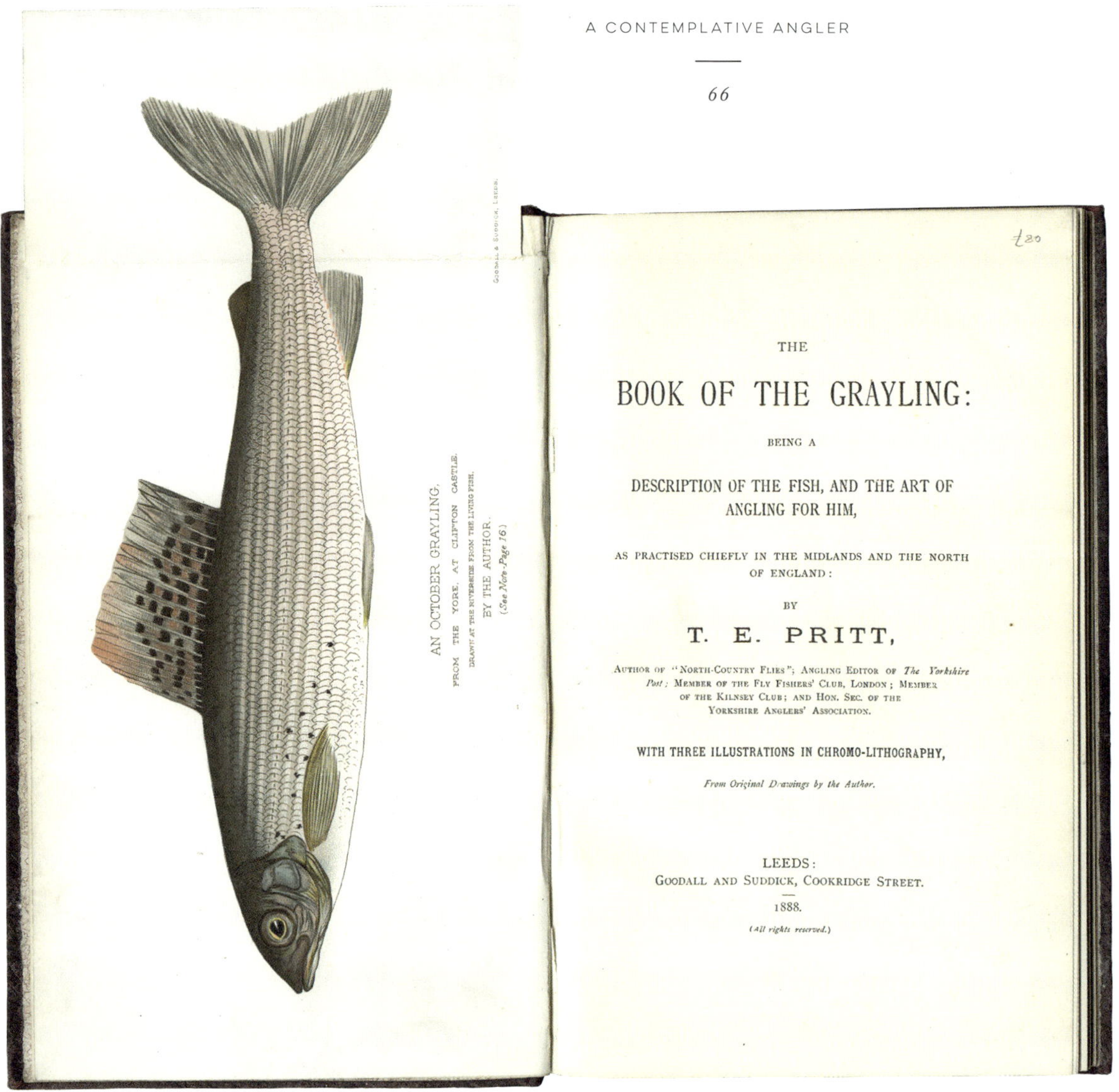
AN OCTOBER GRAYLING.
FROM THE YORE, AT CLIFTON CASTLE.
DRAWN AT THE RIVERSIDE FROM THE LIVING FISH.
BY THE AUTHOR.
(See Note-Page 16.)

THE

BOOK OF THE GRAYLING:

BEING A

DESCRIPTION OF THE FISH, AND THE ART OF ANGLING FOR HIM,

AS PRACTISED CHIEFLY IN THE MIDLANDS AND THE NORTH OF ENGLAND:

BY

T. E. PRITT,

AUTHOR OF "NORTH-COUNTRY FLIES"; ANGLING EDITOR OF *The Yorkshire Post*; MEMBER OF THE FLY FISHERS' CLUB, LONDON; MEMBER OF THE KILNSEY CLUB; AND HON. SEC. OF THE YORKSHIRE ANGLERS' ASSOCIATION.

WITH THREE ILLUSTRATIONS IN CHROMO-LITHOGRAPHY,

From Original Drawings by the Author.

LEEDS:
GOODALL AND SUDDICK, COOKRIDGE STREET.
1888.

(*All rights reserved.*)

20

PRITT, T[HOMAS] E[VAN]. *The Book of the Grayling: Being a Description of the Fish, and the Art of Angling for Him: As Practised Chiefly in the Midlands and the North of England.* LEEDS: GOODALL AND SUDDICK, 1888. [SH 691 G7 P75 1888] 24.7 CM X 15.9 CM

This is the classic text on grayling fishing with three attractive plates: a folding plate of the grayling, a plate of grayling flies, and a plate depicting the grayling's large dorsal fin.

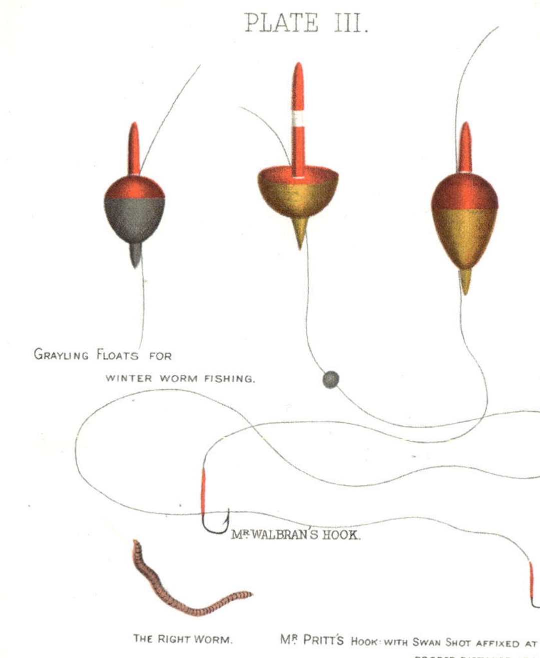

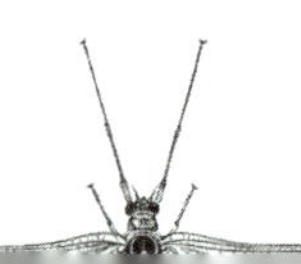

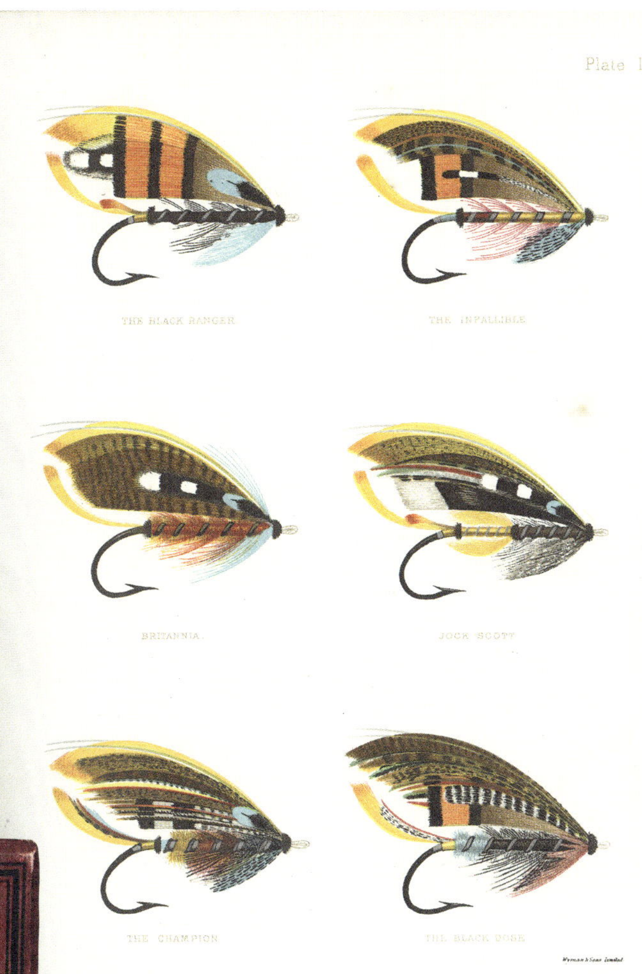

21

KELSON, GEO[RGE] M. *The Salmon Fly: How to Dress It and How to Use It.* LONDON: GEORGE M. KELSON, WYMAN & SONS, 1895. [SH 451 K46 1895] 27.7 CM X 22.5 CM

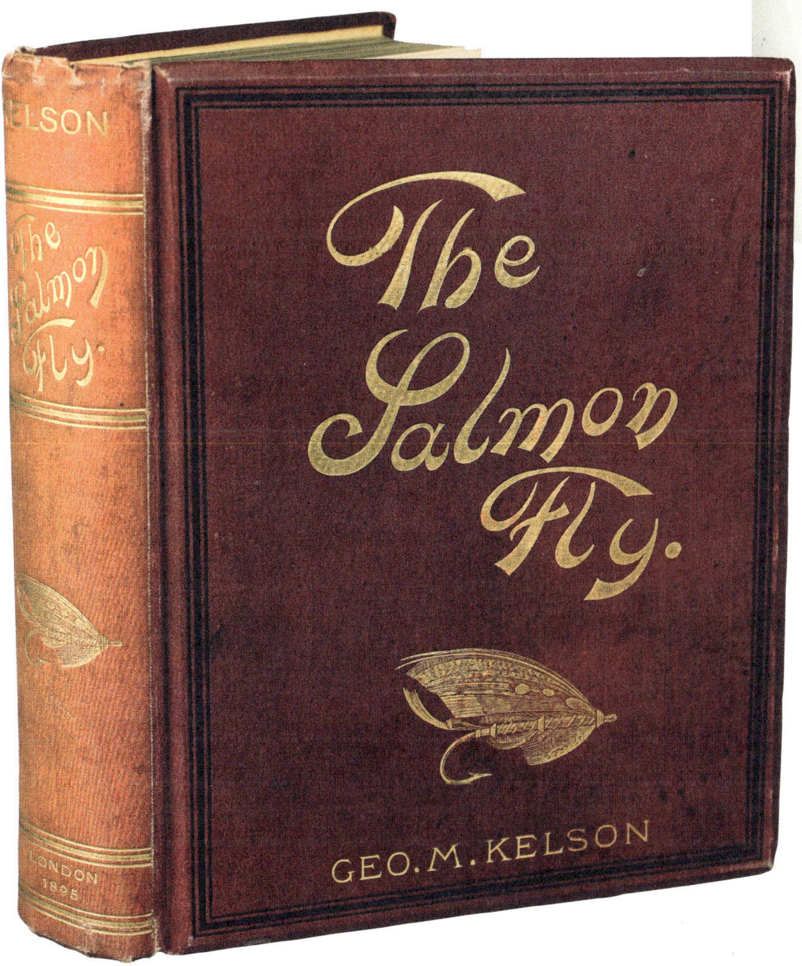

This landmark in the literature of salmon fishing is in the publisher's striking cloth binding. It includes eight colour lithographed plates of salmon flies.

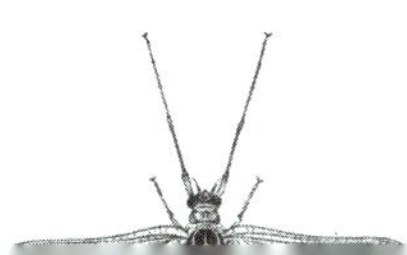

22

GILL, EMLYN M. *Practical Dry-fly Fishing*. NEW YORK: CHARLES SCRIBNER'S SONS, 1912. [SH 456 G56 1912] 19.0 CM X 13.0 CM

This is the first edition of the first American book on dry-fly fishing (Gingrich 210) and an excellent association copy with the bookplate of angling author Joseph Bates. In the first chapter, Gill recounts an anecdote of meeting, at a gathering at Ernest Thompson Seton's estate, a "prominent sportsman," who asked Gill the question, "What is a dry fly?" Gill is taken aback by the question and laments the general absence of dry-fly fishing in North America, despite its common practice in England. Gill draws heavily on the work of Frederic Halford to adapt dry-fly fishing techniques for an American audience (and to make the techniques available to Americans, as the author tried in vain to find Halford's works at New York dealers). Gill does not march blindly behind Halford's banner of dry-fly purism, however, as he remarks, "[a]n American, with a mind capable of seeing humorous features in almost all things, and also at times not beyond the temptation of indulging in ridicule, may easily see an opening for poking fun at the disappointed purist, as he returns at evening without once having cast a fly during the day" (20–21). Gill goes on to say, "[t]he purist's method of angling, sportsmanlike and praiseworthy though it may be, is not, I think, the style of dry-fly fishing that would generally appeal to American anglers, even though conditions on our streams made it all times possible. It is difficult to imagine an American fly-fisherman so patient that he would spend a day on the stream without casting a fly" (22–23). Gill gives techniques for American anglers while calling for a comprehensive "American Entomology" in the vein of Alfred Ronalds's *The Fly-fisher's Entomology*.

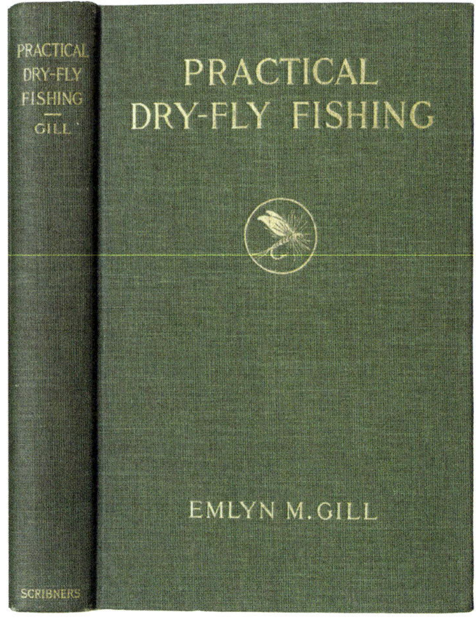

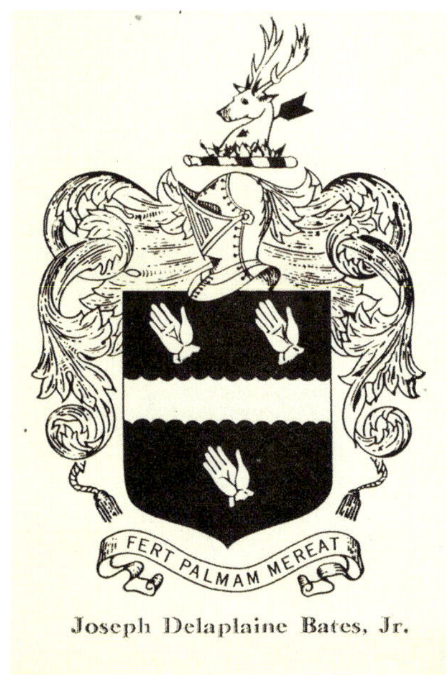

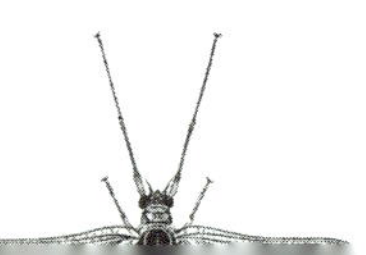

LIMITED EDITIONS

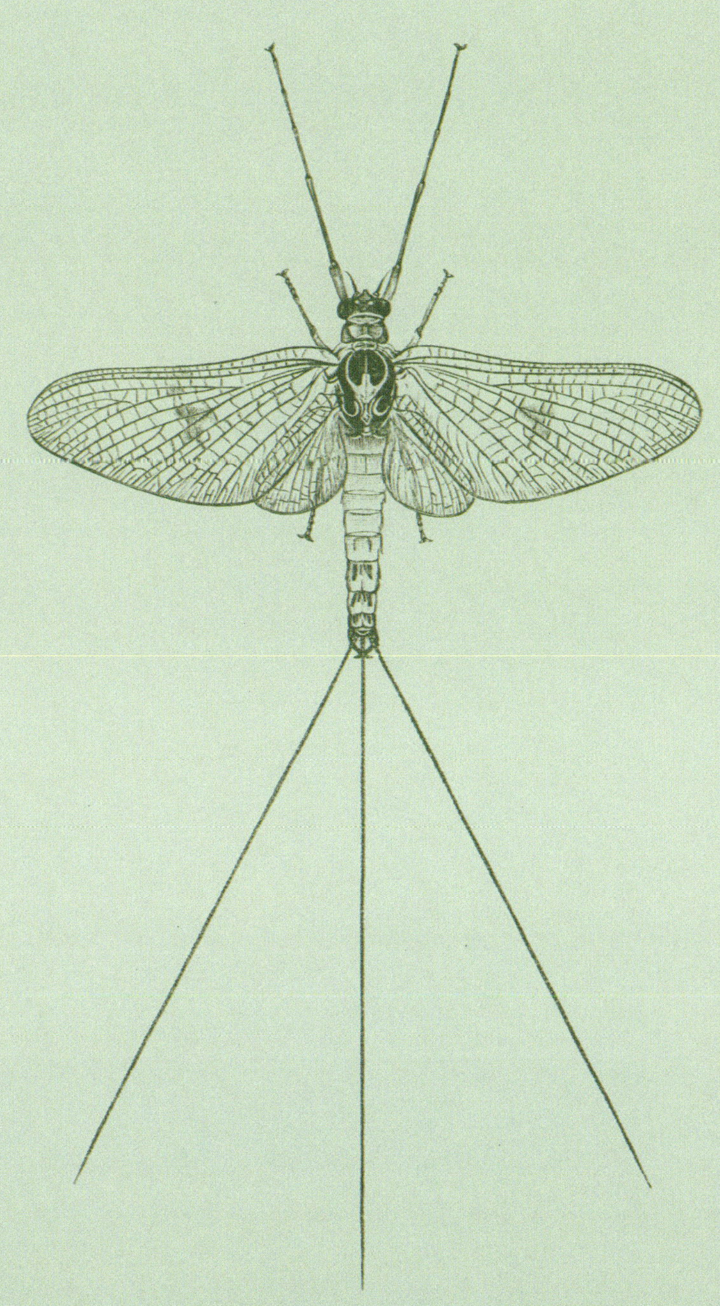

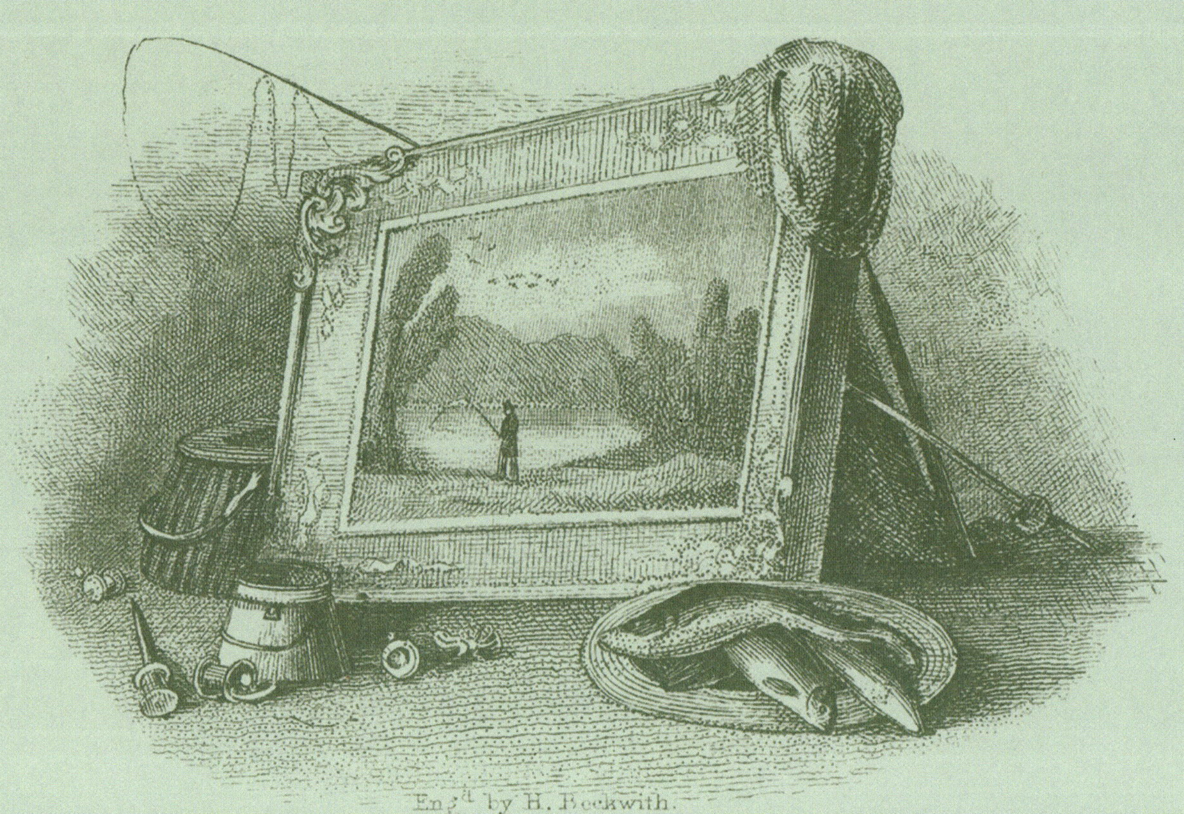

Engd by H. Beckwith.

LIMITED EDITIONS

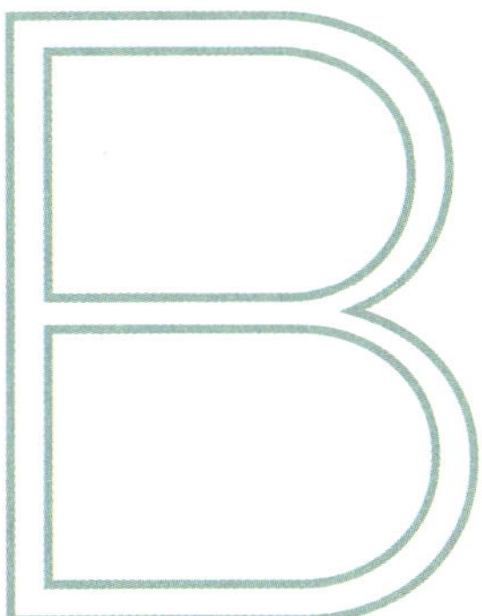

BOOK COLLECTORS have long been lured by limited editions. Lavishly-produced and often issued in only a handful of copies, limited edition books are akin to a trophy fish: beautiful, rare, and, once landed, a prize to show to friends and fellow collectors. This exhibition includes 29 examples of limited editions, spanning nearly 200 years of publishing. The earliest limited editions in the collection differ little from their trade counterparts, although they were often issued in large-paper editions or with different publisher's bindings. Through the late nineteenth and twentieth centuries, the productions became more deluxe with hand-tied flies or examples of fly-tying materials included. Perhaps the most significant items in this category are the series of dry-fly fishing books by Frederick Halford. Foundational works for dry-fly fishermen, these books were issued in deluxe publisher's bindings with hand-tied flies. They were also published in severely limited editions (fewer than 100 copies), further adding to their significance in a collection of angling books. During the latter half of the twentieth century, publishing houses innovated new ways to design limited edition angling books. Books were issued in hand-crafted hardwood boxes, and miniature books with miniature flies were released for the angler's shelf.

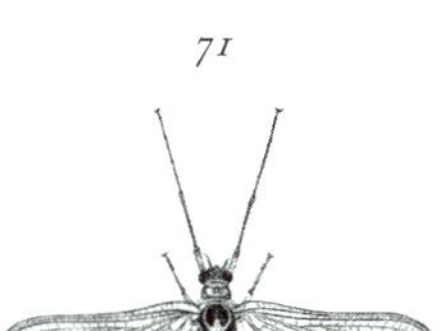

This exhibition is likely the first time that the collection of limited editions included here has been exhibited together. Pay special attention to the unique book designs and construction methods used to present the beautiful hand-tied flies included with many of the books.

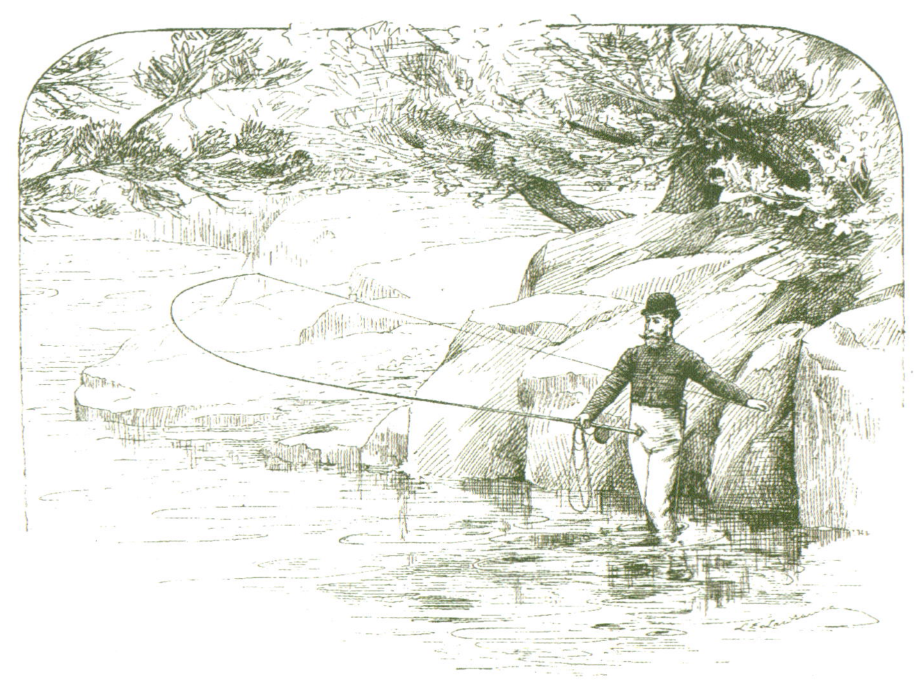

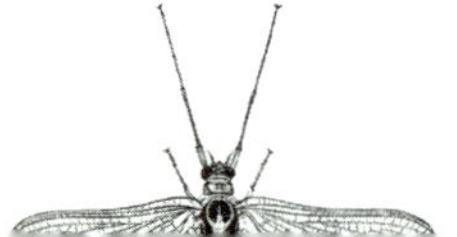

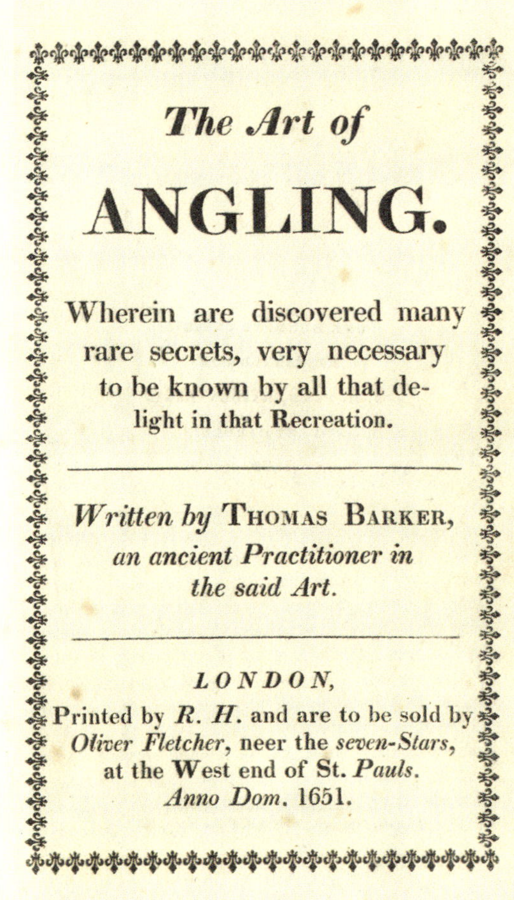
The Art of

ANGLING.

Wherein are discovered many rare secrets, very necessary to be known by all that delight in that Recreation.

Written by THOMAS BARKER, an ancient Practitioner in the said Art.

LONDON,
Printed by R. H. and are to be sold by Oliver Fletcher, neer the seven-Stars, at the West end of St. Pauls.
Anno Dom. 1651.

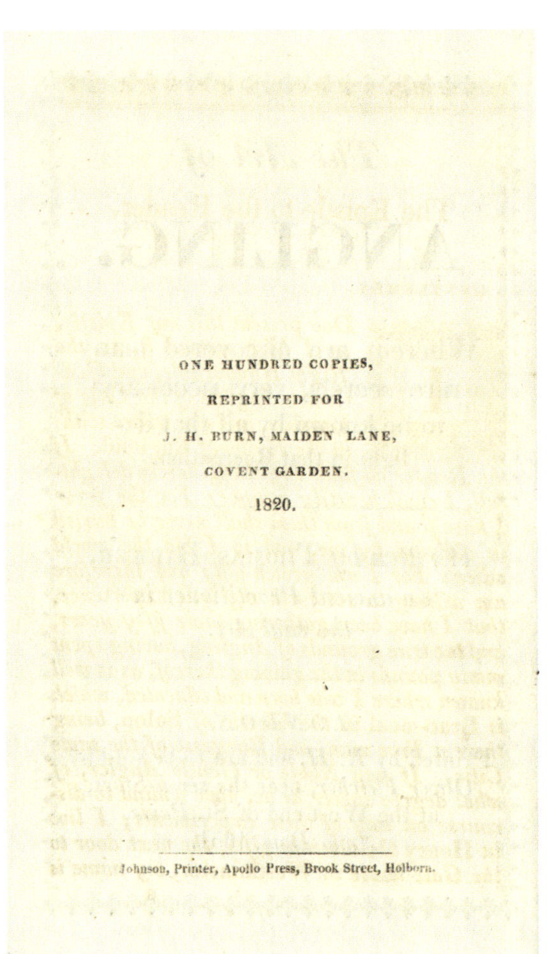
ONE HUNDRED COPIES,
REPRINTED FOR
J. H. BURN, MAIDEN LANE,
COVENT GARDEN.
1820.

Johnson, Printer, Apollo Press, Brook Street, Holborn.

23

BARKER, THOMAS. *The Art of Angling: Wherein Are Discovered Many Rare Secrets, Very Necessary to Be Known by All That Delight in the Recreation.* 1651. LONDON: J.H. BURN, 1820. [SH 437 B35 1820] 16.7 CM X 10.1 CM

This is the earliest book in the collection with a limitation statement and also one of the few "Pre-Waltonian" titles in the collection, with the first edition printed in 1651 (two years prior to *Compleat Angler*). The book contains early descriptions of the use of a reel or "winch" (which was not necessarily common at the time) and also gives instructions on fly tying. Barker was considered "ahead of his time" for his practicality and ingenuity as an angler (Marston 98). Of the run of 100 copies of this edition, a single copy was printed on vellum (Westwood et al. 21).

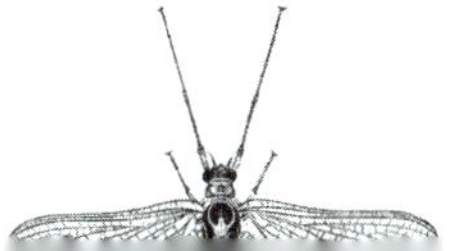

24

WORKS BY JOSEPH CRAWHALL AND AN ASSOCIATION COPY

Joseph Crawhall II was an English artist and printer who produced several limited-edition books during his lifetime (1821–1896). Crawhall's illustrative woodcuts are the most remarkable aspects of his angling titles. They are strangely compelling, both primitive and incredibly modern. This edition of *The Compleatest Angling Booke* is a second edition, which was printed by the author to satisfy his friends who "long cried in vain" for more copies of the original edition (1859), which was only printed in 40 copies (Westwood et al. 70). The reprint, however, would only satisfy the cries of an additional 100 friends, as the plates were destroyed after only 100 copies were printed (Westwood et al. 70). This copy appears never to have been bound and is contained in a cloth folder.

A Collection of Right Merrie Garlands is one of 50 large-paper copies of the trade edition and includes striking woodcuts throughout—both originals of Crawhall's and reproductions of those by Thomas Bewick. One of Crawhall's woodcuts from this title is featured on the bookplate of angling-book collector Joseph Norton.

The copy of *The Coquet-dale Fishing Songs* included here is also a significant association copy. It bears Crawhall's bookplate and was possibly the source copy of some of the garlands in Crawhall's books. Indeed, *A Collection of Right Merrie Garlands* is dedicated by Crawhall to the Coquetdale Angling Club, and *The Coquet-dale Fishing Songs* is referenced in the book's introduction.

24(a)

[CRAWHALL, JOSEPH]. *The Compleatest Angling Booke That Euer Was Writ: Being Done out of Ye Hebrewe and Other Tongvues by a Person of Honor.* 2ND ED. [NEWCASTLE-ON-TYNE]: [JOSEPH CRAWHALL], [1881]. [SH 439 C73 1881]
30.0 CM X 25.5 CM | EDITION OF 100 COPIES

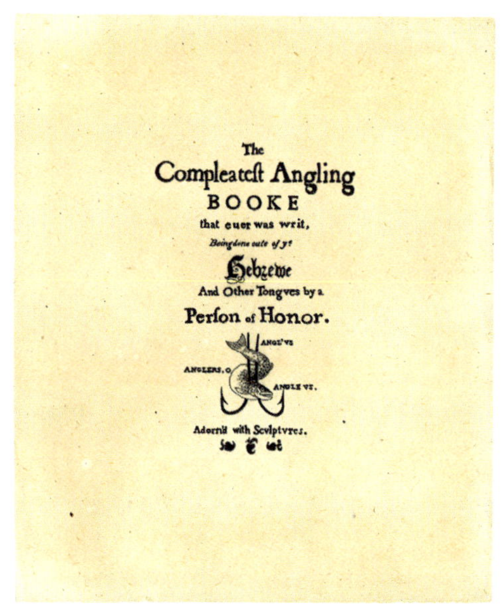

The
Compleatest Angling
BOOKE
that euer was writ,
Hebrewe
And Other Tongves by a
Person of Honor.
ANGLERS, O
ANGLE VE.
Adornd with Sculptures.

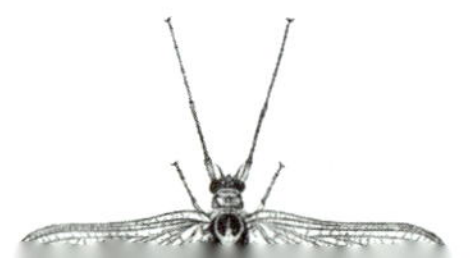

Oft, whilſt practising this moſt scientific mode of Angling on COQUET'S sunny banks, charming to the Angler, the Artiſt, the contemplative Man, or the Philoſopher,—oft have we seen the serenity of a friend's temper seriously diſturbed, as the Reader may imagine from the following

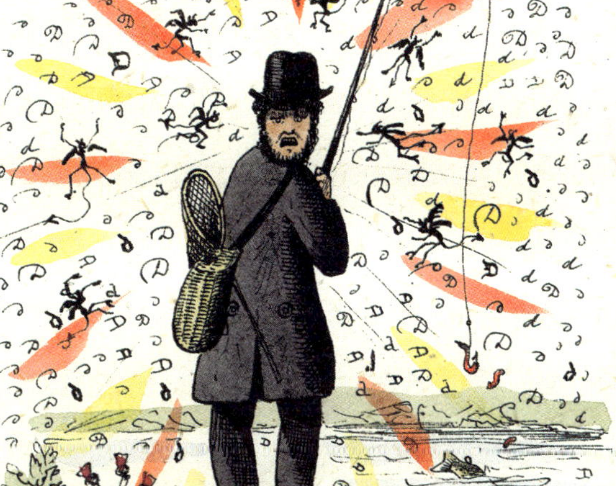

which we introduce as a Tail-piece. N.B. The trouts are suppoſed to be, what is technically called, vigorouſly TAILING the worm, and our friend to be uſing very unparliamentary language, feebly emblematized in his hieroglyphic halo.

clxxxvij

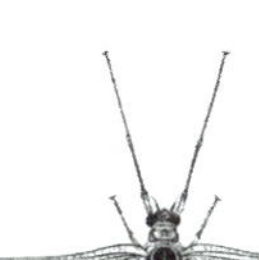

24(b)

CRAWHALL, JOSEPH, ED. *A Collection of Right Merrie Garlands for North Country Anglers.* NEWCASTLE-ON-TYNE: GEORGE RUTLAND, 1864. [PN 6110 A6 C73 1864] 26.6 CM X 21.5 CM | NO. 44 OF 50

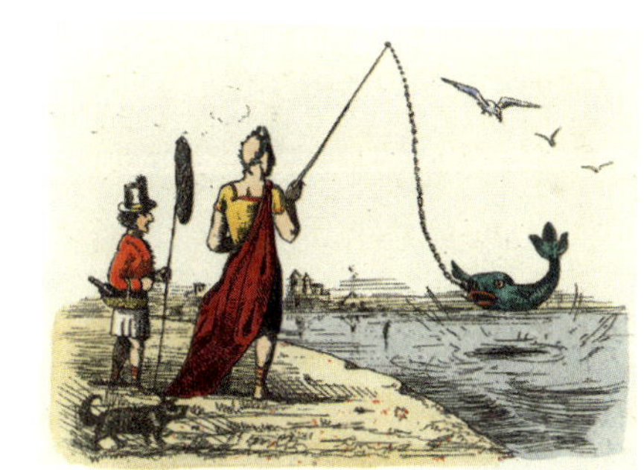

A COLLECTION

OF

RIGHT MERRIE GARLANDS

FOR

North Country Anglers.

EDITED BY

JOSEPH CRAWHALL,

AND CONTINUED TO THIS PRESENT YEAR.

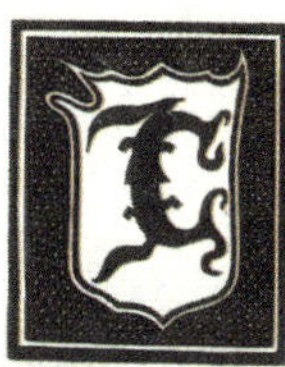

Newcastle-on-Tyne:

GEORGE RUTLAND, 22 BLACKETT STREET

1864.

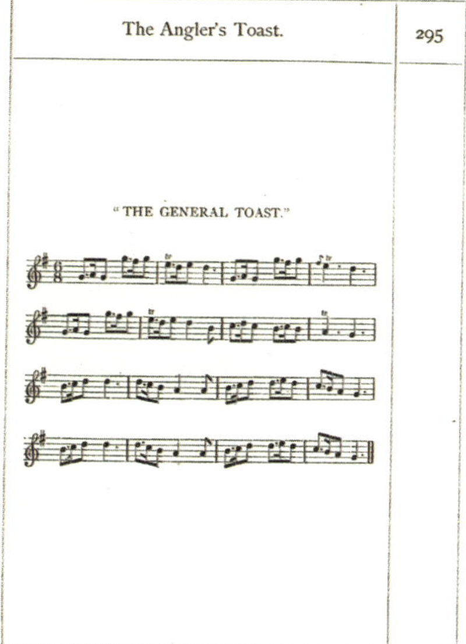

The Angler's Toast. 295

"THE GENERAL TOAST."

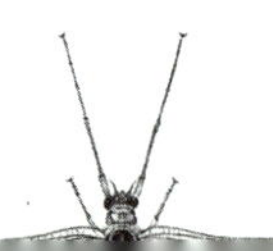

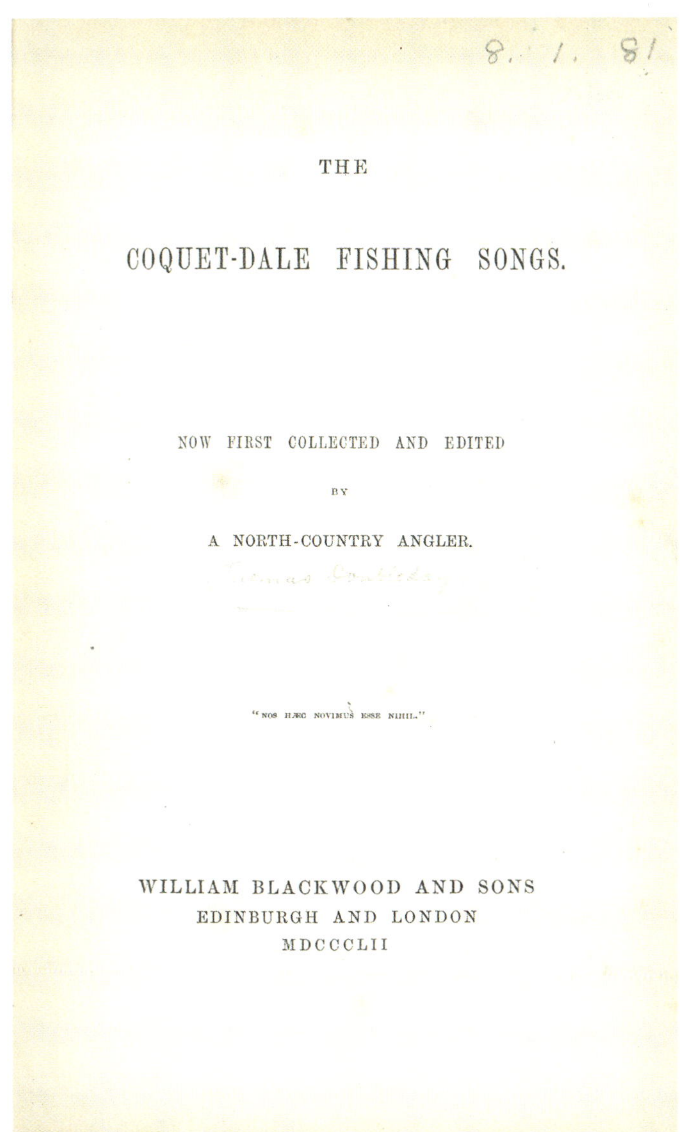
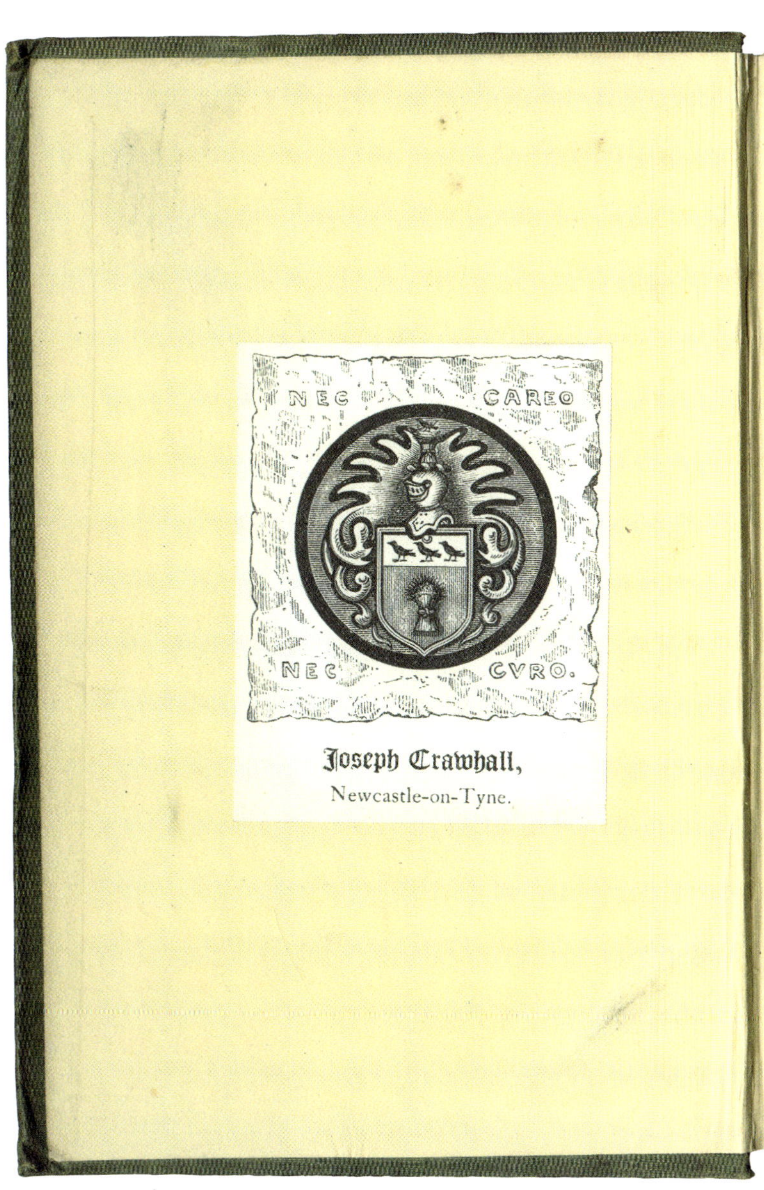

24(c)

[DOUBLEDAY, THOMAS]. *The Coquet-dale Fishing Songs: Now First Collected and Edited by a North-country Angler.* EDINBURGH: WILLIAM BLACKWOOD AND SONS, 1852. [SH 403 C8 D68 1852] 19.0 CM X 13.1 CM

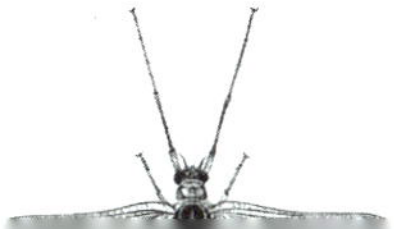

The Old Fisher's Challenge.

TUNE—" Boyne Water," (Old Set.)

O! LET it be in April-tide,
  But one of April's best,
A mornin' that seems made o' May,
  In dews an' sunshine drest;
Frae off the crags o' Simonside,
  Let the fresh breezes blaw,
And let auld Cheviot's sides be green,
  Albeit his head be snaw.
        CHORUS—Frae off the crags, &c.

Let the stream glitter i' the sun;
  The curl be on the pool,
The rash gale rufflin' aye its face
  Aneath the alders cool;
Or if the spring will have her clouds,
  Then let them pass me soon;
Or, if they tak' a thought and stay,
  Then let it be at noon.
        Or if the spring, &c.

O! freshly from his mountain holds
  Comes down the rapid Tyne;
But Coquet's still the stream o' streams,
  So let her still be mine;
There's mony a sawmon lies in Tweed,
  An' mony a trout in Till;
But Coquet—Coquet aye for me,
  If I may have my will.
          There's mony a sawmon, &c.

Let it be "stream an' stream about;"
  Or if that may-na be,
Take off old Coquet where ye like,
  From Thirlmoor to the sea;
But leave to me the streams I love—
  The streams that know my hand,
An' "weight to weight" with the best he
  That's in Northumberland.
          But leave to me, &c.

Let me begin at Brinkburn's stream,
  Fast by the ruins grey,
An' end at bonny Ely-haugh,
  Just wi' the endin' day.
My foremost flee, the heckle red—
  My tried rod springin' free;
An' "creel to creel" wi' ony man
  In a' the north countrie!

[CHORUS.

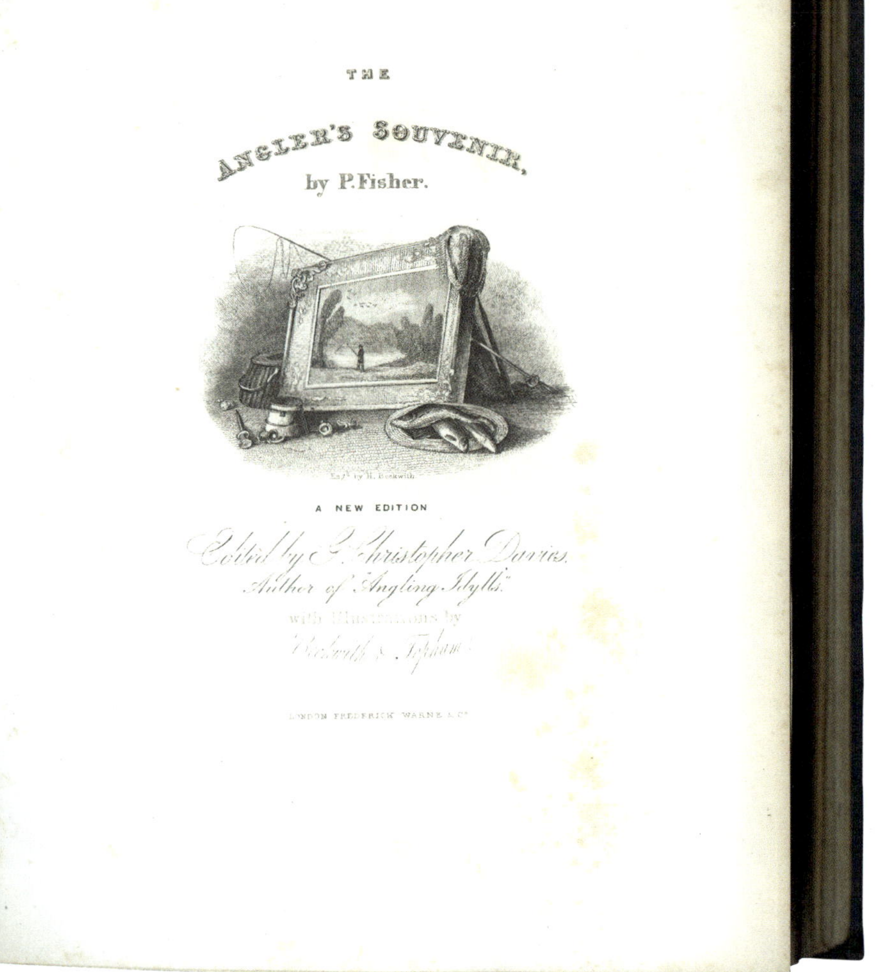
THE

ANGLER'S SOUVENIR,

by P. Fisher.

A NEW EDITION

Edited by G. Christopher Davies,
Author of "Angling Idylls."
with Illustrations by
Beckwith & Topham.

LONDON FREDERICK WARNE & Co.

ANGLER'S SOU

Two hundred and fifty copies printed,

Fifty copies of which are reserved for the American market, and of which this is

No. 55

Frederick Warne & Co.

WITH ILLUSTRATIONS BY BECKWITH

25

[CHATTO, WILLIAM ANDREW]. *The Angler's Souvenir.* LONDON: FREDERICK WARNE & CO., 1886.
[SH 439 C49 1886] 22.0 CM X 18.4 CM | NO. 55 OF 250 COPIES

This is a limited edition reprint of the 1835 edition. The "Introduction" of the edition includes a section musing on the types of people who read angling books:

> There are three classes of men who read angling books. First, and least numerous, are those who care nothing for fishing, but are fond of the country, and like to read those descriptions of country life and scenes which abound in angling books more than others; next come those who are fond of fishing, and are so lucky as to have plenty of it. These, although they cannot keep their hands off a book on their favourite sport, if they see it, look down upon it with some feeling of superiority to it: they know more than it can teach them, and all their lives are passed in the enjoyment to the satiety of what it describes as almost heavenly; and last, there is the large class for which books of this kind are chiefly written—the men who are sportsmen at heart, and passionately devoted to angling, yet have little time, and perhaps less opportunity, to indulge in the pursuit of that which would bring them happiness. These men read with avidity whatever is written upon the gentle art, and so make up in fancy for the loss of the reality (5).

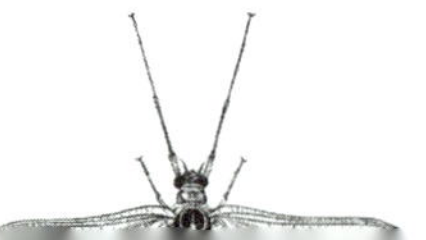

26

LANDMARKS IN DRY-FLY FISHING BY FREDERIC HALFORD

Frederic Halford was the major force behind documenting, articulating, and refining the art of dry-fly fishing. He was immersed almost entirely in the practice and came to believe that "the dry fly had superseded for all time and in all places all other methods of fly fishing, and that those who thought otherwise were either ignorant or incompetent" (John Waller Hills qtd. in Gingrich 202). From humble beginnings as a bait-fisherman, Halford became (and remains) the central figure to promote the art of dry-fly fishing. His books were issued in deluxe limited editions with extremely limited print runs and examples of hand-tied flies. He was also party to one of the greatest debates to rage through the fly-fishing community between dry-fly fisherman (lead by himself) and nymph or "wet fly" fisherman, lead by G.E.M. Skues (see item 35).

Given the importance of these titles, their beauty and desirability, and their rarity, it is remarkable to have them exhibited together.

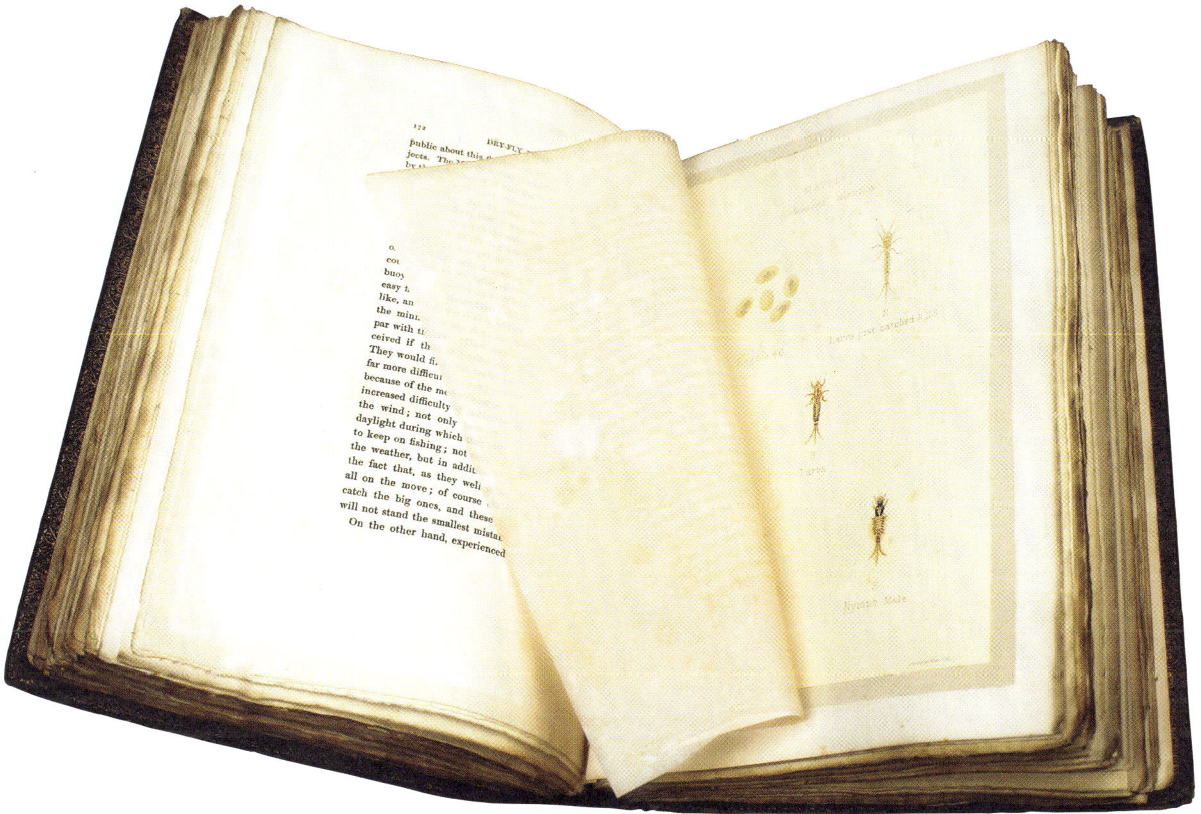

26(b)

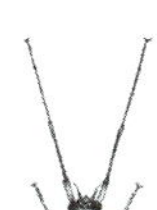

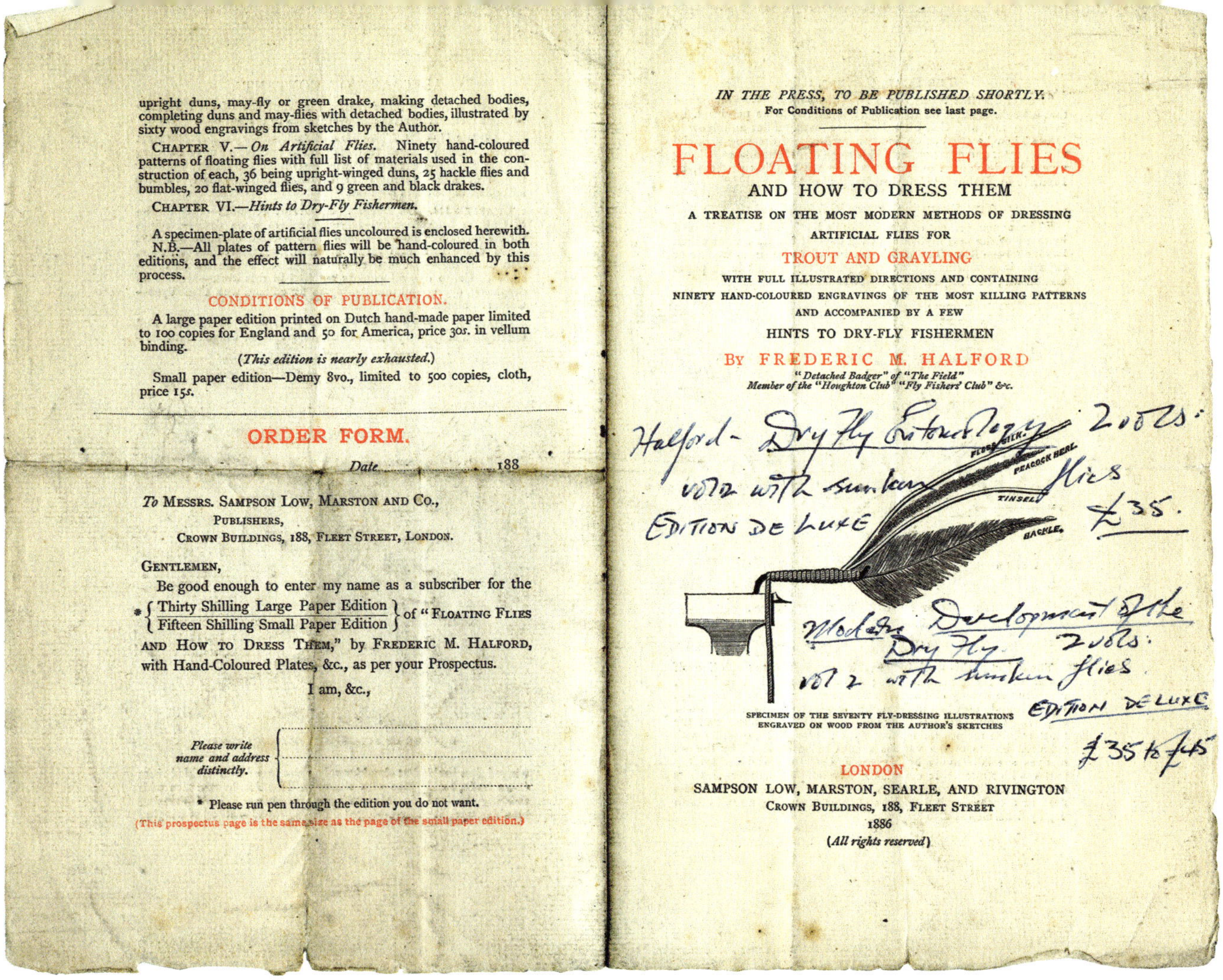

upright duns, may-fly or green drake, making detached bodies, completing duns and may-flies with detached bodies, illustrated by sixty wood engravings from sketches by the Author.

CHAPTER V.—*On Artificial Flies.* Ninety hand-coloured patterns of floating flies with full list of materials used in the construction of each, 36 being upright-winged duns, 25 hackle flies and bumbles, 20 flat-winged flies, and 9 green and black drakes.

CHAPTER VI.—*Hints to Dry-Fly Fishermen.*

A specimen-plate of artificial flies uncoloured is enclosed herewith.

N.B.—All plates of pattern flies will be hand-coloured in both editions, and the effect will naturally be much enhanced by this process.

CONDITIONS OF PUBLICATION.

A large paper edition printed on Dutch hand-made paper limited to 100 copies for England and 50 for America, price 30*s.* in vellum binding.

(*This edition is nearly exhausted.*)

Small paper edition—Demy 8vo., limited to 500 copies, cloth, price 15*s.*

ORDER FORM.

Date..............188

To MESSRS. SAMPSON LOW, MARSTON AND CO.,
PUBLISHERS,
CROWN BUILDINGS, 188, FLEET STREET, LONDON.

GENTLEMEN,

Be good enough to enter my name as a subscriber for the *{ Thirty Shilling Large Paper Edition / Fifteen Shilling Small Paper Edition } of "FLOATING FLIES AND HOW TO DRESS THEM," by FREDERIC M. HALFORD, with Hand-Coloured Plates, &c., as per your Prospectus.

I am, &c.,

Please write name and address distinctly.

* Please run pen through the edition you do not want.

(This prospectus page is the same size as the page of the small paper edition.)

IN THE PRESS, TO BE PUBLISHED SHORTLY.
For Conditions of Publication see last page.

FLOATING FLIES
AND HOW TO DRESS THEM

A TREATISE ON THE MOST MODERN METHODS OF DRESSING ARTIFICIAL FLIES FOR
TROUT AND GRAYLING
WITH FULL ILLUSTRATED DIRECTIONS AND CONTAINING NINETY HAND-COLOURED ENGRAVINGS OF THE MOST KILLING PATTERNS
AND ACCOMPANIED BY A FEW
HINTS TO DRY-FLY FISHERMEN

BY FREDERIC M. HALFORD
"Detached Badger" of "The Field"
Member of the "Houghton Club" "Fly Fishers' Club" &c.

Halford - Dry Fly Entomology 2 vols.
vol 2 with sunken flies
EDITION DE LUXE £35.

FLOSS SILK.
PEACOCK HERL.
TINSEL.
HACKLE.

Modern Development of the Dry Fly 2 vols.
vol 2 with sunken flies
EDITION DE LUXE
£35 to £45

SPECIMEN OF THE SEVENTY FLY-DRESSING ILLUSTRATIONS ENGRAVED ON WOOD FROM THE AUTHOR'S SKETCHES

LONDON
SAMPSON LOW, MARSTON, SEARLE, AND RIVINGTON
CROWN BUILDINGS, 188, FLEET STREET
1886
(*All rights reserved*)

26(a)

HALFORD, FREDERIC M[ICHAEL]. *Floating Flies and How to Dress Them: A Treatise on the Most Modern Methods of Dressing Artificial Flies for Trout and Grayling: With Full Illustrated Directions and Containing Ninety Hand-coloured Engravings of the Most Killing Patterns: Together with a Few Hints to Dry-fly Fishermen.* LONDON: SAMPSON LOW, MARSTON, SEARLE AND RIVINGTON, 1886. [SH 451 H335 1886] 26.1 CM X 17.6 CM

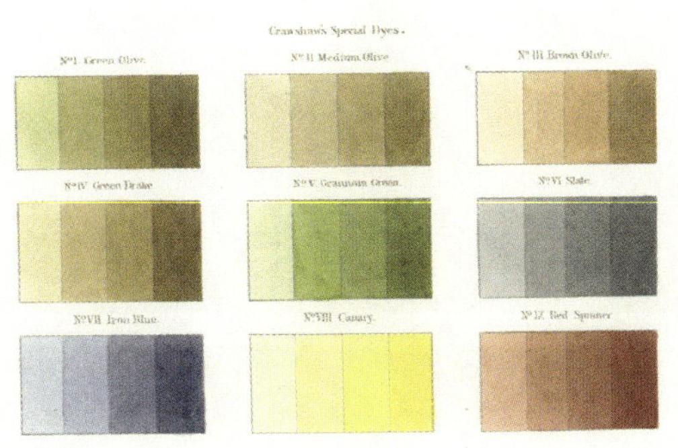

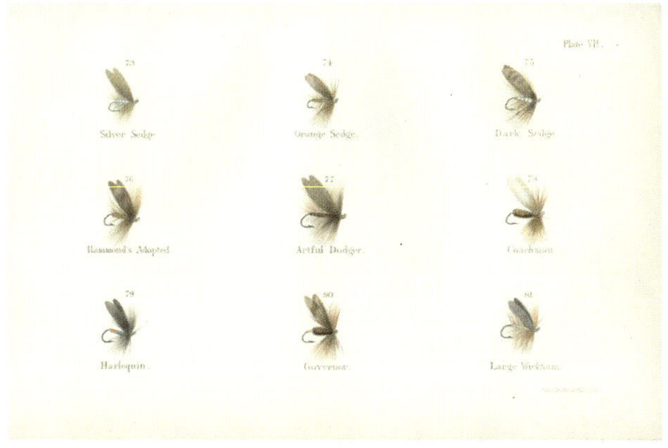

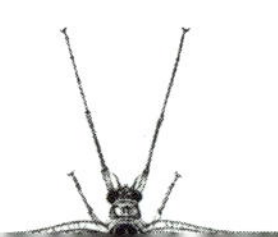

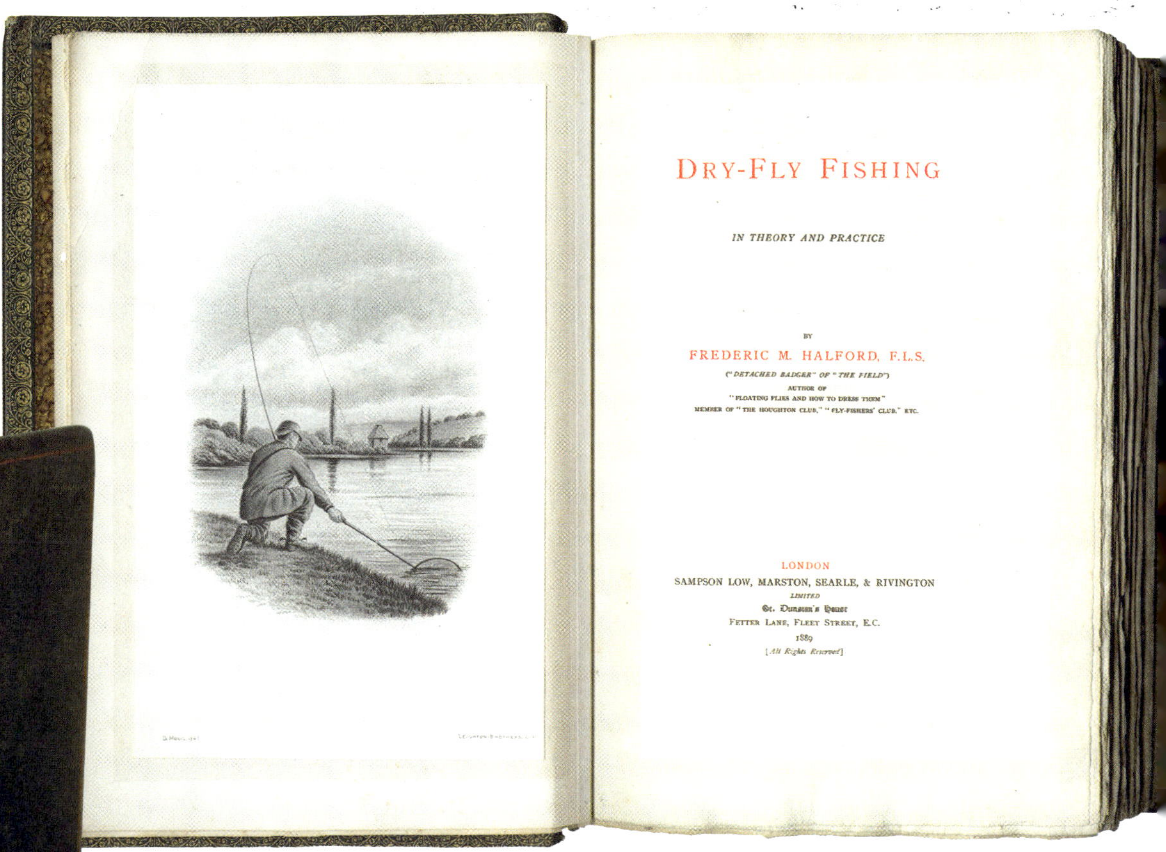

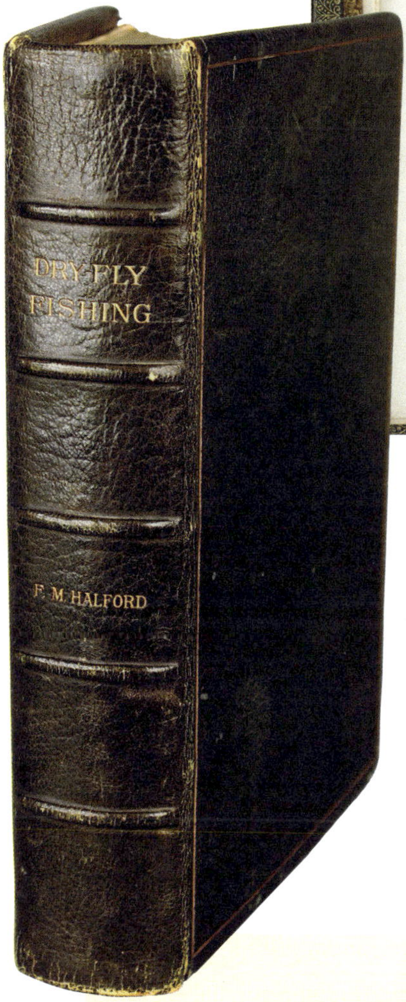

DRY-FLY FISHING

IN THEORY AND PRACTICE

BY

FREDERIC M. HALFORD, F.L.S.

LONDON

SAMPSON LOW, MARSTON, SEARLE, & RIVINGTON

1889

26(b)

HALFORD, FREDERIC M[ICHAEL]. *Dry-fly Fishing in Theory and Practice*. LONDON: SAMPSON LOW, MARSTON, SEARLE & RIVINGTON LTD., 1889. [SH 456 H25 1889] 28.6 CM X 20.1 CM NO. 3 OF 100 COPIES

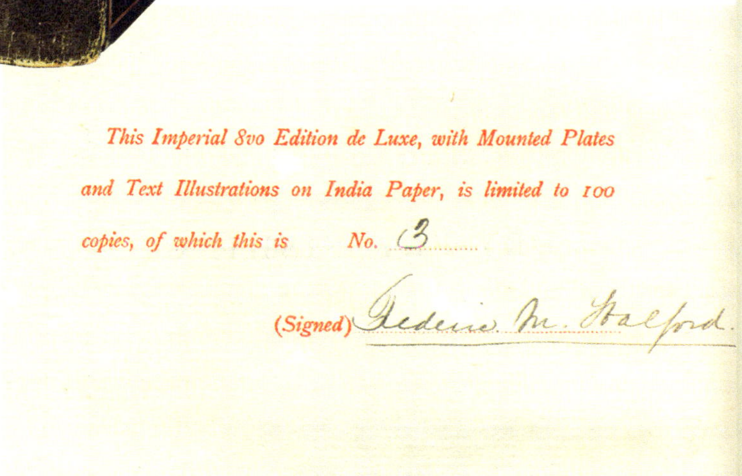

This Imperial 8vo Edition de Luxe, with Mounted Plates and Text Illustrations on India Paper, is limited to 100 copies, of which this is No. 3

(Signed) Frederic M. Halford

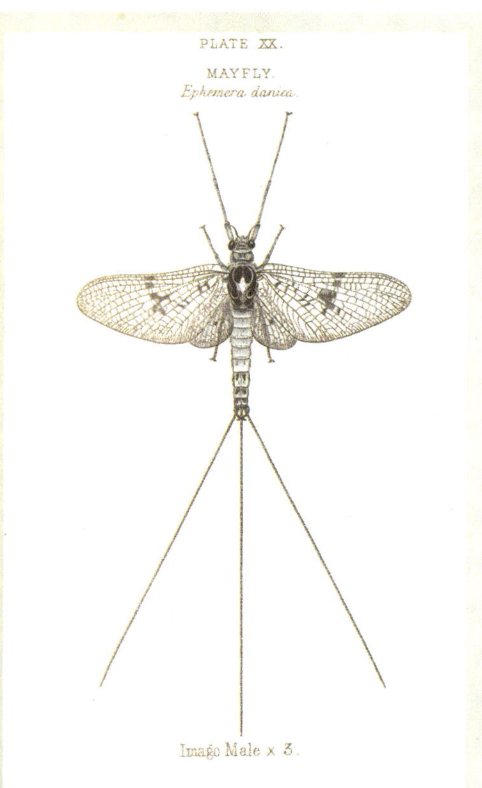

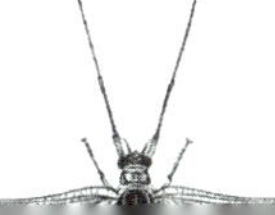

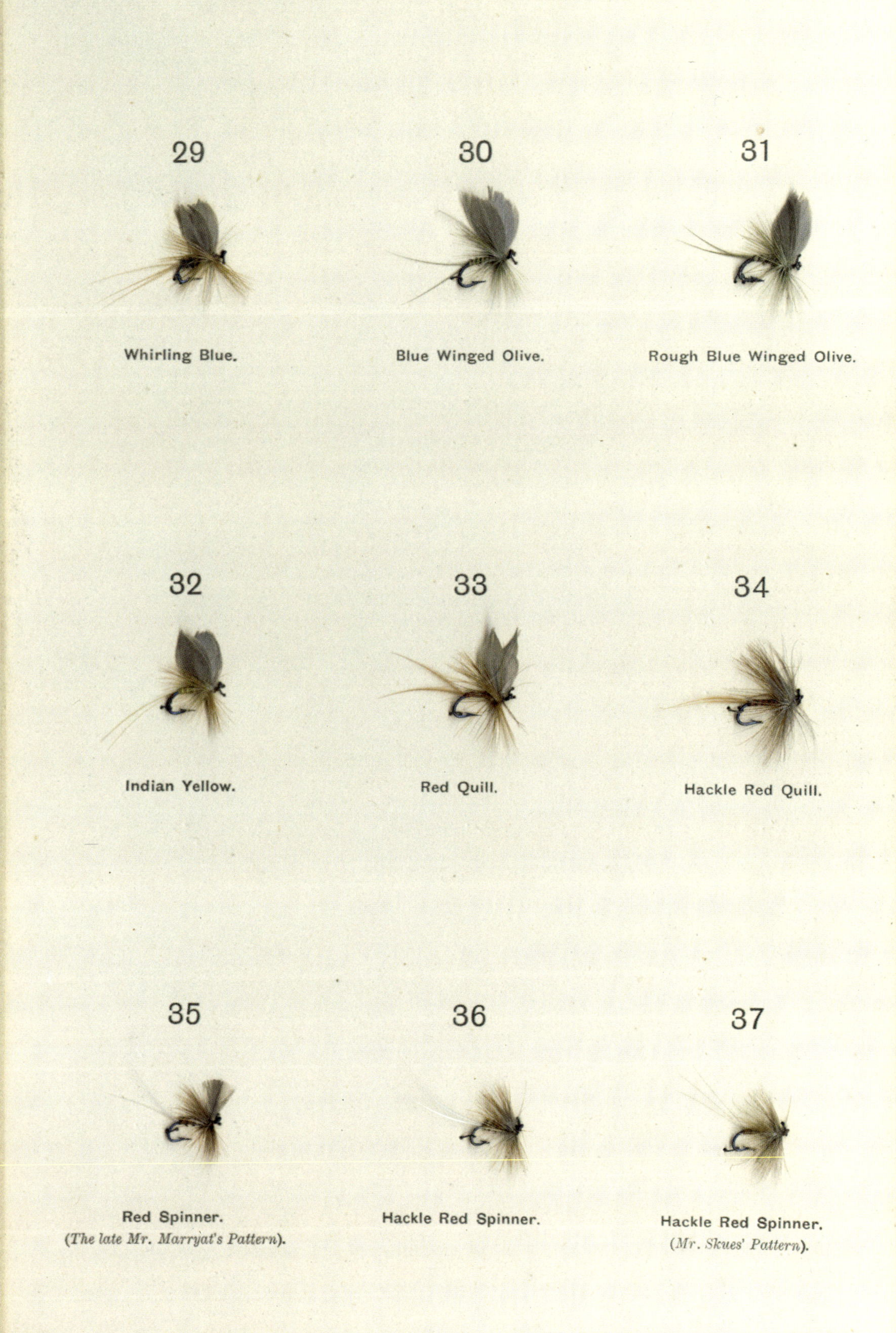
29
30
31
Whirling Blue.
Blue Winged Olive.
Rough Blue Winged Olive.
32
33
34
Indian Yellow.
Red Quill.
Hackle Red Quill.
35
36
37
Red Spinner.
(The late Mr. Marryat's Pattern).
Hackle Red Spinner.
Hackle Red Spinner.
(Mr. Skues' Pattern).

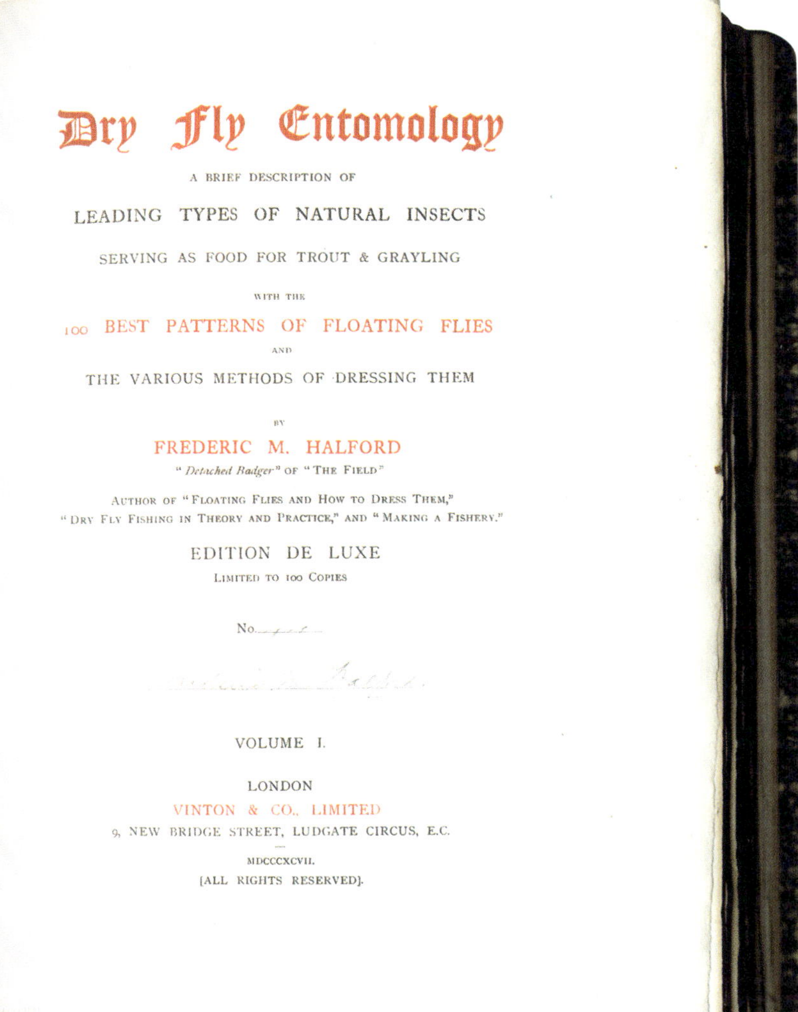

Dry Fly Entomology

A BRIEF DESCRIPTION OF

LEADING TYPES OF NATURAL INSECTS

SERVING AS FOOD FOR TROUT & GRAYLING

WITH THE

100 BEST PATTERNS OF FLOATING FLIES

AND

THE VARIOUS METHODS OF DRESSING THEM

BY

FREDERIC M. HALFORD

"*Detached Badger*" OF "THE FIELD"

AUTHOR OF "FLOATING FLIES AND HOW TO DRESS THEM," "DRY FLY FISHING IN THEORY AND PRACTICE," AND "MAKING A FISHERY."

EDITION DE LUXE

LIMITED TO 100 COPIES

No.

VOLUME I.

LONDON

VINTON & CO., LIMITED

9, NEW BRIDGE STREET, LUDGATE CIRCUS, E.C.

MDCCCXCVII.

[ALL RIGHTS RESERVED].

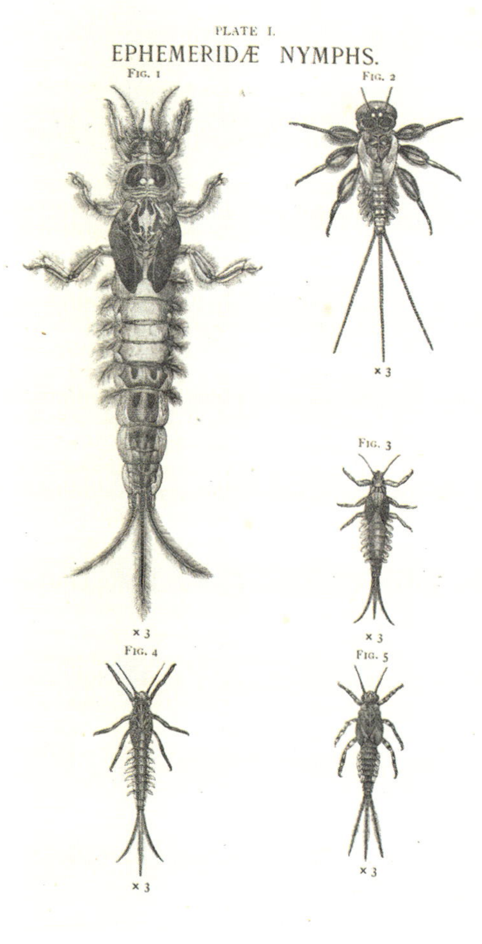

26(c)

HALFORD, FREDERIC M[ICHAEL]. *Dry Fly Entomology: A Brief Description of Leading Types of Natural Insects Serving as Food for Trout & Grayling: With the 100 Best Patterns of Floating Flies and the Various Methods of Dressing Them.* 2 VOLS. LONDON: VINTON & CO., 1897. [SH 451 H33 1897 V.1–2] 29.0 CM X 21.0 CM | NO. 44 OF 100 COPIES

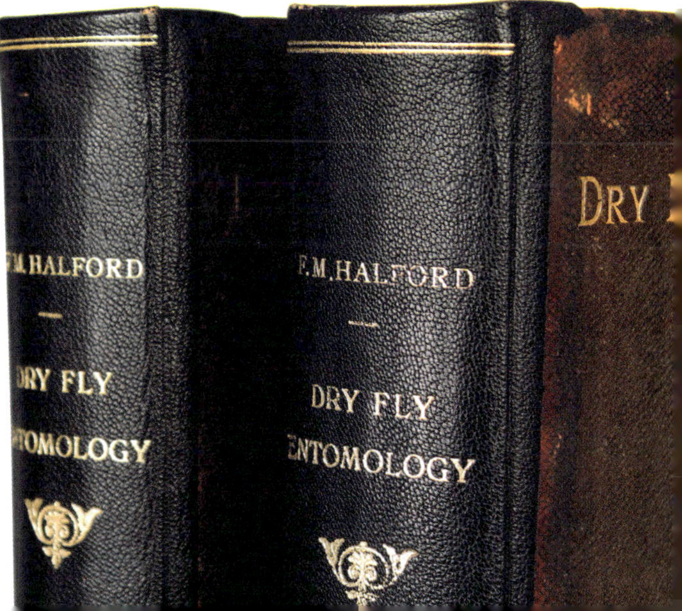

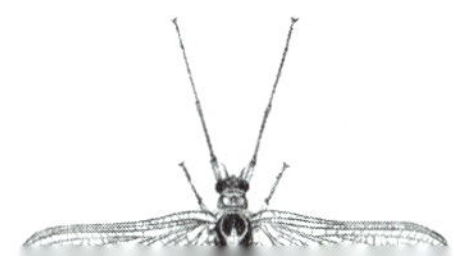

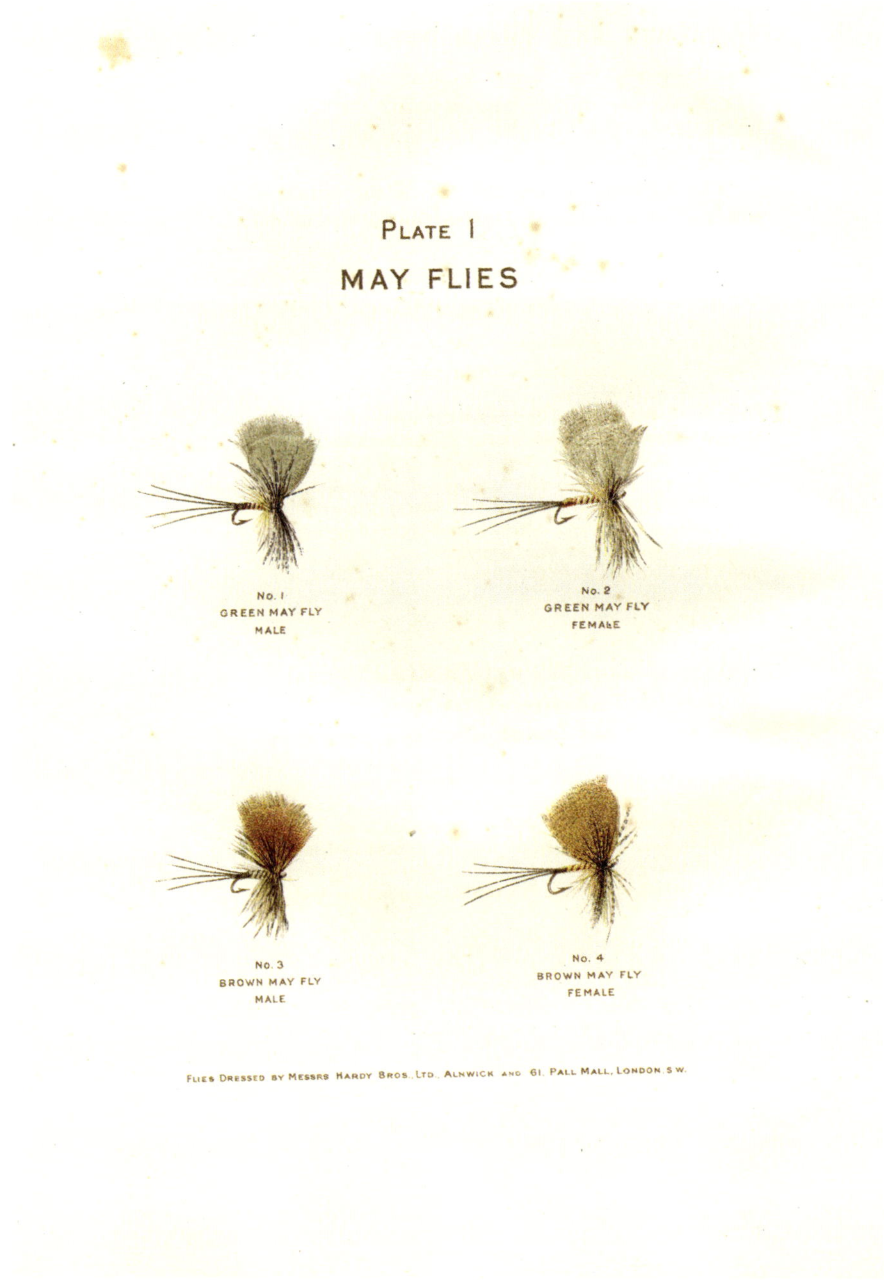

26(d)

HALFORD, FREDERIC M[ICHAEL]. *Modern Development of the Dry Fly: The New Dry Fly Patterns, the Manipulation of Dressing Them and Practical Experiences of Their Use.* 2 VOLS.
LONDON: GEORGE ROUTLEDGE AND SONS LTD., [1910]. [SH 451 H34 1910 V.1–2]
28.1 CM X 23.0 CM | NO. 74 OF 75 COPIES

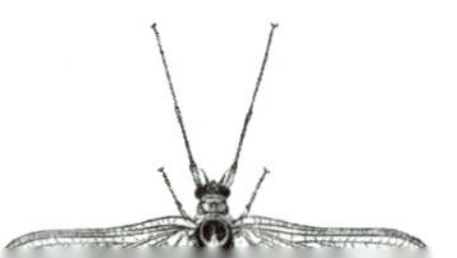

27

JOHNSON, FRANK M[ACKIE]. *Forest, Lake and River: The Fishes of New England & Eastern Canada.* 2 VOLS. BOSTON: N.P., 1902. [SH 461 J7 1902 V.1–2] 27.3 CM X 22.0 CM | NO. 43 OF 350 COPIES

This set is notorious for its fragile suede binding, and many sets are in poor condition. Although the original suede "clasps" are missing, this is an excellent example. Charles Wetzel, in his *American Fishing Books*, calls this "the most sumptuous angling work that had yet appeared in this country" outside of Dean Sage's *The Ristigouche and Its Salmon Fishing* (160). The set features numerous colour plates, silk endpapers, and gilt dentelles. Like nearly all extant copies, it lacks the large portfolio of plates.

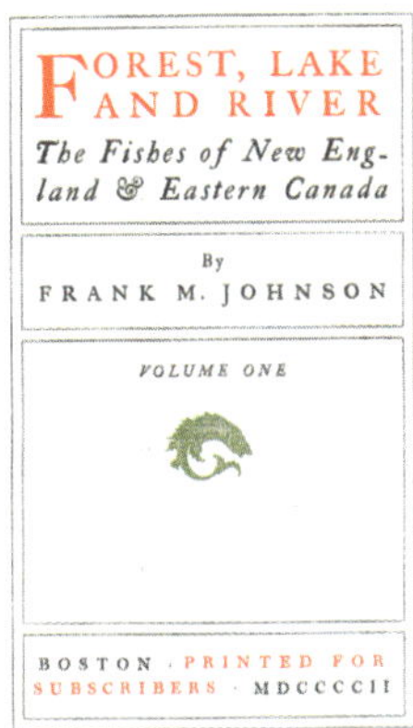
FOREST, LAKE AND RIVER

The Fishes of New England & Eastern Canada

By

FRANK M. JOHNSON

VOLUME ONE

BOSTON · PRINTED FOR SUBSCRIBERS · MDCCCCII

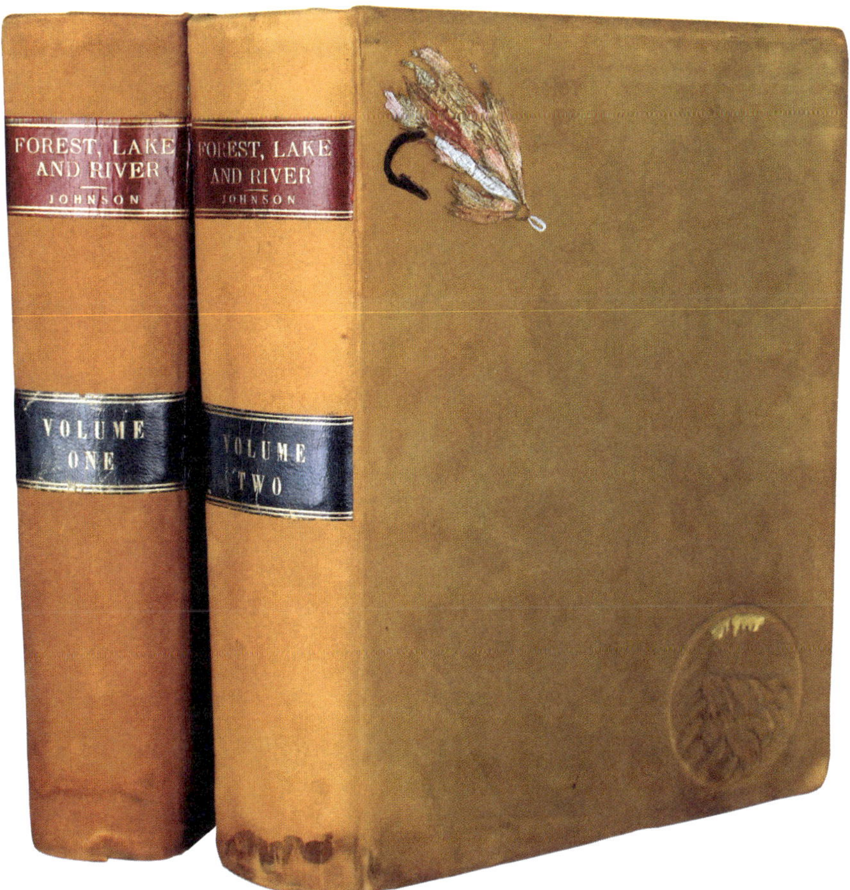

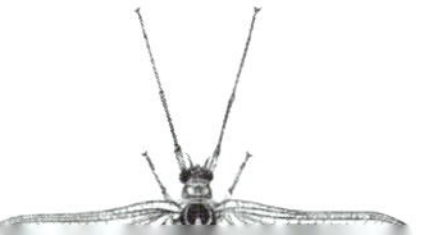

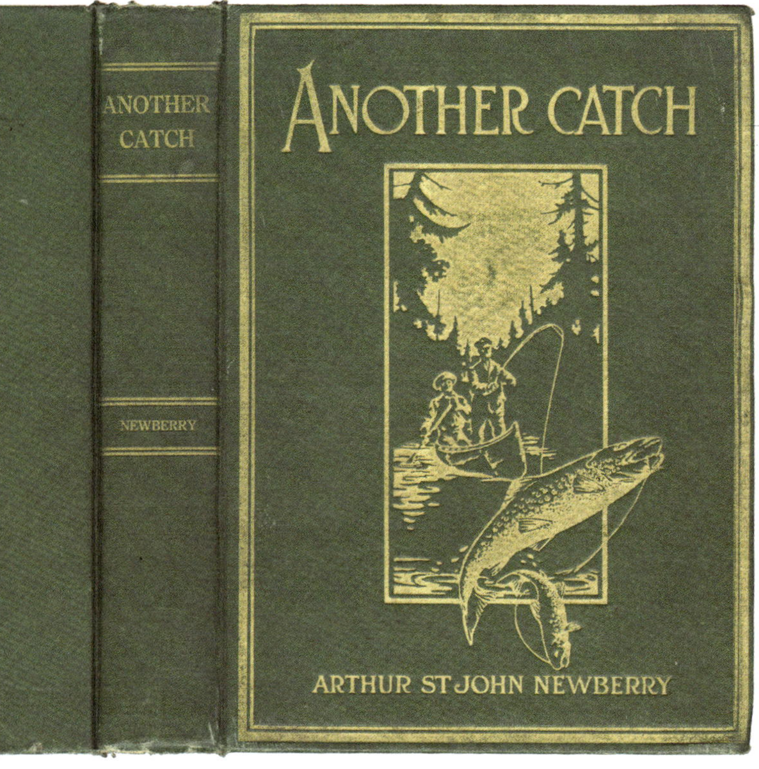

28

NEWBERRY, ARTHUR ST. JOHN. *Another Catch: More Fugitive Notes on Sport and Other Things.* CLEVELAND: N.P., 1914. [SH 34 N49 1914] 21.2 CM X 16.4 CM | EDITION OF 75 COPIES

Newberry's *Another Catch* is a scarce title with an ornate, heavily-gilt publisher's cloth binding. The book was privately printed for the author's widow for her distribution (Wetzel 187) and contains stories of her husband's angling and hunting exploits.

29

HILLS, JOHN WALLER. *A Summer on the Test.* LONDON: PHILIP ALLAN & CO., [1924]. [SH 688 G7 H55 1924 F] 32.5 CM X 25.7 CM NO. 24 OF 25 COPIES

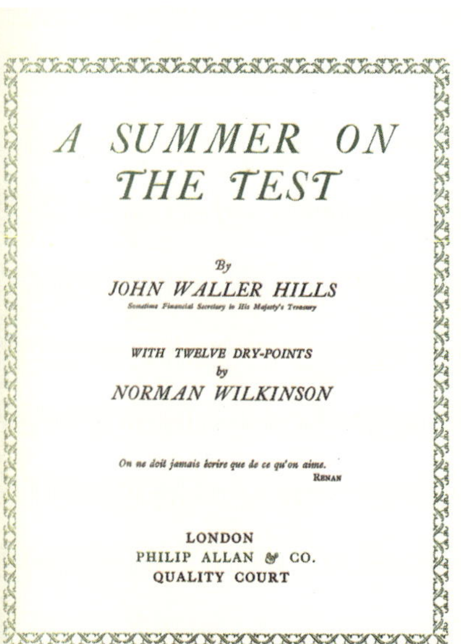
A SUMMER ON THE TEST

By
JOHN WALLER HILLS

WITH TWELVE DRY-POINTS
by
NORMAN WILKINSON

LONDON
PHILIP ALLAN & CO.
QUALITY COURT

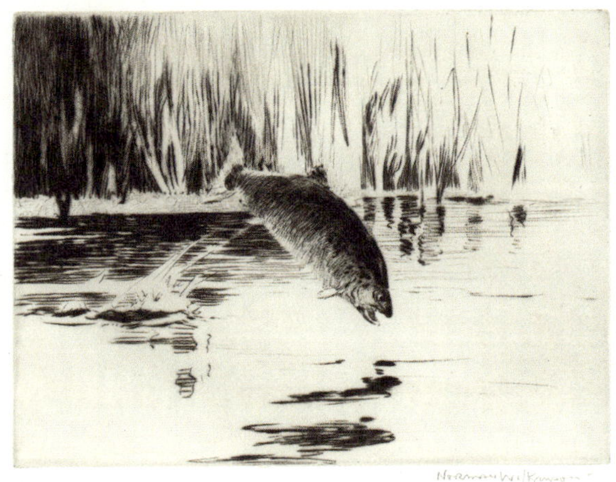

This is a fine, heavily-limited edition with all plates signed by the artist, Norman Wilkinson, whose twelve drypoints evoke quiet days angling on the River Test. Hills was also a historian of angling and remarks in the book's introduction, "[f]ishing has always been a progressive pursuit; it has always had a special attraction for the leisure intellectuals, and each age has added to its development. Some periods have added more, some less; but progress has never stopped and each age has added to its development" (vii). This title is one of the high points of twentieth-century angling literature, both for its content and for this beautiful limited edition.

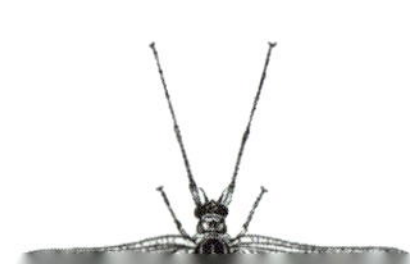

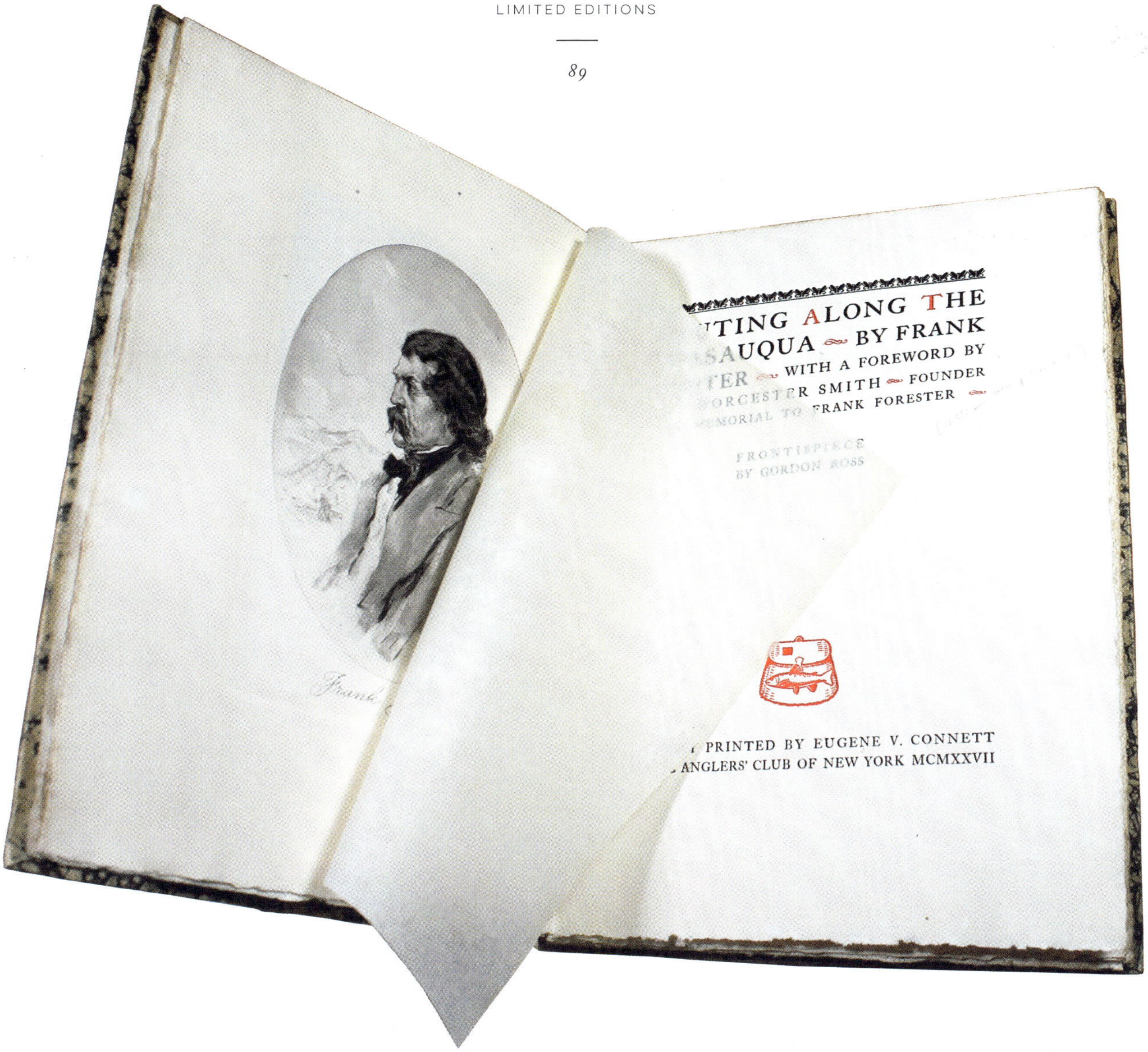

30

FORESTER, FRANK. *Trouting along the Catasauqua*. [NEW YORK, N.Y.]: ANGLERS' CLUB OF NEW YORK, 1927. [SH 688 U5 H47 1927]

This title was printed by Eugene V. Connett for the Anglers' Club of New York in the same year as *Magic Hours*, the first book to carry Connett's Derrydale Press imprint. Connett was dismayed that many of the early American fishing books had perished because they "were so insignificant-looking that they had been thrown away during spring cleaning" (Connett 12). So he decided to issue fine limited editions through his press. He "knew that if they were to be beautiful enough to warrant preservation, they would cost more than the general public would pay . . .;" however, ". . . . a limited number of people would be willing to add them to their libraries if they not only looked nice but their contents were of real significance" (12). The press was in operation from 1926 to 1942 and printed significant new additions to the sporting cannon as well as reprints of classic titles.

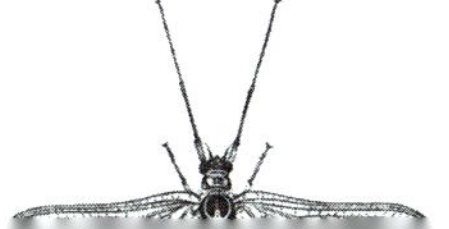

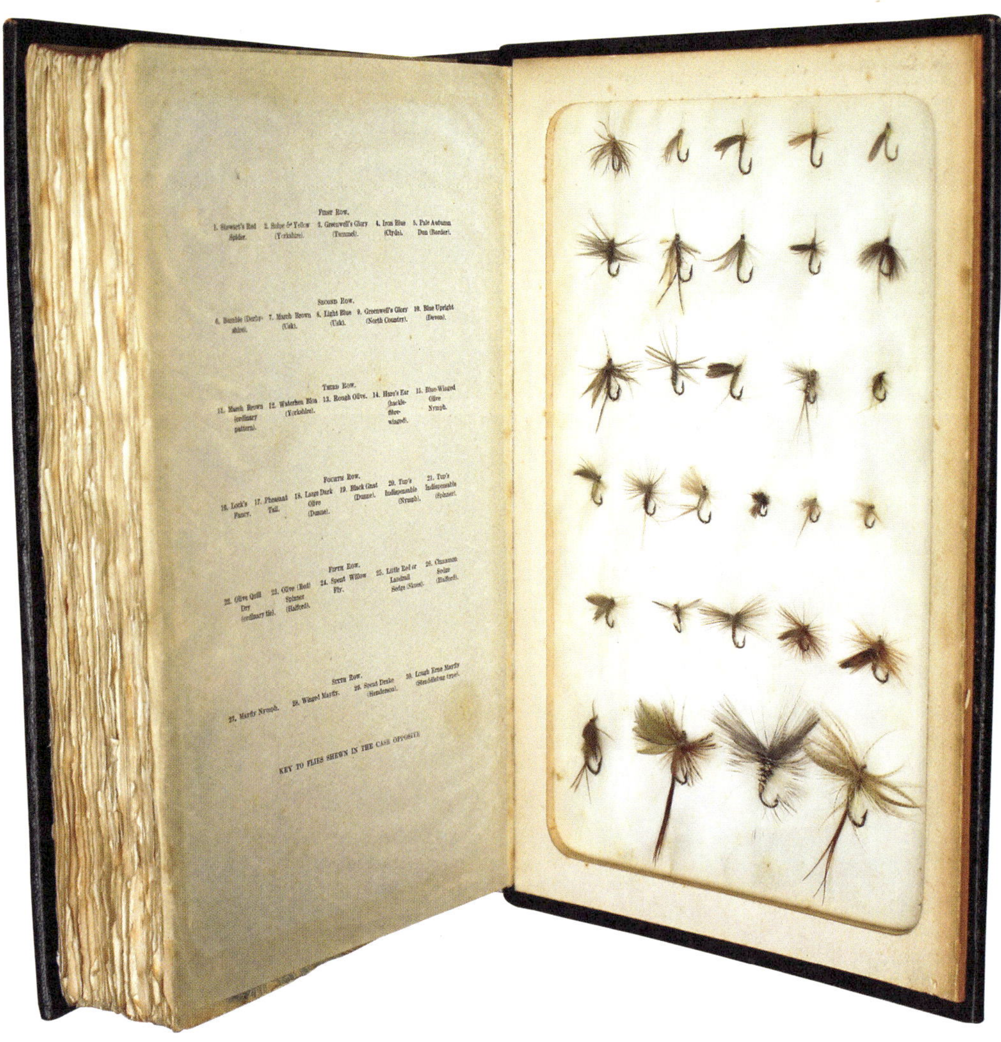

31

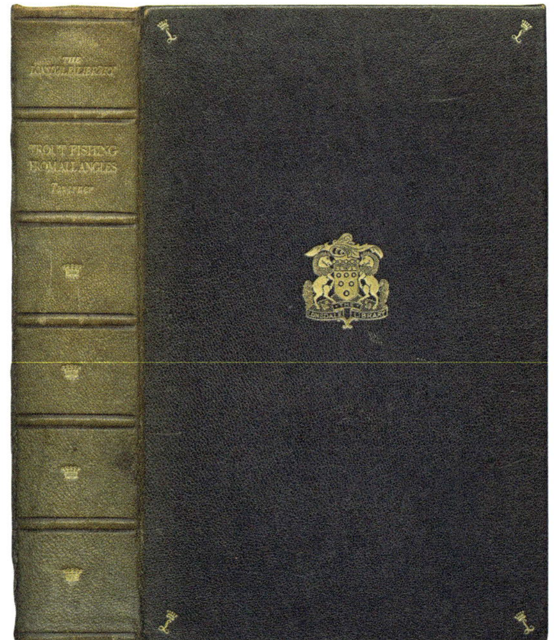

TAVERNER, ERIC. *Trout Fishing from All Angles: A Complete Guide to Modern Methods.* LONDON: SEELEY, SERVICE & CO. LTD., 1929. [SH 687 T38 1929] 25.8 CM X 17.8 CM NO. 181 OF 375 COPIES

This limited edition includes 30 hand-tied flies intended to show characteristics of different schools of fly dressing, including both dry flies and nymphs. The book also includes extensive sections on the natural histories of organisms eaten by trout.

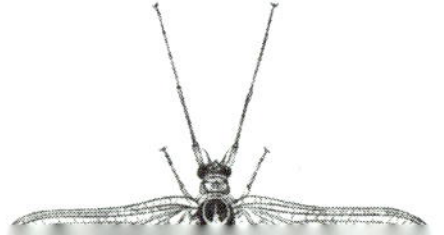

32

BAIGENT, W[ILLIAM]. *A Book on Hackles for Fly Dressing.* [ENGLAND]: N.P., [1935?].
[SH 451 B35 1935] 24.0 CM X 20.3 CM

This is an early "hackle book" that contains actual examples of hackles—the neck feathers of roosters and other birds—used to tie flies. The book is heavily-limited with no more than 80, and possibly as few as 40, copies produced. Dr Baigent was a fly-tier and breeder of gamefowl whose "notes on tying" are also included in this exhibition (item 33). Baigent provides serious and studied discussion of the nature of hackles and the way that their characteristics could be true to—or betray—the insects each fly was intended to imitate.

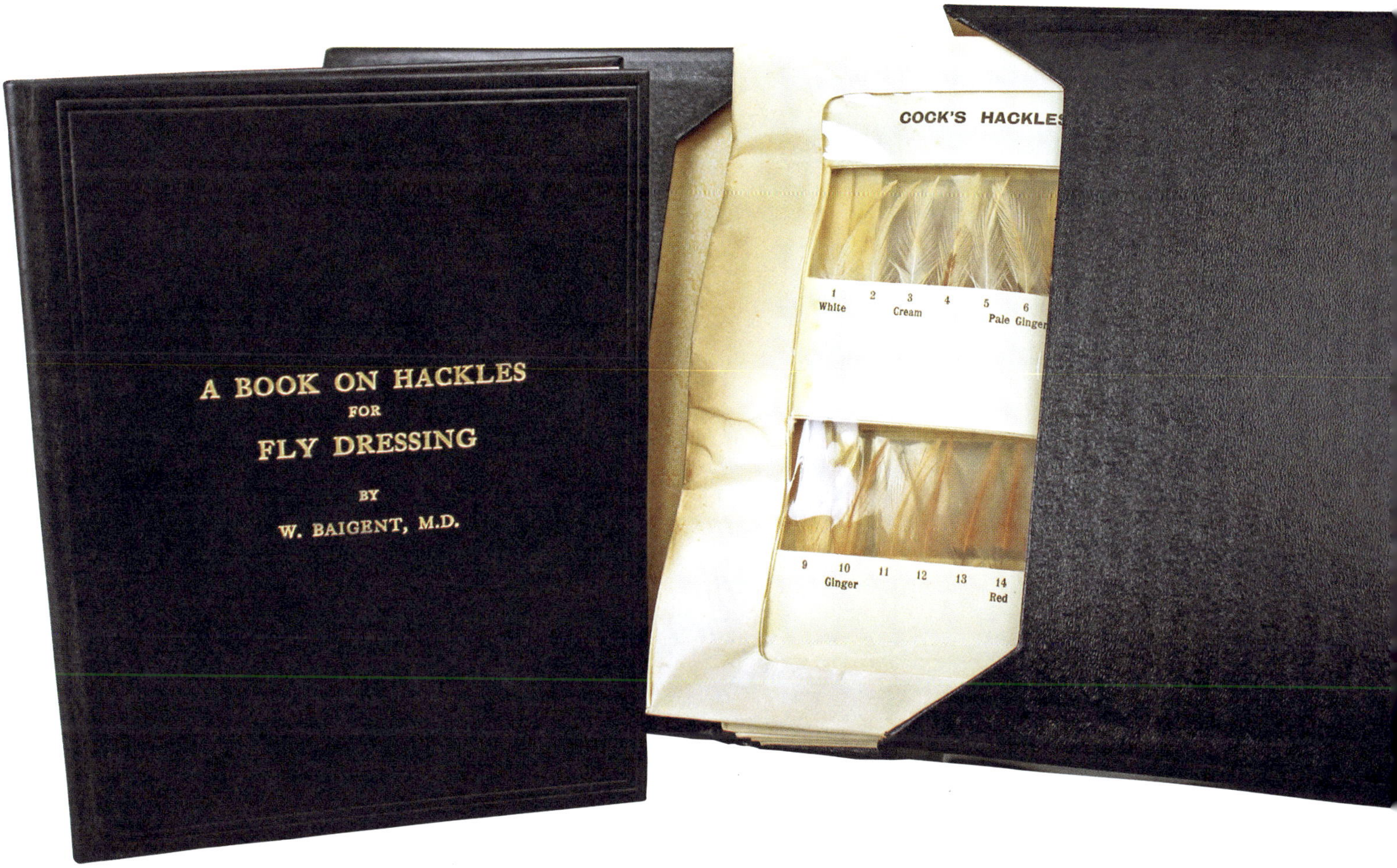

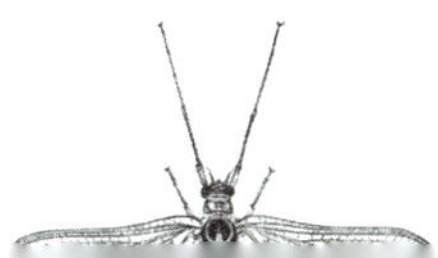

33

BAIGENT, W[ILLIAM]. *Notes on the Tying of Certain Flies.* COPY OF TYPESCRIPT WITH ADDED PREFACE BY A.H. THOMPSON DATED AUGUST 1943.
[SH 451 B36 1943] 22.9 CM X 17.9 CM

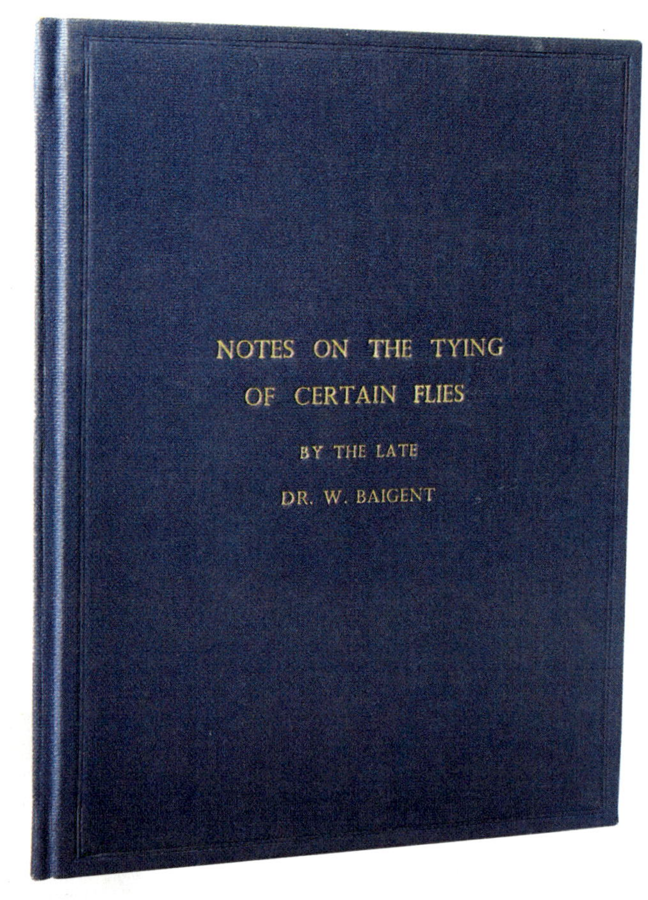

P R E F A C E

Owing to the kindness of Mrs. Jane S.Baigent, widow of Dr. Baigent, these notes on the tying of artificial flies have been lent to me.

In a letter dated the 26th July, 1943, Mrs. Baigent said:-

"I enclose the directions for the dressing of flies - for your own use - I have no objection to your copying them, but will you please not give them to any professional fly dresser. My husband gave these to Hardy's of Alnwick".

I gave an undertaking that Mrs.Baigent's wishes should be respected, and therefore should any angling friends see these notes I expect them to act in a similar manner.

A.H. THOMPSON.

AUGUST 1943.

This title is a facsimile of the privately-printed issue of Dr Baigent's notes on fly-tying. The notes were originally compiled and printed by Arthur Howard Thompson circa 1943 after he obtained them from Baigent's wife, Jane S. Baigent. This facsimile, bound to resemble the original, is undated but was likely produced in the 1960s.

34

SCHWIEBERT, ERNEST. *Salmon of the World.* NEW YORK: WINCHESTER PRESS, 1970.
[QL 638 S2 S36 1970 FOLIO] 41.7 CM X 31.7 CM | NO. 11 OF 750

Ernest Schwiebert was one of the preeminent angling figures of the latter half of the twentieth century and a true angling polymath—author, historian, artist, and lay entomologist and ichthyologist. William Kaufman says of the author in his review of Schwiebert's *Trout* (1978), "[s]urely no other fly fisherman in human history can have fished more widely than Ernest Schwiebert has, and surely no one else has combined angling, artistic and writing talents to better advantage."

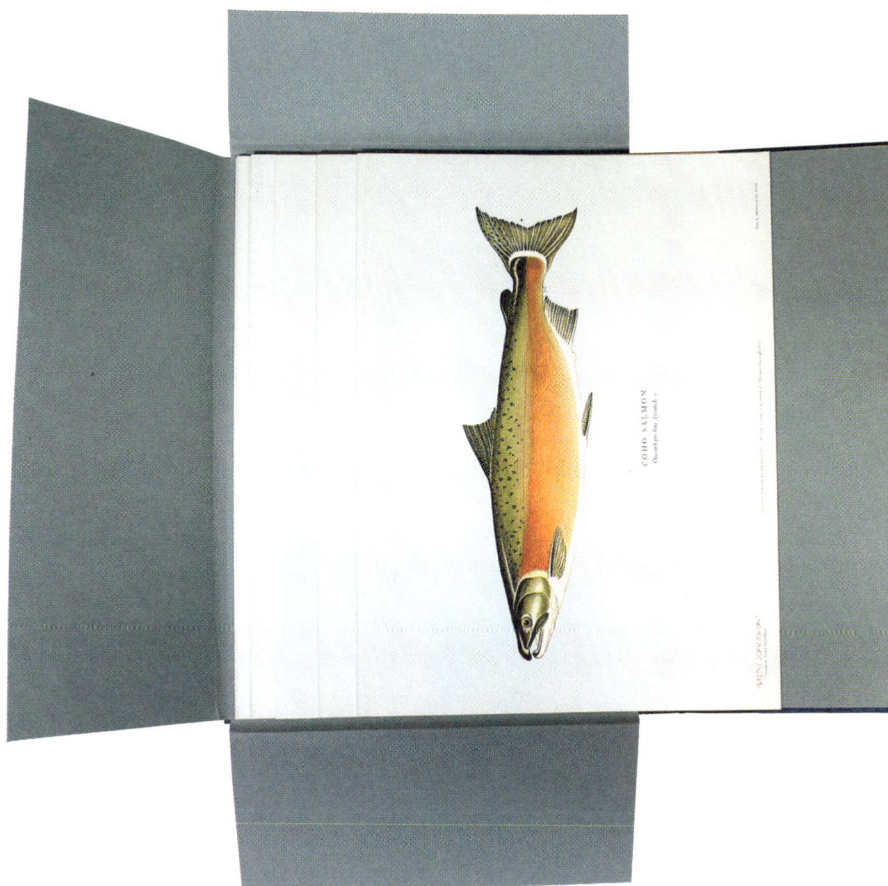

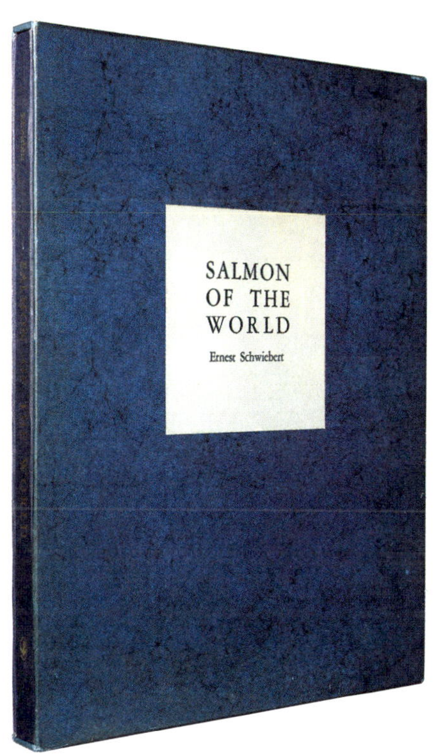

This book is a presentation copy that includes a long angling-related inscription reminiscing over the locations that the recipient, "Gene," and Schwiebert have fished, including Canadian locales like Ungava, the Cascapedia, and the Restigouche. The book also includes a hand-tied salmon fly, a colour drawing by Schwiebert, and 30 large colour plates of salmon. The "Gene" in the dedication is outdoor author Gene Hill.

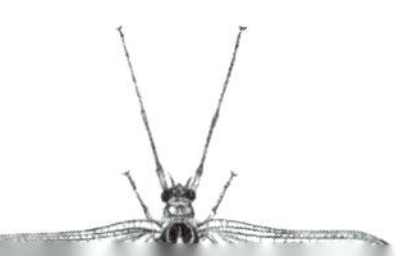

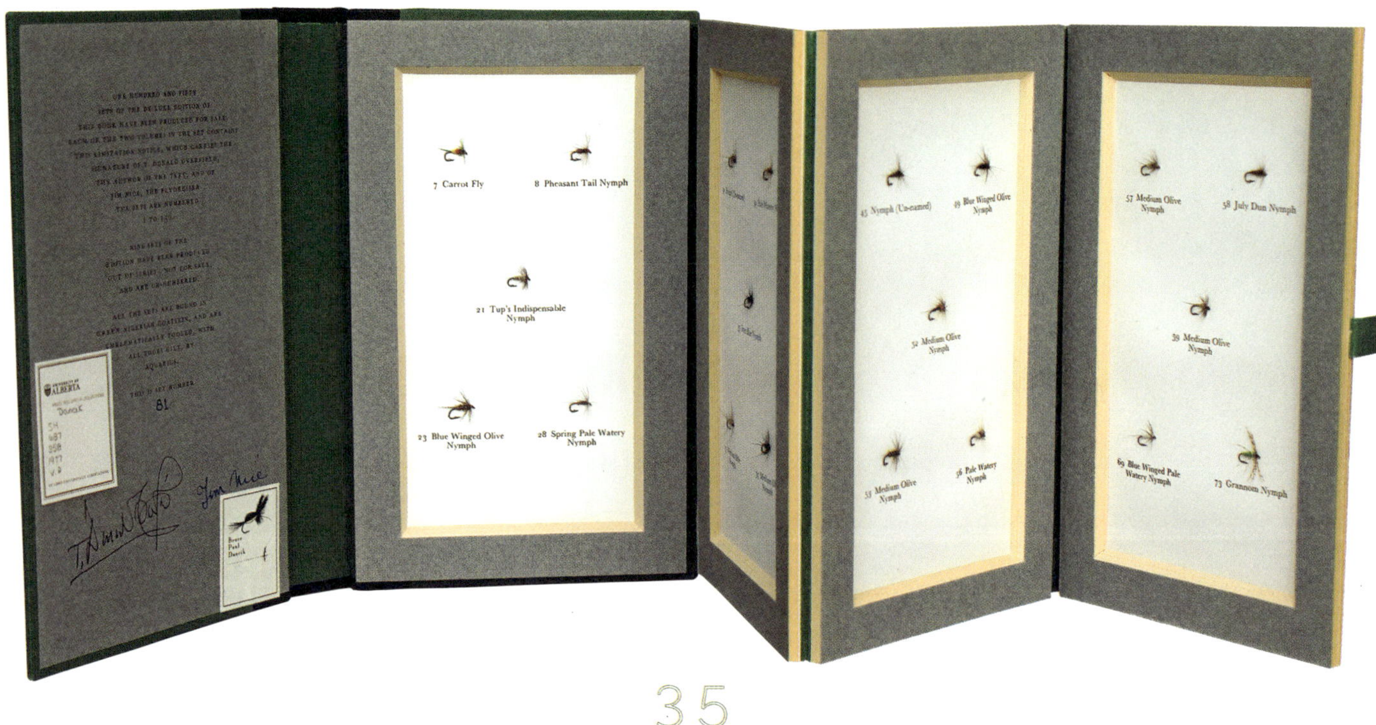

35

SKUES, GEORGE EDWARD MACKENZIE. *The Way of a Man with a Trout*. 2 VOLS. LONDON: ERNEST BENN LTD., 1977. [SH 687 S58 1977 V.1–2] 22.0 CM X 14.5 CM | NO. 81 OF 150

These elegantly-bound volumes collect seventy-one articles and thirty letters by Skues that had not yet been presented in book form. The companion to the text volume contains 20 nymphs tied by English fly-tier Jim Nice after Skues's patterns with materials supplied, in part, by Frank Elder (see item 36). Skues was a proponent of nymph or "wet fly" fishing at a time when dry-fly fishing was exalted as the ultimate and "true" expression of fly fishing. Skues and Frederick Halford refined their wet and dry fly-fishing techniques somewhat in tandem, and Skues's advocacy for nymph fishing rankled the cadre of dry-fly purists. Debate raged within the fly-fishing community, pitting dry-fly purists against those who accepted nymph-fishing as a practical—and often necessary—technique to catch actively-feeding fish that were not rising. Of Skues, Hill writes in his *A Summer on the Test* (item 29),

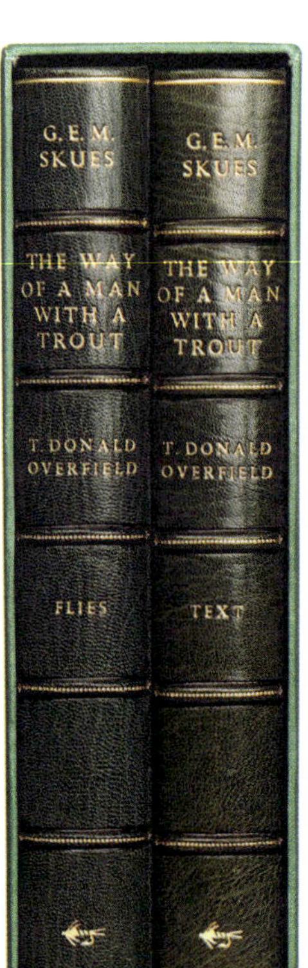

> Mr. Skues ... effected a revolution. The dry fly was at the height of its intolerant dictatorship and the other method [nymph fishing] was discarded and ridiculed to such an extent that enthusiasts of the school of Halford regarded Mr. Skues as a dangerous heresiarch. Much water has flown under the bridges since then, and in that water many are the trout which have been caught on a sunk fly which would not have fallen to a dry. More and more each year does nymph fishing become a part of the modern angler's equipment, and he who does not possess the art is gravely handicapped. And at the same time has come the realization that this art is both difficult and delightful. (230)

It is true that a perfectly-laid cast to a rising fish is an ultimate pleasure in angling; however, the angler who has both wet and dry flies in his or her tackle box will be able to catch fish more effectively during more times of the year than an angler who eschews one technique for the other. This exhibition includes examples of flies tied to the patterns of both Skues and Halford (items 26c–26d) that were the centre of such controversy in the angling world.

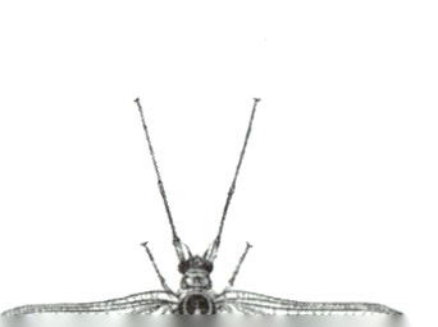

36

ELDER, FRANK. *The Book of the Hackle*. EDINBURGH: SCOTTISH ACADEMIC PRESS, 1979. [SH 451 E42 1979] 24.3 CM X 15.7 CM

Frank Elder was a breeder of gamecocks for their hackles to be used for fly-tying. The book includes detailed descriptions of different hackles and 29 actual examples of feathers mounted on five cards in the rear of the book. Elder supplied some of the tying materials used in *The Way of a Man with a Trout* in this exhibition (item 35).

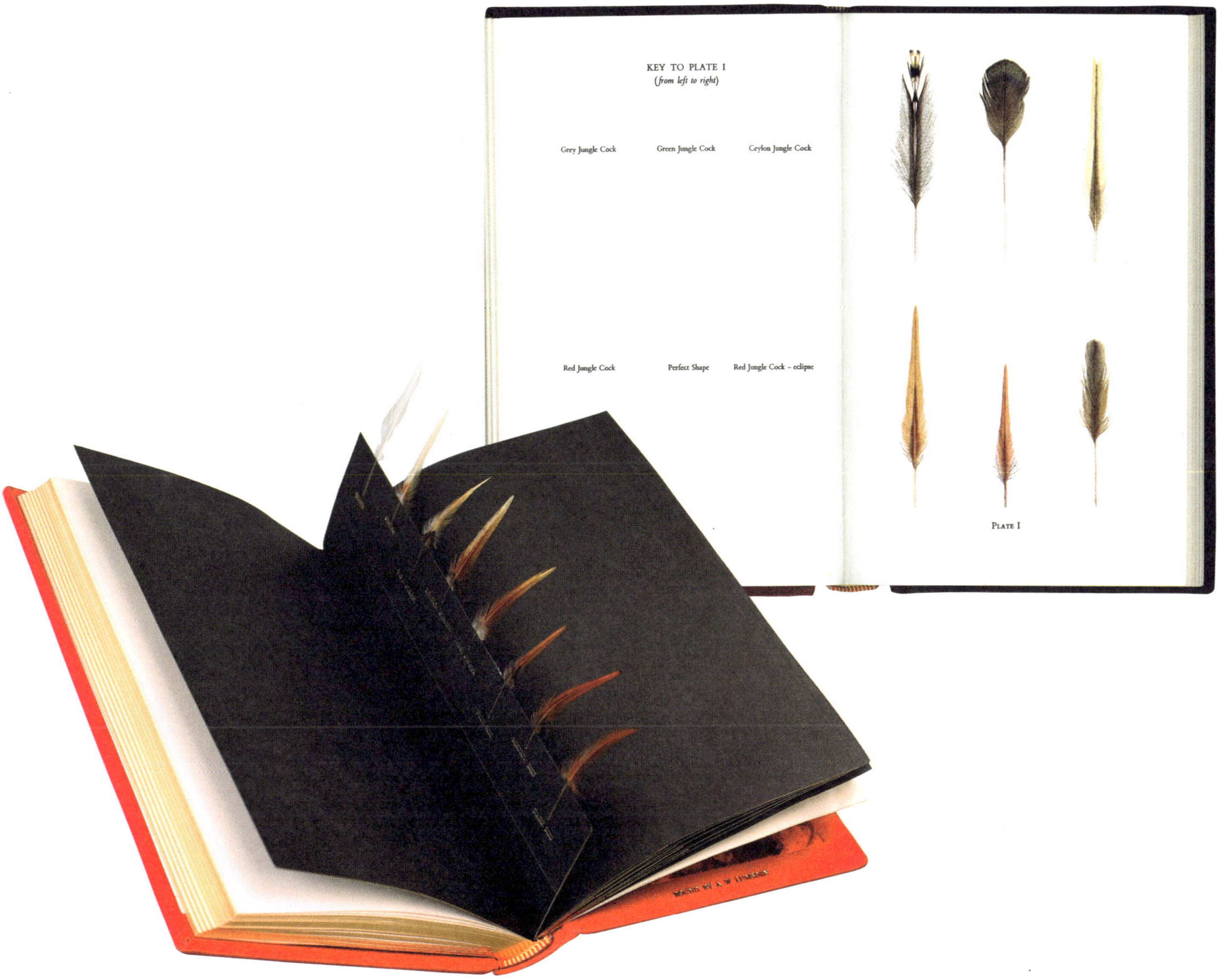

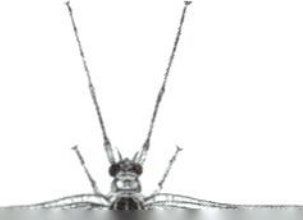

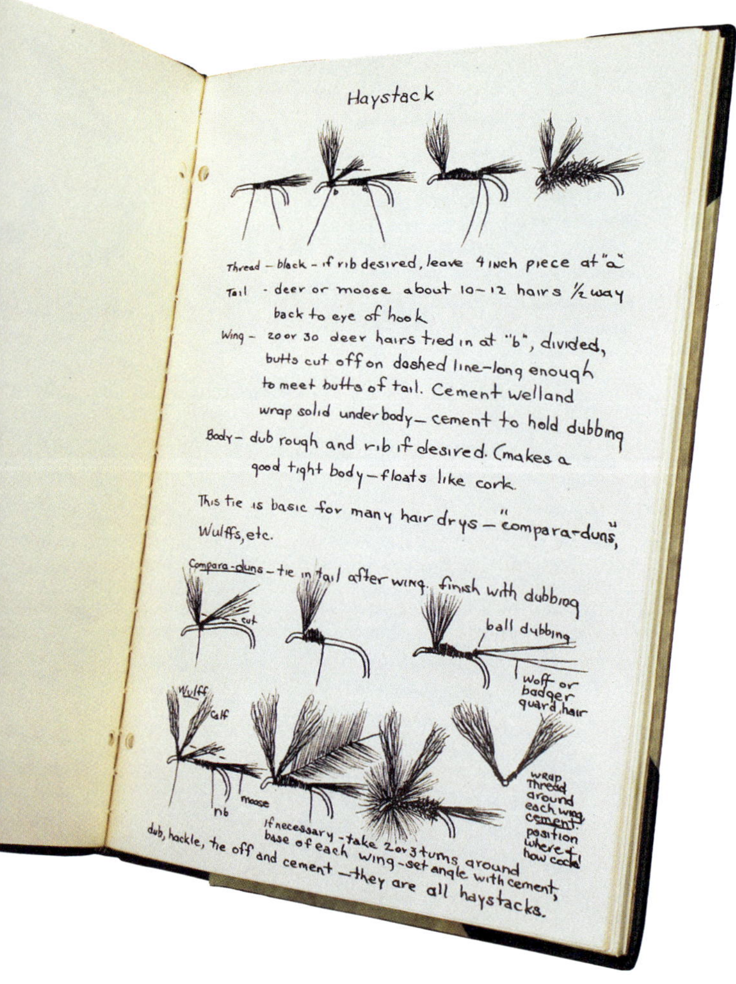
Haystack

Thread - black - if rib desired, leave 4 inch piece at "a"
Tail - deer or moose about 10-12 hairs ½ way back to eye of hook
Wing - 20 or 30 deer hairs tied in at "b", divided, butts cut off on dashed line—long enough to meet butts of tail. Cement well and wrap solid underbody—cement to hold dubbing
Body - dub rough and rib if desired. (makes a good tight body—floats like cork.
This tie is basic for many hair drys—"compara-duns", Wulffs, etc.
Compara-duns - tie in tail after wing. finish with dubbing
cut
ball dubbing
Wolf or badger guard hair
Wulff
calf
rib
moose
wrap thread around each wing, cement, position where—how cocked
If necessary - take 2 or 3 turns around base of each wing - set angle with cement,
dub, hackle, tie off and cement—they are all haystacks.

37

MICHL, LEO. *Some Favorite Flies.* [LEBANON, MO]: [LEO MICHL], 1979. [SH 451 M43 1979 FOLIO]
30.4 CM X 22.0 CM | EDITION OF 20 COPIES

Leo Michl presented this copy to Jack Heddon, publisher of angling books (item 38) and included a long inscription on the back of the book's mailing envelope. The inscription explains that the book (a collection of fly-tying notes and drawings) was "written for my grandson, Patrick, or so I pretend, but mainly just for myself." The book is a facsimile of the original in the author's own handwriting and contains 16 hand-tied flies mounted on the rear board.

Some Favorite flies

From time to time, someone drops in to ask "how in hell do you tie that fly Sam's tearing them up with?" Of course Sam could tear 'em up with a clothes pin, but I don't have to tell them that. Truth is I enjoy telling people how to tie flies – especially some flies, but, with the sobering thought; I wont always be here to show 'em, or Sam to catch 'em, I thought I'd best get some of this down and out to friends – especially to that promising neophyte Patrick who may, someday, have both Sam's and my responsibilities.

I make no claim to originating many of these – I give credit where I can – neither do I offer these sheets as art – 40 years and more ago I'd have shown them to no one. but old skills fall into disuse and fingers stiffen – at this late date – they'll just have to do.

Lee

Merry Christmas
1979

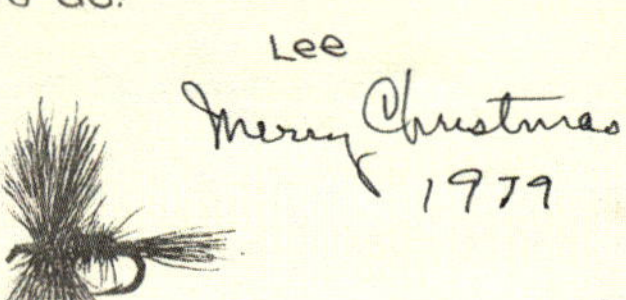

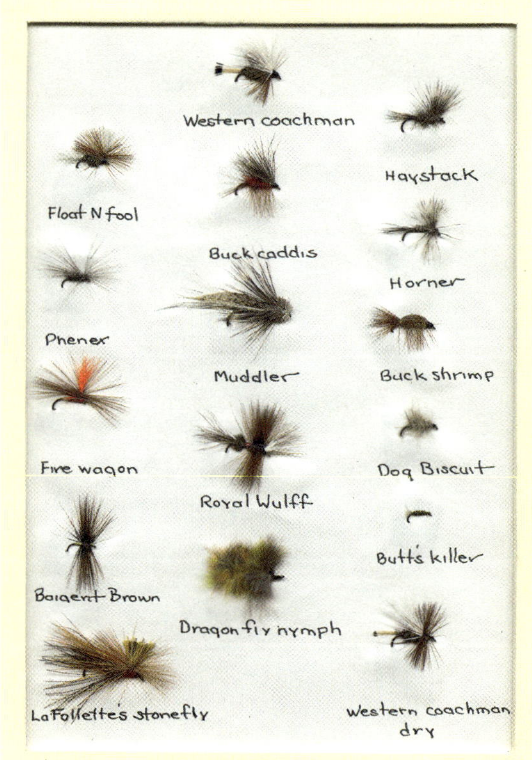

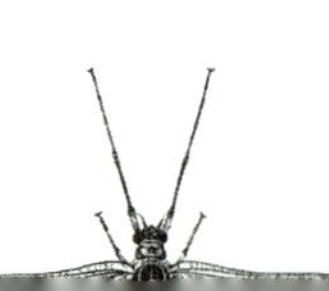

hackles, however, tend to the form shown in Fig. 1, the fibres from the butt to about three-quarters of the length of the mid rib become gradually longer and then shorten towards the point. As long as this fault is not greatly accentuated it will not make much difference to the appearance or form of a fly tied with this type of hackle."

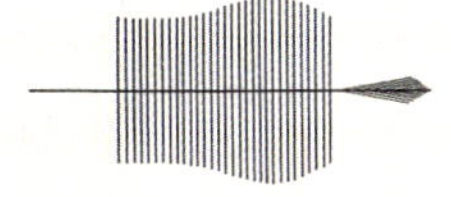

Fig. 1.

His method was to strip the fluff from the butt of a hackle, leaving enough of the tip to be gripped in a pair of hackle pliers and draw back the remaining barbs to about right-angles to the stem (see Fig. 2). AB, called "the useful length" and AC, "the length of the barb", were measured and the Hackle Index obtained by dividing the useful length by the length of barb.

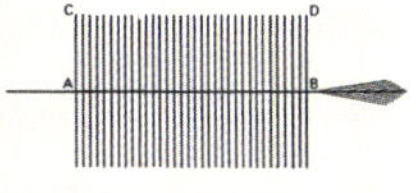

Fig. 2.

As an example, if we assume the useful length (AB) to be 45 millimetres and the length of barb (AC) to be 15 millimetres, we get:

$$\text{Hackle Index} = \frac{\text{Useful length}}{\text{Barb length}}$$

$$= \frac{AB}{AC} = \frac{45}{15}$$

$$\therefore \text{ H.I.} = 3.0$$

It will be seen that the larger the H.I. number the better the hackle shape. If in the above example the barb had measured 12 mm, the H.I. would have been 3.8; had the hackle been of an even better shape and the length of barb 10 mm, the H.I. would have been 4.5.

Frank Elder appreciated the value of the Hackle Index several years ago and has simplified and improved upon the original method. We exchanged several latters upon the subject and I am grateful for his permission to quote the following extracts:

"...Taking a series of hackles from the centre of a good cape, a typical series of H.I. figures from crown to base of a cape might well be – 3.4, 3.7, 4.6, 3.8, 4.6, 5.6 – one always seems to get better figures from the large hackles and a drop in the middle is not uncommon."

"...to standardise hackle measurements one would have to specify the total length of the feather to be used as standard – I would suggest either 45 mm or 50 mm – and the length of barb must be measured at the middle of the hackle. I would classify as follows:
under 3.0 – poor; 3.0 to 3.5 – good; 3.5 to 4.0 – very good; and anything over 5.0 – excellent."

47

SPECIMEN HACKLES

33 Grizzle or cuckoo cock hackle. Another incredible shape, H.I. about 7.0. Rather soft web, especially towards the butt.

34 Black hen hackle. A most useful colour.

35 Pale furnace hen hackle. The colour used by James Wright of Sprouston to dress Canon Greenwell's "Glory". A finely marked hackle.

36 Badger hen hackle. Another superbly marked hen hackle, pure black with white edges.

37 Pale blue-dun hen hackle.

38 Medium blue-dun hen hackle.

39 Dark blue-dun hen hackle.

40 Honey dun hen hackle. I have rarely seen cock hackles with colouring as fine as this – whereas I have seen many hen capes with hackles at least as good. However, hen hackles are often of a better colour than cock's, as can be seen from the hen hackles in this section.

33
34
35
36
37
38
39
40

38

HEDDON, JACK, ED. *John Henderson's Hackle Book: An Account of Twenty Years Breeding Old English Game Fowls for Their Hackles.* TWICKENHAM: HONEY DUN PRESS LTD., 1980. [SH 451 H38 1980]
29.9 CM X 21.6 CM | NO. 88 OF 180 COPIES

This title is a technical treatise on using hackles for fly tying, with a "hackle index" that describes the quality of a hackle by dividing its useful length by its barb length. It includes 40 samples of feathers mounted on cards in the back of the book.

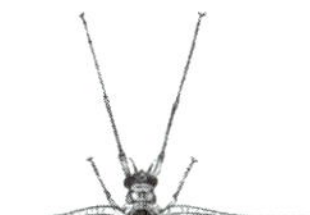

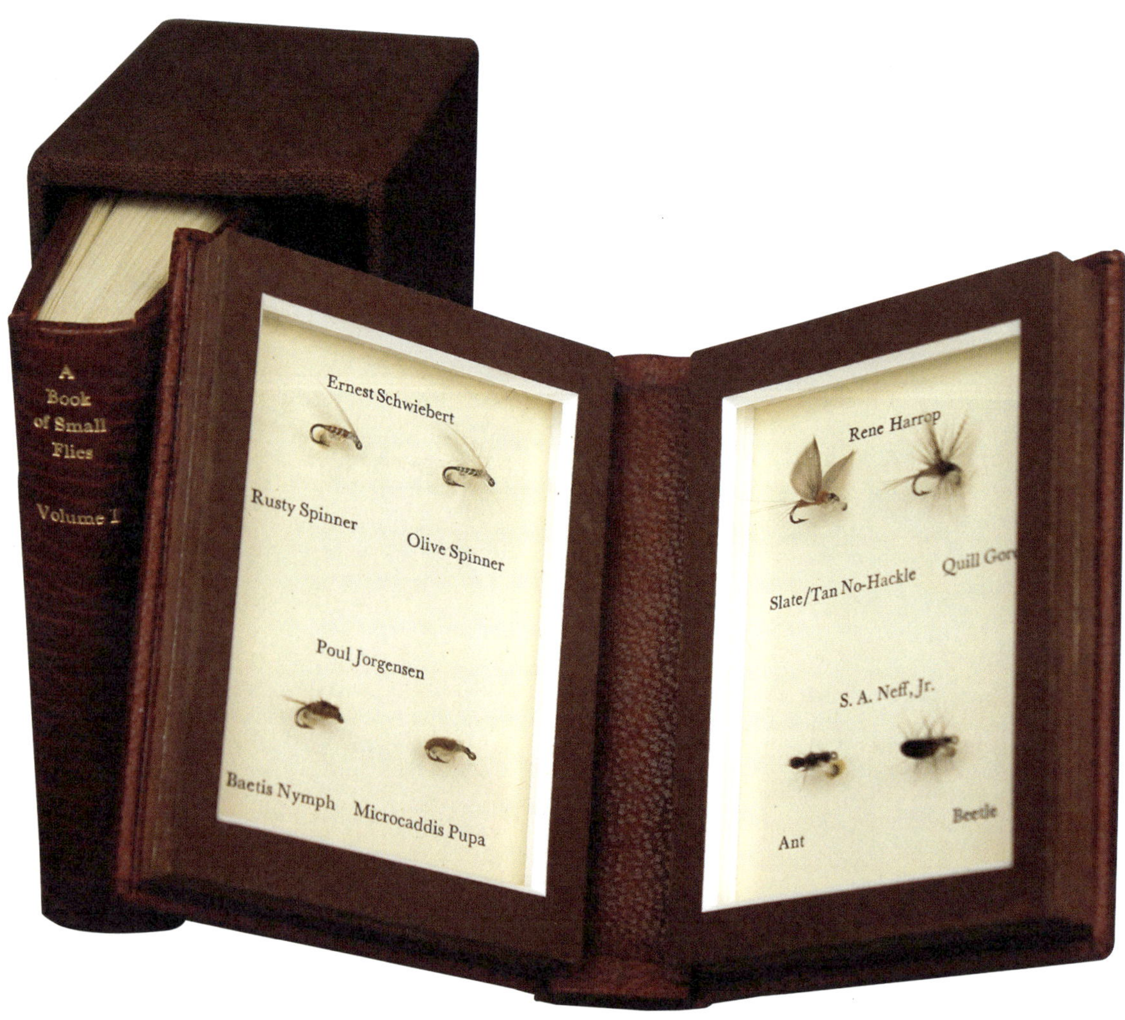

39

HARROP, RENE, POUL JORGENSEN, ERIC LEISER, JOHN MERWIN, S.A. NEFF, JR., AND ERNEST SCHWIEBERT. *A Book of Small Flies*. 2 VOLS. ARLINGTON: ISAAC OELGART, 1983.
[SH 451 H38 1983 V.1–2] 8.6 CM X 6.8 CM | EDITION OF 60 COPIES

This is a delightful marriage of book design and content issued in a very limited edition. The second volume features two miniature flies tied by each of Ernest Schwiebert, Poul Jorgensen, Rene Harrop, and S.A. Neff, Jr. The text volume contains descriptions of each fly written by its tier and also includes examples of feathers mounted to text leaves and a colour engraving by Al Barker.

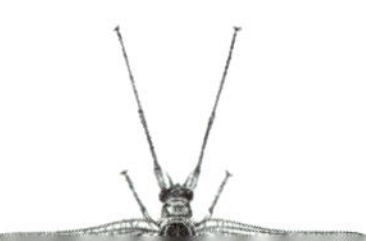

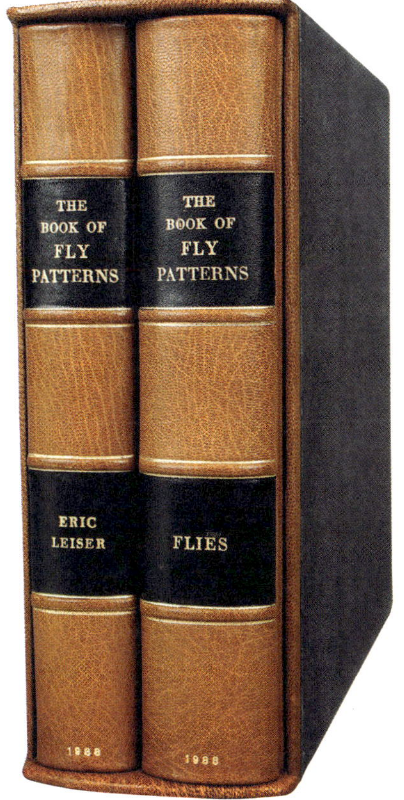

40

LEISER, ERIC. *The Book of Fly Patterns*. 2 VOLS.
NEW YORK: ALFRED A. KNOPF, 1987. [SH 451 L417 1987B V.1–2]
23.1 CM X 26.8 CM | NO. II OF 12

Leiser's *The Book of Fly Patterns* is one of the standard fly-tying reference books and illustrates more than 1000 flies. This heavily-limited set is finely bound in half leather and marbled boards and includes 25 flies tied by Leiser in one volume and the text in the second volume. An interesting mix of flies is included in the second volume, from the tiny Jessid dry fly to the enormous Black Angus.

The Book of
FLY PATTERNS
BY ERIC LEISER

PHOTOGRAPHS BY MATTHEW VINCICUERRA
DRAWINGS BY ERNEST LUSSIER

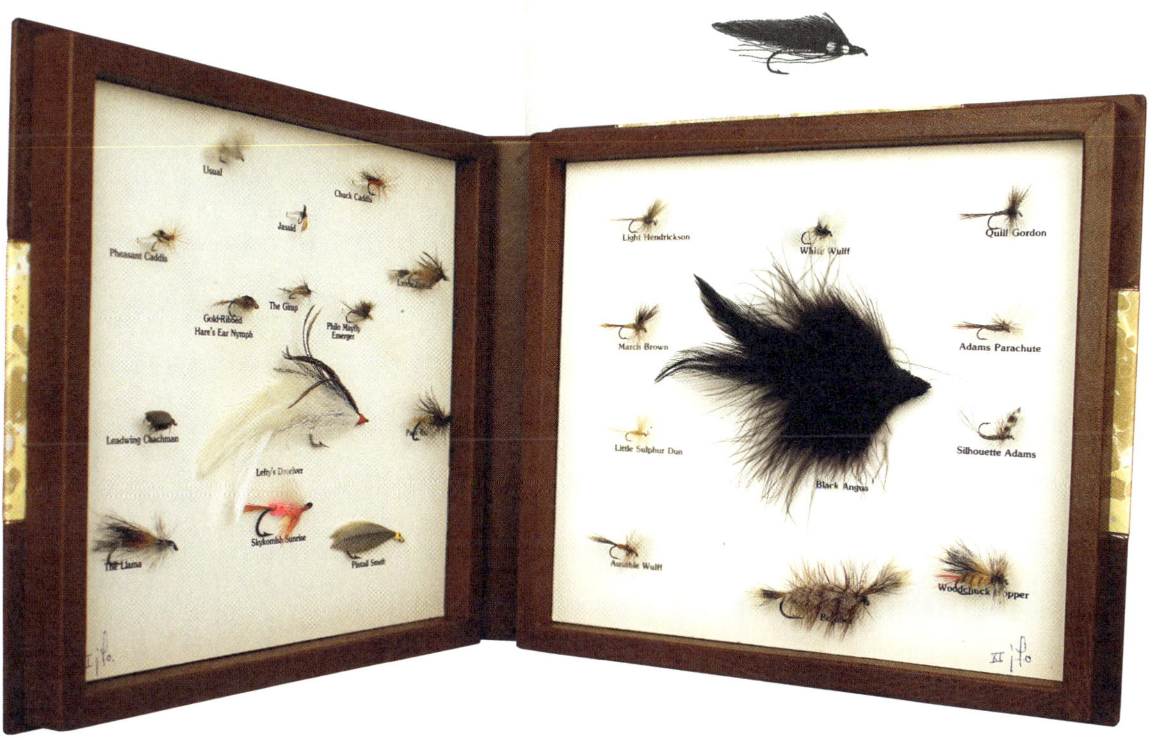

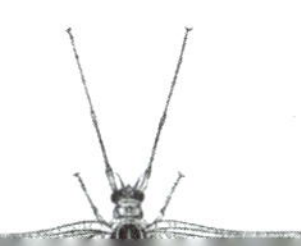

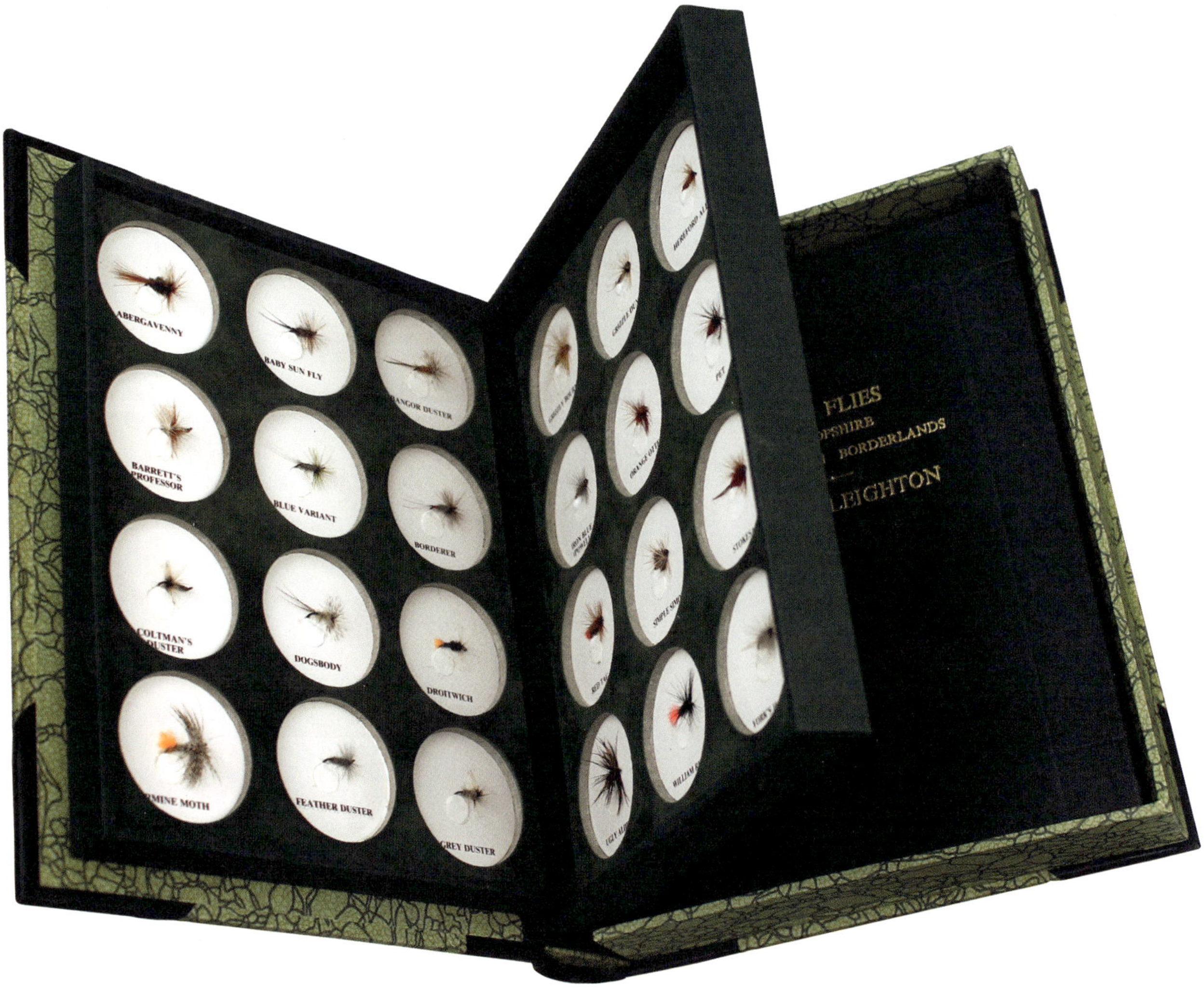

41

LEIGHTON, MICHAEL. *Trout Flies of Shropshire and the Welsh-Borderlands.* SHREWSBURY: REDVERSE LTD., 1987. [SH 451 L38 1987]
22.1 CM X 18.4 CM | NO. 28 OF 50 COPIES

This limited edition has an interesting design. A folding box contains the small text volume, and the flies are contained in two "hinged leaves" attached to the box. This is number 28 of 50 copies, although apparently only 30 were produced. The 24 flies are tied by Martin Bailey of Welshpool.

ABERGAVENNY (Plate 4)

The first pattern in the book, and what a cracking Border fly it is!

During its migration from Yorkshire to Herefordshire, the John Storey fly underwent various changes in its dressing, in particular acquiring a red silk rib. Dressed thus, it became a popular pattern on the Border streams. James Evans, author of the best guide yet written to Border stream fishing, used to fish for trout on the Usk above Abergavenny on Wednesdays, where he found this pattern very effective. Unfortunately the fly did not float as well as he would have preferred on the fast, rough Usk waters. So James decided to modify the dressing still further, and produce a better floating fly. And so the Abergavenny was born, out of John Storey, by the Usk! It is now widely used throughout the South Shropshire/Herefordshire border region. As is apparent from the dressing, it is rather heavily hackled, so that it floats as well as its inventor hoped on the rough stickles of the Border streams, and is very easy to see.

The dressing is—
Hook 10-14
Silk .... Bright Red
Whisks .... A very large bunch of red cock hackle fibres
Body .... Bronze peacock herl ribbed with tying silk
Hackles ...... Red cock hackle wound in front of a badger cock hackle. (Use 2 Red cock hackles on size 10 hook.)

I have recently seen this fly tied with the addition of a small, upright white polypropylene wing to aid visibility on the fast water, and the old angler using it claimed the modification did not detract from its fish-catching abilities.

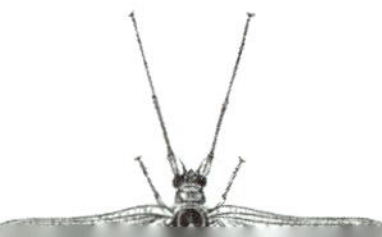

42

BORGER, GARY A. *Designing Trout Flies*. WAUSAU: TOMORROW RIVER PRESS, 1991.
[SH 687 B65 1991 FOLIO] 33.9 CM X 26.4 CM | NO. 20 OF UNKNOWN COPIES

This is the most lavish production in the exhibition, all housed in a walnut box in a slipcase. One half of the box contains the text volume (also in a slipcase) and the other half contains 50 examples of flies behind glass imitating a large fly box. An impressive variety of flies is represented, including two damselfly patterns, which are rarely featured in fly-tying books.

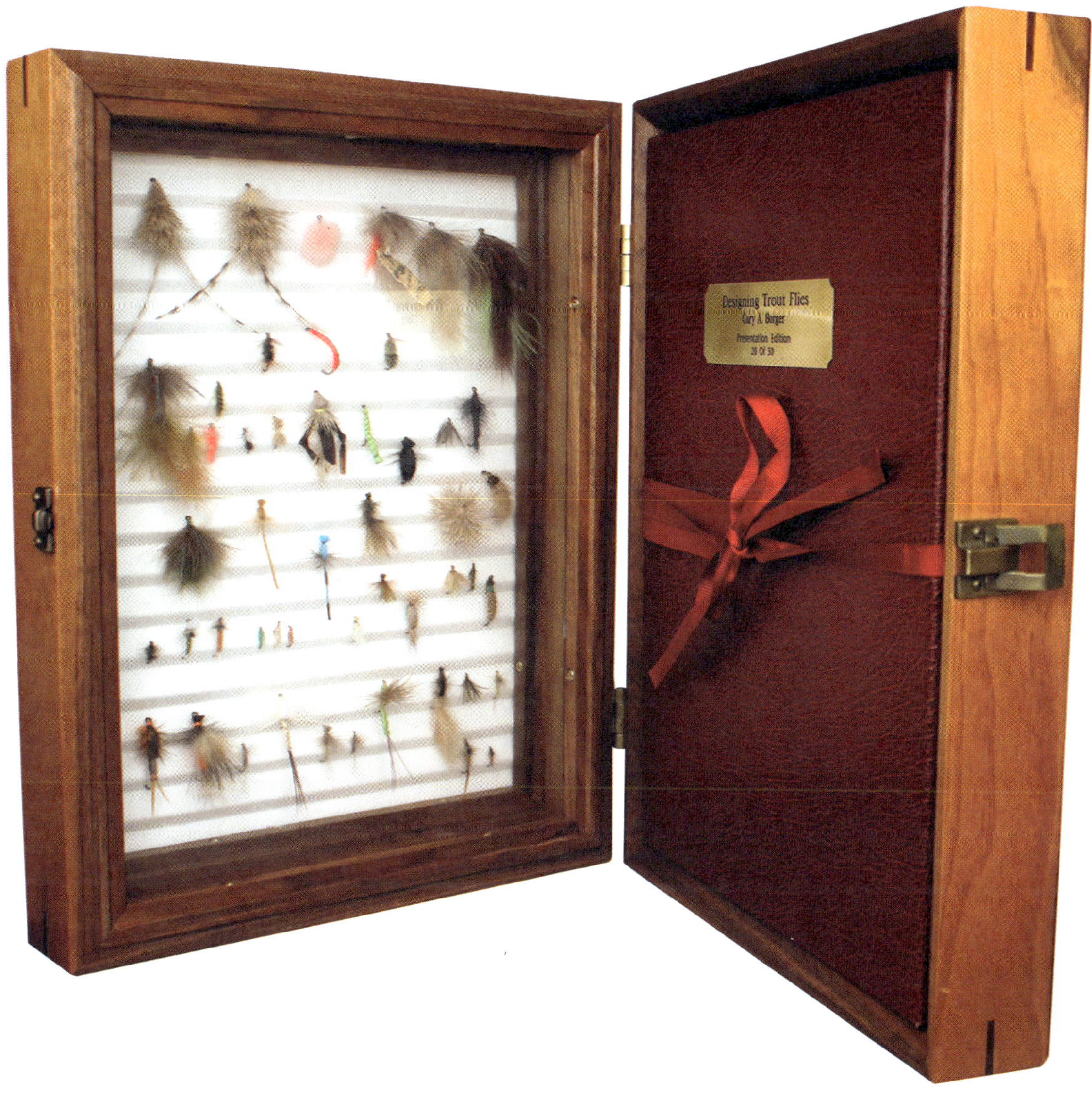

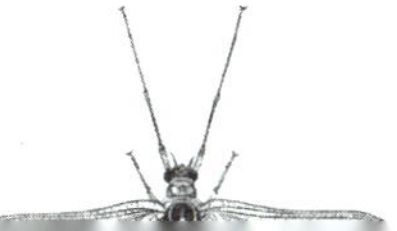

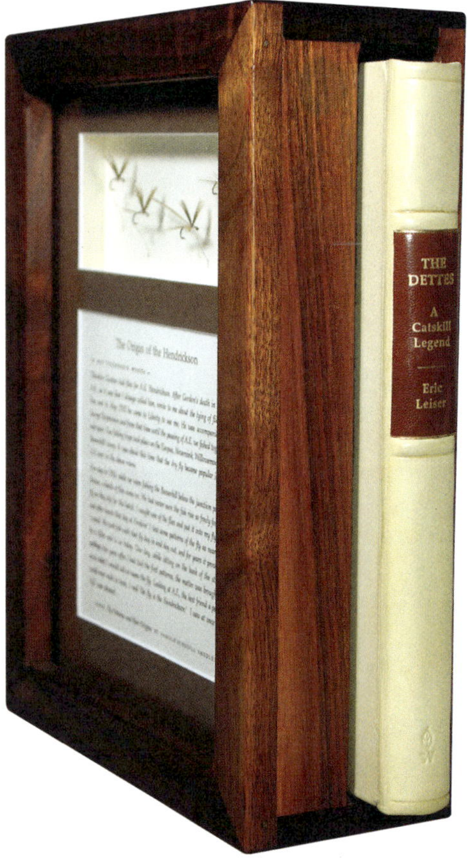

43

LEISER, ERIC. *The Dettes: A Catskill Legend.* NEW YORK: WILLOWKILL PRESS, 1992. [SH 451 L42 1992]
27.8 CM X 21.1 CM | NO. J OF Z

This limited edition includes a walnut box with flies mounted in a window built into its side. The box also serves as a slipcase for the text volume. Walt and Winnie Dette and their daughter Mary were a "first family" of fly fishing in the Catskill Mountains of New York. This volume is a biography of the Dette family and a history of their fly tying and fly fishing in the Catskills. It is signed by Eric Leiser, Walt, Winnie, and Mary Dette and includes flies tied by the Dettes.

44

LYONS, NICK. "CONNECTIONS." 28 MAY 1995. MS. BRUCE PEEL SPECIAL COLLECTIONS, UNIVERSITY OF ALBERTA.
[SH 441 L94 1995 FOLIO] 36.8 CM X 26.1 CM

This manuscript is for a story, "Connections," published in *Field and Stream* magazine in 1995. It is the first draft and includes a handwritten note to Dr Lyons's son, Tony. Nick Lyons is a fly-fisherman, author, and publisher; this exhibition includes both a book written by him (item 46) and a book from his publishing house (item 45). Lyons's passion for fly-fishing has pervaded his life; however, he told the *The New York Times*, "I never glamorize fly-fishing. . . . There is a lot of ego involved in this sport. People like to name flies after themselves or take credit for being the first to do this or that. All that seems so silly." (Lawson).

for F&S
possibly last page

Nick Lyons
Lyons & Burford
31 West 21 Street
New York, Ny 10010

CONNECTIONS

Nick Lyons

A friend, a naturalist who has not fished since he was a teenager and won't, on "moral grounds," asked me last week if I had to fish to be close to nature. Wasn't it cruel? Wasn't it unnecessary? I said hastily that this was one reason why I went to rivers. "But there's so much to see and touch and understand," he argued. "Must you pursue fish, too?"

Though I have fished since before memory and have never needed a "reason," his questions itched me and the more I thought about them the more I realized I didn't really go to rivers to "connect" with the natural world but to catch fish. I went with tackle that I had assembled over a course of many years: a rod I bought only last year because of its Space Age power and lightness, an old reel I'd found at a country red-tag sale thirteen years ago that worked like a fine watch; some flies

-1-

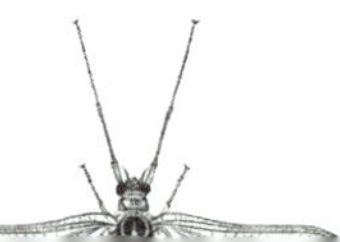

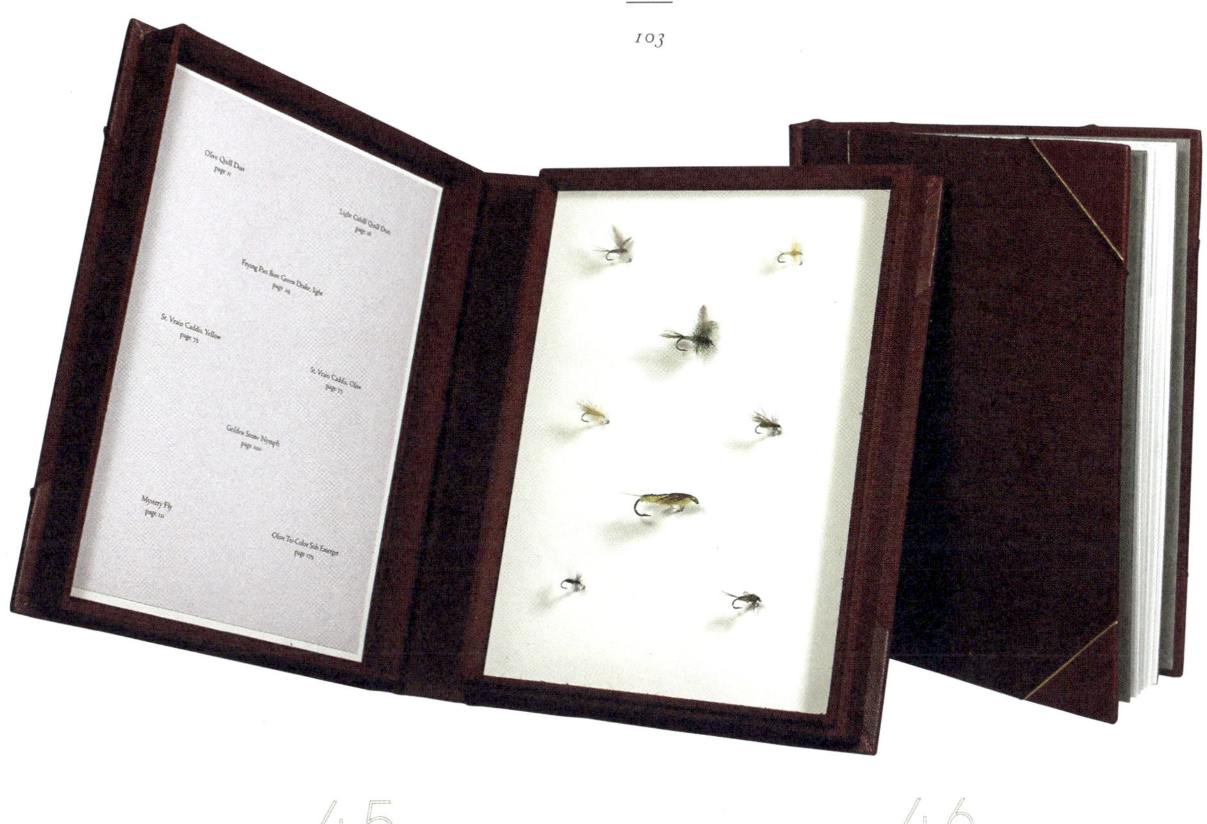

45

BEST, A.K. *A. K.'s Fly Box*. 2 VOLS. NEW YORK: LYONS & BURFORD, 1996. [SH 451 B4525 1996 V.1–2] 26.7 CM X 20.5 CM | NO. 8 OF 10 COPIES

This is the smallest limitation in the collection—number 8 of 10 copies! It includes a folding box with one volume of text and a second volume of eight flies tied by A.K. Best. It is signed by several people including Best, John Gierach, Nick Lyons, and others. Best is a master fly-tier and has written several books on fly tying.

46

LYONS, NICK. *Hemingway's Many-hearted Fox River*. [NEW YORK]: TIMKEN PUBLISHERS, 1998. [SH 441 L943 1998] 26.0 CM X 18.4 CM
LETTER V OF 100 COPIES
(NUMBERED 1–74 AND A–Z)

This is a limited edition of Nick Lyons's story of fishing the Fox River in Michigan's Upper Peninsula, the former fishing grounds of Ernest Hemingway. The book includes an original signed watercolour by Lyons's wife, Mary Lyons.

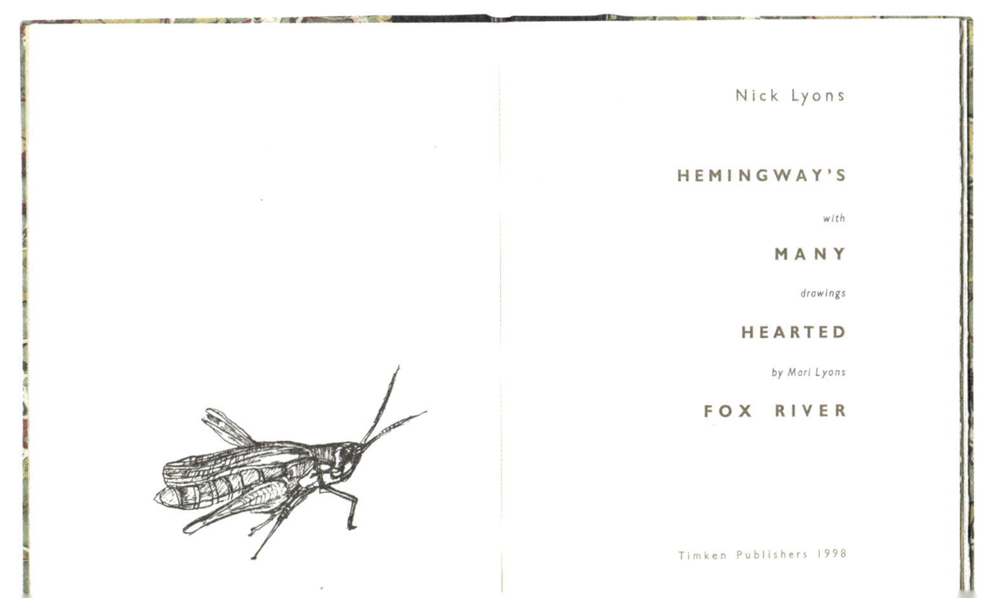

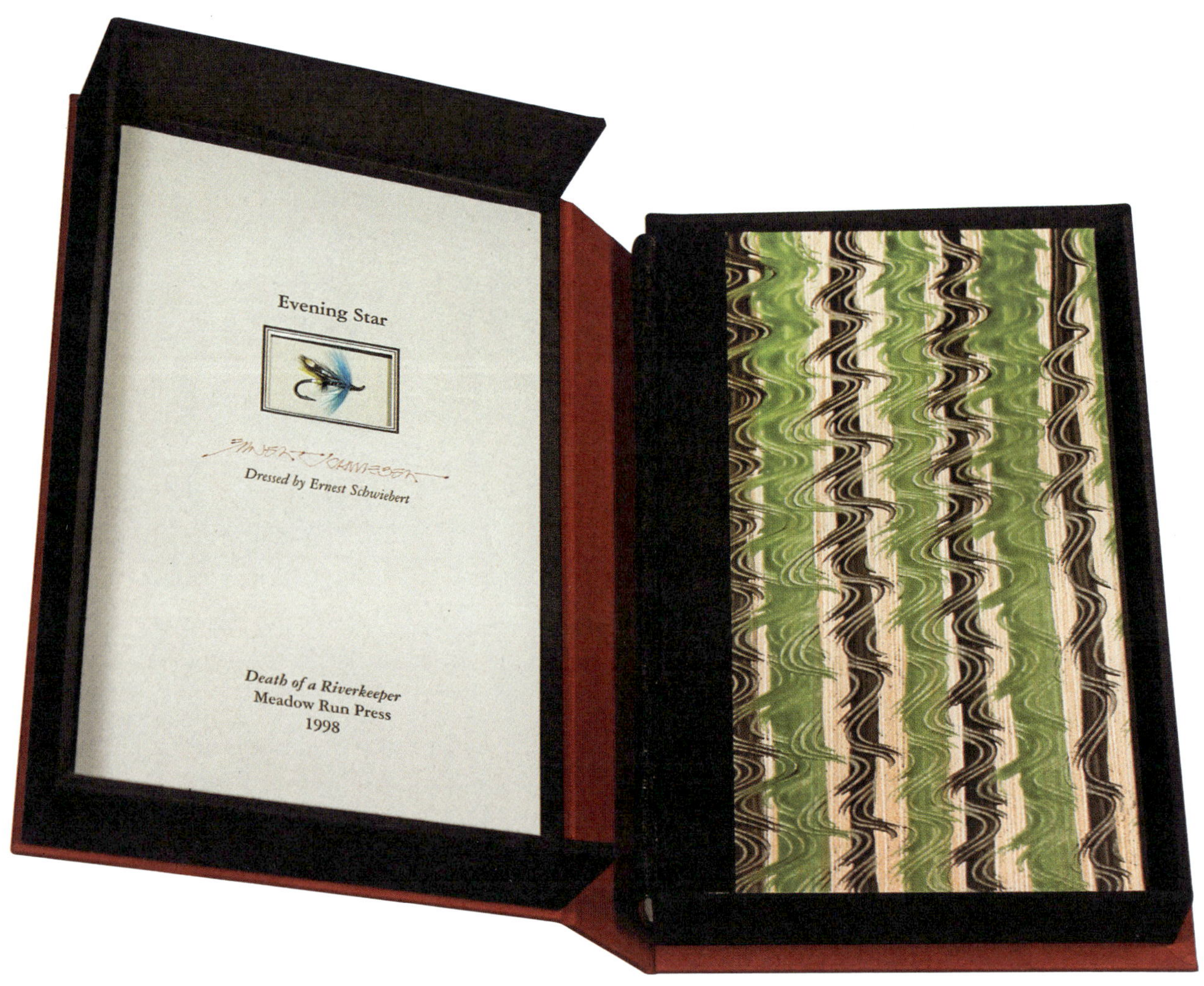

47

SCHWIEBERT, ERNEST. *Death of a Riverkeeper.* [FAR HILLS]: MEADOW RUN PRESS, 1998.
[SH 441 S387 1998] 20.9 CM X 14.0 CM | NO. 8 OF 35 COPIES

This is the limited edition reprint of Ernest Schwiebert's classic *Death of a Riverkeeper* that collects several stories and recollections of Schwiebert's angling travels around the world.

This volume includes a finely-bound copy of the book, a fly dressed by Schwiebert, and an illustration signed by Schwiebert, all in a folding box.

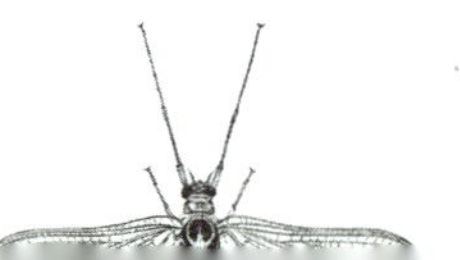

ANGLING AS ADVENTURE

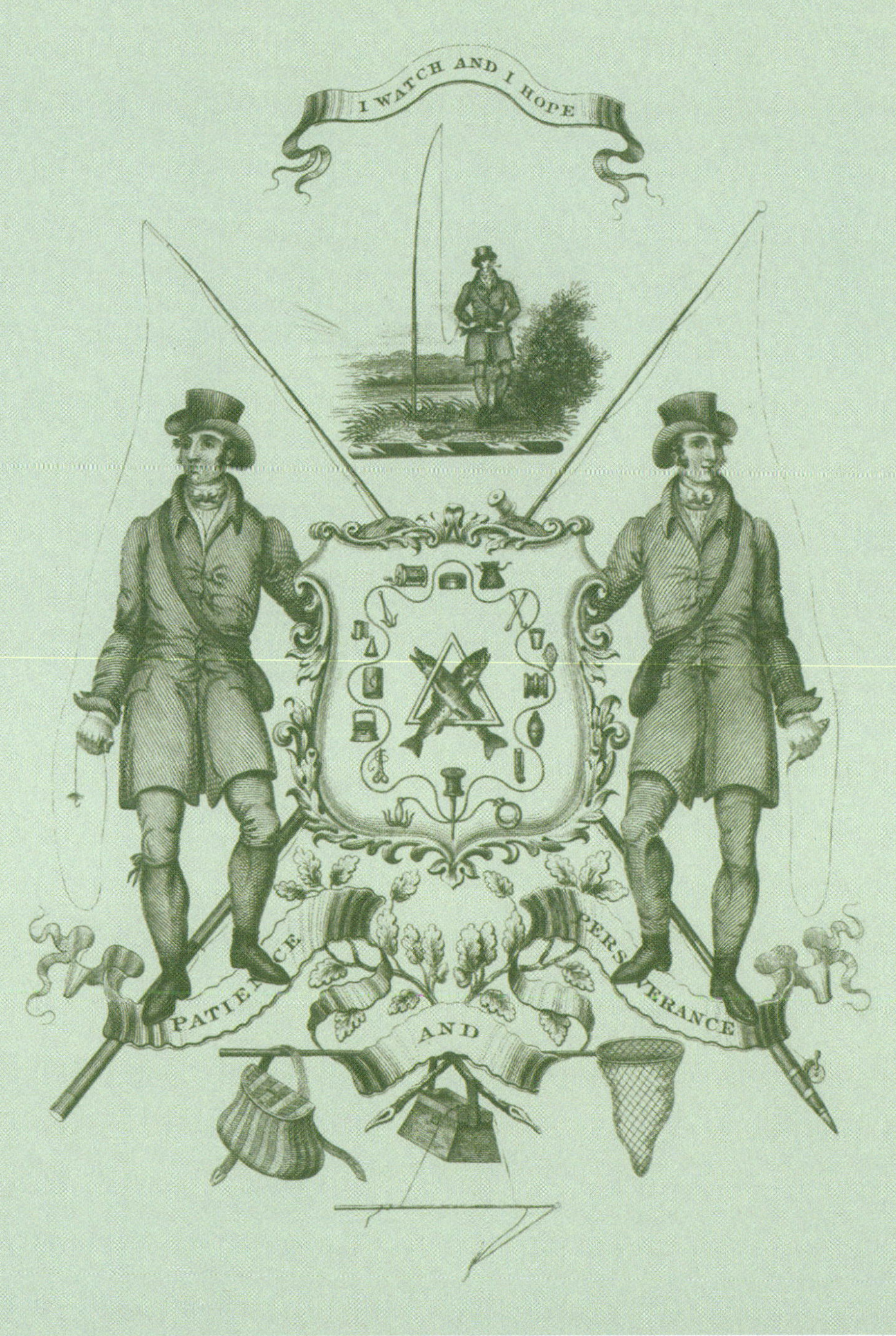

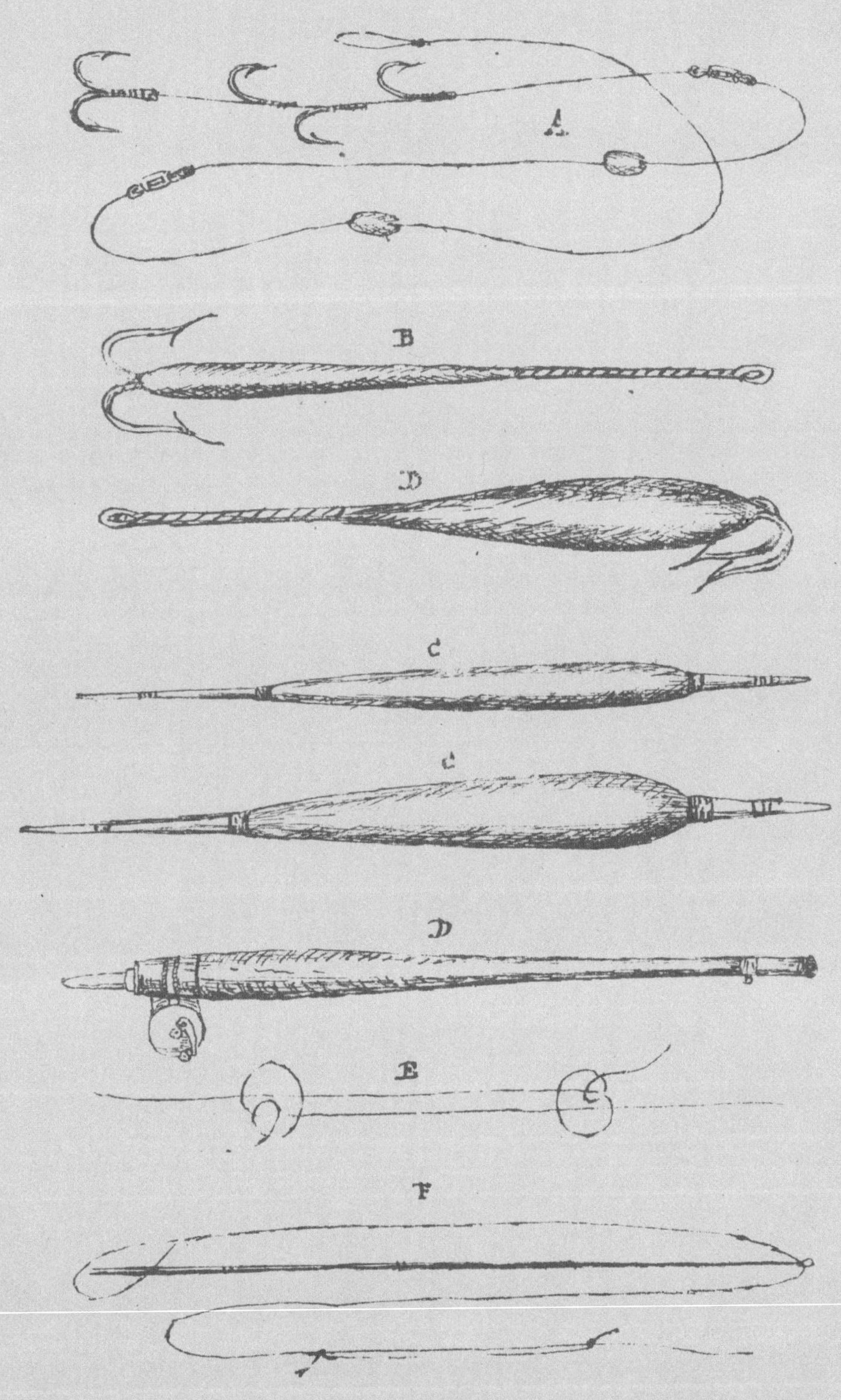
A
B
D
C
C
D
E
F

ANGLING AS ADVENTURE

FOR MANY, angling is as much about adventure as it is about catching fish. Most people live within a short distance of fishable water, yet anglers will travel to the most remote, wildest (and sometimes most dangerous) corners of the earth to pursue fish. The opening of the Rocky Mountains in Canada and the United States was accomplished, in part, by railways bringing adventure-seeking anglers into the wilderness, and lodges around the world (in Tierra del Fuego, Mongolia, the Canadian high arctic islands, Alaska, and countless other locales) lure anglers from local streams for the opportunity to catch exotic fishes in beautiful locales.

The books in this section span over 100 years and include travel narratives, travel guides, and brochures for the adventuresome angler. Some of these items are carefully curated advertisements by rail companies, some are guidebooks for the angler to create his or her own trips, while others provide vicarious adventures into the wilderness for the armchair angler. All of the books in this section are evidence of the siren song that lures anglers from the comforts of home to seek angling experiences around the world.

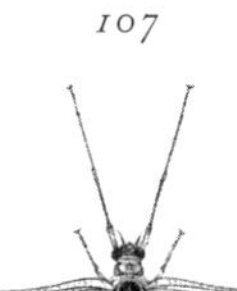

48

[BADDELEY, JOHN]. *The London Angler's Book, or Waltonian Chronicle: Containing Much Original Information to Anglers Generally, Combined with Numerous Amusing Songs and Anecdotes of Fish and Fishing, Never before Published: Together with an Entirely New Description of the Thames, from London Bridge to Staines, the Lea from the Thames to Hertford, the Wandle, the Mole, the Wey, the Colne, the Brent, the Roding, and Every River and Stream within 20 Miles of London, Worth Fishing in*. LONDON: JOHN BADDELEY, 1834. [SH 439 B13 1834] 18.5 CM X 11.5 CM

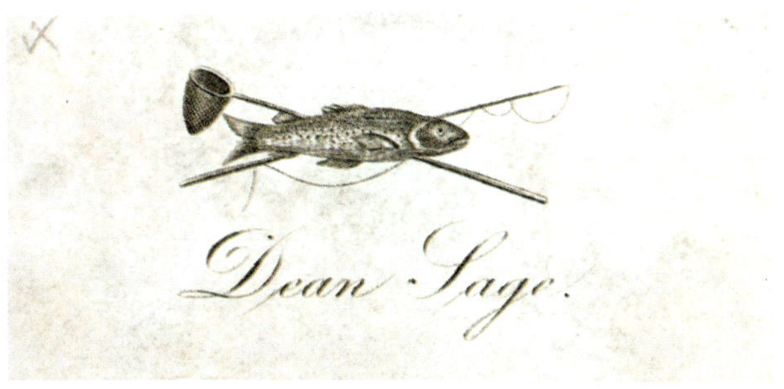

As the extended title says, Baddeley's guide gives a description of "every river and stream within 20 miles of London worth fishing in." Although the book does include a section on flies and fly fishing, Baddeley was convinced that authors of the day were overcomplicating fly fishing. He states,

> … many excellent fly fishers would still wish this art to be shrouded in all the long prevailing nonsensical complication, some asserting that a certain fly on such a day of the month, in such a stream, at such an hour, will alone take fish; and at two hours after, another fly, most minutely described, is the only one that will do any good; in half an hour, 3 minutes, and 5 seconds, there will be a necessity for another change, which must be made with all the accustomed nicety of shade and size. It is all quackery and nonsense. Throw a light line, keep out of sight as much as possible, use some of the few flies above recommended, and in any stream in England, at some part of the day, if the fish are inclined to rise at all, you may kill Dace, Chub, and Trout, as well as though you had all the tackle that was ever made to choose from (91–92).

The book bears the bookplate of angling author and book collector Dean Sage.

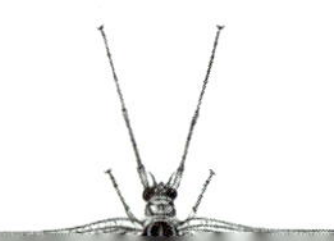

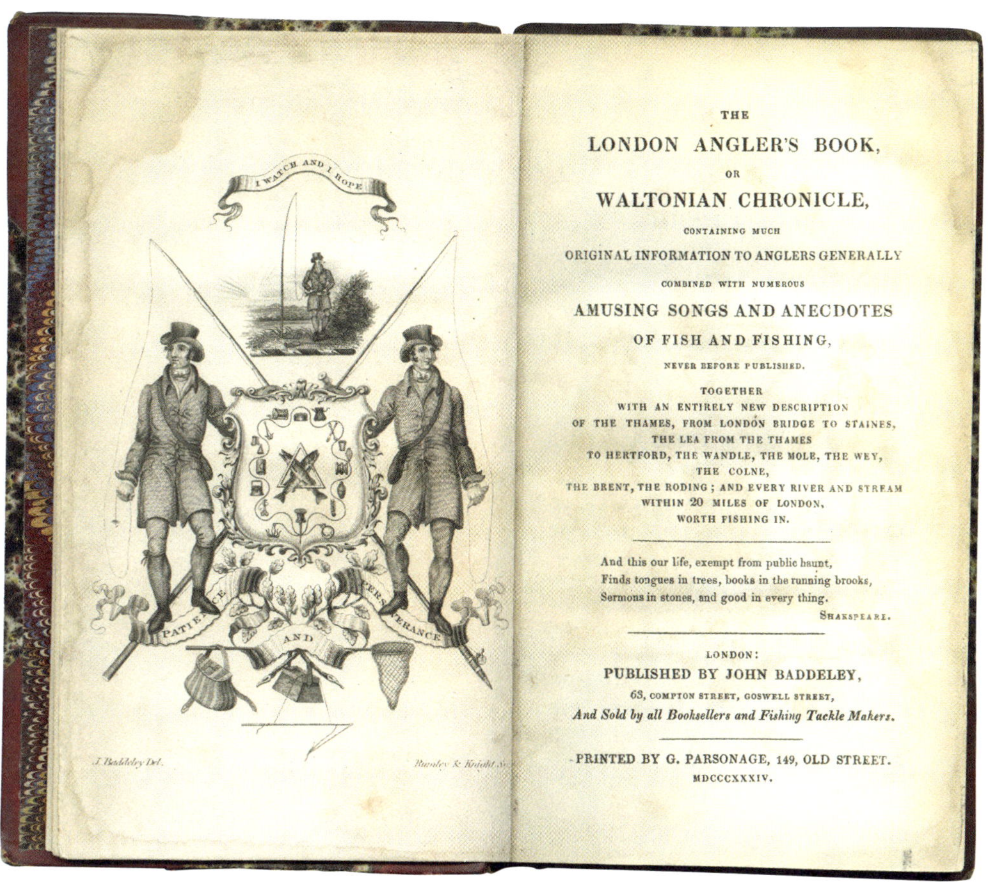

THE

LONDON ANGLER'S BOOK,

OR

WALTONIAN CHRONICLE,

CONTAINING MUCH

ORIGINAL INFORMATION TO ANGLERS GENERALLY

COMBINED WITH NUMEROUS

AMUSING SONGS AND ANECDOTES

OF FISH AND FISHING,

NEVER BEFORE PUBLISHED.

TOGETHER

WITH AN ENTIRELY NEW DESCRIPTION
OF THE THAMES, FROM LONDON BRIDGE TO STAINES,
THE LEA FROM THE THAMES
TO HERTFORD, THE WANDLE, THE MOLE, THE WEY,
THE COLNE,
THE BRENT, THE RODING; AND EVERY RIVER AND STREAM
WITHIN 20 MILES OF LONDON,
WORTH FISHING IN.

And this our life, exempt from public haunt,
Finds tongues in trees, books in the running brooks,
Sermons in stones, and good in every thing.
SHAKSPEARE.

LONDON:

PUBLISHED BY JOHN BADDELEY,

63, COMPTON STREET, GOSWELL STREET,

And Sold by all Booksellers and Fishing Tackle Makers.

PRINTED BY G. PARSONAGE, 149, OLD STREET.

MDCCCXXXIV.

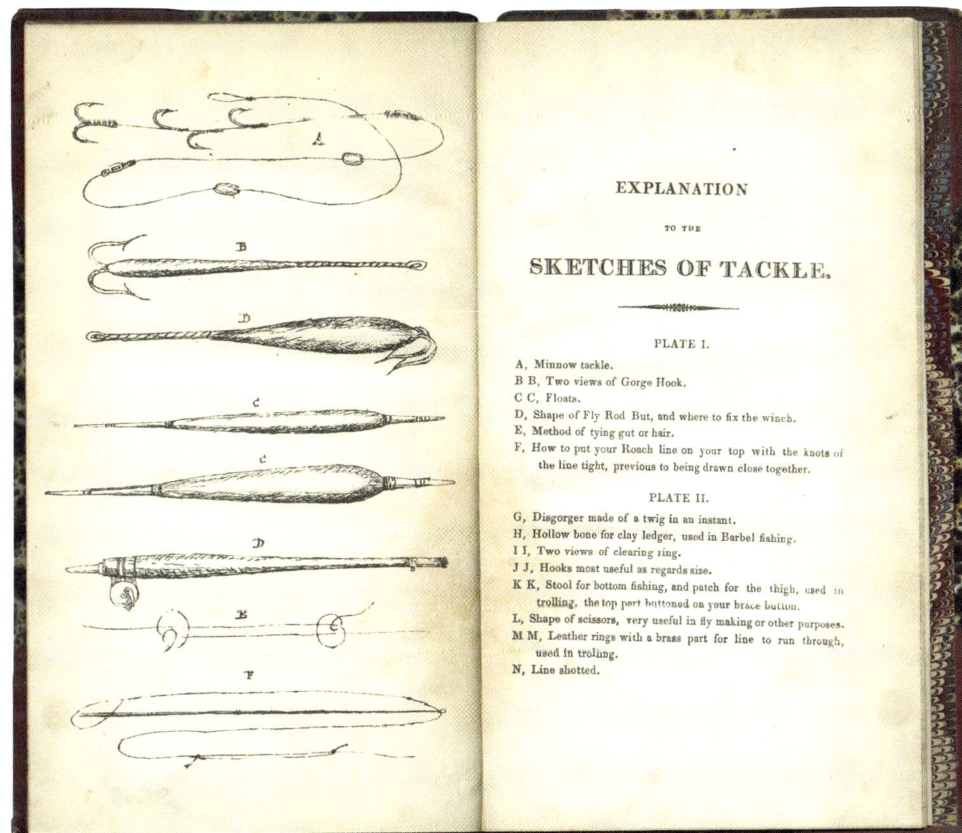

EXPLANATION

TO THE

SKETCHES OF TACKLE.

PLATE I.

A, Minnow tackle.
B B, Two views of Gorge Hook.
C C, Floats.
D, Shape of Fly Rod But, and where to fix the winch.
E, Method of tying gut or hair.
F, How to put your Roach line on your top with the knots of the line tight, previous to being drawn close together.

PLATE II.

G, Disgorger made of a twig in an instant.
H, Hollow bone for clay ledger, used in Barbel fishing.
I I, Two views of clearing ring.
J J, Hooks most useful as regards size.
K K, Stool for bottom fishing, and patch for the thigh, used in trolling, the top part buttoned on your brace button.
L, Shape of scissors, very useful in fly making or other purposes.
M M, Leather rings with a brass part for line to run through, used in trolling.
N, Line shotted.

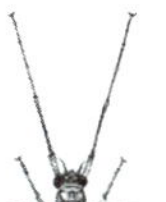

ANGLING STREAMS

AND

ANGLING QUARTERS

IN THE

SCOTTISH LOWLANDS

With Maps & Plain Directions to Trout Fishers

BY

J. ROBERTSON, LEITH

EDINBURGH
JOHN MENZIES
2 SOUTH HANOVER STREET
MDCCCLIX

49

LEITH, J[OHN] ROBERTSON. *Angling Streams and Angling Quarters in the Scottish Lowlands with Maps and Plain Directions to Trout Fishers.* EDINBURGH: JOHN MENZIES, 1859. [SH 609 R63 1859] 17.1 CM X 11.4 CM

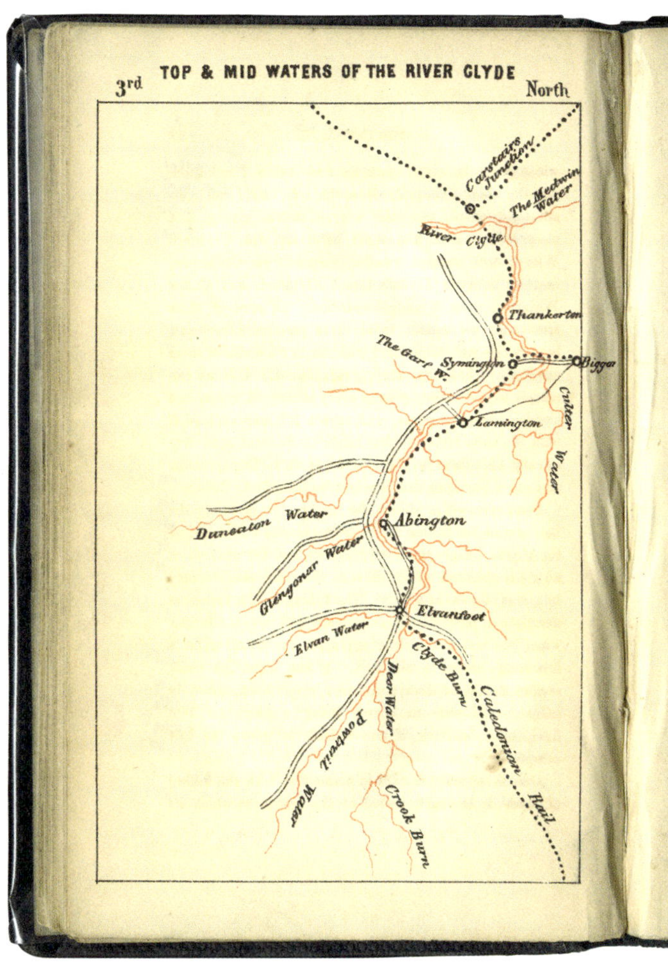

Robertson's guide provides maps and, as the title says, "plain directions to trout fishers" to reach streams in the Scottish lowlands. The full-page maps are printed in red and black and include roads that can be used to reach recommended angling locations.

50

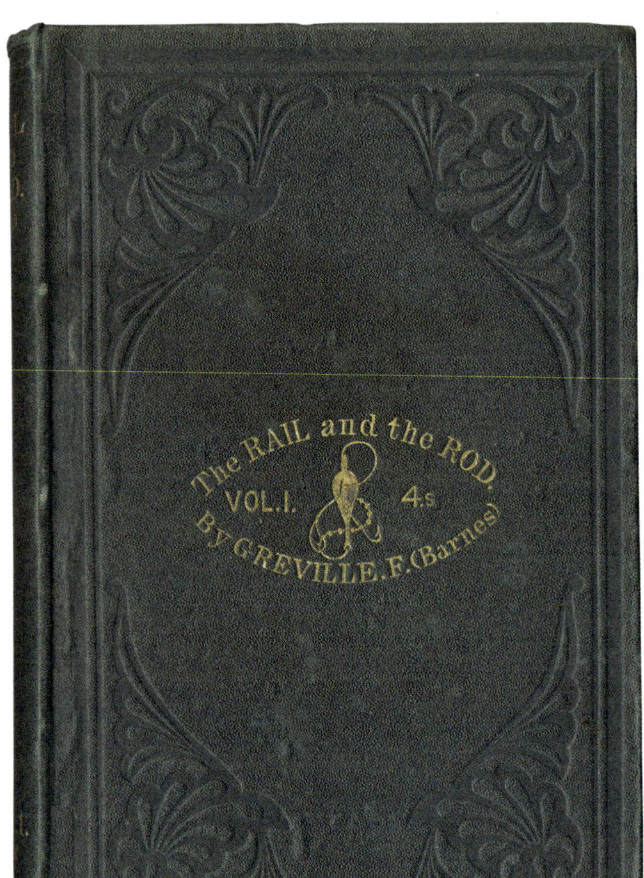

[FENNELL, JOHN GREVILLE]. *The Rail and the Rod, or, Tourist-Angler's Guide to Waters and Quarters Thirty Miles Around London.* LONDON: HORACE COX, 1867. [SH 606 F46 1867 V.1] 20.5 CM X 13.8 CM

This book is a guide to angling waters near London accessible via railway. The work was issued in parts (at least six parts were issued between 1867 and 1871), with each part highlighting a different railway (Westwood et al. 89–90). This copy includes parts I through III: Great Eastern Railway, Great Western Railway, and South Western Railway. All parts are scarce.

51

ALLERTON, R[EUBEN] G[ERMAN]. *Brook Trout Fishing: An Account of a Trip of the Oquossoc Angling Association to Northern Maine in June, 1869*. NEW YORK: R. G. ALLERTON, 1869. [SH 403 O6 A66 1869] 19.0 CM X 12.0 CM

The book is an account of the author's trip to Northern Maine in pursuit of large brook trout, which he certainly found. Fish up to nine pounds were landed, and the book's publication resulted in a "trout rush" of anglers descending upon the region (Wetzel 58). This example is complete with the attractive folding plate of a brook trout, which is often absent in other copies.

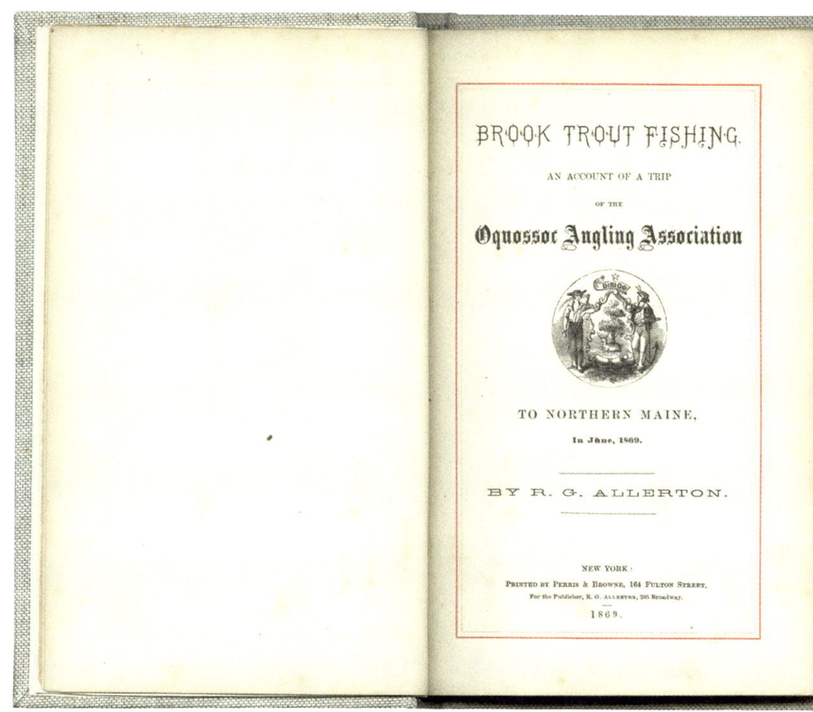

BROOK TROUT FISHING.

AN ACCOUNT OF A TRIP

OF THE

Oquossoc Angling Association

TO NORTHERN MAINE,

In June, 1869.

BY R. G. ALLERTON.

NEW YORK:

PRINTED BY PERRIS & BROWNE, 164 FULTON STREET,

For the Publisher, R. G. ALLERTON, 285 Broadway.

1869.

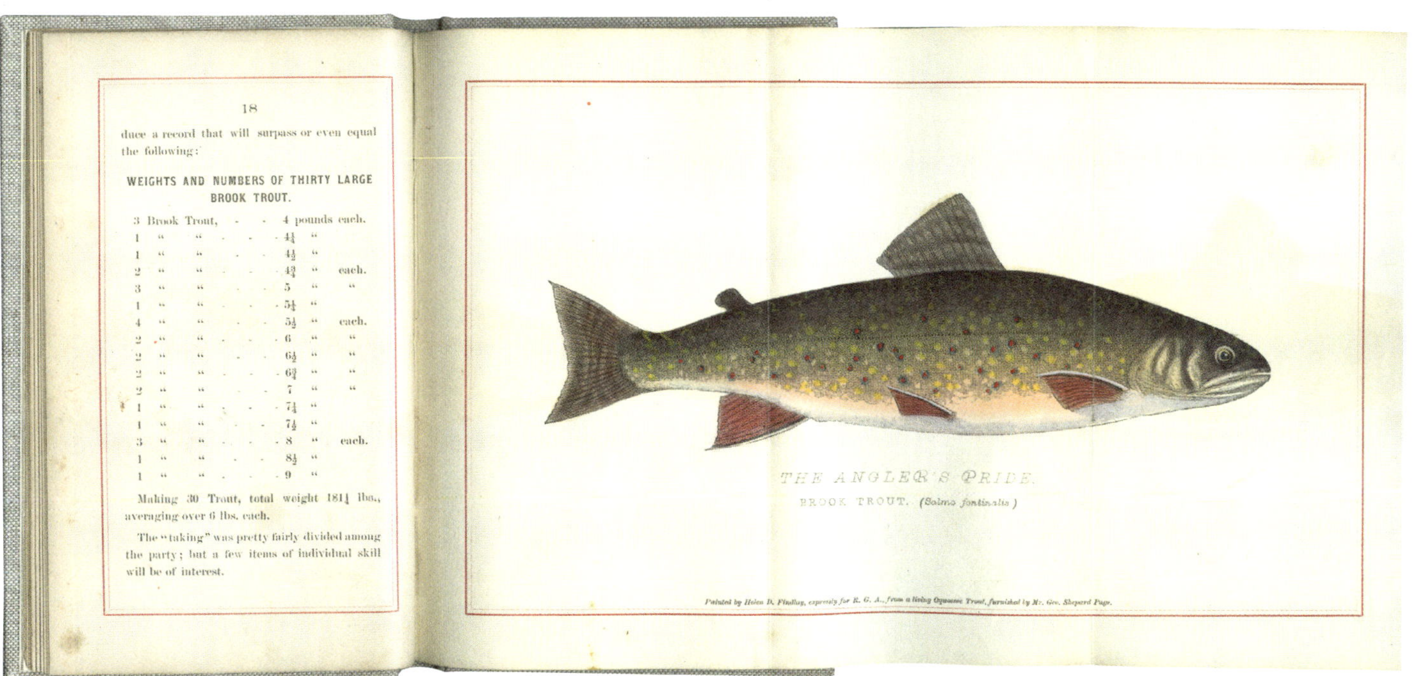

18

duce a record that will surpass or even equal the following:

WEIGHTS AND NUMBERS OF THIRTY LARGE BROOK TROUT.

3	Brook	Trout,	4	pounds	each.
1	"	"	4¼	"	
1	"	"	4½	"	
2	"	"	4¾	"	each.
3	"	"	5	"	"
1	"	"	5¼	"	
4	"	"	5½	"	each.
2	"	"	6	"	"
2	"	"	6½	"	"
2	"	"	6¾	"	"
2	"	"	7	"	"
1	"	"	7¼	"	
1	"	"	7½	"	
3	"	"	8	"	each.
1	"	"	8½	"	
1	"	"	9	"	

Making 30 Trout, total weight 181¼ lbs., averaging over 6 lbs. each.

The "taking" was pretty fairly divided among the party; but a few items of individual skill will be of interest.

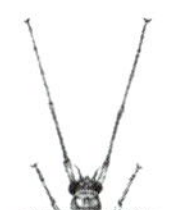

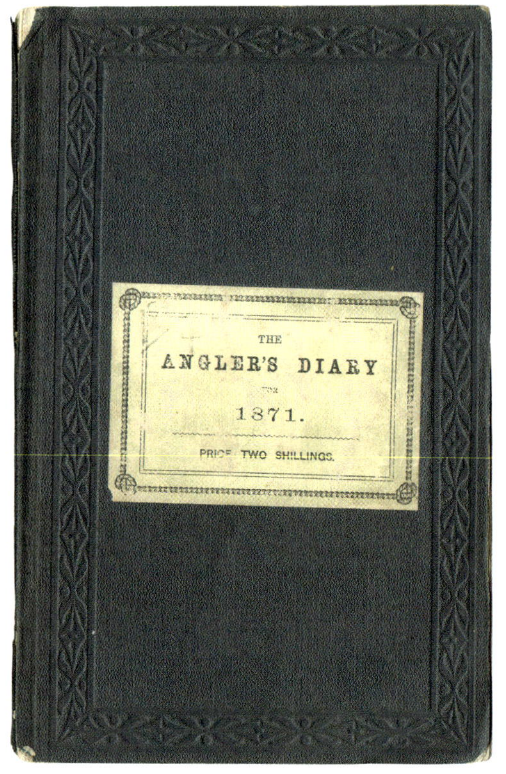

52

C[OX], I[RWIN] E[DWIN] B[AINBRIDGE]. *The Angler's Diary and Fisherman's Guide to the Rivers and Lakes of the World: to Which Are Added Forms for Registering the Fish Taken during the Year.* LONDON: HORACE COX, 1871. [SH 401 A54 1871] 18.9 CM X 12.1 CM

This is an ambitious little title, claiming to be an angler's guide to the "rivers and lakes of the world." It includes a blank diary for anglers to record their catches. Diaries were apparently issued yearly from 1869 to 1881 (Westwood et al. 8), and one can imagine a daydreaming angler reading of exotic fishing locales around the world by the fire on a cold winter day. Unfortunately, this example does not have any entries in the diary.

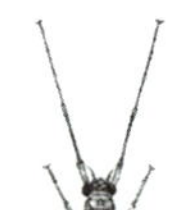

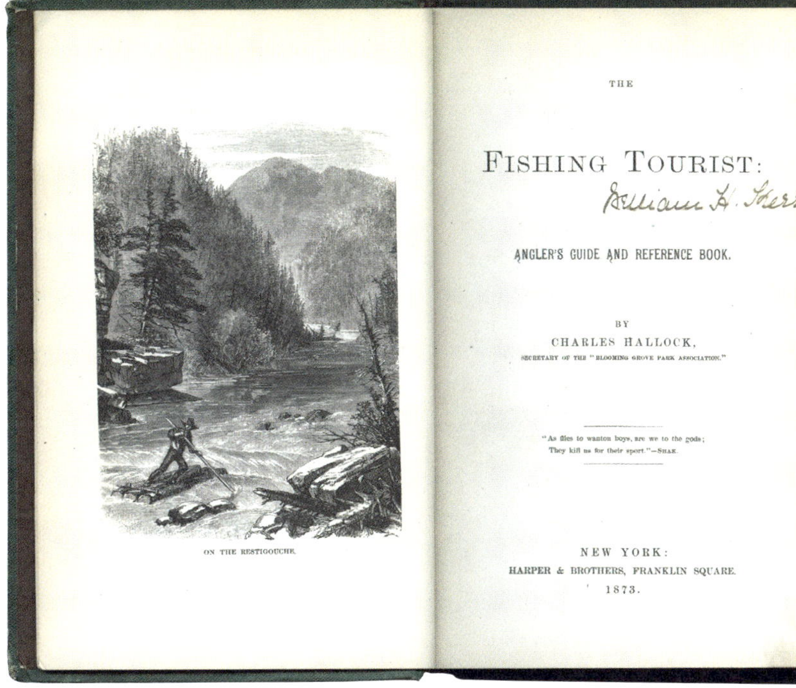

53

HALLOCK, CHARLES. *The Fishing Tourist: Angler's Guide and Reference Book*. NEW YORK: HARPER & BROTHERS, 1873.
[SH 441 H16 1873 C.2] 21.0 CM X 14.1 CM

This was one of the more popular guides for anglers in the late nineteenth century, focusing on the Eastern United States and Canada. For the modern reader, it provides insight into nineteenth-century angling, including the distribution of various fish species. The title is also infamous for introducing and describing the Michigan grayling and its rivers (Wetzel 61). The grayling was a well-known species in England, but the North American species had been previously thought only to reside in northern portions of Canada and Alaska. Anglers were enchanted by the description of the grayling, and they arrived in Michigan in great numbers to harvest the fish. After overfishing, habitat loss, and introduction of non-native species, the Michigan grayling was extinct by the 1930s.

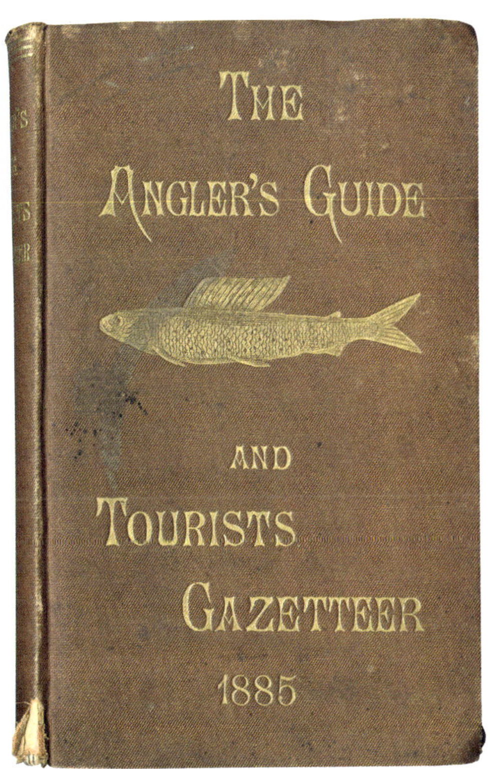

54

HARRIS, WILLIAM C. *The Angler's Guide Book and Tourists' Gazetteer of the Fishing Waters of the United States and Canada. 1885*. NEW YORK: THE AMERICAN ANGLER, 1885.
[SH 463 H26 1885] 19.3 CM X 12.4 CM

This title was issued eight years after Hallock's fishing guide (item 53). It also provides specific locations to catch Michigan grayling and even features a Michigan grayling in gilt on the front board. Approximately fifty years after the book's publication, the Michigan grayling would be extinct. The binding of this copy is a bit rough, potentially evidence of its intended use as a guidebook.

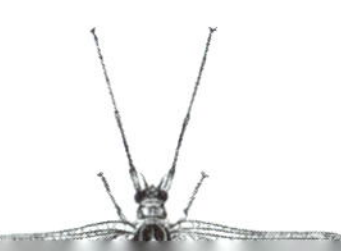

ing: April, May, Sept. and Oct. best; hotels $2 p. d.; Indians as guides; boat plenty and cheap.

Selkirk West (Can. P.)—Red r. near station; Lake Winnipeg 15 m.; last name best; pike, pickerel, golden eye (moon-eye), perch and coarse fish; pike and pick erel most numerous; baits used, meat, minnows and trolling; June and Septembe best; hotels $1 p. d.; guides cheap; boats and canoes plentiful.

Stonewall (Can. P.)—Jackfish cr. near station; pike most numerous; trollin mostly; May and June best; hotel reasonable; boats cheap.

Winnipeg (Can. P.)—Red r. and Assiniboine r. near station; last named bes pike, golden eye, (moon-eye) catfish etc.; usual baits; June, July, August and Sep best; hotels at moderate prices; boats plenty at 20c. p. h.

Province of New Brunswick.

Andover (New B.)—There is good fishing at certain seasons, say in June, f salmon and trout at the mouth of Tobique r., and 15 or 20 m. up it. In 1884 tw rods scored 17 salmon in Aug. on the main Tobique. During the latter part of th month and in Sept. there is good fishing, also in June and July, when the blackf is not so troublesome. The trip can be made up the Tobique and down t Nepisiquit to Bathurst in about 16 days and good fishing can be had during t passage. There are also several lakes that can be reached by canoe in 8 to 10 da which give excellent fishing. Salmon can be caught in the above waters, but tro are most numerous and very abundant. June and September are the best month hotels at Andover $1.50 to $2 p. d.; guides, including boat $1.75 p. d., and boar Address J. A. Perley Esq., Andover, Victoria Co., N. B., for information. Addre the Gen. Pass Agent of the road, as to public waters for salmon and trout.

Barnaby River (Intercolonial)—S. W. branch of Miramichi r. 4 m.; salmon a trout; salmon most numerous; artificial flies; July and August best months; boa can be had.

Bathurst (Intercolonial)—Nepisiquit or Big r. 3 m.; Tete-a-gouche r. 2½ n Middle r. 2 m.; first named best; salmon and trout; salmon most numerous; arti cial flies used; June 15 to September 15 best; hotels $1 p. d.; guides plenty, $1. p. d.; canoes with men easily procured. The fishing is said to be good in Big r. f salmon from the mouth to Grand Falls 21 m. A number of good trout streams a in this section.

Belledune (Intercolonial)—Bay Chaleur and Belledune r. accessible; fi named best; salmon, trout, codfish, mackerel and herring; the two last mo numerous; clams, herring etc. as baits; September best; no regular hotel, b board can be obtained very cheap; guide with boat $2.50 p. d. The trout a scarce, and the salmon are caught only in nets. The mackerel take the hook a give fine play.

Campbellton (Intercolonial)—Trout as large as 6¼ lbs. have been caught wi bait in the Restigouche r. at this point. They are also taken with the artificial f Parker l. from 3 to 7 m. distant, abound in speckled trout of large size, and t same is likewise true of Mission l., some 4 m. distant from Campbellton. The se tion around this point is full of fine fishing waters. In the Restigouche here salm may also be caught at times, and some of the pools are subject to day lea Indian guides $2.50 p. d., including board, or $3 p. d. and board themselves. Hot $1.25 to $1.50 p. d., from which a day's good fishing can be had on the waters ad cent.

Canaan (Intercolonial)—Canaan r. 1 m.; trout; worms usual bait; June a July best.

Charlo (Intercolonial)—River Charlo, North and South branches; accessib North branch best; sea trout, speckled trout, grilse and salmon; sea trout m numerous; worms and flies used as bait; July and August best; hotels $1 p. guide at moderate charge; boats unnecessary; bait easily obtained and is m killing than the artificial fly.

Dalhousie Junc., (Intercolonial)—Robinson's l. 2 m.; Restigouche r. near s tion; first named best; trout, salmon, perch, smelts etc.; trout and salmon m numerous; artificial fly used mostly; June and July best; hotels $1 p. d.; gu $1.25 p. d.; boats and bait at small cost. The fishing is good and accommodati ample.

Frederickton, (New B.)—This is a centre point for anglers visiting New Bru wick. The r. r. runs as far as Edmundston 156 m. above Frederickton. Outf uides etc., can be had at Grand Falls, 120 m. from Fredericton, and good hotels ill be found there, and at Edmundston also, where the Madawaska r. joins the St. ohns r. The Toledi r. empties into a lake near by, and the r. can be navigated by noes for 50 m. It has several branches and many lakes where a fly has never een cast. 8 m. below Edmundston is the Green r., having numerous l and branches nptying into the St. Johns. The above waters teem with trout of good size, and the l. may be found lake trout. From the last of June until Aug. is the best ason. The St. Francis, 30 m. above Edmundston, is a branch of the St. Johns, d gives for 50 m. or more, noble trout fishing. The above section is probably the st trouting ground in Eastern America.

Hampton (Intercolonial)—Henry l. accessible; trout; worms and flies as bait; ptember and October best; hotel accommodations not extensive.

Henry's Lake (St. M. & U.)—See St. Martin's N. B.

Jacquet River (Intercolonial)—Jacquet r. 1 m.; Belledune r. 4 m.; Armstrong . ½ m.; first named best; brook and sea trout and salmon; sea trout most numer- as; ordinary flies for trout and salmon used; June, July and August best; hotels to $5 p. w.; guides $3 p. d., with canoe; mackerel fishing with hook and line in ep water about 2 m. from shore, is much indulged in, and for which speckled rring chopped fine is used as bait. The trout of the fresh waters are of small ze but are numerous. Those in Jacquet r. run large; 4 and 5 lbs. fish having been ught there.

New Mills (Intercolonial)—New Mills r. ¼ m.; Benjamine r. 1 m.; last named st; salmon and trout, last most numerous; flies and worms as bait; June and ly best; hotels at moderate charge; guides $1 p. d.; boats and bait reasonable.

Painsec Junc (Intercolonial)—Painsec l. 1 m.; trout; worms and flies as bait; ne and July best; hotel at reasonable rate. The l. is small, but trout from 1 to 2 s. are taken from it. No public boats.

Petitcodiac (Intercolonial)—Posett r. 4 m.; Little r. 8 m.; North r. 2 m.; New naan r. 12 m.; Anagance Mill p. and str. ½ m.; Elgin ls. 15 m.; first named best; out only; usual lures; June best; hotels $1 p. d.; guides at moderate charges; ats not needed. This is a good trout section, the fish do not run large but they e abundant.

Petite Roche (Intercolonial)—Elm Tree r. 2 m.; Negadoo r. 3 m.; Mill str. 6 m.; o last named best; trout only; worms and fly in use; July and August best; hotel p. d.; guides and boats not needed.

Point Du Chene (Intercolonial)—Harbor (immediate vicinity) Dickies p. 3 m.; iiths Mill 4 m.; Gilberts Mill 10 m.; last named best for trout; perch, smelts, ss, mackerel, sea trout and brook trout; bass and mackerel most numerous; rgies as bait for mackerel and bright baits for bass; August and September best onths; hotels $1.50 p. d.; guides at moderate charge; boats $1 p. d. Excellent hing.

St. George (Grand So.)—Lake Utopia connected with Trout l., Mill l., Red Rock Sparks l., McDougall l., Magaquadane r., at station; all good; brook and lake out, perch etc.; trout most numerous; flies, worms, and grasshoppers are baits ed; May, June, August and Sept. best; hotels reasonable and camping out is actised; guides in abundance, $1 to $1.50 p. d.; boats and baits moderate. These comparatively virgin waters. See THE AMERICAN ANGLER, Dec. 27, 1884.

St. John (Intercolonial)—St. John r., Hammond r. and Salmon r.; first named st; salmon, trout, b. b. and pickerel; trout and bass most numerous; flies used r salmon; worms and small fish for the others; June, August and September best; tels at moderate prices; guides easily procured and boats plentiful.

St. Leonards (New B.)—Green Brier r. 15 m.; Restigouche r. 24 m.; (the last st;) both give excellent trout fishing; trout only in Green Brier r.; July and Sep- nber best months; guides $1.50 p. d.; salmon are caught in this section of the stigouche r. The favorite grounds of local anglers on the latter r. is between tle and Big Forks, a distance of 35 m. The distances from St. Leonard's to the mon waters are as follows: Soldiers Gulch 50 m.; Little Cross Point 65 m.; acey br. 60 m.; Devils Half-Acre 68 m.; Catapediac Pool 70 m. Write to Genl. ss Agent of railroad as to open waters for salmon and trout; leases and ownership ange so constantly that it would mislead visiting anglers for us to state the privi- es existing at the time we go to press with the guide book.

St. Martin's (St. M. & U.)—Henry l. at station; Wood l. 1 m.; a number of os and streams from 1 to 10 miles from St. Martin's all equally good; trout prin-

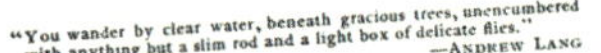

"You wander by clear water, beneath gracious trees, unencumbered with anything but a slim rod and a light box of delicate flies."
—Andrew Lang

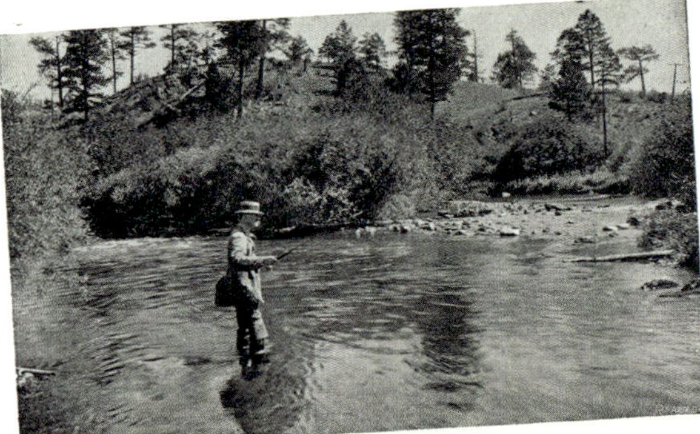

WAITING FOR A RISE
NEAR BUFFALO PARK

"It is not disinclination that keeps so many away from the pleasures and delights of the woods and running streams, but rather the idea that they can not get away."

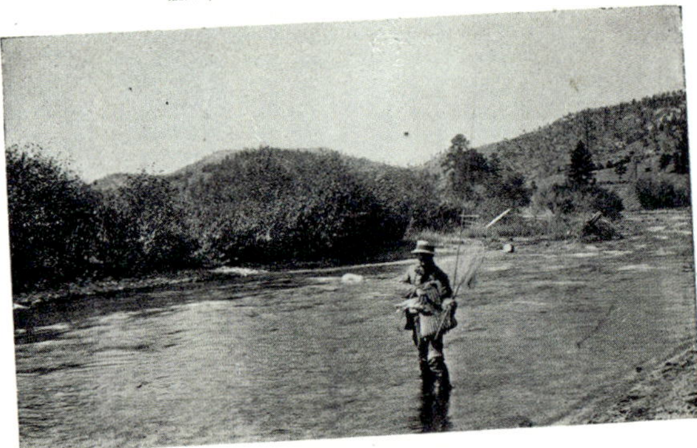

AN AMPLE REWARD
BELOW PINE GROVE

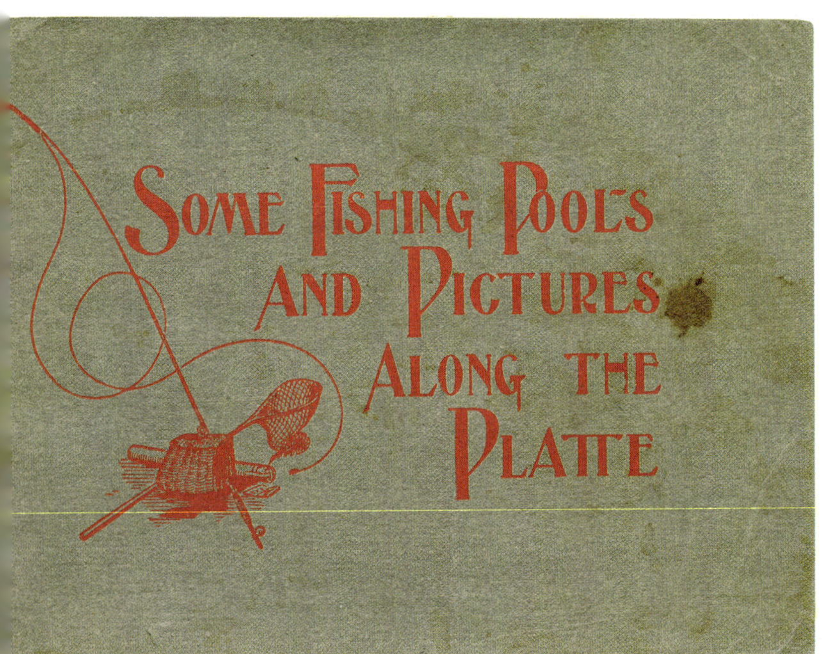

55

[FISHER, T.E.]. *Some Fishing Pools and Pictures along the Platte.* DENVER: COLORADO & SOUTHERN RAILWAY, [1900-1903?]. [F 782 S7 S66 1900Z] 14.7 CM X 19.6 CM

This scarce pictorial pamphlet was issued to entice anglers to fish the Platte River in Colorado. It includes 21 photographs of angling scenes, each with a quotation from a famous angling author. This pamphlet is only included in a handful of additional institutional collections around the world.

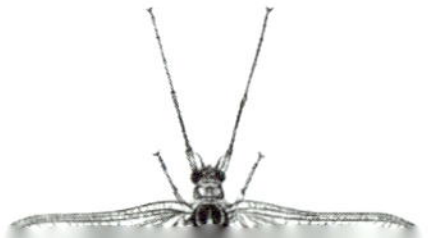

56

MAPS OF THE RIVER THAMES

Two excellent fold-out maps of the River Thames intended for reference by anglers and oarsman. However, manipulating the fold-out map on a windy, rainy day in a rowboat would present a formidable challenge. These examples are undated, but Westwood et al. (174) record editions published in 1861 and 1867.

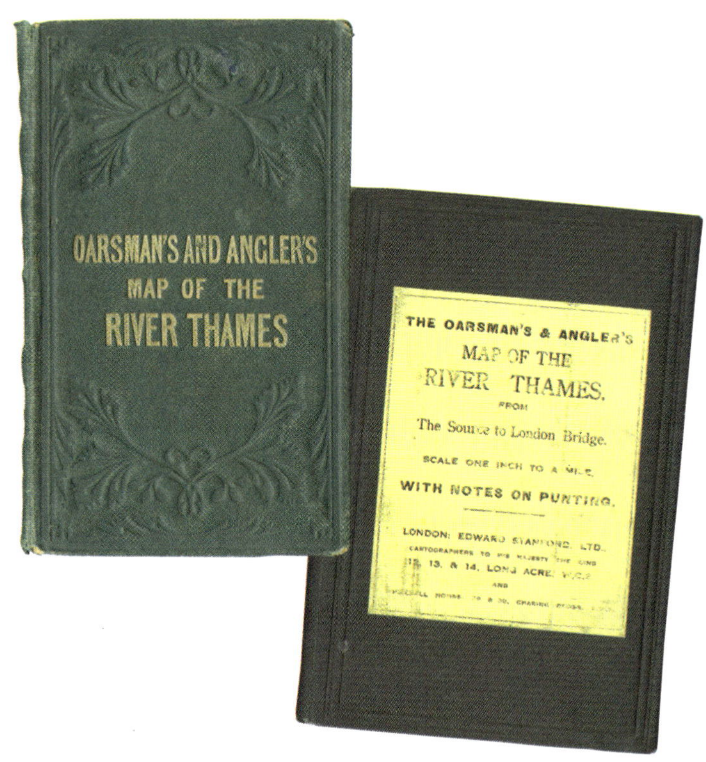

56(a)

RAVENSTEIN, E[RNST] G[EORG]. *The Oarsman's and Angler's Map of the River Thames.* LONDON: JAMES REYNOLDS, [1870?]. [G 5752 T4 P5 1870] 17.0 CM X 10.5 CM

56(b)

The Oarsman's and Angler's Map of the River Thames from Its Source to London Bridge. LONDON: EDWARD STANFORD, LTD., [1927]. [G 5752 T4 P5 1927] 16.3 CM X 10.8 CM

56(a)

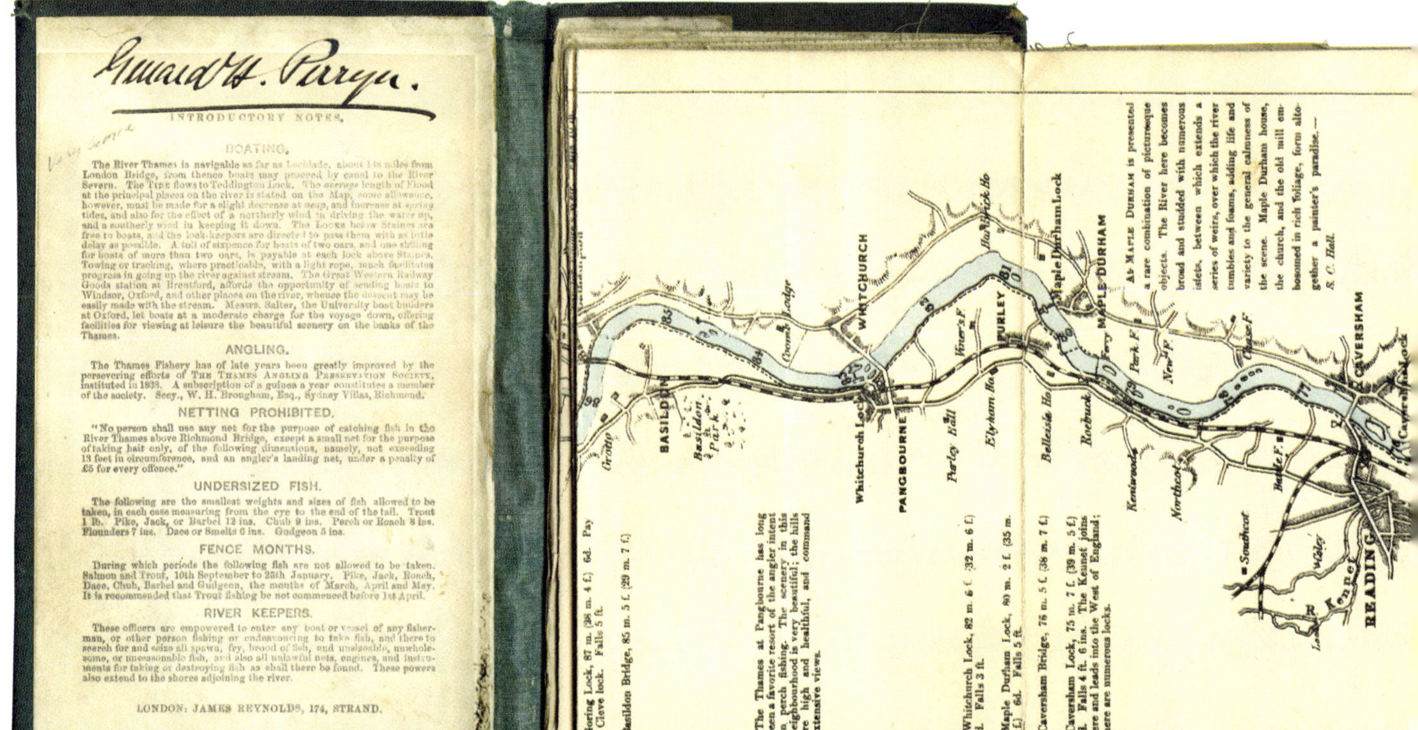

57

RAILWAY EPHEMERA

These are examples of ephemera issued by Canadian and American railways intended to lure anglers to vacation destinations along their lines. The brochures use attractive graphics of outdoor scenes to promise a sportsman's paradise at their advertised destination. Pamphlets like these were a significant driver of immigration into the wilderness (Schwantes) and also facilitated the expansion of the Canadian Rocky Mountain National Parks to accommodate visitors arriving in great numbers on the newly-opened railways (Lothian 32). These brochures were not often saved and survive in relatively small numbers.

57(a)

CANADIAN NATIONAL RAILWAYS. *Nipigon Lodge, Orient Bay, Ontario.* [MONTRÉAL]: CANADIAN NATIONAL RAILWAYS, [1925]. [FC 3095 N54 N54 1925] 23.2 CM X 10.7 CM

57(b)

CANADIAN NATIONAL RAILWAYS. *Nipigon.* [MONTRÉAL?]: CANADIAN NATIONAL RAILWAYS, [BETWEEN 1920 AND 1925?]. [FC 3095 N54 N54 1920Z] 23.6 CM X 10.9 CM

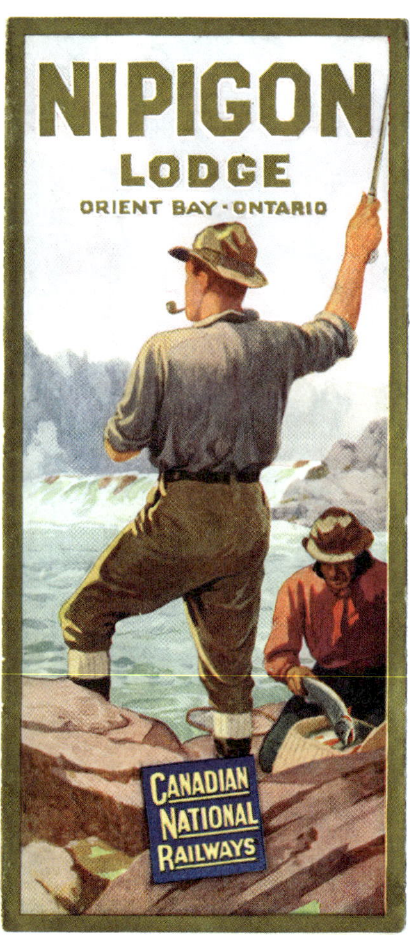

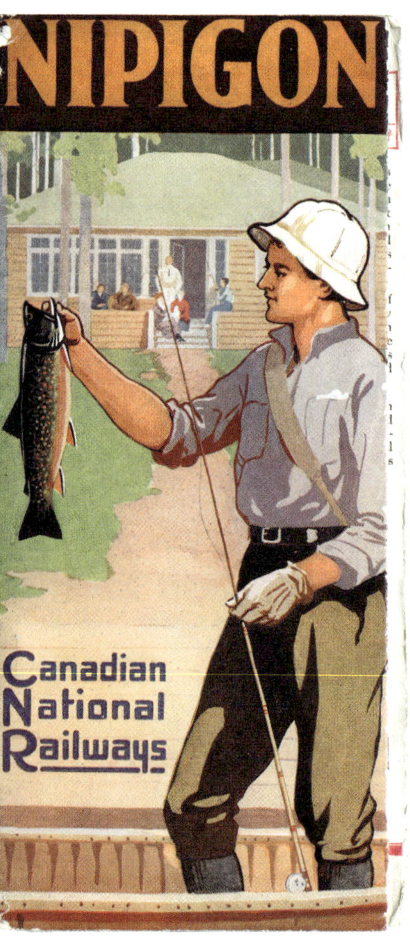

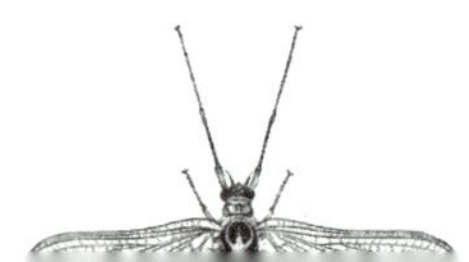

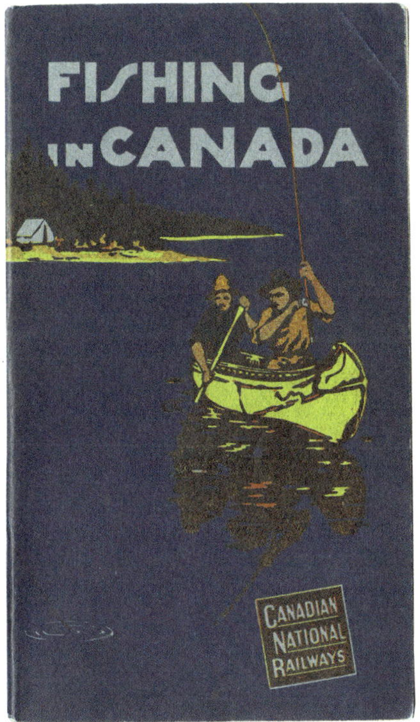

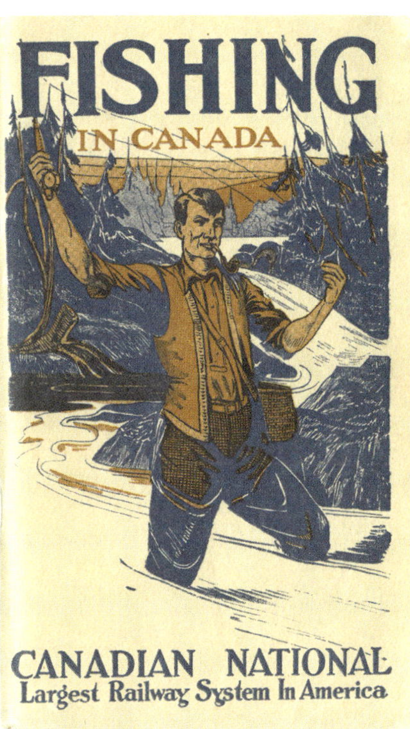

57(c)

CANADIAN NATIONAL RAILWAYS. *Fishing in Canada*. [MONTRÉAL]: CANADIAN NATIONAL RAILWAYS, [1923?]. [SH 571 F57 1923] 20.4 CM X 11.7 CM

57(d)

CANADIAN NATIONAL RAILWAYS. *Fishing in Canada*. [MONTRÉAL]: CANADIAN NATIONAL RAILWAYS, [1929?]. [SH 571 F57 1929] 20.6 CM X 11.8 CM

57(e)

A Guide to Inyo Mono Counties: The Eastern Slope of the Scenic High Sierras: Fishing, Hunting, Camping. N.P.: WILKINS & LARSON, 1925. [F 868 I6 G85 1925] 22.7 CM X 10.3 CM

TAMARACK LODGE

In the Heart of the Sierras

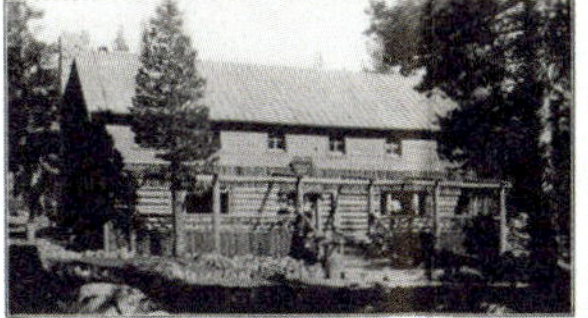

The Ideal Mountain Camp for Rest and Relaxation

TRANSPORTATION

By Rail—Southern Pacific to Lone Pine; O. V. T. Stage to Bishop, then Bishop-Mono Lake Stage to Tamarack Lodge.

By Auto—Los Angeles to Bishop, then 50 miles good road to Twin Lakes.

From Yosemite Park or Lake Tahoe—Yosemite Transportation System Stage to Mono Lake, then Bishop-Mono Lake Stage to the Lodge.

The Lodge with its cheerful fireplace, rustic lobby and dining room is located on the shore of Twin Lakes, in the Mammoth Lakes District, Inyo National Forest.

The Cabins are scattered among the towering Tamaracks, have the best of beds, are very inviting and comfortable.

Accommodations, summer 1925, for 50 guests. For reservations or information, address Tamarack Lodge, G. M. Gee, Mgr., Twin Lakes, Bishop, Cal.

The store carries complete stock of groceries and supplies for campers, fishermen and hunters.

Gasoline and oil.

Row boats for fishing.

Saddle and pack stock and guides for side trips.

Adjoins a Forest Service Public Auto Camp.

This is a central point for the start of side trips to many very interesting places and scenes in the back country of the high and rugged "Sierras."

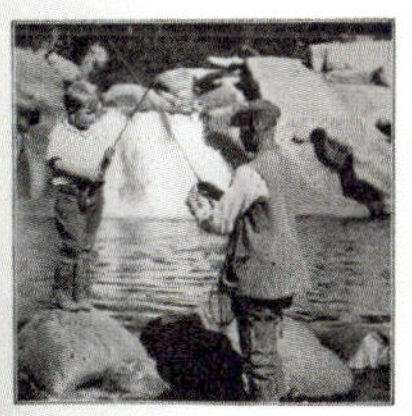

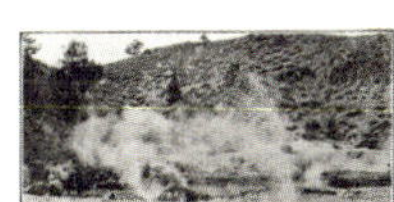

Hot Creek Geysers

is an inspiring one. We view the great ice crevasses, hundreds of feet in depth, and the magnificent ice caves fill us with awe. We can hardly appreciate the wonder of the scene. Here we stand on a body of perpetual ice over two miles long, over one mile wide, with a depth estimated at over 700 feet—a solid block of ice that has lain here for ages—while far below us and visible in the distance are beautiful, green fields of alfalfa and corn in the valley. Returning to Big Pine and continuing north on the highway, which still follows the west side of the valley, we soon come to the artistic stone column that directs us to

KEOUGHS RADIUM HOT SPRINGS

Here we leave the highway for the Springs, one-half mile distant. As we first leave the highway we look for but cannot see anything that denotes anything of importance until we clear the gradual raise and can look into the pretty enclosed nook containing the springs, hotel and cabins, surrounded by a vineyard and fruit trees. This is the spot that the traveler will always enjoy to visit. This is a resort that is not one in name only, but one that compares with the best in appointments. Here we take a bath in the big plunge, which is very refreshing as well as cleansing after the long drive.

Returning to the highway we continue on and soon arrive at Bishop, 59 miles from Lone Pine—182 miles from Mojave.

BISHOP

Bishop is the chief business center of Eastern California. It is the outfitting point for tourists going into Mono County and the upper country. Here can be had everything for the fisherman and camper, including fishing tackle of the right type and information concerning the country beyond.

Here we find a thriving, up-to-date town with hotels, garages, repair shops and stores of all kinds. A new hotel, the Kittie Lee Inn, has just been completed at a cost of $100,000.00, having 55 guest rooms, and is thoroughly modern in every detail. A unique feature is a fountain,

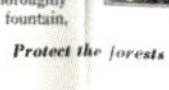

Protect the forests

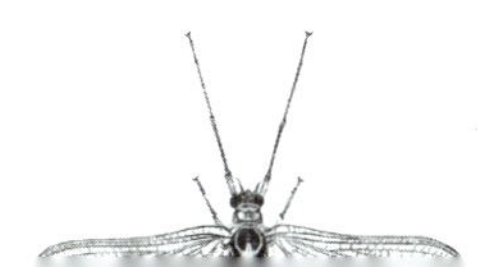

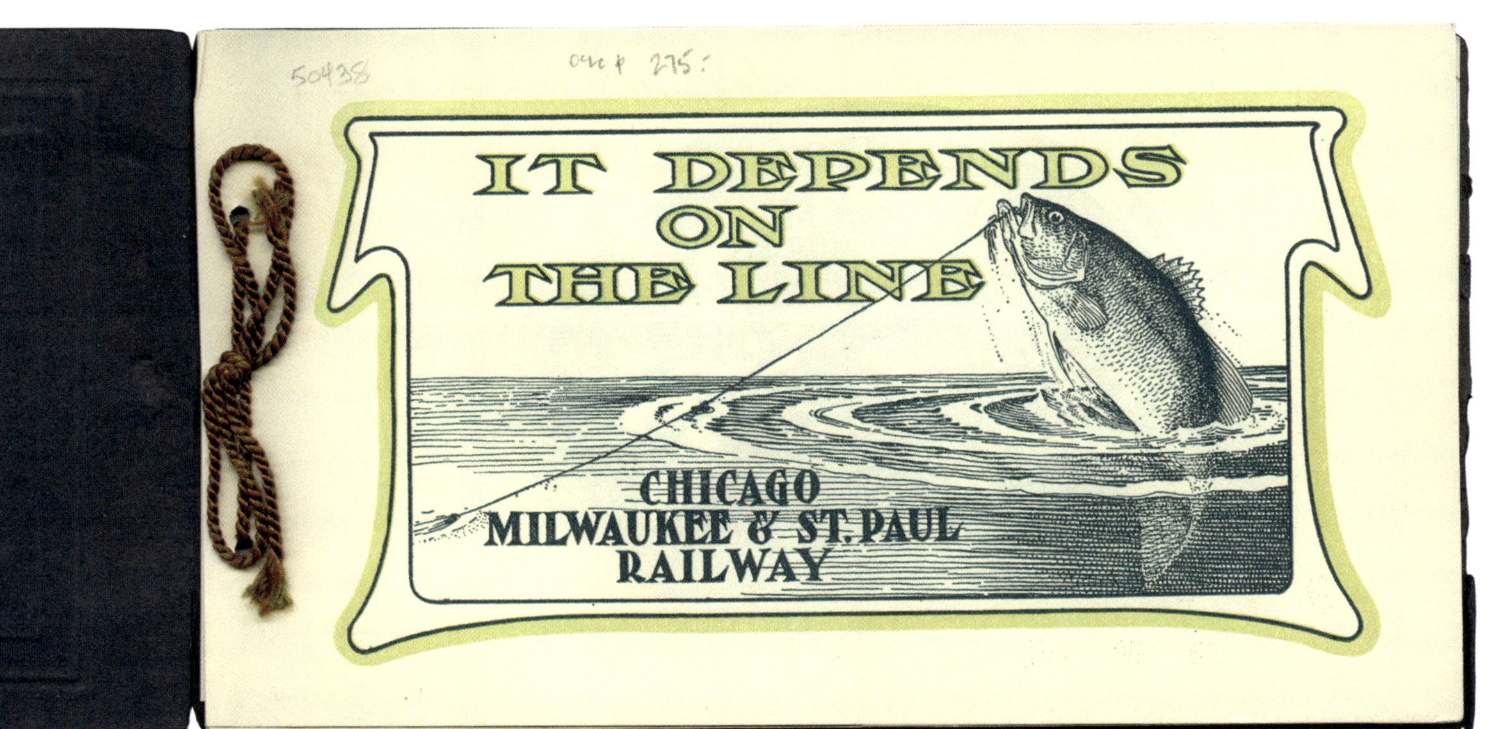

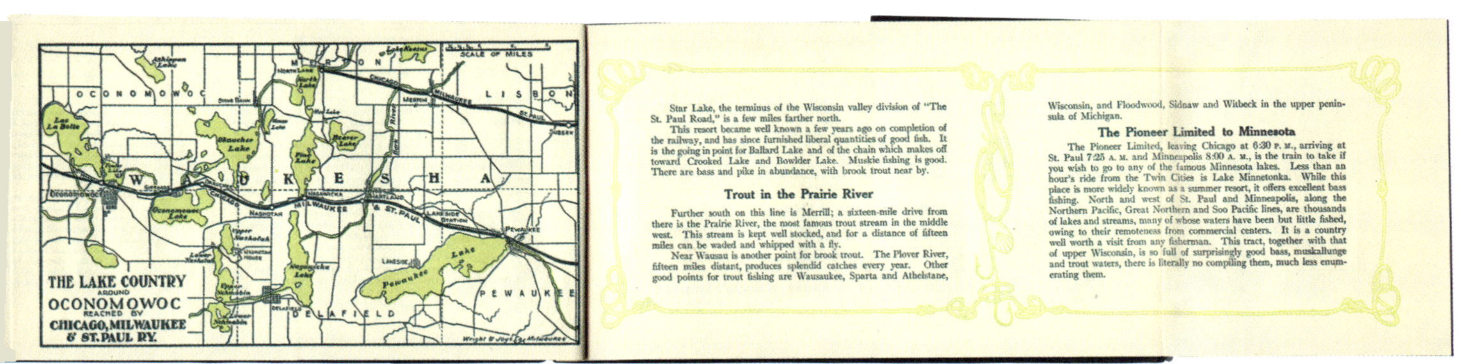

Star Lake, the terminus of the Wisconsin valley division of "The St. Paul Road," is a few miles farther north.

This resort became well known a few years ago on completion of the railway, and has since furnished liberal quantities of good fish. It is the going in point for Ballard Lake and of the chain which makes off toward Crooked Lake and Bowlder Lake. Muskie fishing is good. There are bass and pike in abundance, with brook trout near by.

Trout in the Prairie River

Further south on this line is Merrill; a sixteen-mile drive from there is the Prairie River, the most famous trout stream in the middle west. This stream is kept well stocked, and for a distance of fifteen miles can be waded and whipped with a fly.

Near Wausau is another point for brook trout. The Plover River, fifteen miles distant, produces splendid catches every year. Other good points for trout fishing are Wausaukee, Sparta and Athelstane, Wisconsin, and Floodwood, Sidnaw and Witbeck in the upper peninsula of Michigan.

The Pioneer Limited to Minnesota

The Pioneer Limited, leaving Chicago at 6:30 P. M., arriving at St. Paul 7:25 A. M. and Minneapolis 8:00 A. M., is the train to take if you wish to go to any of the famous Minnesota lakes. Less than an hour's ride from the Twin Cities is Lake Minnetonka. While this place is more widely known as a summer resort, it offers excellent bass fishing. North and west of St. Paul and Minneapolis, along the Northern Pacific, Great Northern and Soo Pacific lines, are thousands of lakes and streams, many of whose waters have been but little fished, owing to their remoteness from commercial centers. It is a country well worth a visit from any fisherman. This tract, together with that of upper Wisconsin, is so full of surprisingly good bass, muskallunge and trout waters, there is literally no compiling them, much less enumerating them.

57(f)

CHICAGO, MILWAUKEE, & ST. PAUL RAILWAY. *It Depends on the Line.* [CHICAGO]: CHICAGO, MILWAUKEE, & ST. PAUL RAILWAY, [1905?]. [SH 464 M53 18 1905] 11.4 CM X 20.8 CM

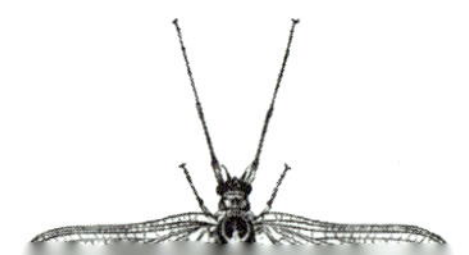

58

MATUZAKI, MEIZI. *Angling in Japan*. TRANS. R. OKADA. [TOKYO]: BOARD OF TOURIST INDUSTRY, JAPANESE GOVERNMENT RAILWAYS, 1940. [SH 659 M32 1940] 19.8 CM X 13.5 CM

This guide to angling in Japan was issued by the Japanese Government Railways as part of their Tourist Library. The guide includes sections on Japanese culture and traditional fishing methods as well as angling opportunities for the traveller. It is targeted at a western audience despite its printing during World War II.

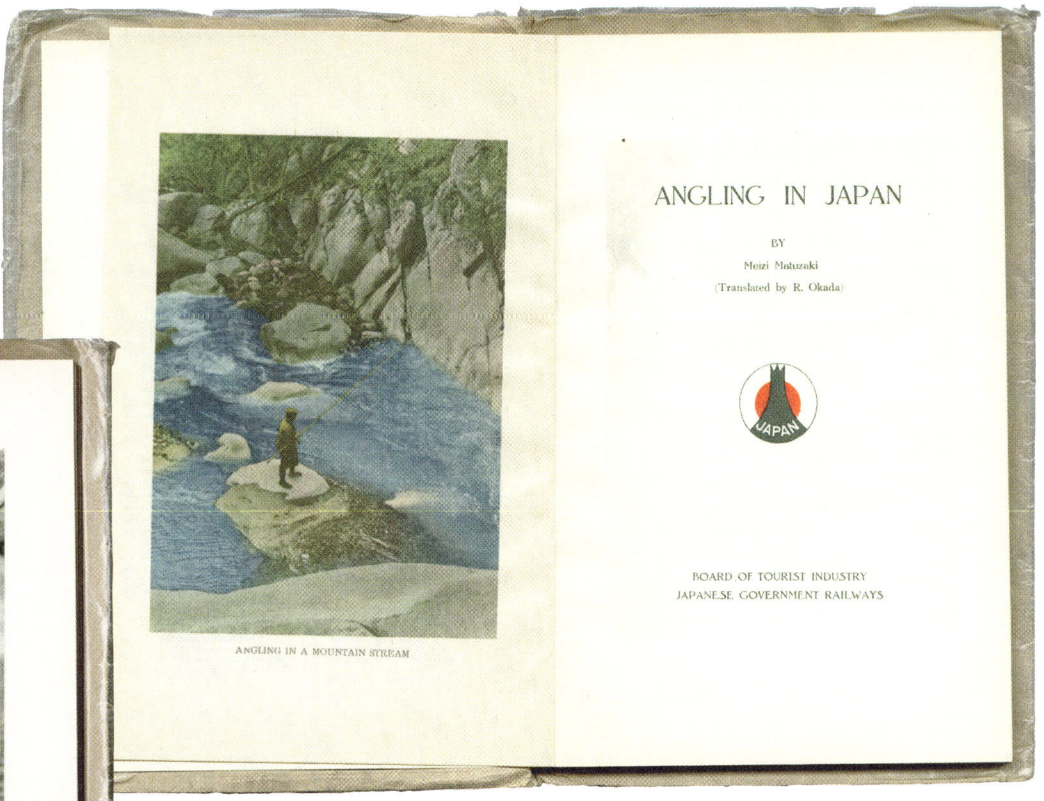

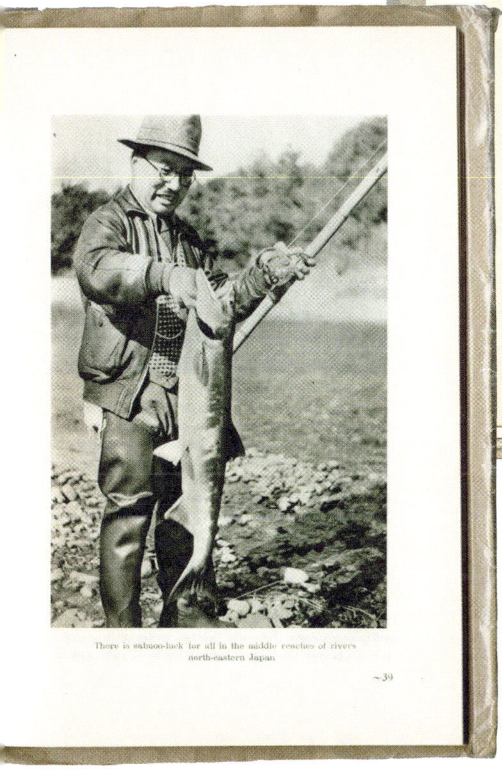

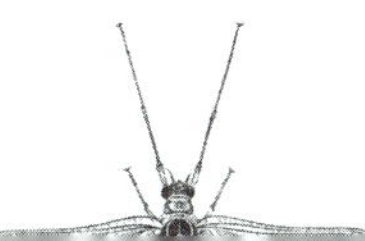

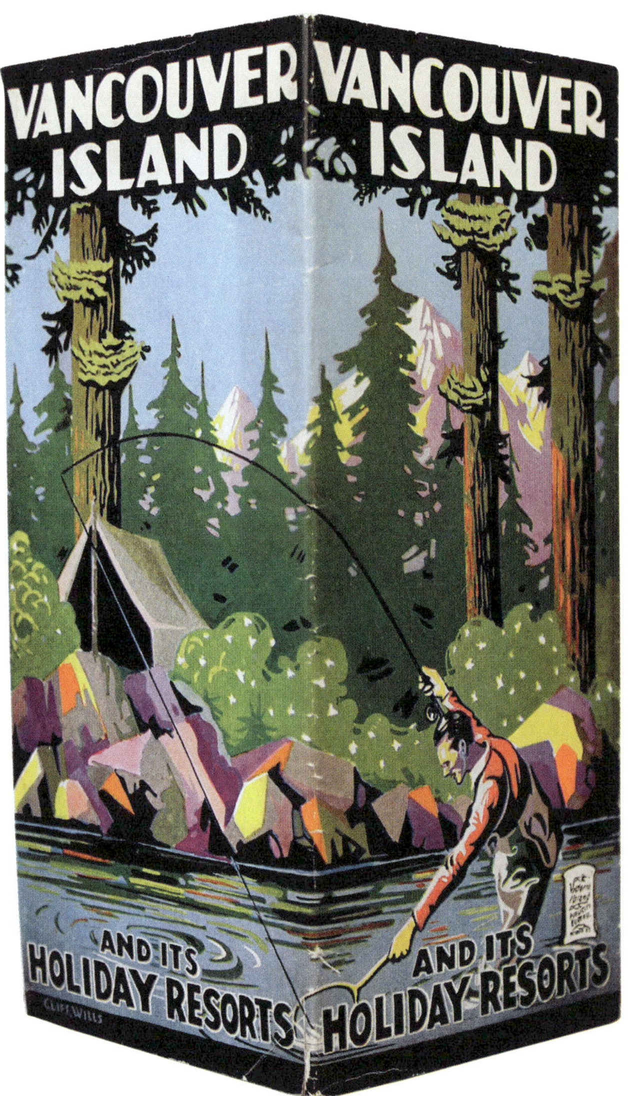

59

VICTORIA & ISLAND PUBLICITY BUREAU. *Vancouver Island and Its Holiday Resorts.* VICTORIA: VICTORIA & ISLAND PUBLICITY BUREAU, [BETWEEN 1921 AND 1930?]. [FC 3844.2 V36 1920Z] 23.4 CM X 11.0 CM

Similar to the railway ephemera, regional tourism organizations also issued brochures targeting anglers and sportsmen. This example is an attractive pamphlet issued by the Victoria & Island Publicity Bureau to entice anglers to its resorts.

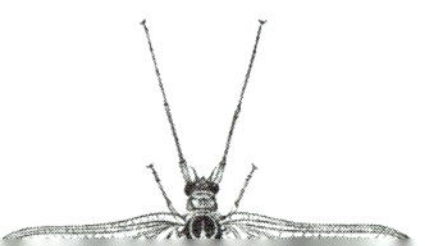

CANADIAN ANGLING

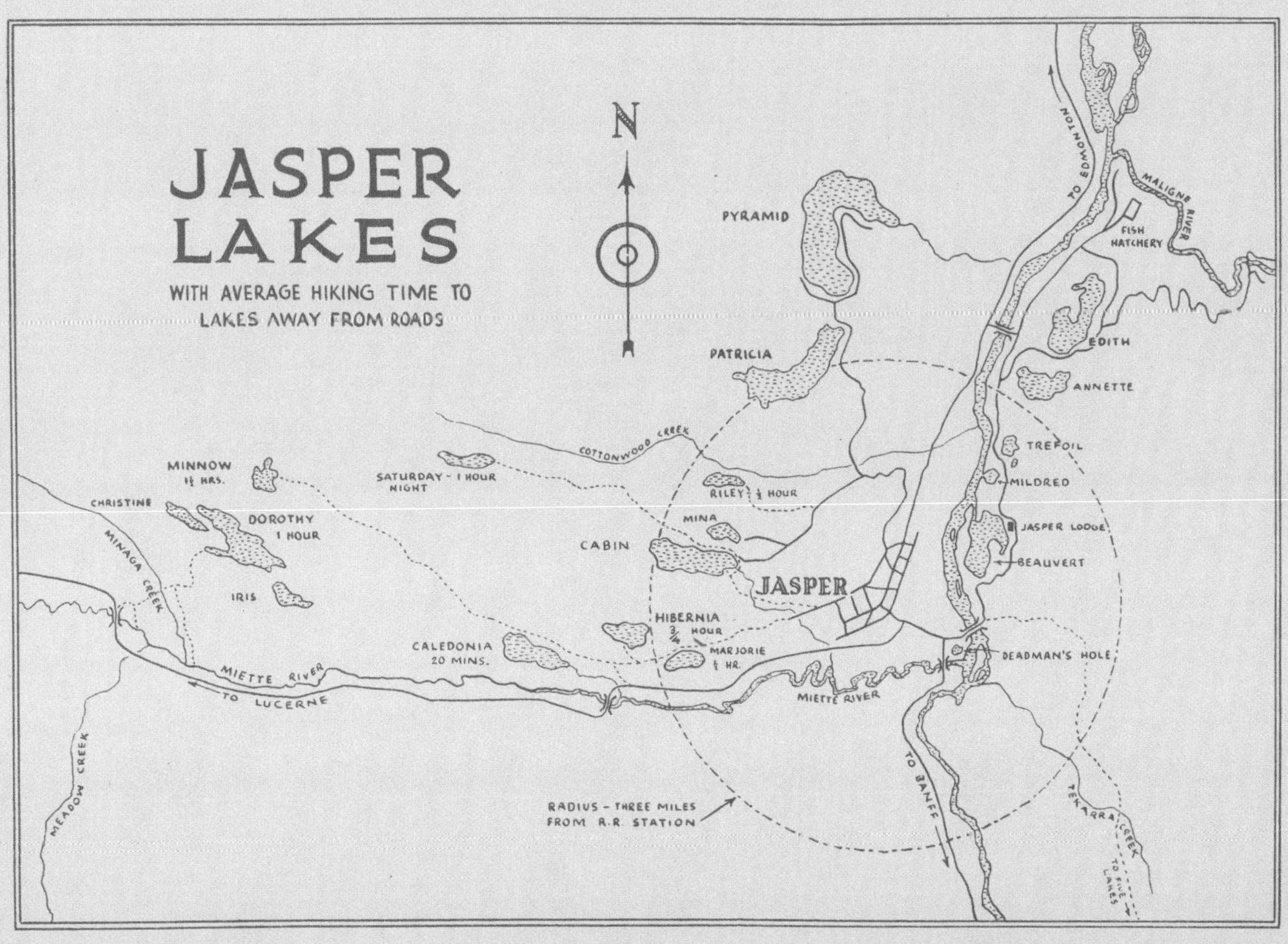

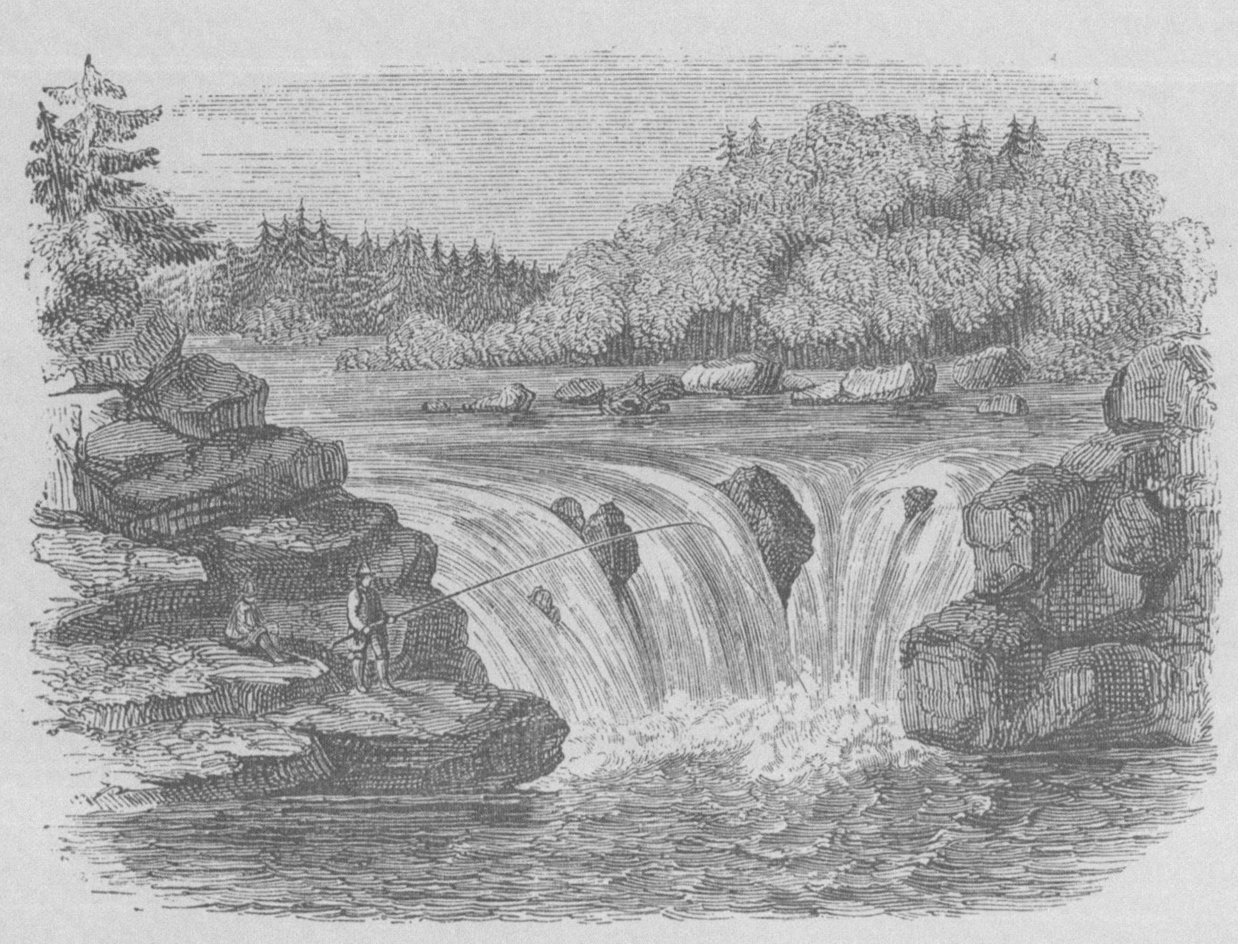

THE CHUTE-EN-HAUT

CANADIAN ANGLING

THIS SECTION PRESENTS BOOKS spanning nearly 150 years of Canadian angling. It includes early accounts of fishing in eastern Canada, works by Roderick Haig-Brown, and guidebooks to fishing specific locales in Alberta. Several of the titles presented here have made important contributions to the canon of angling literature and are cornerstones for the angling library.

Some books would also be at home in the "Angling as Adventure" section; however, they are included here for their primary importance to angling in Canada. Early books on recreational angling in Canada were often travel narratives penned by visitors from Europe. News of Canada's spectacular fishing opportunities—especially for salmon—spread quickly, and numerous titles were printed about Canadian angling in the late nineteenth and early twentieth centuries. One of the most desirable angling books on any topic—Dean Sage's *The Ristigouche and Its Salmon Fishing*—is a Canadian fishing book.

60

TOLFREY, FREDERIC. *The Sportsman in Canada.* 2 VOLS. LONDON: T.C. NEWBY, 1845. [FC 72 T649 1845 V.1–2] 19.0 CM X 12.6 CM

This scarce book is an account of Frederic Tolfrey's deployment to Quebec with the British military from 1816 to 1820. In addition to details of his fishing and hunting exploits, Tolfrey makes observations on every-day Canadian life. The book includes descriptions of fishing for trout and salmon (which would be familiar targets for a Briton visiting Canada); however, it is notable for a very early description of "musky" fishing in Canada. Tolfrey refers to the muskellunge as "muskanungee, a kind of mammoth pike" (80), and gives a lively account of hooking, playing, and landing a 42-pound musky in Lake Champlain:

> I have hooked and played a shark many a times on the broad Atlantic in calm weather, but my arms never ached more from exertion than on the occasion I am recording. Having incautiously handled my rod after the European fashion, my fingers were cruelly cut by the line being whisked through them with such extraordinary velocity: the excitement as well as the novelty of the affair prevented my noticing the inconvenience at the time: I shall never forget the sensation I experienced on feeling such a monster at the end of my line. (84–85)

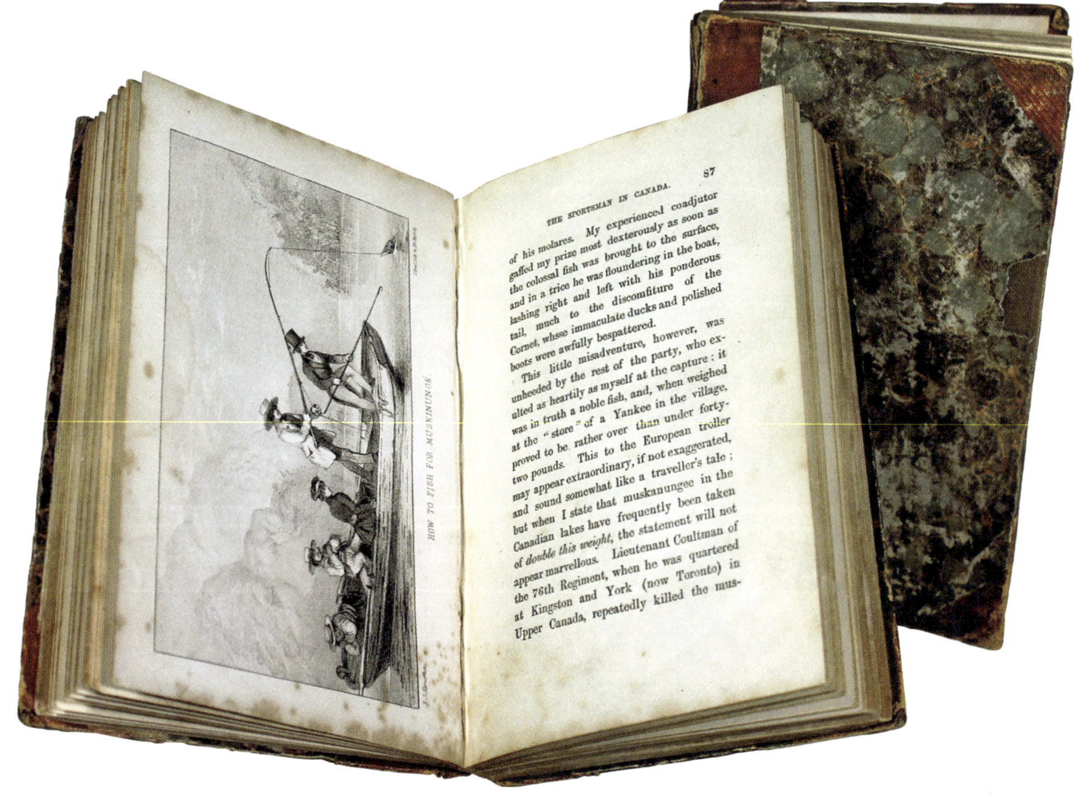

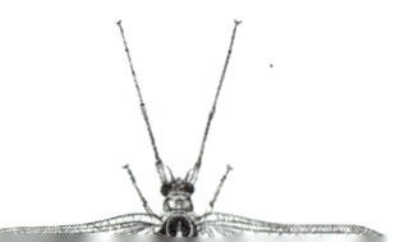

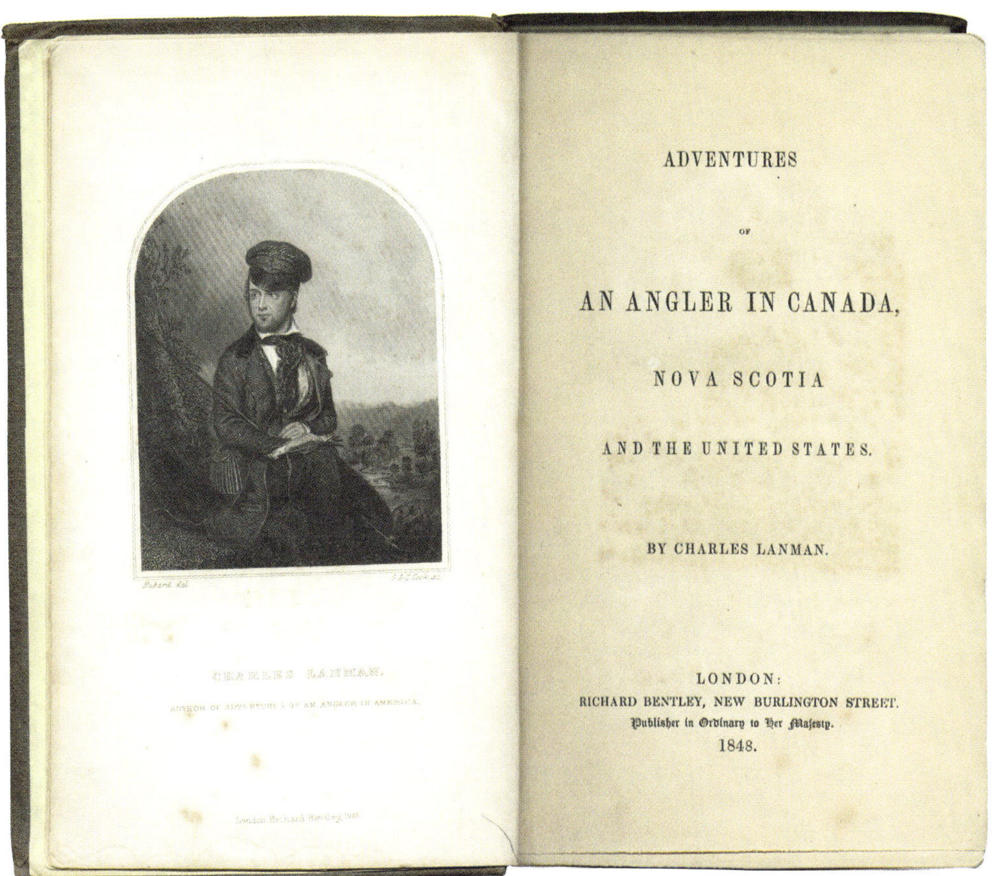

ADVENTURES

OF

AN ANGLER IN CANADA,

NOVA SCOTIA

AND THE UNITED STATES.

BY CHARLES LANMAN.

LONDON:
RICHARD BENTLEY, NEW BURLINGTON STREET.
Publisher in Ordinary to Her Majesty.
1848.

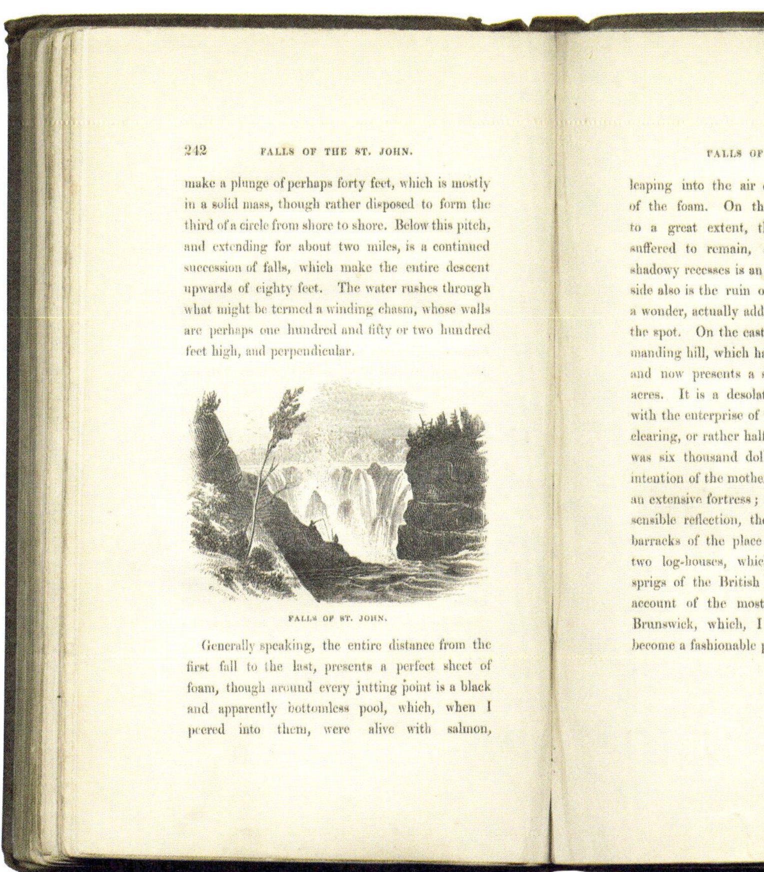

242 FALLS OF THE ST. JOHN.

make a plunge of perhaps forty feet, which is mostly in a solid mass, though rather disposed to form the third of a circle from shore to shore. Below this pitch, and extending for about two miles, is a continued succession of falls, which make the entire descent upwards of eighty feet. The water rushes through what might be termed a winding chasm, whose walls are perhaps one hundred and fifty or two hundred feet high, and perpendicular.

FALLS OF ST. JOHN.

Generally speaking, the entire distance from the first fall to the last, presents a perfect sheet of foam, though around every jutting point is a black and apparently bottomless pool, which, when I peered into them, were alive with salmon,

61

LANMAN, CHARLES. *Adventures of an Angler in Canada, Nova Scotia and the United States.* LONDON: RICHARD BENTLEY, 1848. [SH 572 Q4 L26 1848] 20.8 CM X 13.3 CM

Like Tolfrey's, Lanman's book provides early observations on recreational salmon fishing in Canada, including on the Saguenay River in Quebec. Lanman published several books on angling and other adventures in the Canadian and American wildernesses.

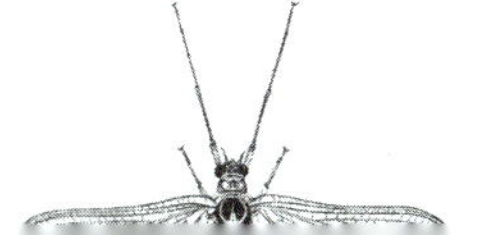

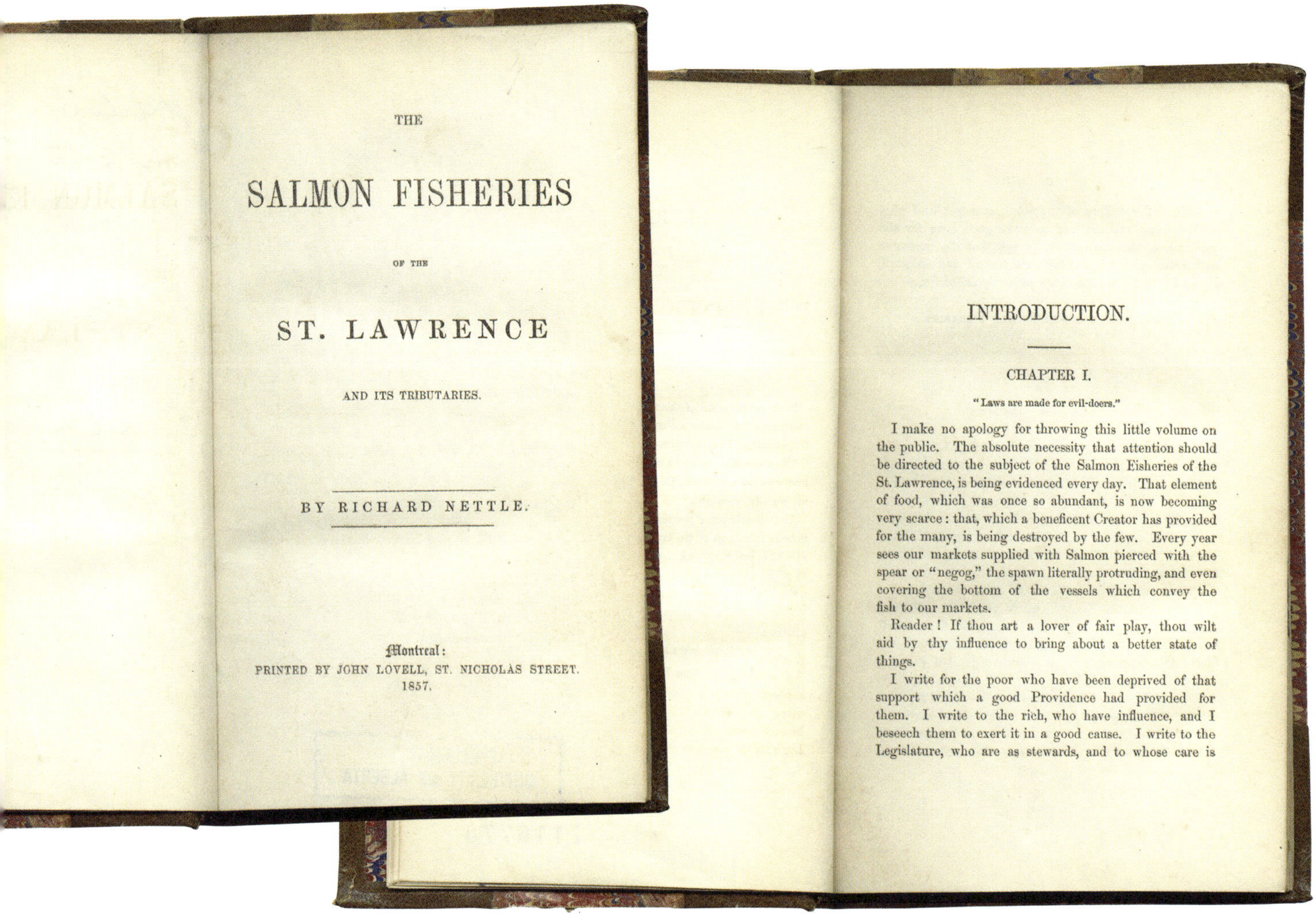

62

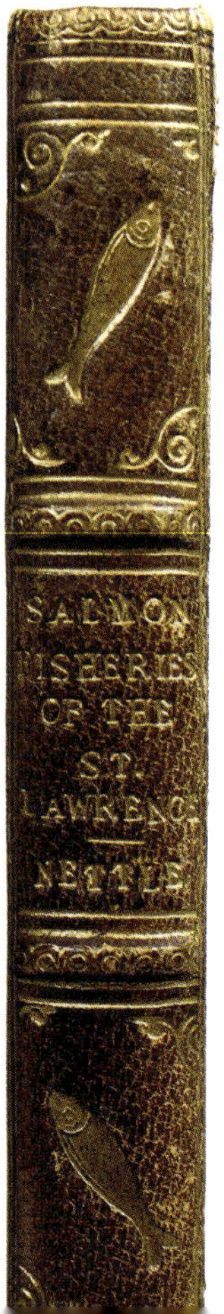

NETTLE, RICHARD. *The Salmon Fisheries of the St. Lawrence and Its Tributaries.* MONTREAL: N.P., 1857. [SH 346 N47] 19.1 CM X 11.6 CM

Nettle's book provides an introduction to the salmon fisheries of the St. Lawrence River and some of its tributaries. It includes descriptions of fishing with artificial flies and of trout fishing, but it is notable for many admonitions against overfishing, such as this strongly-worded passage: "Man, the destroyer man—commenced a war of extermination, hunted [salmon] with nets of all description, —with spear, with hook, with lister, poisoned them with lime, spearing them by torch-light, mangling and wounding as many as he killed—and to crown all—denied them a right of way, by building Dams—and thus destroyed their fisheries indeed" (8).

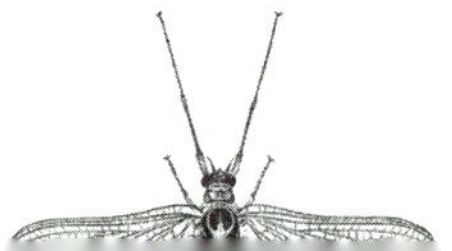

63

[ADAMSON, WILLIAM AGAR]. *Salmon-fishing in Canada by a Resident.* LONDON: LONGMAN, GREEN, LONGMAN, AND ROBERTS, 1860. [SH 571 A22 C.3] 18.7 CM X 12.8 CM

James Edward Alexander, the book's editor, was an explorer and soldier in the British Army. He served in Canada, where he collected some of the information and advice presented in this book. Alexander poses the remarkable question, "Is there salmon fishing in Canada?" as the title of the second chapter. Subsequent chapters give advice on salmon flies suitable for Canadian waters and the location of salmon rivers.

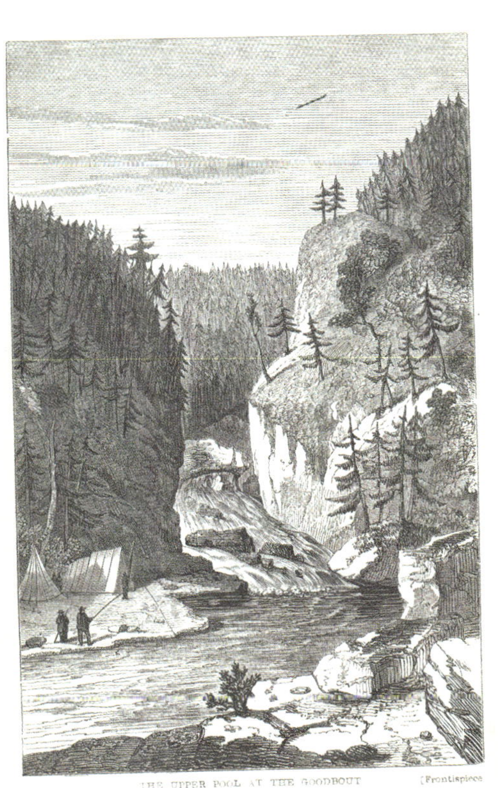

THE UPPER POOL AT THE GODBOUT [Frontispiece

Adamson, W. A.

SALMON-FISHING

IN CANADA

BY A RESIDENT

EDITED BY

COLONEL SIR JAMES EDWARD ALEXANDER

KNT. K.C.L.S. 14TH REGT.

AUTHOR OF 'EXPLORATIONS IN AMERICA, AFRICA, ETC.'

WITH ILLUSTRATIONS

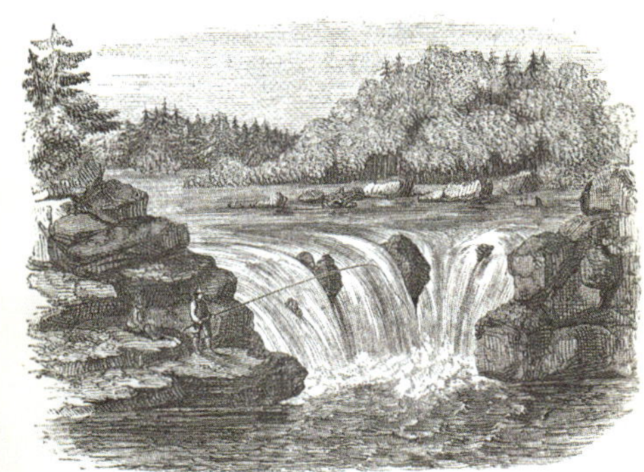

THE CHUTE-EN-HAUT

LONDON

LONGMAN, GREEN, LONGMAN, AND ROBERTS

1860

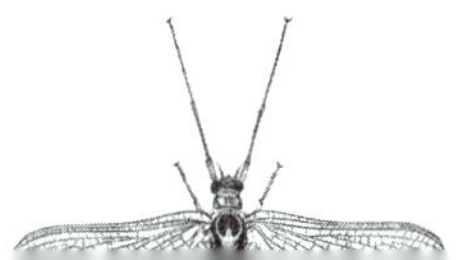

64

DEAN SAGE ON SALMON AND TROUT

Dean Sage was born into a wealthy New York family and showed an interest in fishing and book collecting at an early age. Sage made his first trip from New York to New Brunswick's Ristigouche River in 1875, where he fell in love with the river and its fishing. Sage was to return to the Ristigouche every year until his death in 1902 (Ledlie 1976). Sage's *The Ristigouche and Its Salmon Fishing* was lavish when it was published in 1888 and retailed for an impressive $100. One-hundred and five copies were printed; 50 of these were made available for sale publicly (25 in England and 25 in the United States), 50 were reserved for private presentation, and 5 copies were for public libraries (Ledlie 1977). The book immediately sold well and has remained one of the most desired angling books of any era. The book is celebrated for its design and illustrations and also as "the saga of a man and the river he loved – a potpourri of his personal adventures centered around a gentleman's retreat in the 'wilds' of Canada" (Ledlie 1977). While *The Ristigouche* was Sage's love letter to Canada and the river, his essays collected in *Salmon and Trout*, originally published in 1902, focused more on the technical aspects of Atlantic salmon fishing (Ledlie 1977).

Sage also assembled a renowned collection of fishing books, including many great rarities, that was sold at auction by Parke-Bernet Galleries in 1942. Sage's son commissioned the sale after continuing to build the collection himself. Sage's bookplate is present in *The London Angler's Book* exhibited here (item 48).

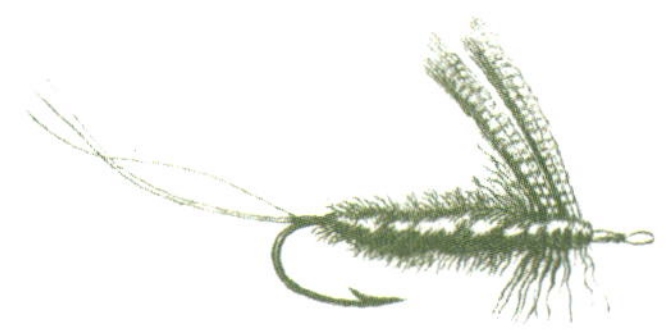

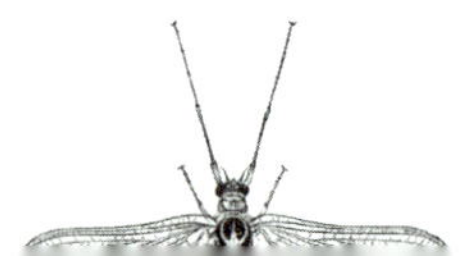

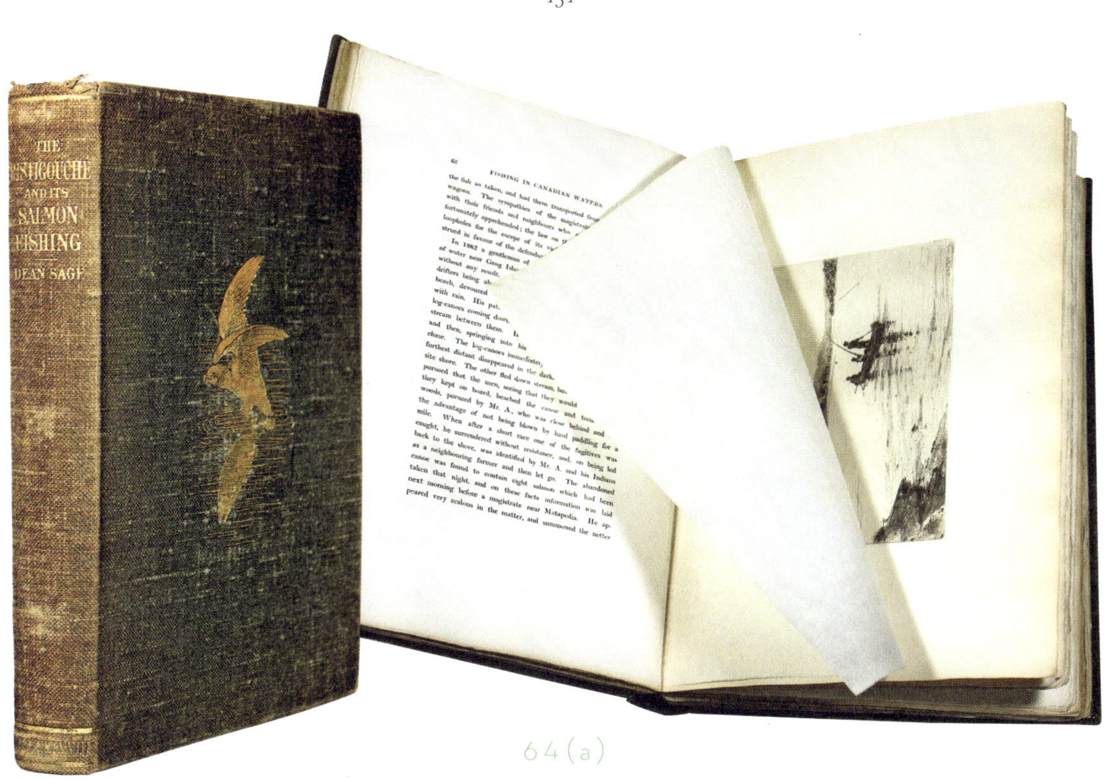

64(a)

SAGE, DEAN. *The Ristigouche and Its Salmon Fishing: With a Chapter on Angling Literature.* EDINBURGH: DAVID DOUGLAS, 1888. [SH 685 S24 R5 1888 FOLIO] 33.1 CM X 23.9 CM

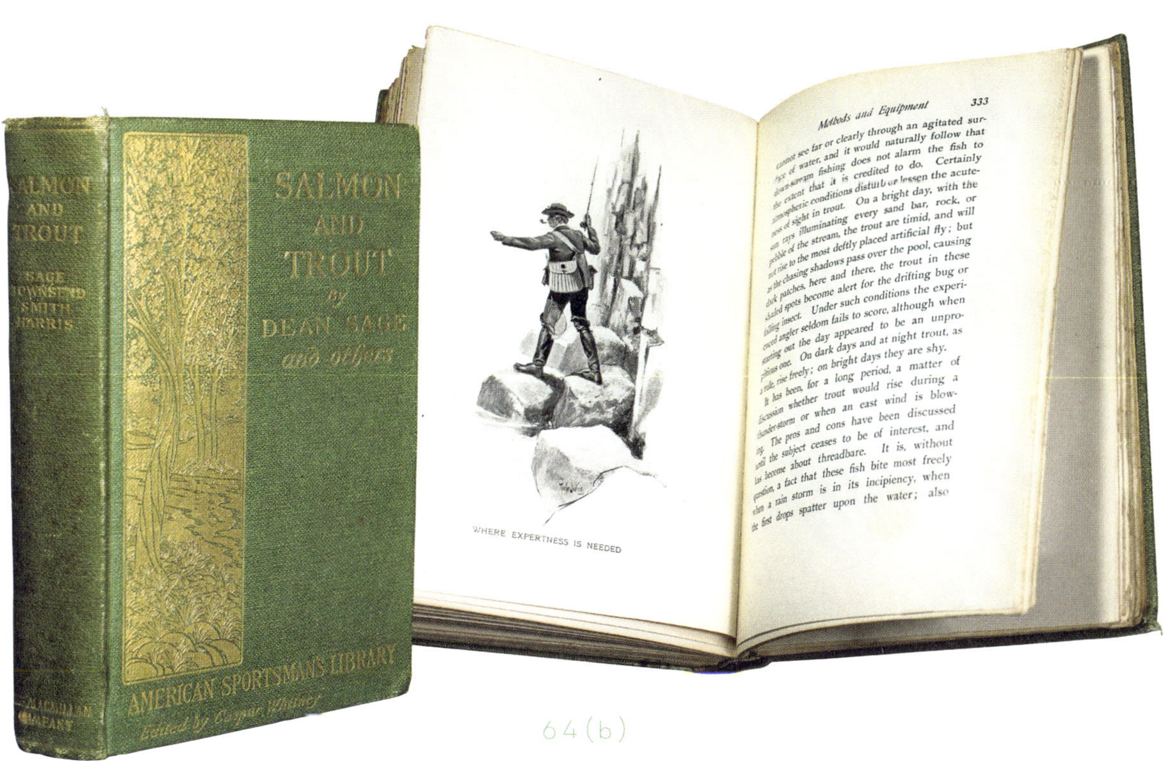

64(b)

SAGE, DEAN, C. H. TOWNSEND, H. M. SMITH, AND WILLIAM C. HARRIS. *Salmon and Trout.* NEW YORK: THE MACMILLAN COMPANY, 1904. [SH 441 S17 1904] 20.7 CM X 14.6 CM

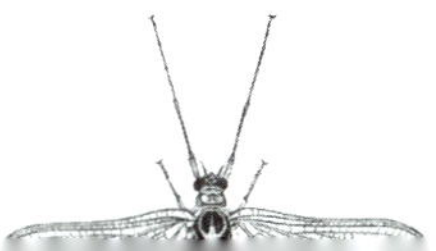

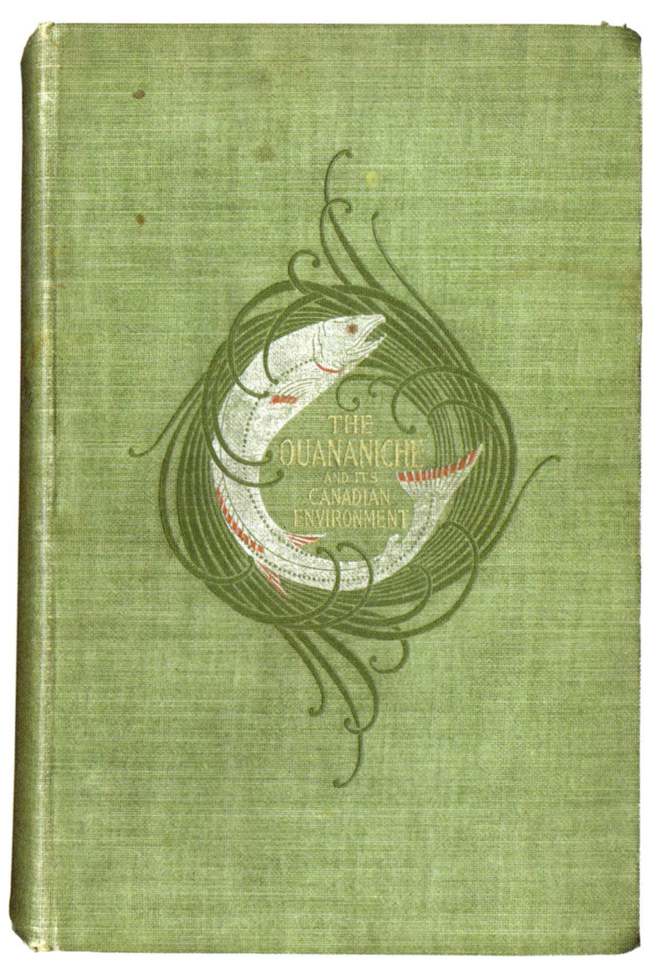

65

CHAMBERS, E[DWARD] T[HOMAS] D[AVIES]. *The Ouananiche and Its Canadian Environment*. NEW YORK: HARPER & BROTHERS, 1896. [SH 685 C44]
21.5 CM X 14.4 CM

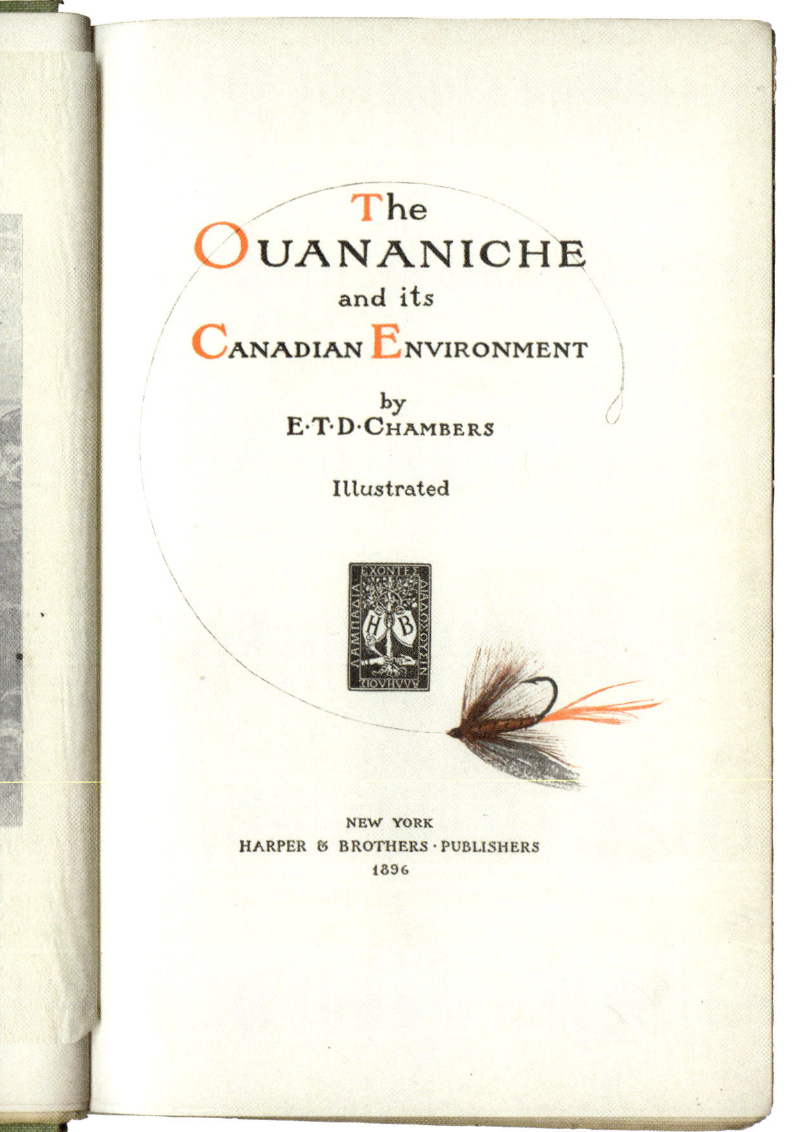

This is one of the few complete works dedicated to the ouananiche, the landlocked Atlantic salmon of Eastern Canada and the United States. The publisher's binding features a stylized cartouche of a salmon.

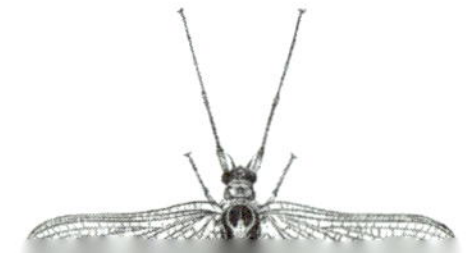

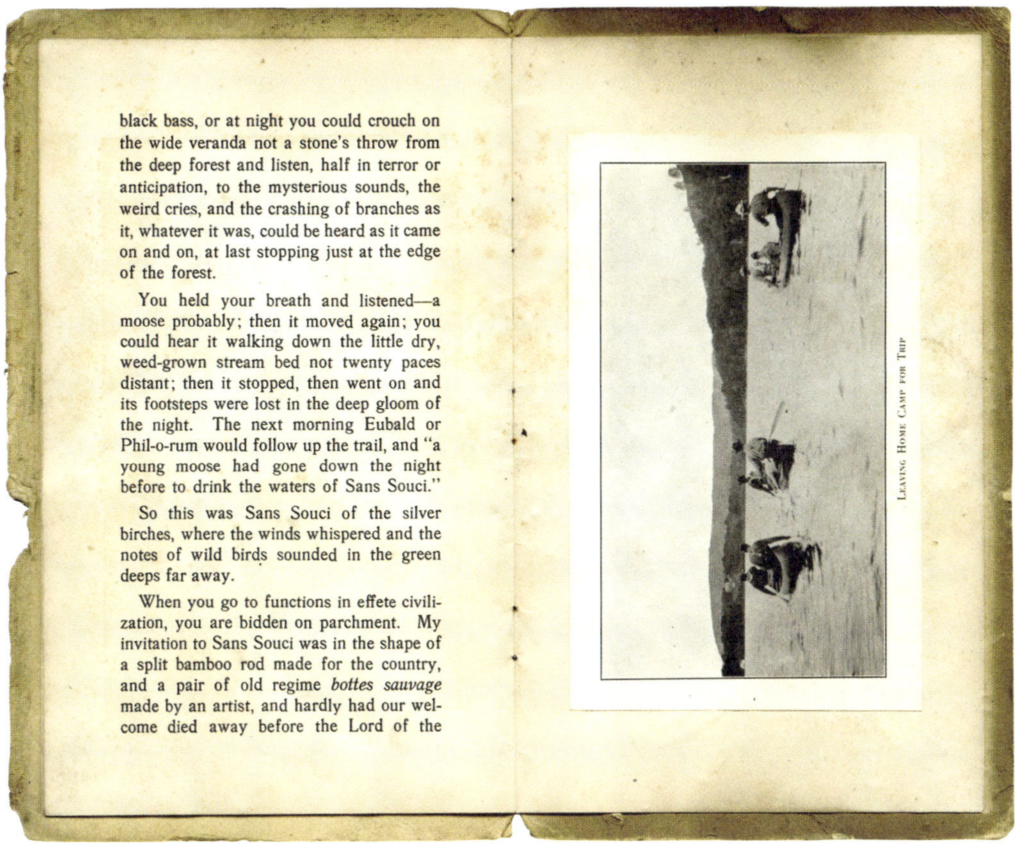
black bass, or at night you could crouch on the wide veranda not a stone's throw from the deep forest and listen, half in terror or anticipation, to the mysterious sounds, the weird cries, and the crashing of branches as it, whatever it was, could be heard as it came on and on, at last stopping just at the edge of the forest.

You held your breath and listened—a moose probably; then it moved again; you could hear it walking down the little dry, weed-grown stream bed not twenty paces distant; then it stopped, then went on and its footsteps were lost in the deep gloom of the night. The next morning Eubald or Phil-o-rum would follow up the trail, and "a young moose had gone down the night before to drink the waters of Sans Souci."

So this was Sans Souci of the silver birches, where the winds whispered and the notes of wild birds sounded in the green deeps far away.

When you go to functions in effete civilization, you are bidden on parchment. My invitation to Sans Souci was in the shape of a split bamboo rod made for the country, and a pair of old regime *bottes sauvage* made by an artist, and hardly had our welcome died away before the Lord of the

Leaving Home Camp for Trip

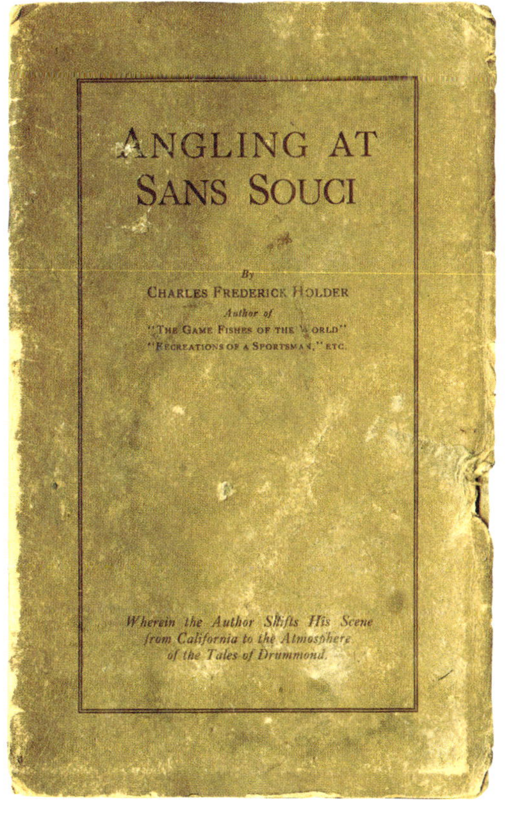
Angling at Sans Souci

By

Charles Frederick Holder

Author of

"The Game Fishes of the World"

"Recreations of a Sportsman," etc.

Wherein the Author Shifts His Scene from California to the Atmosphere of the Tales of Drummond.

66

HOLDER, CHARLES FREDERICK. *Angling at Sans Souci: Wherein the Author Shifts His Scene from California to the Atmosphere of the Tales of Drummond.* N.P.: N.P., [BETWEEN 1913 AND 1915?]. [SH 572 Q3 H66 1910Z] 20.3 CM X 12.7 CM

This is a very scarce, undated pamphlet with a story by angling author, zoologist, and "inventor" of deep-sea fishing, Charles Frederick Holder. It includes a short tale of travel and fishing in Sans Souci in Georgian Bay, Ontario. Only two other copies of this pamphlet are found in institutional collections, The Huntington Library and the University of Southern California.

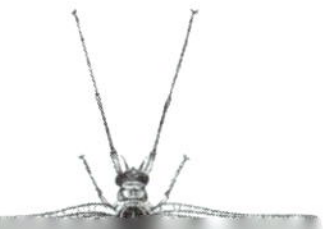

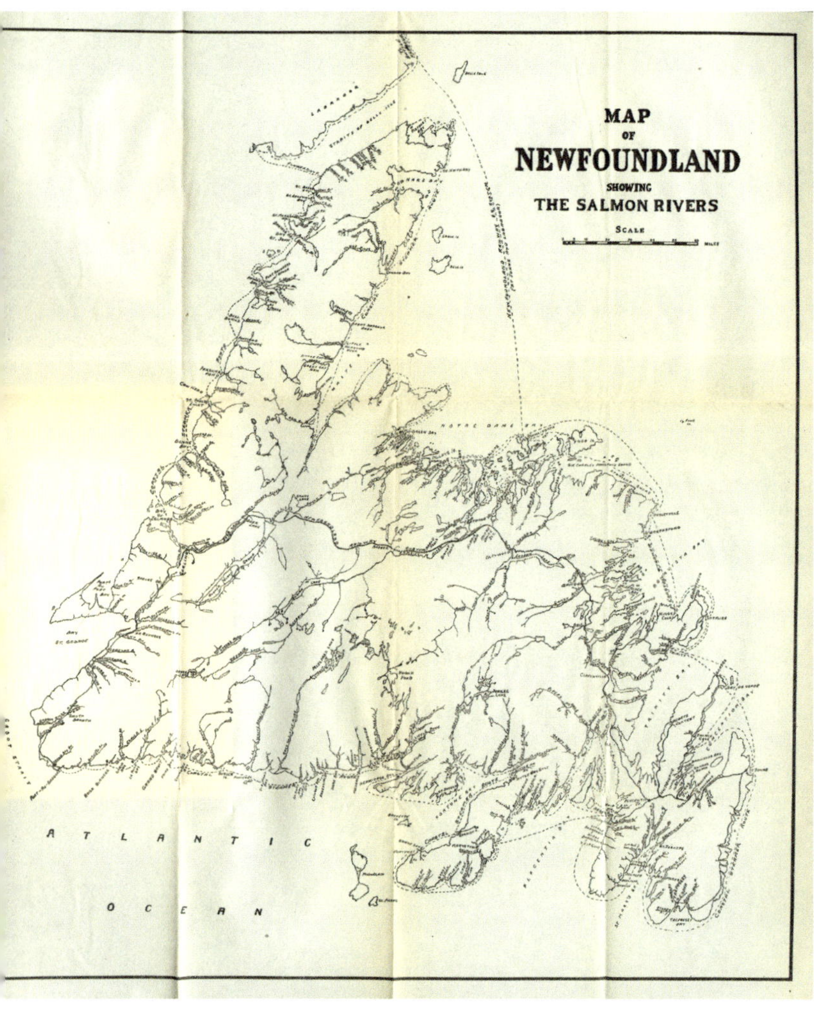

67

PALMER, C.H. *The Salmon Rivers of Newfoundland: A Descriptive Account of the Various Rivers of the Island.* BOSTON: N.P., 1928. [SH 685 P17 1928] 20.5 CM X 13.9 CM

Inside this book's unassuming paper wraps are scores of partially coloured, hand-sketched maps of rivers in Newfoundland. Many of the maps include local landmarks and names of specific pools and reaches.

SERPENTINE RIVER

Location—

On the West Coast 12 miles from the entrance to Bay of Islands.

Accessibility—

Readily reached by motor boat from Curling in Bay of Islands, on the Newfoundland Railway, a total distance of approximately 30 miles.

Accommodation—

Good hotel accommodation is available in Bay of Islands. There is no accommodation available on the river. Camping outfit with necessary supplies, canoes, etc., have to be brought from Curling.

Supplies, Boats, Canoes, Guides, etc.—

Bagg Bros., and Ayre & Sons, Ltd., general dealers at Curling, make a specialty of outfitting sportsmen and they will readily make all arrangements as to outfit, supplies, guides, canoes, motor boats, etc. Mr. Whittington of the Log Cabin, Spruce Brook, also outfits parties for this river.

Season—

Any time during July and August is a good time for fishing this river.

General Remarks—

This is a well-known river to which many anglers, from abroad, return year after year. It offers excellent fishing and the run of salmon is large, fish of 40 lbs. in weight having been caught. From the falls, a distance of approximately 5 miles, to the mouth of the river, are located many excellent pools and are the most readily accessible. Other pools are located above the falls to the outlet at Serpentine Lake. A trail leads from the lower pools to the falls. Excellent sea-trout fishing can be had in June and July at the mouth of the river. Camping sites along the river are numerous.

66

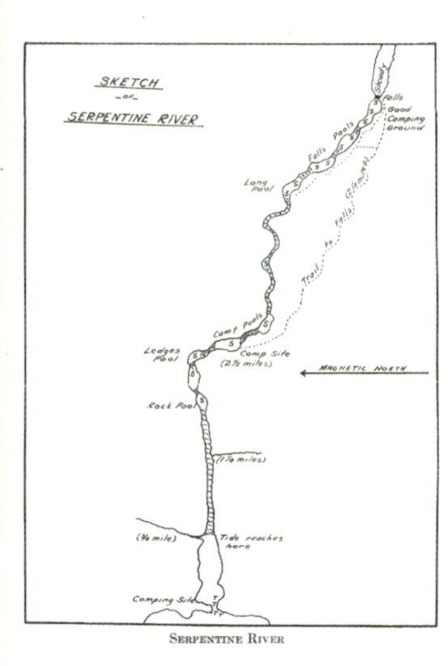

SERPENTINE RIVER

67

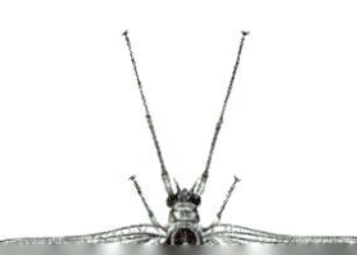

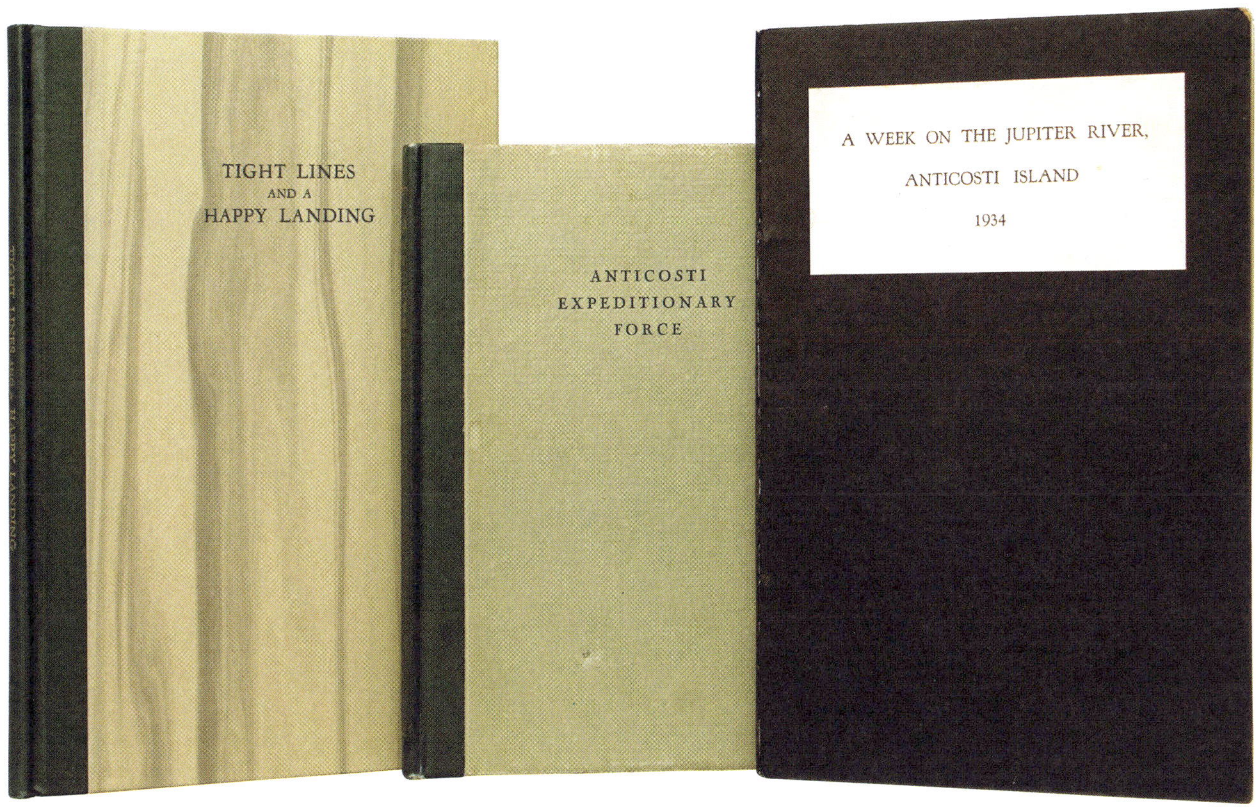

68

SALMON ADVENTURES ON ANTICOSTI ISLAND

These three titles are privately-printed examples of anglers' "expeditions" to Anticosti Island for its famed wilderness and Atlantic salmon fishing. Although larger than Prince Edward Island, *L'Île-d'Anticosti* is home to fewer than 250 permanent residents. All three titles are uncommon and describe incredible numbers of salmon taken by the angling parties.

A Week on the Jupiter River is a presentation copy from Vere Brabazon Ponsonby, 9th Earl of Bessborough to Colonel J.S. O'Meers, presented when Bessborough was 14th Governor General of Canada. Additional provenance from Bessborough's time as Governor General is tipped into the book, including an invitation to attend a luncheon and a signed letter from Eric Mackenzie, Comptroller of Government House in Ottawa, who was also on the trip. *A.E.F.: Anticosti Expeditionary Force* is inscribed by Ted and Marg Leisenring, with additional paper and pencil notes inlaid identifying individuals in photos.

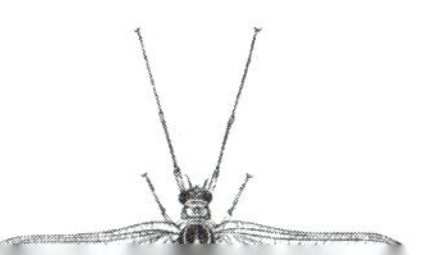

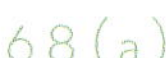

[PONSONBY, VERE BRABAZON]. *A Week on the Jupiter River, Anticosti Island by Baldemec.* N.P.: N.P., 1934. [SH 572 Q4 B35 1934] 23.2 CM X 15.3 CM NO. 60 OF 100 COPIES

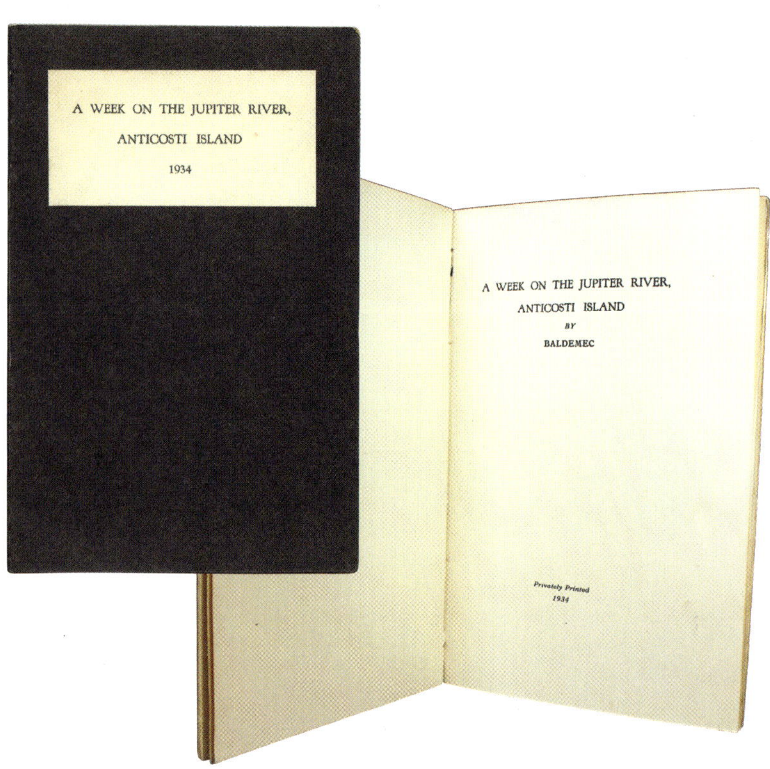

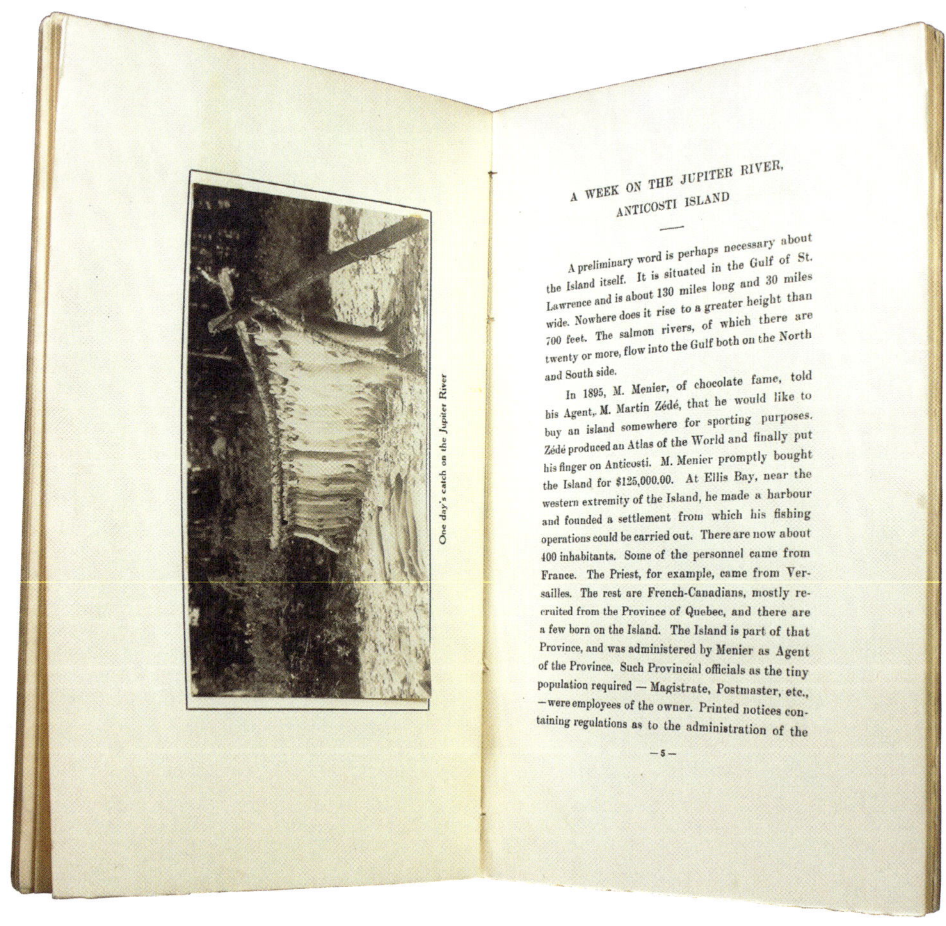

One day's catch on the Jupiter River

A WEEK ON THE JUPITER RIVER,
ANTICOSTI ISLAND

A preliminary word is perhaps necessary about the Island itself. It is situated in the Gulf of St. Lawrence and is about 130 miles long and 30 miles wide. Nowhere does it rise to a greater height than 700 feet. The salmon rivers, of which there are twenty or more, flow into the Gulf both on the North and South side.

In 1895, M. Menier, of chocolate fame, told his Agent, M. Martin Zédé, that he would like to buy an island somewhere for sporting purposes. Zédé produced an Atlas of the World and finally put his finger on Anticosti. M. Menier promptly bought the Island for $125,000.00. At Ellis Bay, near the western extremity of the Island, he made a harbour and founded a settlement from which his fishing operations could be carried out. There are now about 400 inhabitants. Some of the personnel came from France. The Priest, for example, came from Versailles. The rest are French-Canadians, mostly recruited from the Province of Quebec, and there are a few born on the Island. The Island is part of that Province, and was administered by Menier as Agent of the Province. Such Provincial officials as the tiny population required — Magistrate, Postmaster, etc., — were employees of the owner. Printed notices containing regulations as to the administration of the

— 5 —

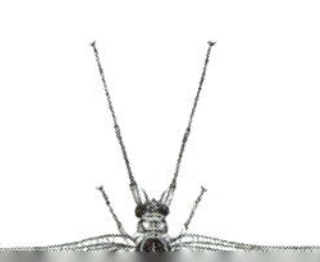

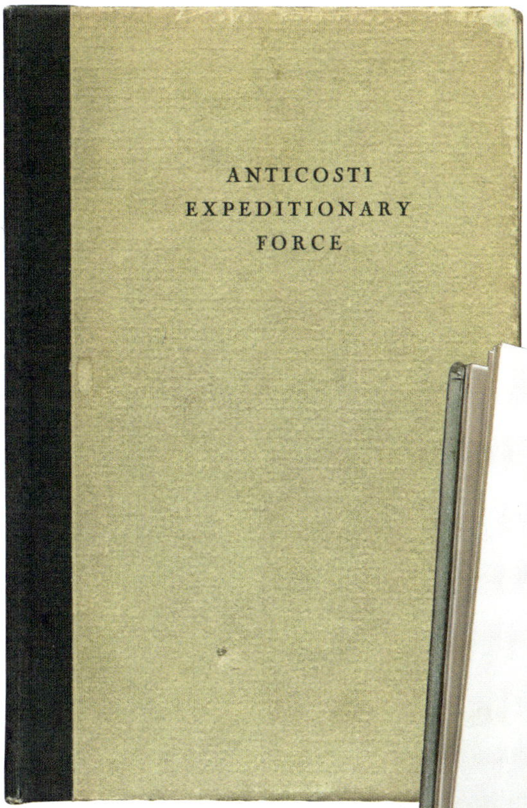

68(b)

PEW, ALBERTA C. *A.E.F.: Anticosti Expeditionary Force.* N.P.: N.P., 1935. [SH 572 Q3 P49 1935] 19.8 CM X 13.2 CM
NO. 27 OF 300 COPIES

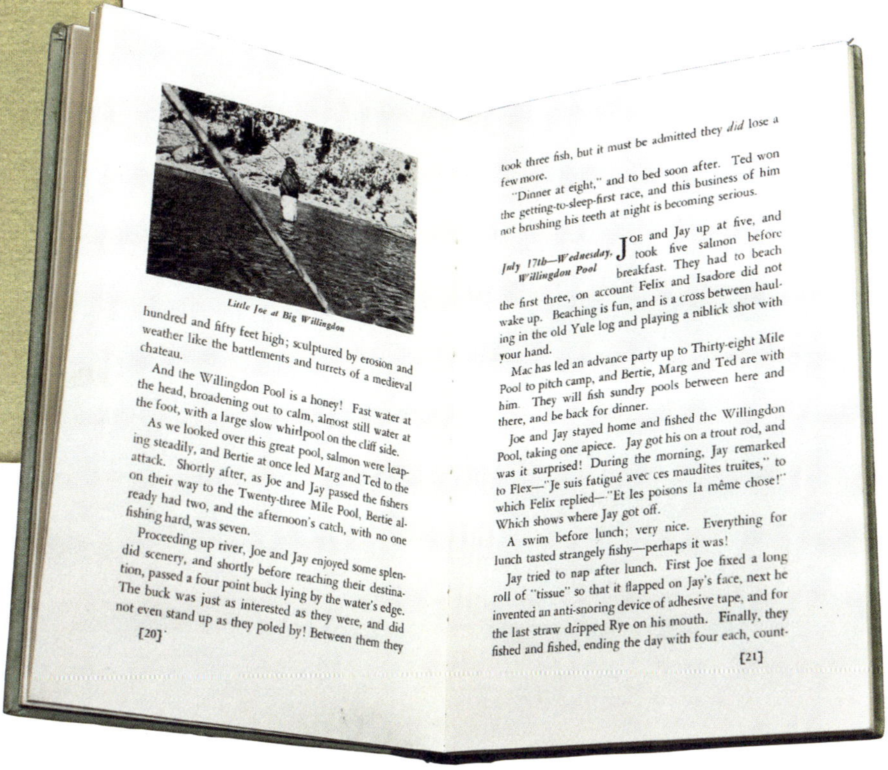

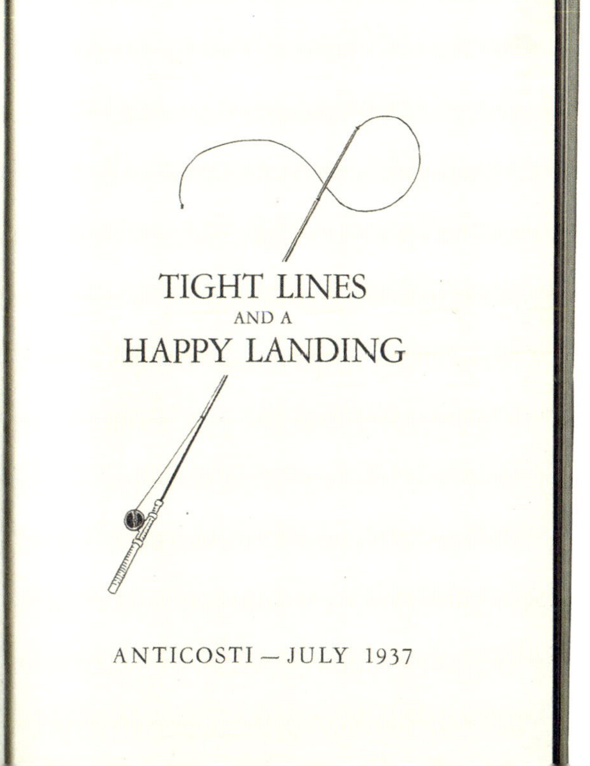

68(c)

[BRUCE, HOWARD]. *Tight Lines and a Happy Landing: Anticosti - July 1937.* N.P: N.P., [1937?]. [SH 685 T55 1937] 23.5 CM X 15.7 CM
NO. 227 OF 300 COPIES

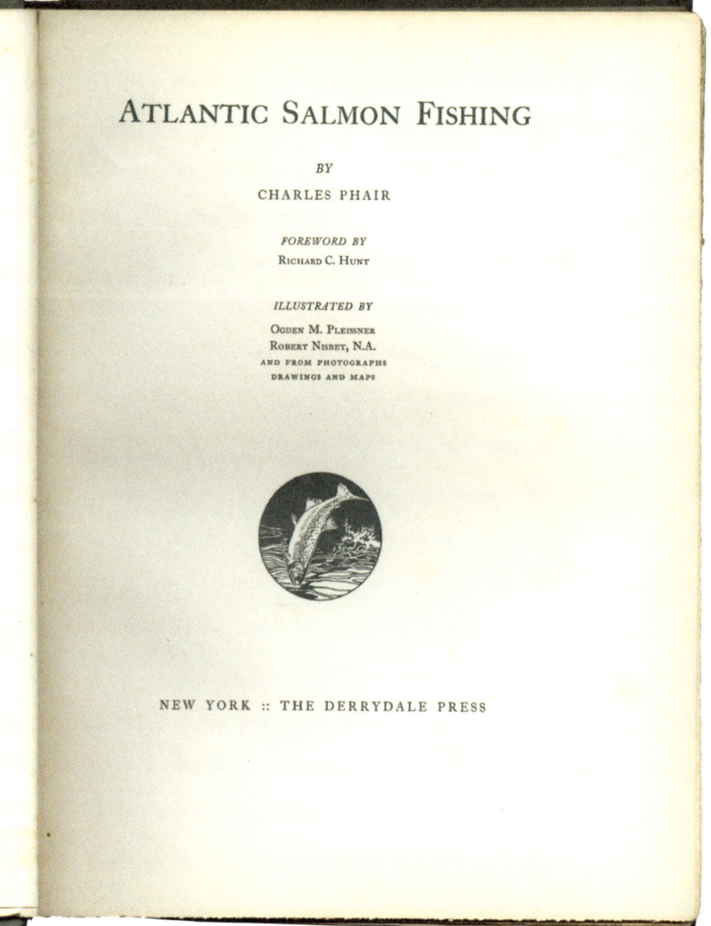

ATLANTIC SALMON FISHING

BY

CHARLES PHAIR

FOREWORD BY

RICHARD C. HUNT

ILLUSTRATED BY

OGDEN M. PLEISSNER

ROBERT NISBET, N.A.

AND FROM PHOTOGRAPHS

DRAWINGS AND MAPS

NEW YORK :: THE DERRYDALE PRESS

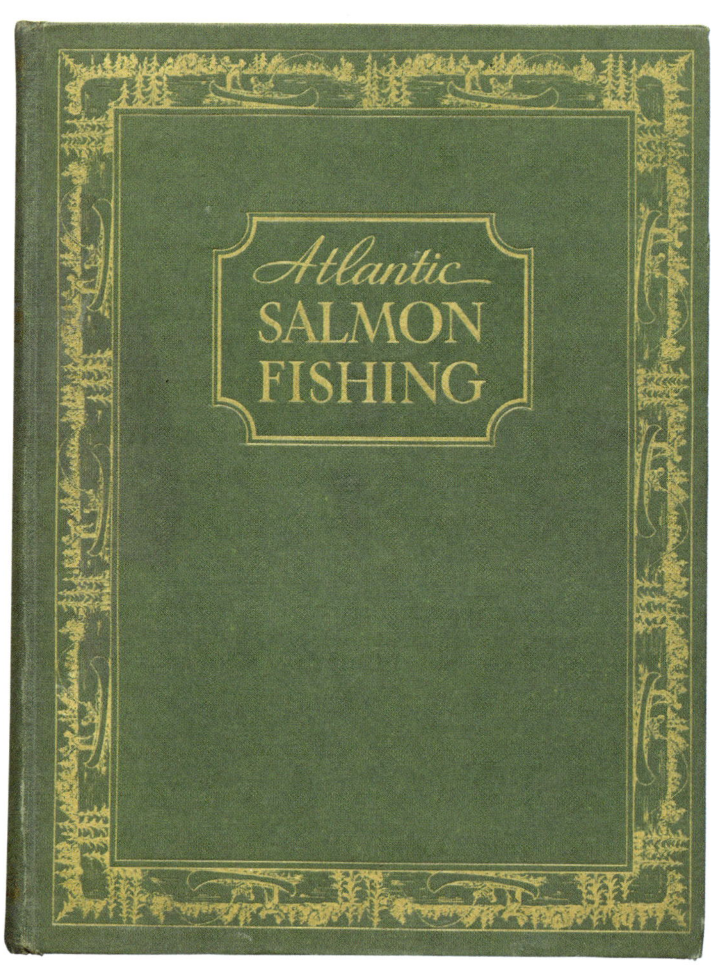

69

PHAIR, CHARLES. *Atlantic Salmon Fishing*. NEW YORK: DERRYDALE PRESS, 1937.
[SH 635 P5 1937 FOLIO] 32.3 CM X 24.9 CM | EDITION OF 950 COPIES

This classic Derrydale Press title lacks the dust jacket but is inscribed by Phair to his boss, Alan Rutherford Stuyvesant. *Atlantic Salmon Fishing* focuses on fishing in New Brunswick, Nova Scotia, Newfoundland, Labrador, and Maine with numerous plates, eight of which are full colour. This copy has additional ephemera laid in, including a map of the Mo River in Norway and an invitation to attend a "happy party" at the Anglers' Club of New York celebrating Lee Wulff's life.

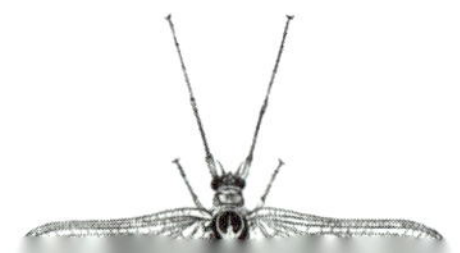

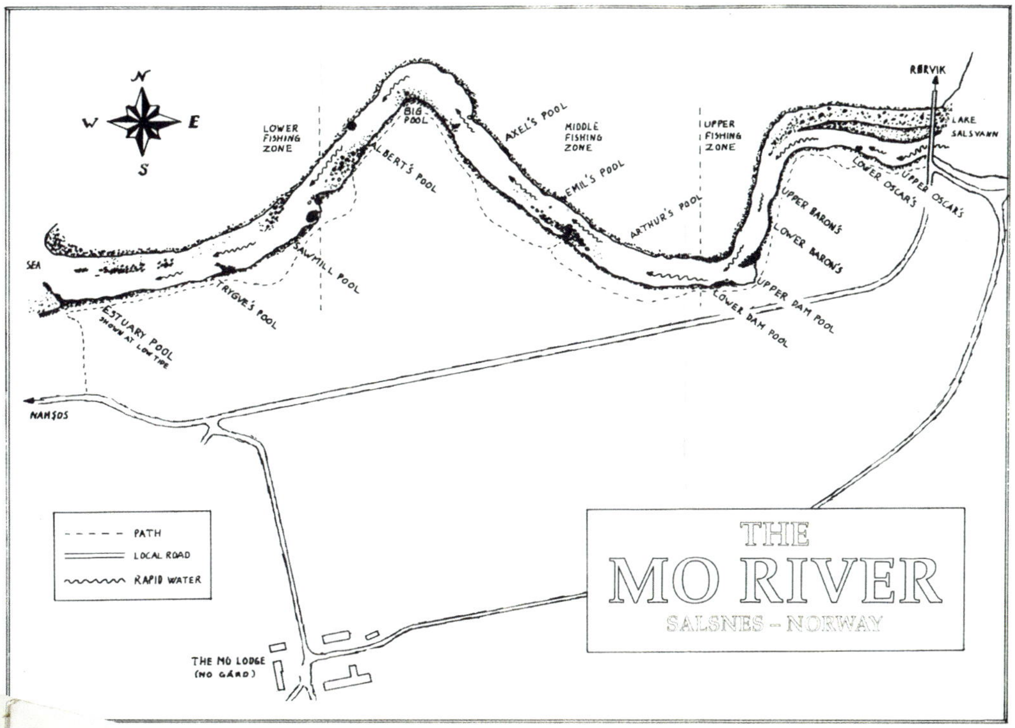

THE
MO RIVER
SALSNES — NORWAY

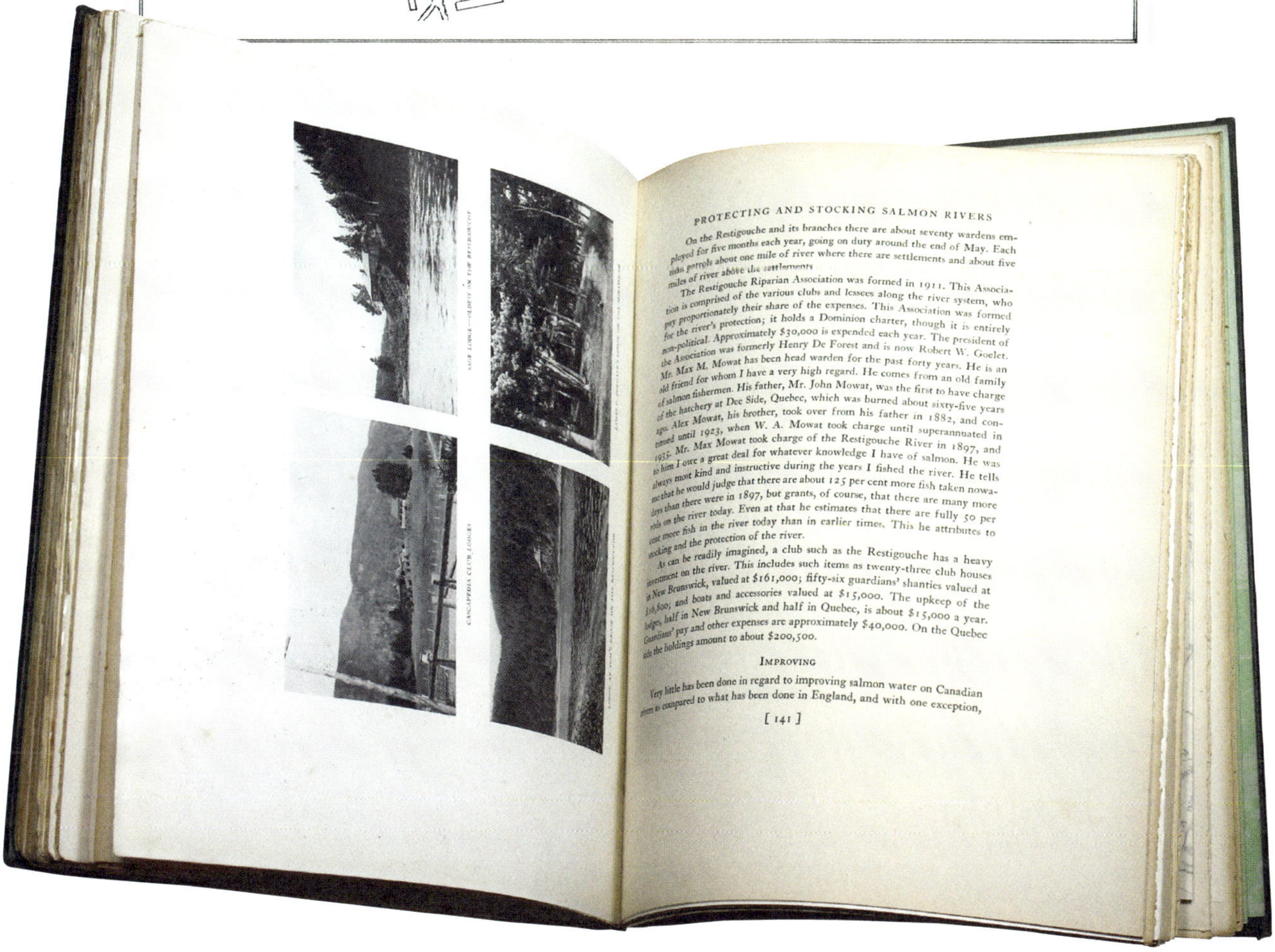

N
W
E
S
RØRVIK
LAKE SALSVANN
LOWER FISHING ZONE
MIDDLE FISHING ZONE
UPPER FISHING ZONE
BIG POOL
AXEL'S POOL
ALBERT'S POOL
EMIL'S POOL
ARTHUR'S POOL
UPPER BARON'S
LOWER BARON'S
LOWER OSCAR'S
UPPER OSCAR'S
SAWMILL POOL
TRYGVE'S POOL
ESTUARY POOL SHOWN AT LOW TIDE
UPPER DAM POOL
LOWER DAM POOL
SEA
NAMSOS
PATH
LOCAL ROAD
RAPID WATER
THE MO LODGE (MO GÅRD)

PROTECTING AND STOCKING SALMON RIVERS

On the Restigouche and its branches there are about seventy wardens employed for five months each year, going on duty around the end of May. Each man patrols about one mile of river where there are settlements and about five miles of river above the settlements.

The Restigouche Riparian Association was formed in 1911. This Association is comprised of the various clubs and lessees along the river system, who pay proportionately their share of the expenses. This Association was formed for the river's protection; it holds a Dominion charter, though it is entirely non-political. Approximately $30,000 is expended each year. The president of the Association was formerly Henry De Forest and is now Robert W. Goelet. Mr. Max M. Mowat has been head warden for the past forty years. He is an old friend for whom I have a very high regard. He comes from an old family of salmon fishermen. His father, Mr. John Mowat, was the first to have charge of the hatchery at Dee Side, Quebec, which was burned about sixty-five years ago. Alex Mowat, his brother, took over from his father in 1882, and continued until 1923, when W. A. Mowat took charge until superannuated in 1935. Mr. Max Mowat took charge of the Restigouche River in 1897, and to him I owe a great deal for whatever knowledge I have of salmon. He was always most kind and instructive during the years I fished the river. He tells me that he would judge that there are about 125 per cent more fish taken nowadays than there were in 1897, but grants, of course, that there are many more rods on the river today. Even at that he estimates that there are fully 50 per cent more fish in the river today than in earlier times. This he attributes to stocking and the protection of the river.

As can be readily imagined, a club such as the Restigouche has a heavy investment on the river. This includes such items as twenty-three club houses in New Brunswick, valued at $161,000; fifty-six guardians' shanties valued at $16,800; and boats and accessories valued at $15,000. The upkeep of the lodges, half in New Brunswick and half in Quebec, is about $15,000 a year. Guardians' pay and other expenses are approximately $40,000. On the Quebec side the holdings amount to about $200,500.

IMPROVING

Very little has been done in regard to improving salmon water on Canadian rivers as compared to what has been done in England, and with one exception,

[141]

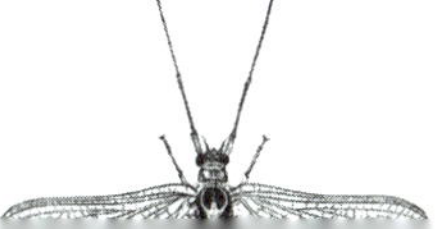

70

ANGLING LITERATURE AND OTHER WORKS BY RODERICK HAIG-BROWN

Roderick Haig-Brown is among Canada's most celebrated anglers, naturalists, and authors. He is the author of dozens of books and articles, both fiction and non-fiction, for children and adults and winner of the Governor General's Literary Award for *Saltwater Summer* (1948). Although Haig-Brown's work is primarily about angling and the outdoors, his writing transcends simple "outdoor" or "fishing" writing. Arnold Gingrich lists Haig-Brown and Izaak Walton as the two primary examples of "fishing authors" entering the realm of literature with a capital "L" (Gingrich 3 and 319). As well, a British Columbia literary prize is named in his honour, The Haig-Brown Heritage House in Campbell River is maintained as a museum with a yearly writer in residence, and Canada recently designated Haig-Brown as a National Historic Figure. On top of his literary accomplishments, Haig-Brown was a significant public advocate for conservation during the rapid industrialization of British Columbia in the middle of the twentieth century (Keeling 239).

This exhibition presents several works by Haig-Brown, starting with his first book, *Silver: The Life Story of an Atlantic Salmon*, which follows the protagonist, Silver, from birth until capture by an angler. *Return to the River* tells a similar story, but from the viewpoint of a Chinook Salmon on Canada's West Coast. *A River Never Sleeps* and Haig-Brown's Seasons Cycle (items 70d-70g) include the angler's musings on fishing, rivers, salmon, and natural history. The spectacular *The Salmon: Canada's Plea for a Threatened Species*, designed by Robert Reid and David Denbigh, is a portfolio that includes a deluxe edition of Haig-Brown's *The Salmon* and several large prints, including five silkscreens by Bill Reid. Finally, *Fly Patterns of Roderick Haig-Brown* presents patterns fished by Haig-Brown with a fly tied by Art Lingren.

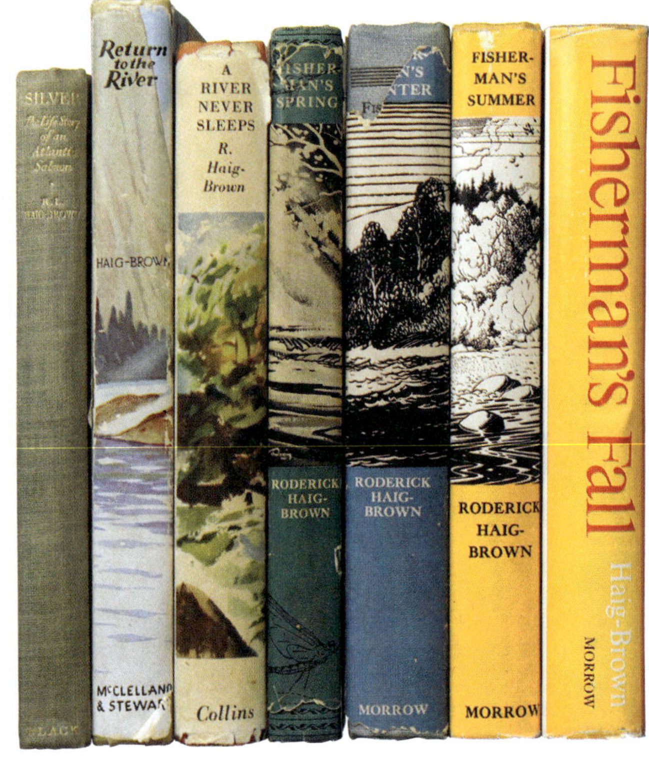

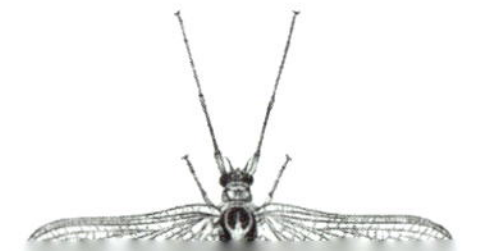

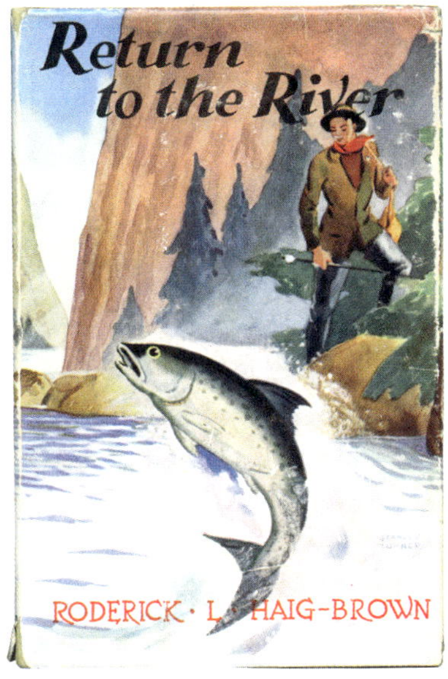

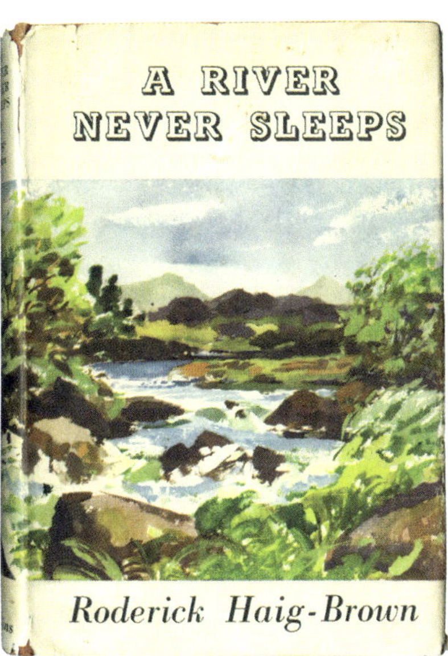

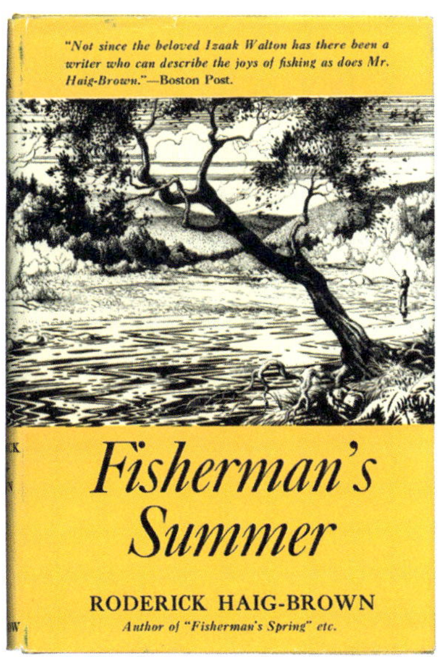

70 (a)

HAIG-BROWN, R[ODERICK] L. *Silver: The Life Story of an Atlantic Salmon*. LONDON: A. & C. BLACK, LTD., 1931. [QL 795 F7 H14 1931] 19.8 CM X 14.0 CM

70 (b)

HAIG-BROWN, RODERICK L. *Return to the River: A Story of the Chinook Run*. TORONTO: MCCLELLAND & STEWART LTD., 1946. [QL 795 F7 H1 1946] 22.0 CM X 14.8 CM

70 (c)

HAIG-BROWN, RODERICK. *A River Never Sleeps*. LONDON: COLLINS, 1948. [SH 441 H14 1948] 20.7 CM X 14.6 CM

70 (d)

HAIG-BROWN, RODERICK. *Fisherman's Spring*. TORONTO: COLLINS, 1951. [SH 443 C2 H14 1951] 21.0 CM X 14.3 CM

70 (e)

HAIG-BROWN, RODERICK. *Fisherman's Winter*. NEW YORK: WILLIAM MORROW & CO., 1954. [SH 587 H14] 21.0 CM X 14.2 CM

70 (f)

HAIG-BROWN, RODERICK. *Fisherman's Summer*. NEW YORK: WILLIAM MORROW & CO., 1959. [SH 441 H144] 21.0 CM X 14.6 CM

70 (g)

HAIG-BROWN, RODERICK. *Fisherman's Fall*. NEW YORK: WILLIAM MORROW & CO., 1964. [SH 462 H3 1964B] 20.8 CM X 14.6 CM

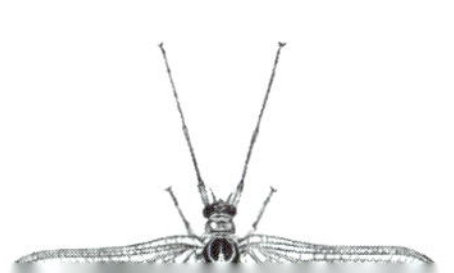

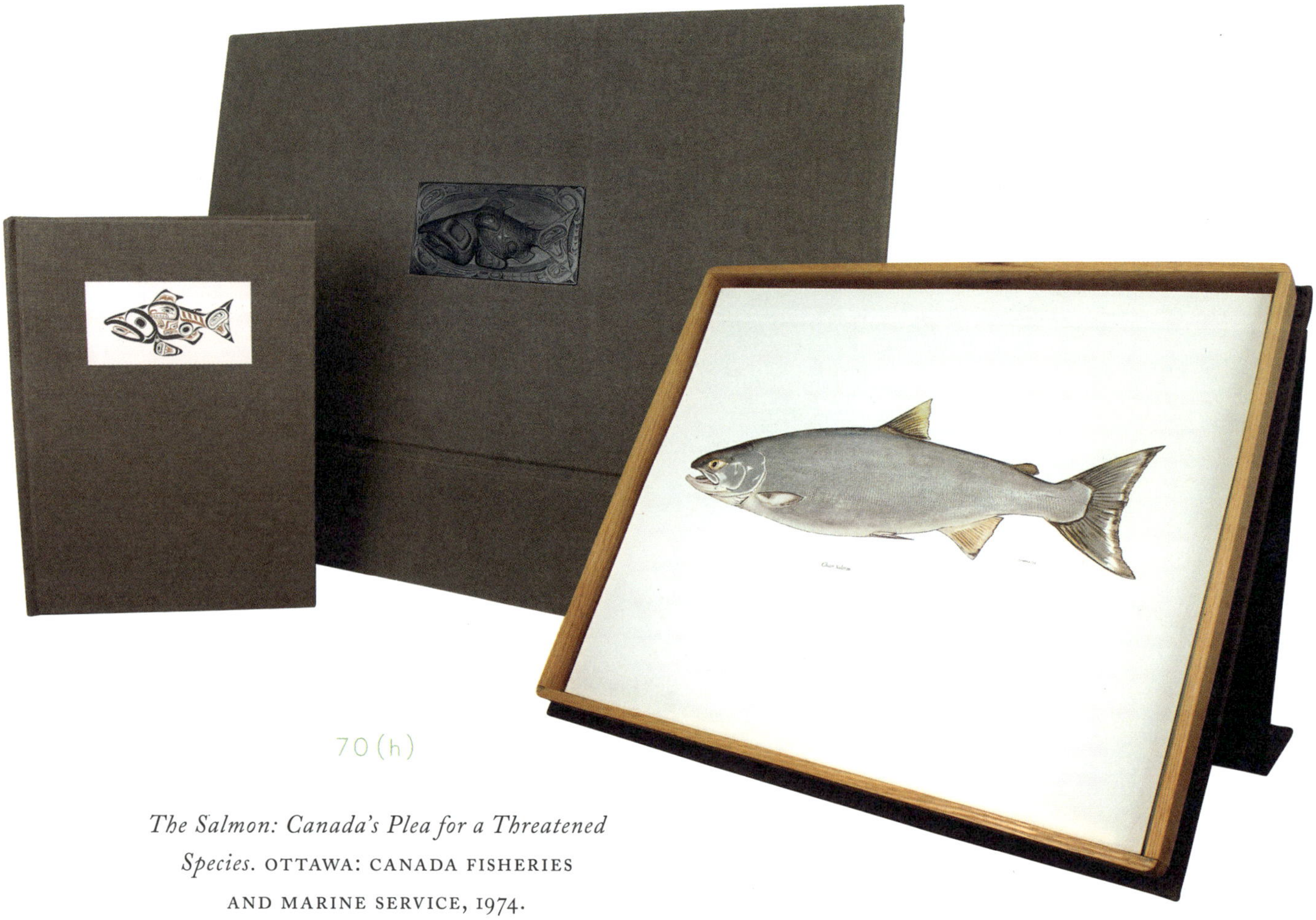

70(h)

The Salmon: Canada's Plea for a Threatened Species. OTTAWA: CANADA FISHERIES AND MARINE SERVICE, 1974. [SH 346 C212 1974 FOLIO] 61.1 CM X 47.4 CM

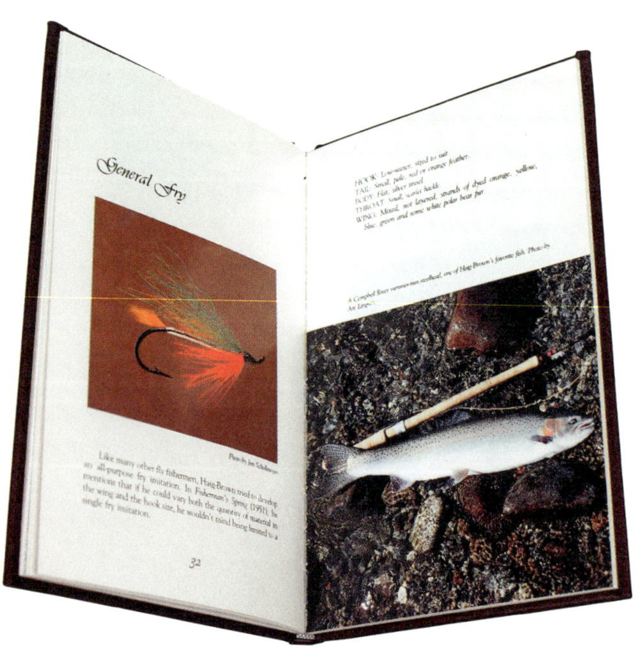

70(i)

LINGREN, ARTHUR JAMES. *Fly Patterns of Roderick Haig-Brown*. PORTLAND: RANK AMATO, 1993. [SH 451 L55 1993] 22.0 CM X 14.3 CM | NO. 10 OF 100 COPIES

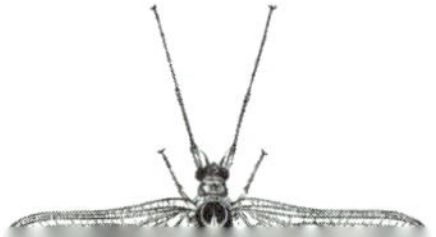

71

ANGLING IN ALBERTA

These five titles are ephemera issued as guides to fishing in Alberta, including the Rocky Mountain Parks and Edmonton. Ephemeral guides such as these were often discarded after use, and all these titles are scarce. The trout-fishing guide to Edmonton is particularly interesting, as it provides a snapshot of the trout-stocking program near Edmonton at the time.

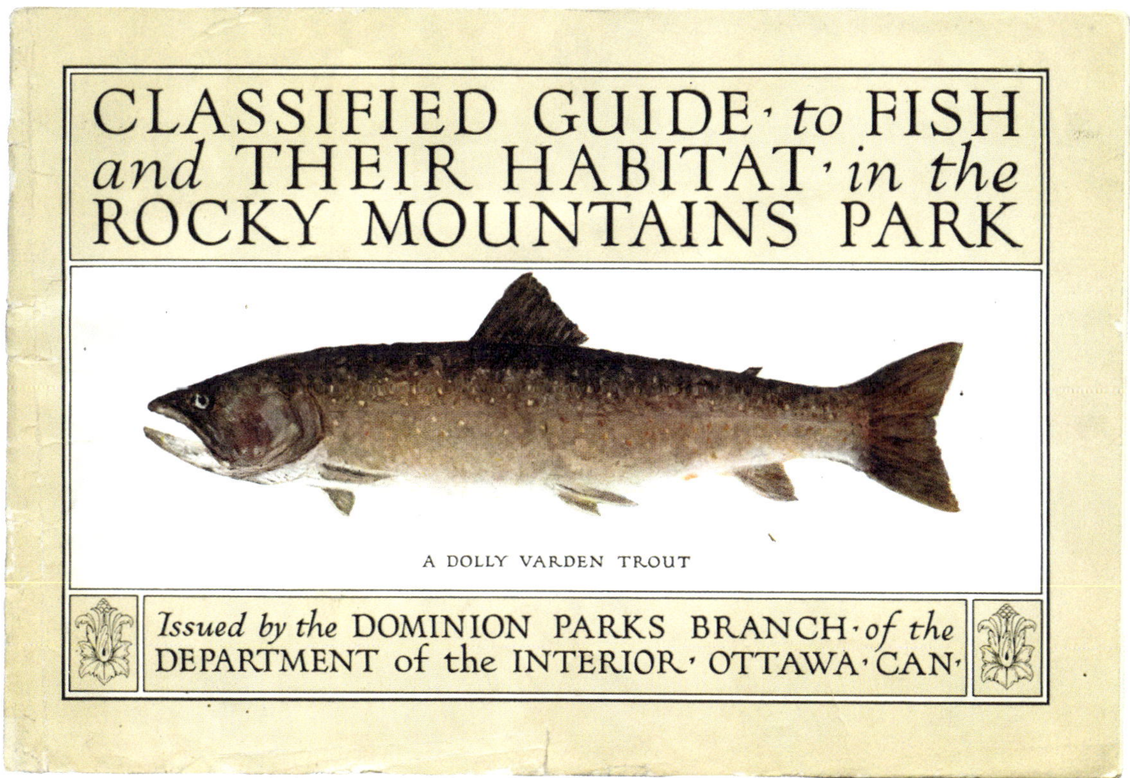

71(a)

VICK, S.C. *Classified Guide to Fish and Their Habitat in the Rocky Mountains Park.*
OTTAWA: DOMINION PARKS BRANCH, DEPARTMENT OF THE INTERIOR, [1913].
[QL 626.5 A3 V53 1913] 15.4 CM X 23.0 CM

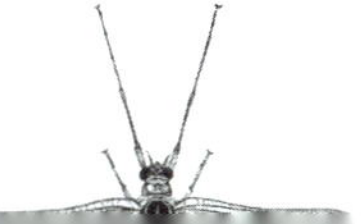

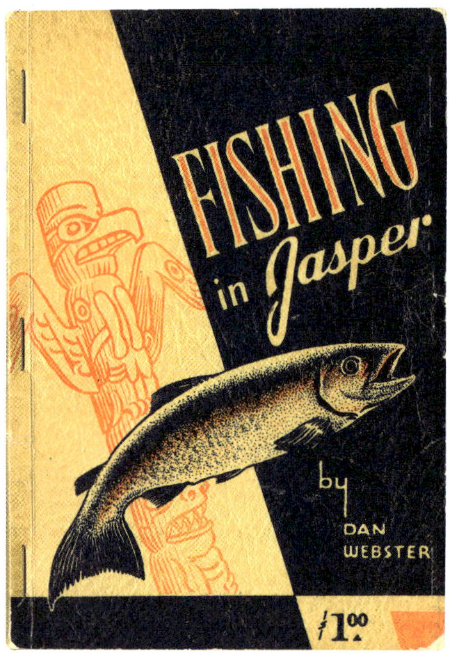

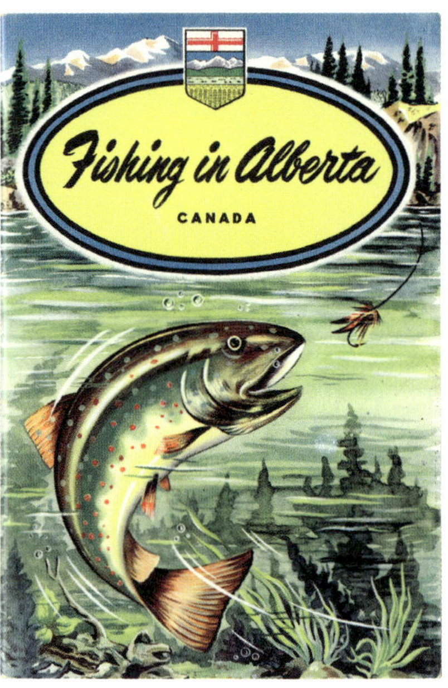

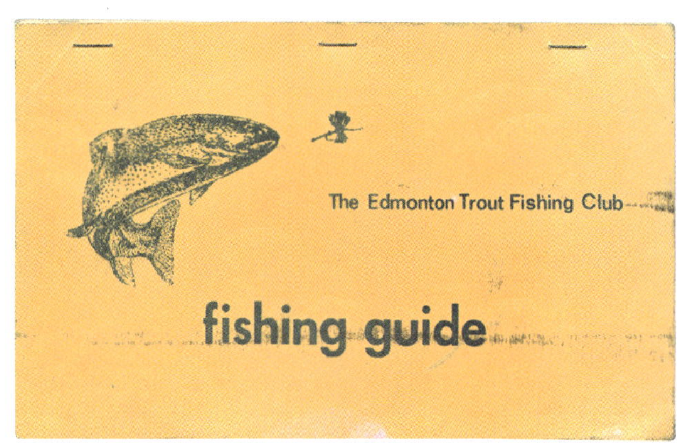

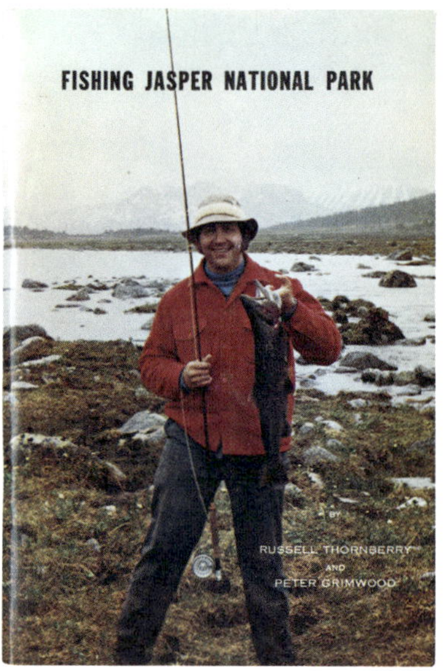

71(b)

WEBSTER, DAN. *Fishing in Jasper.* CALGARY: KELLAWAY PRINTING LTD., [1947?]. [SH 688 C2 W43 1947] 17.2 CM X 12.2 CM

71(c)

MACDONALD, W.H. *Fishing in Alberta.* [EDMONTON]: ALBERTA TRAVEL BUREAU, [1951]. [SH 572 A3 M145 1951] 22.6 CM X 15.2 CM

71(d)

SHEA, LLOYD, ED. *The Edmonton Trout Fishing Club Fishing Guide.* 2ND ED. [EDMONTON]: [THE EDMONTON TROUT FISHING CLUB], [1974]. [SH 688 C2 E46 1974] 13.2 CM X 21.6 CM

71(e)

THORNBERRY, RUSSELL, AND PETER GRIMWOOD. *Fishing Jasper National Park.* [CANADA]: GREENHORN PUBLISHING LTD., [197-?]. [SH 572 A3 T5 1970Z] 22.5 CM X 15.1 CM

Facing page: Bruce Peel Special Collections, SH 456 B46 1833

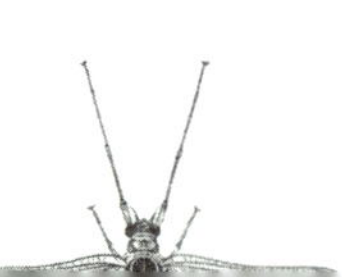

SCIENTIFIC ANGLING

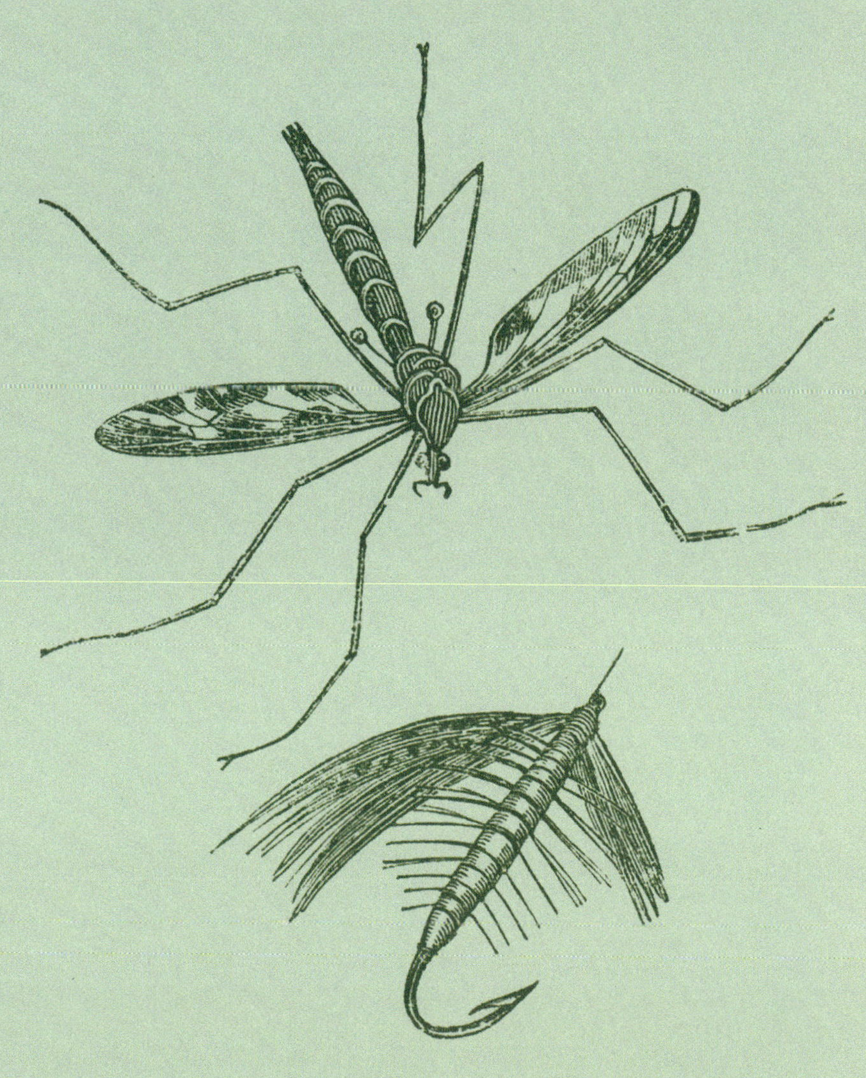

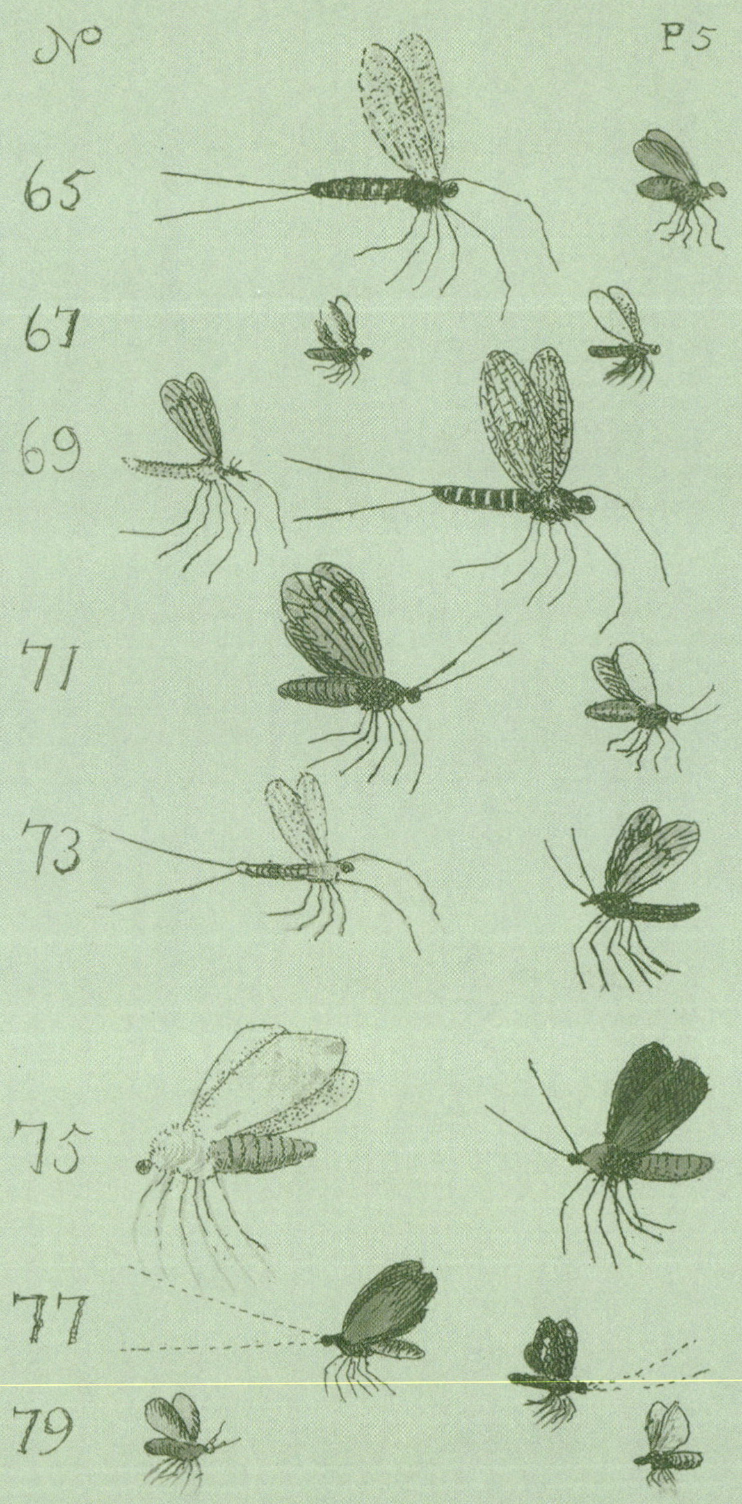
No
P5
65
67
69
71
73
75
77
79

SCIENTIFIC ANGLING

THE ANGLER-NATURALIST has for centuries studied the biology of fish and their prey to increase his or her success on the water. The following books have been chosen for their specific focus on science or their important role in advancing the "entomology of angling," including significant contributions to British and American angler-entomologies. Some of the books feature colour plates of insects for the angler to study while tying flies, while other titles present advice to the angler on how to create and manage a fishery or explain phylogenetic relationships among popular gamefish species.

Alfred Ronalds's *The Fly-fisher's Entomology* is the most significant title in this section and is the first book credited with making the connection between the scientific names of insects and the common names used by anglers (Gingrich 112). This advancement provided a common entomological language for anglers across Britain, but the American equivalent did not appear for an additional 100 years (item 80). Angling is truly a science and an art, and the following titles were all intended to advance the art of angling through science.

Facing page: Bruce Peel Special Collections, SH 439 C35 1818

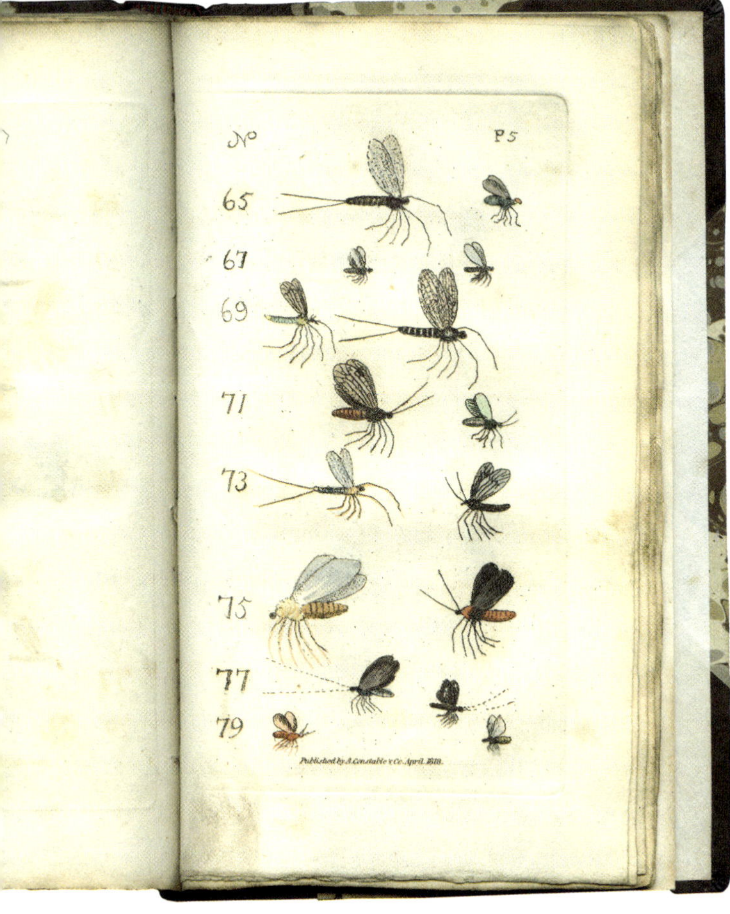

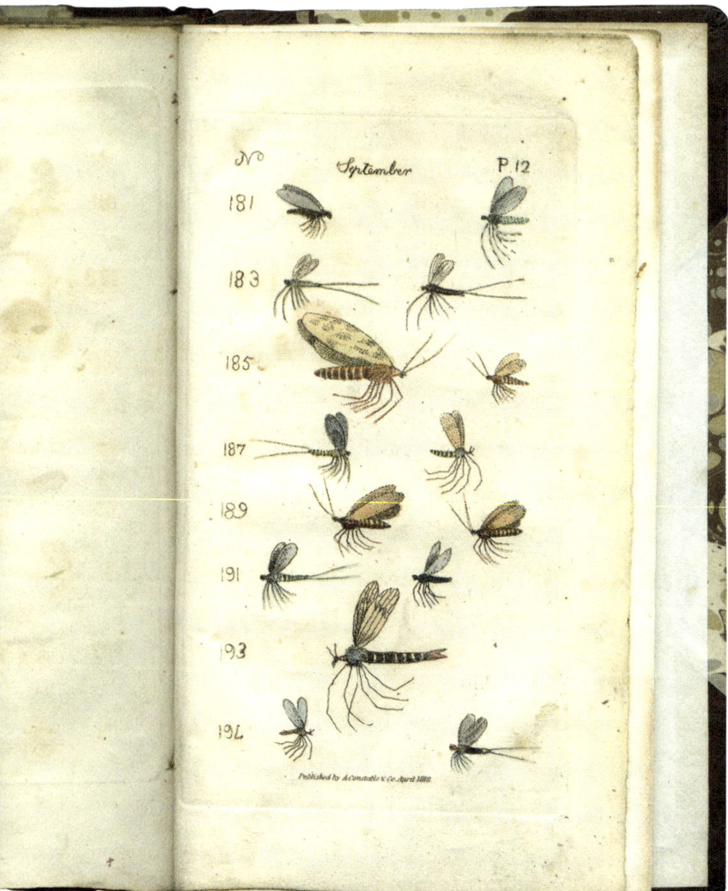

72

CARROLL, W. *The Angler's Vade Mecum: Containing a Descriptive Account of the Water Flies, Their Seasons, and the Kind of Weather That Brings Them Most on the Water: The Whole Represented in Twelve Coloured Plates: To Which is Added a Description of the Different Baits Used in Angling and Where Found.* EDINBURGH: ARCHIBALD CONSTABLE AND CO., 1818. [SH 439 C35 1818] 20.2 CM X 12.8 CM

This early contribution to scientific angling has 12 colour plates depicting 194 aquatic insects so that the angler can tie matching artificial flies. The book's purpose was to describe "water flies" and the seasons and specific weather conditions that cause each insect to hatch. The engravings are rather crudely executed, but they are hand-coloured. This early attempt at a systematic entomology for anglers preceded Ronalds's landmark *The Fly-fisher's Entomology* by 18 years.

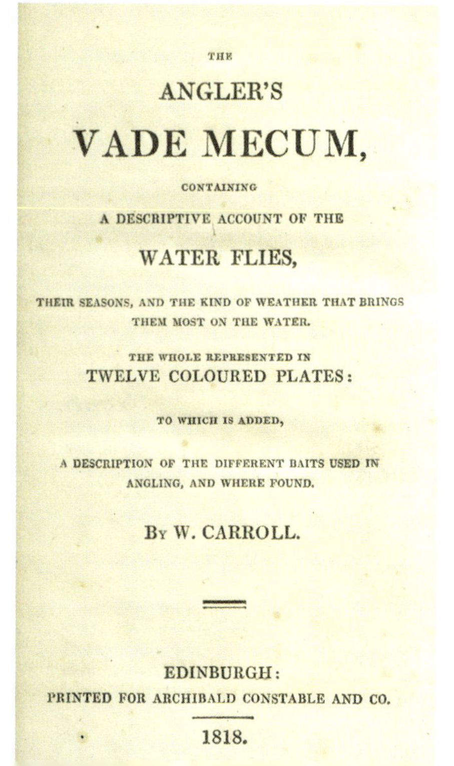
THE

ANGLER'S

VADE MECUM,

CONTAINING

A DESCRIPTIVE ACCOUNT OF THE

WATER FLIES,

THEIR SEASONS, AND THE KIND OF WEATHER THAT BRINGS THEM MOST ON THE WATER.

THE WHOLE REPRESENTED IN

TWELVE COLOURED PLATES:

TO WHICH IS ADDED,

A DESCRIPTION OF THE DIFFERENT BAITS USED IN ANGLING, AND WHERE FOUND.

BY W. CARROLL.

EDINBURGH:

PRINTED FOR ARCHIBALD CONSTABLE AND CO.

1818.

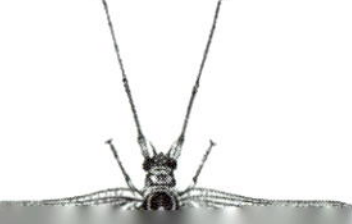

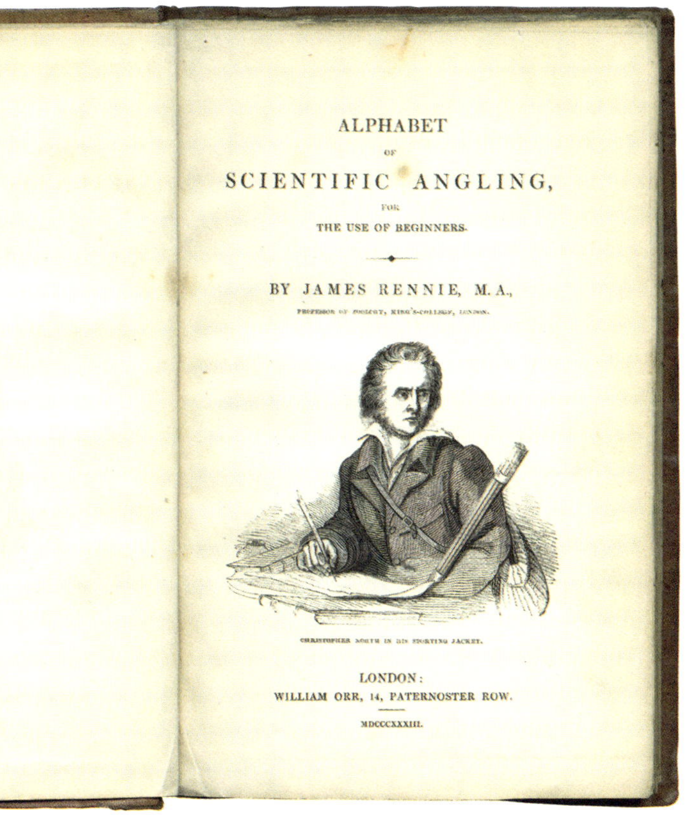

ALPHABET

OF

SCIENTIFIC ANGLING,

FOR

THE USE OF BEGINNERS.

BY JAMES RENNIE, M.A.,

PROFESSOR OF ZOOLOGY, KING'S-COLLEGE, LONDON.

CHRISTOPHER NORTH IN HIS SPORTING JACKET.

LONDON:

WILLIAM ORR, 14, PATERNOSTER ROW.

MDCCCXXXIII.

73

RENNIE, JAMES. *Alphabet of Scientific Angling for the Use of Beginners.* LONDON: WILLIAM ORR, 1833. [SH 456 R46 1833] 15.7 CM X 10.6 CM

Rennie was a professor of zoology at King's College London, and this book was his attempt to translate his scientific knowledge of fish for strategic use by anglers. Topics include the following: taste, smell, sight, and hearing in fishes; attention to colour in fishes; and various remarks on prey, including insects. Although Rennie acknowledges that this goes against the conventional thinking of the day, he advocates matching primarily the colours of prey insects rather than focusing on the morphology of a species.

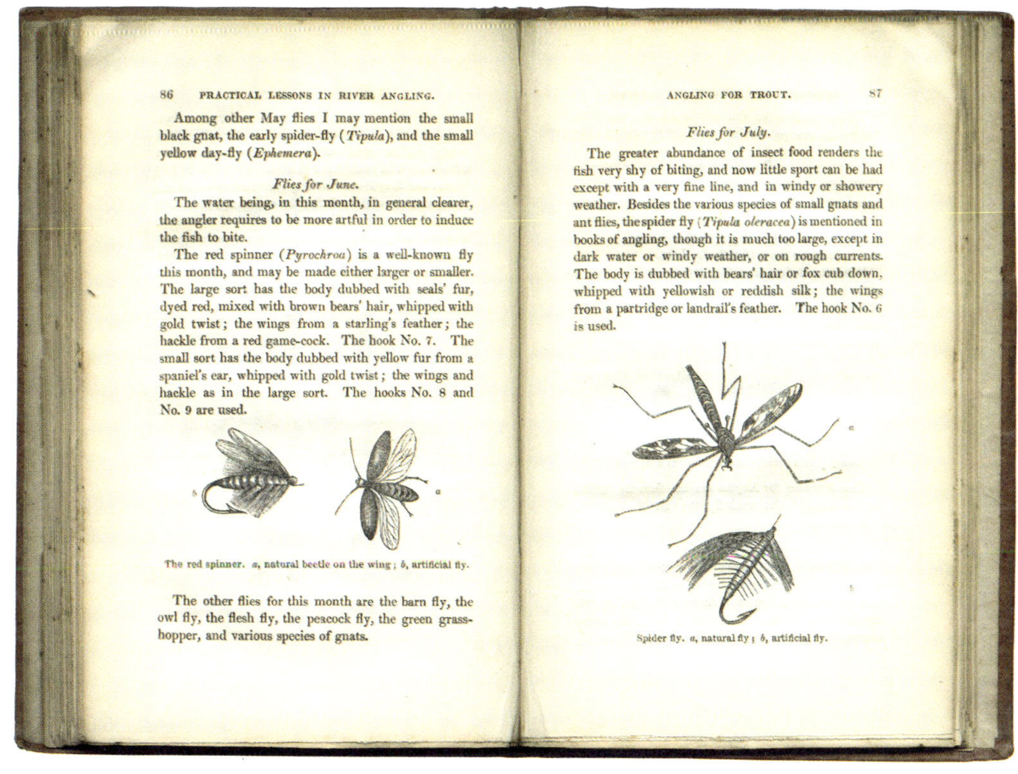

86 PRACTICAL LESSONS IN RIVER ANGLING.

Among other May flies I may mention the small black gnat, the early spider-fly (*Tipula*), and the small yellow day-fly (*Ephemera*).

Flies for June.

The water being, in this month, in general clearer, the angler requires to be more artful in order to induce the fish to bite.

The red spinner (*Pyrochroa*) is a well-known fly this month, and may be made either larger or smaller. The large sort has the body dubbed with seals' fur, dyed red, mixed with brown bears' hair, whipped with gold twist; the wings from a starling's feather; the hackle from a red game-cock. The hook No. 7. The small sort has the body dubbed with yellow fur from a spaniel's ear, whipped with gold twist; the wings and hackle as in the large sort. The hooks No. 8 and No. 9 are used.

The red spinner. *a*, natural beetle on the wing; *b*, artificial fly.

The other flies for this month are the barn fly, the owl fly, the flesh fly, the peacock fly, the green grass-hopper, and various species of gnats.

ANGLING FOR TROUT. 87

Flies for July.

The greater abundance of insect food renders the fish very shy of biting, and now little sport can be had except with a very fine line, and in windy or showery weather. Besides the various species of small gnats and ant flies, the spider fly (*Tipula oleracea*) is mentioned in books of angling, though it is much too large, except in dark water or windy weather, or on rough currents. The body is dubbed with bears' hair or fox cub down, whipped with yellowish or reddish silk; the wings from a partridge or landrail's feather. The hook No. 6 is used.

Spider fly. *a*, natural fly; *b*, artificial fly.

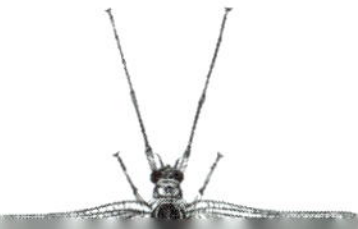

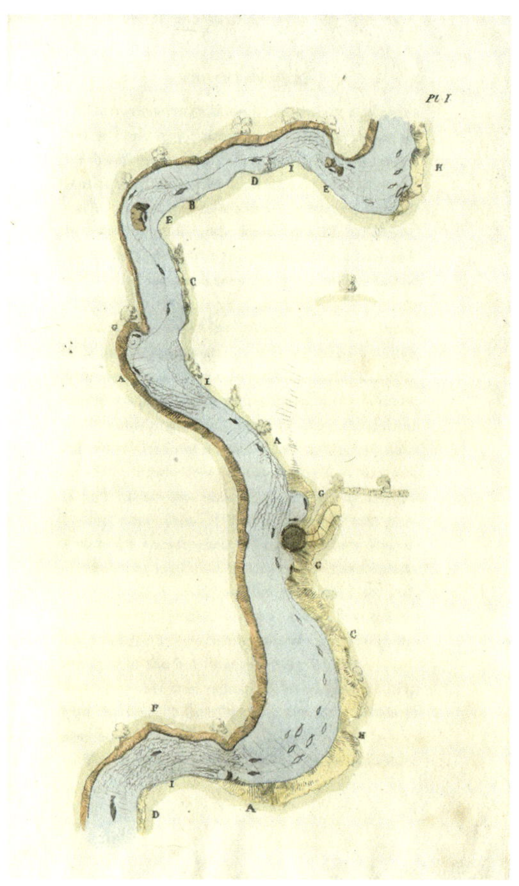

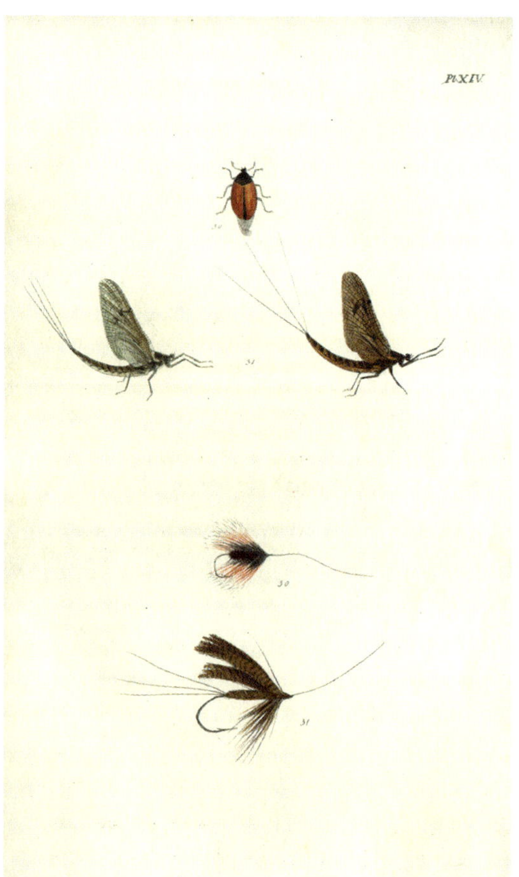

74

RONALDS, ALFRED. *The Fly-fishers Entomology: Illustrated by Coloured Representations of the Natural and Artificial Insect. And Accompanied by a Few Observations and Instructions Relative to Trout-and-Grayling Fishing.* LONDON: LONGMAN, REES, ORME, BROWN, GREEN, AND LONGMAN, 1836. [SH 451 R66 1836] 22.7 CM X 14.7 CM

This title is significant as the first true "angler's entomology," with 19 coloured engravings, each illustrating natural insects above their tied imitations. Westwood et al. praise the book as a "rare combination of piscatorial and entomological science" (178), and Gingrich states that "it's because of Ronalds, largely, that you and I fish with the kinds of flies we use today . . ." (112). Over five editions and twenty years, Ronalds linked the vernacular used by anglers with each insect's scientific name, and, in doing so, he "gave for the first time a systematic and scientific basis of distinguishing one fly from another" (Gingrich 112). Today, many serious fly-fisherman are also avid students of entomology and can respectably discuss insect anatomy, biology, and ecology with an academic entomologist; it was Ronalds who solidified this tradition of the angler-entomologist.

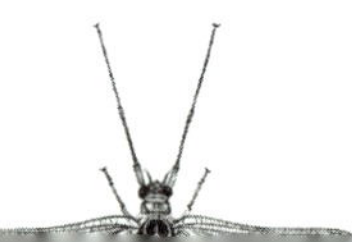

75

WRIGHT, W[ILLIAM]. *Fishes and Fishing: Artificial Breeding of Fish, Anatomy of Their Senses, Their Loves, Passions, and Intellects. With Illustrative Facts.* LONDON: THOMAS CAUTLEY NEWBY, 1858. [SH 439 W95 1858] 17.9 CM X 11.5 CM

This book has a goal similar to Rennie's *Alphabet of Scientific Angling*. Wright, a lecturer of anatomy, discusses the anatomy of fish senses and, as the title says, their "loves, passions, and intellects" to inform the angler.

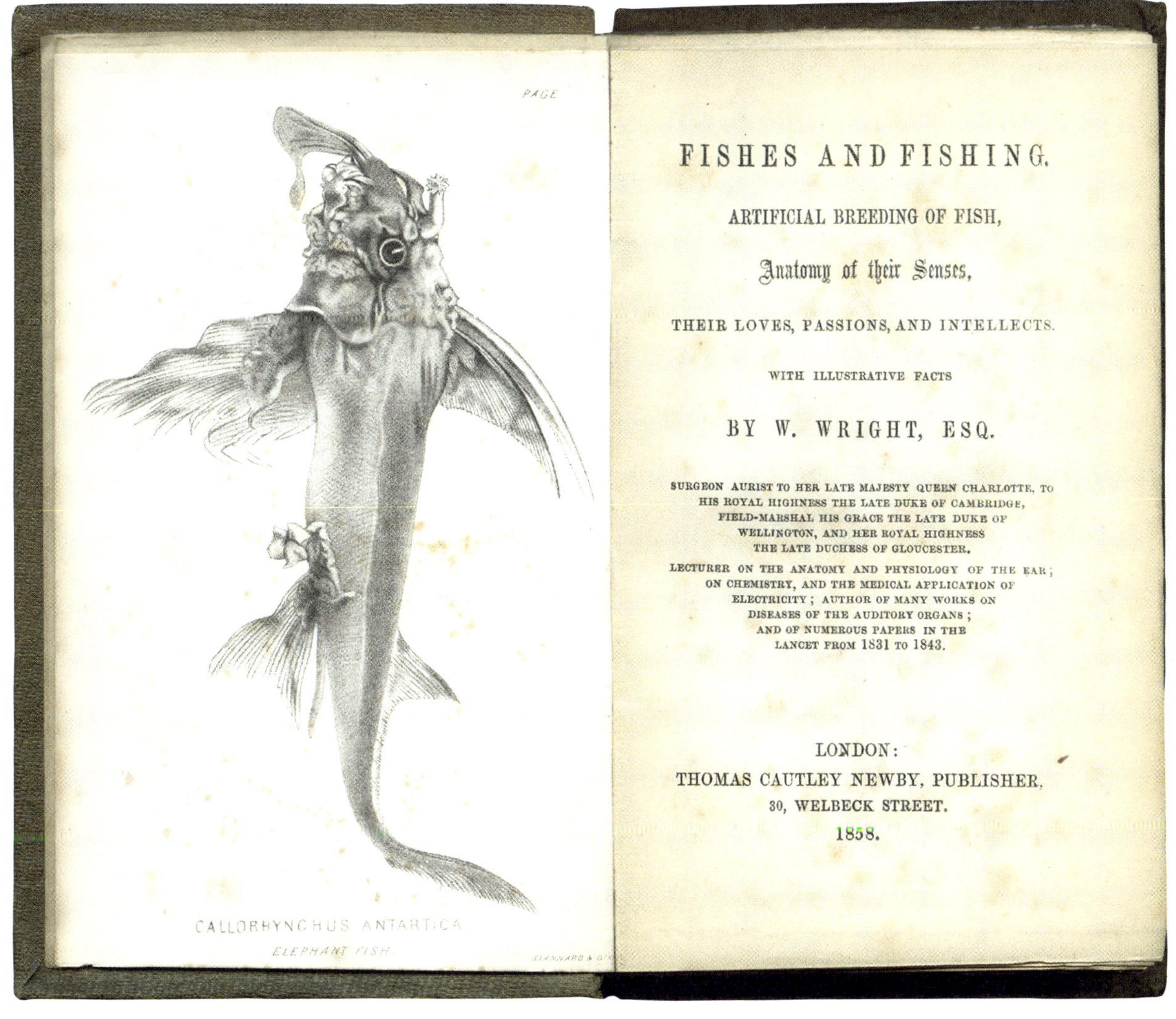

FISHES AND FISHING.

ARTIFICIAL BREEDING OF FISH,

Anatomy of their Senses,

THEIR LOVES, PASSIONS, AND INTELLECTS.

WITH ILLUSTRATIVE FACTS

BY W. WRIGHT, ESQ.

SURGEON AURIST TO HER LATE MAJESTY QUEEN CHARLOTTE, TO HIS ROYAL HIGHNESS THE LATE DUKE OF CAMBRIDGE, FIELD-MARSHAL HIS GRACE THE LATE DUKE OF WELLINGTON, AND HER ROYAL HIGHNESS THE LATE DUCHESS OF GLOUCESTER.

LECTURER ON THE ANATOMY AND PHYSIOLOGY OF THE EAR; ON CHEMISTRY, AND THE MEDICAL APPLICATION OF ELECTRICITY; AUTHOR OF MANY WORKS ON DISEASES OF THE AUDITORY ORGANS; AND OF NUMEROUS PAPERS IN THE LANCET FROM 1831 TO 1843.

LONDON:
THOMAS CAUTLEY NEWBY, PUBLISHER,
30, WELBECK STREET.
1858.

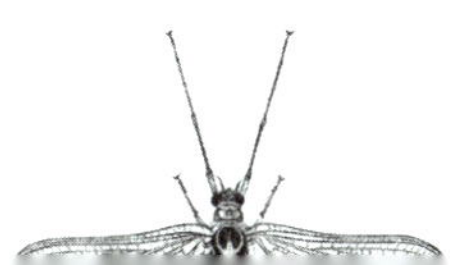

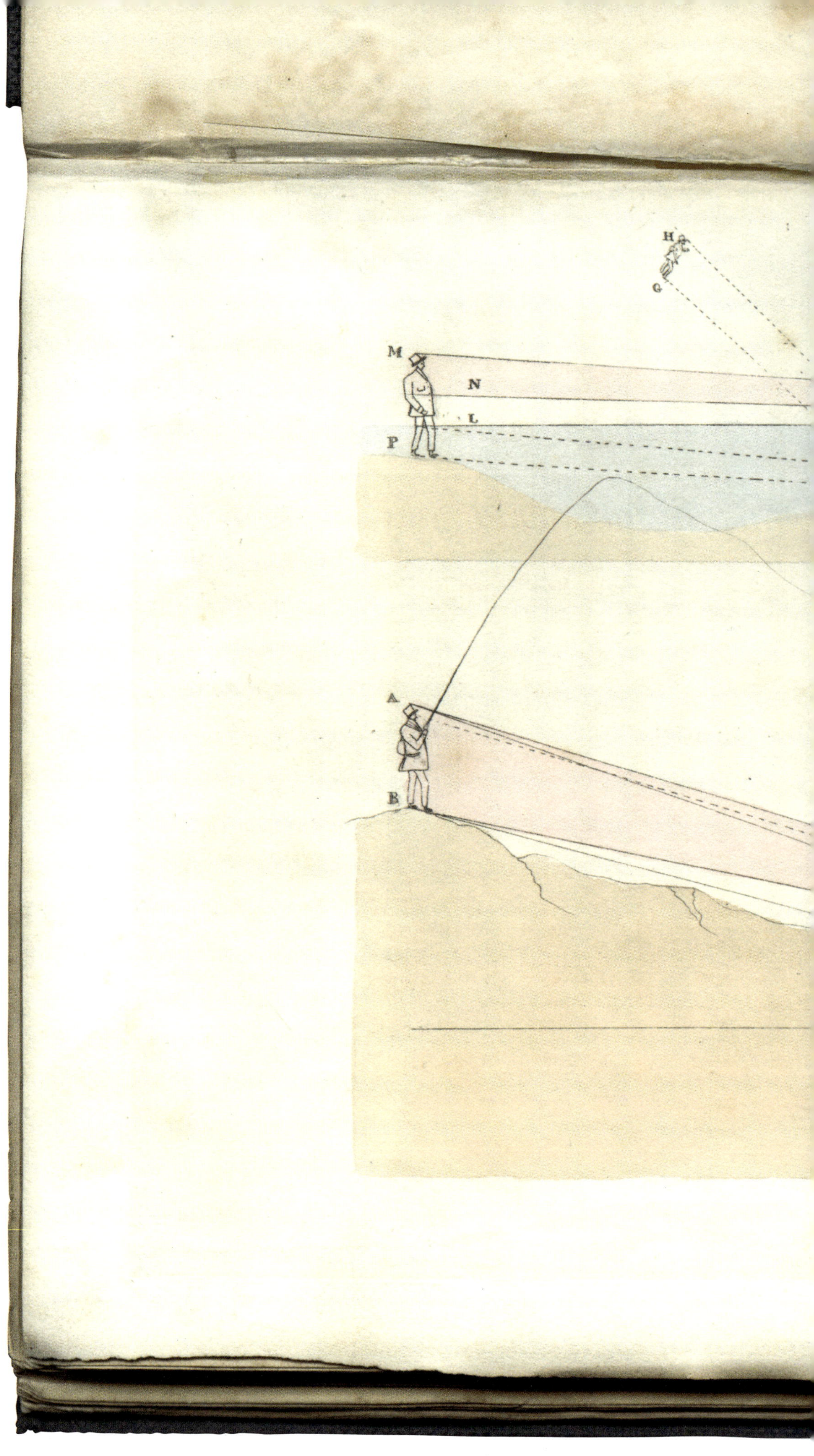
H
G
M
N
L
P
A
B

Pl. II

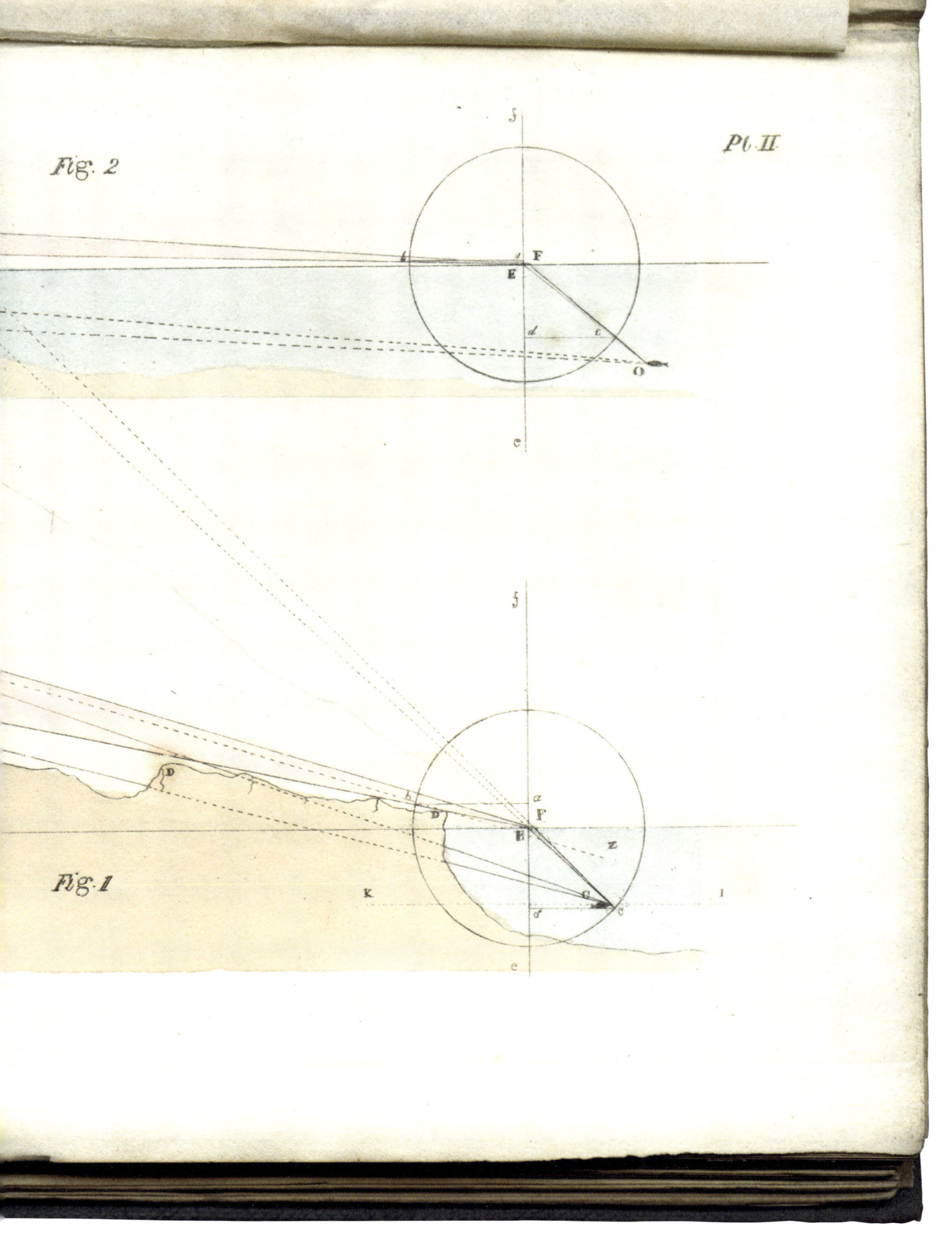

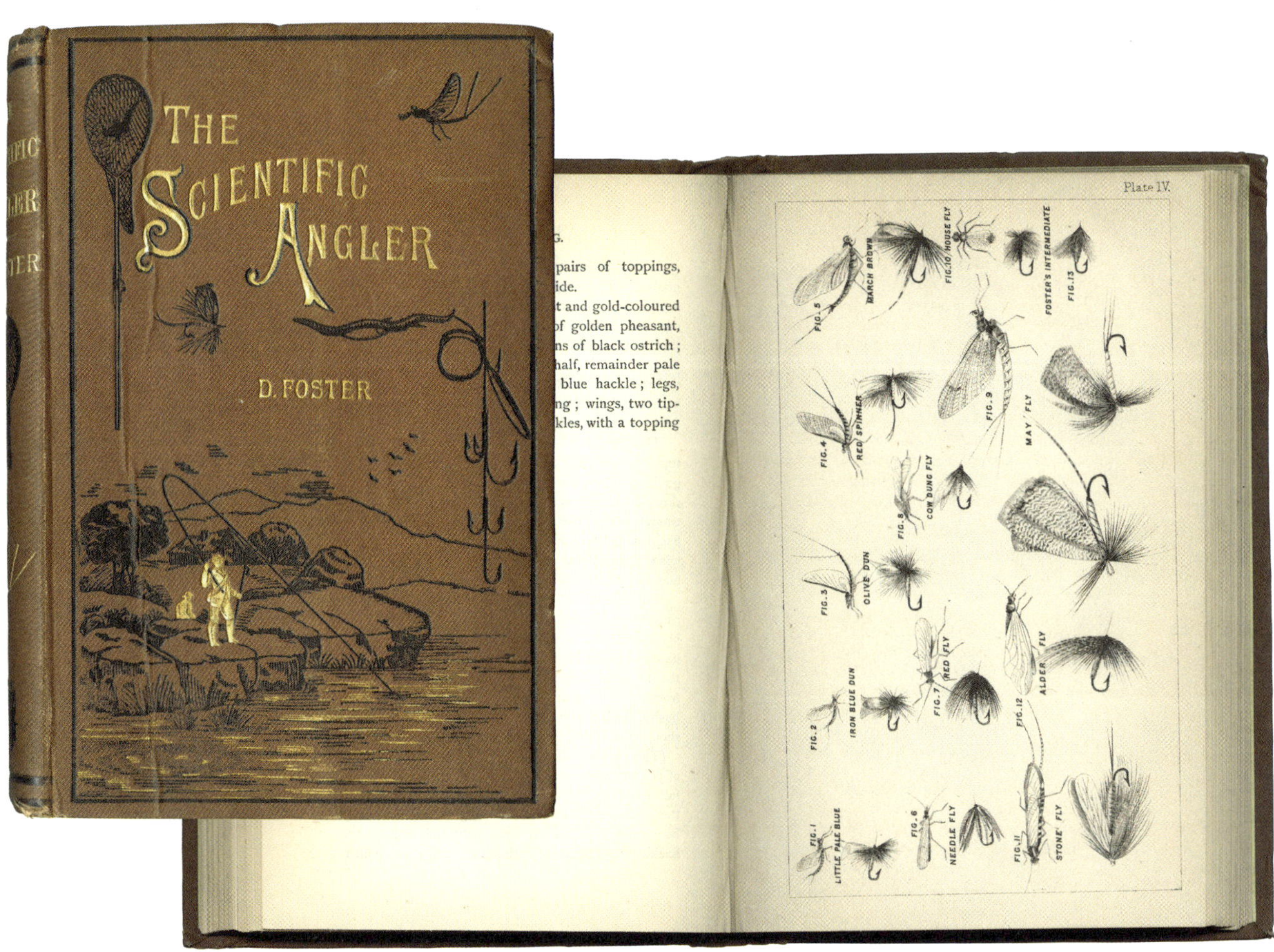

76

FOSTER, DAVID. *The Scientific Angler: Being a General and Instructive Work on Artistic Angling.* LONDON: BEMROSE & SONS, [1882]. [SH 439 F75 1882] 19.0 CM X 13.3 CM

Foster's sons published this book to share their father's lifetime of fishing knowledge. In the book's introduction, Foster is described as naturalist who "applied himself with great energy and ingenuity to the improvement of fishing with the artificial fly; the study of aquatic insects; the forms and colours of flies found on certain waters; the times of their appearance and departure; and the methods of imitation" (viii). Foster also worked at the Allcock company (see item 19a) and invented and refined several advancements in fishing tackle, primarily hooks and lines (vii). The book includes a section on the "Angler's Entomology" and a plate illustrating several natural streamside insects next to their tied imitations.

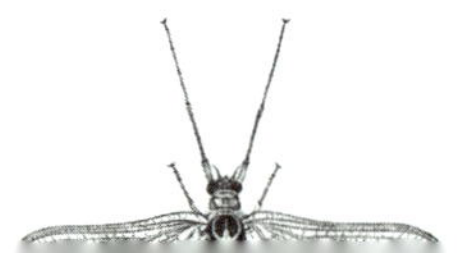

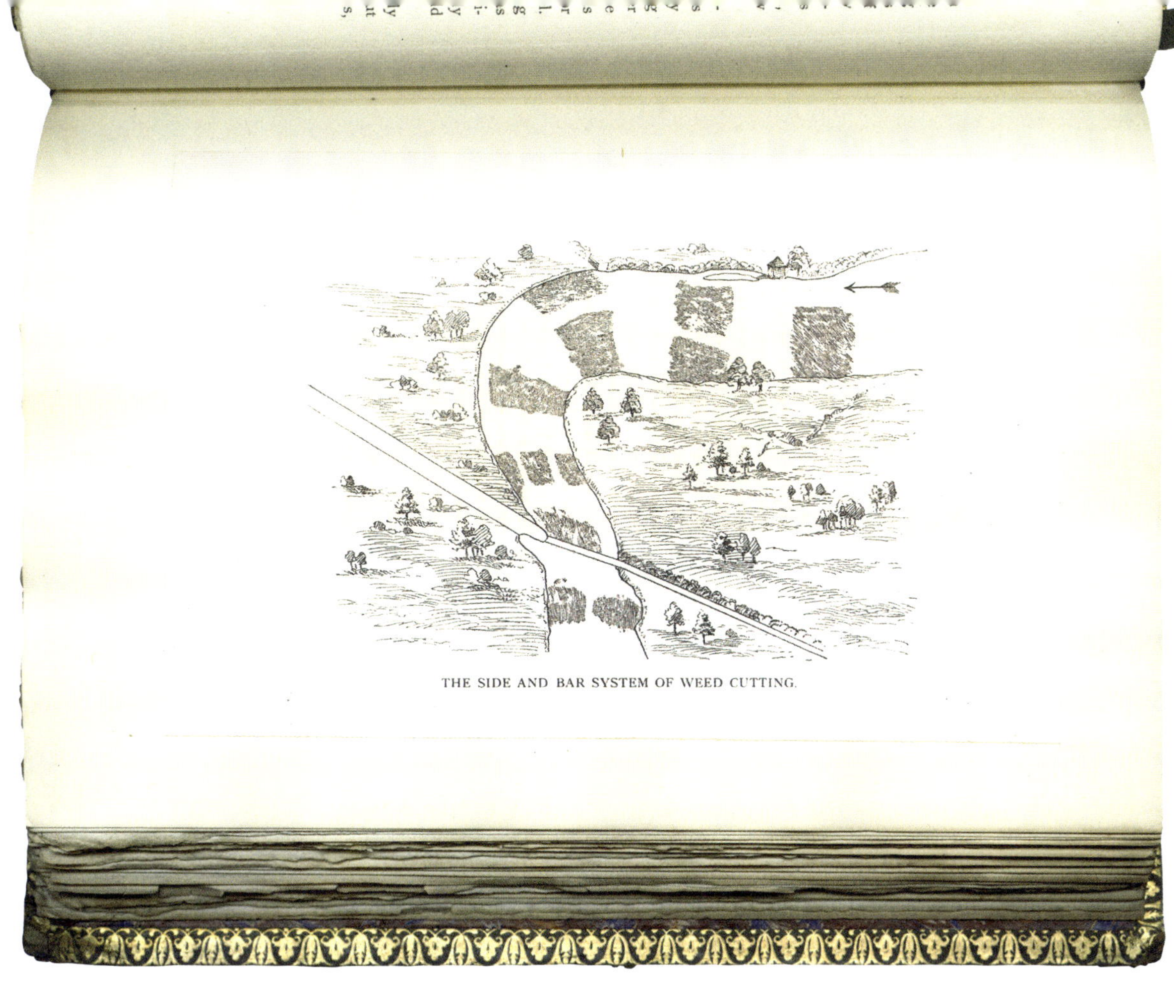

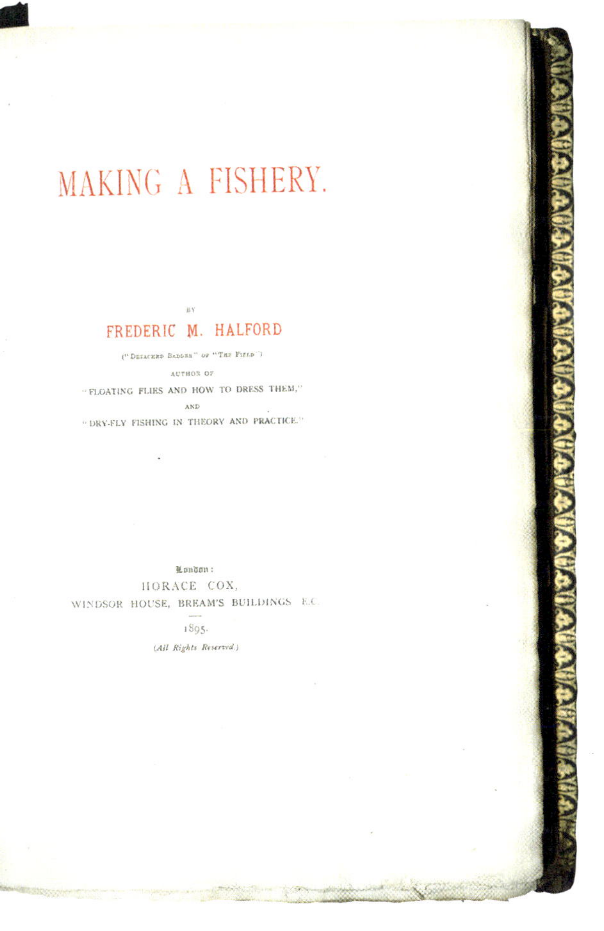

MAKING A FISHERY.

BY

FREDERIC M. HALFORD

("DETACHED BADGER" OF "THE FIELD")

AUTHOR OF

"FLOATING FLIES AND HOW TO DRESS THEM,"

AND

"DRY-FLY FISHING IN THEORY AND PRACTICE."

London:

HORACE COX,

WINDSOR HOUSE, BREAM'S BUILDINGS E.C.

1895.

(All Rights Reserved.)

77

HALFORD, FREDERIC M[ICHAEL]. *Making a Fishery*. LONDON: HORACE COX, 1895.
[SH 159 H25 1895] 29.4 CM X 20.1 CM
NO. 48 OF 150 COPIES

Halford was critical of the mismanagement of rivers in England and offers his own advice on managing trout streams, with sections on weed management, stocking, and netting for populations estimates.

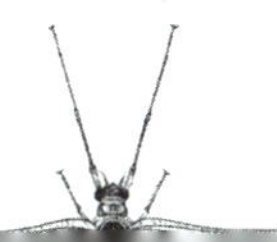

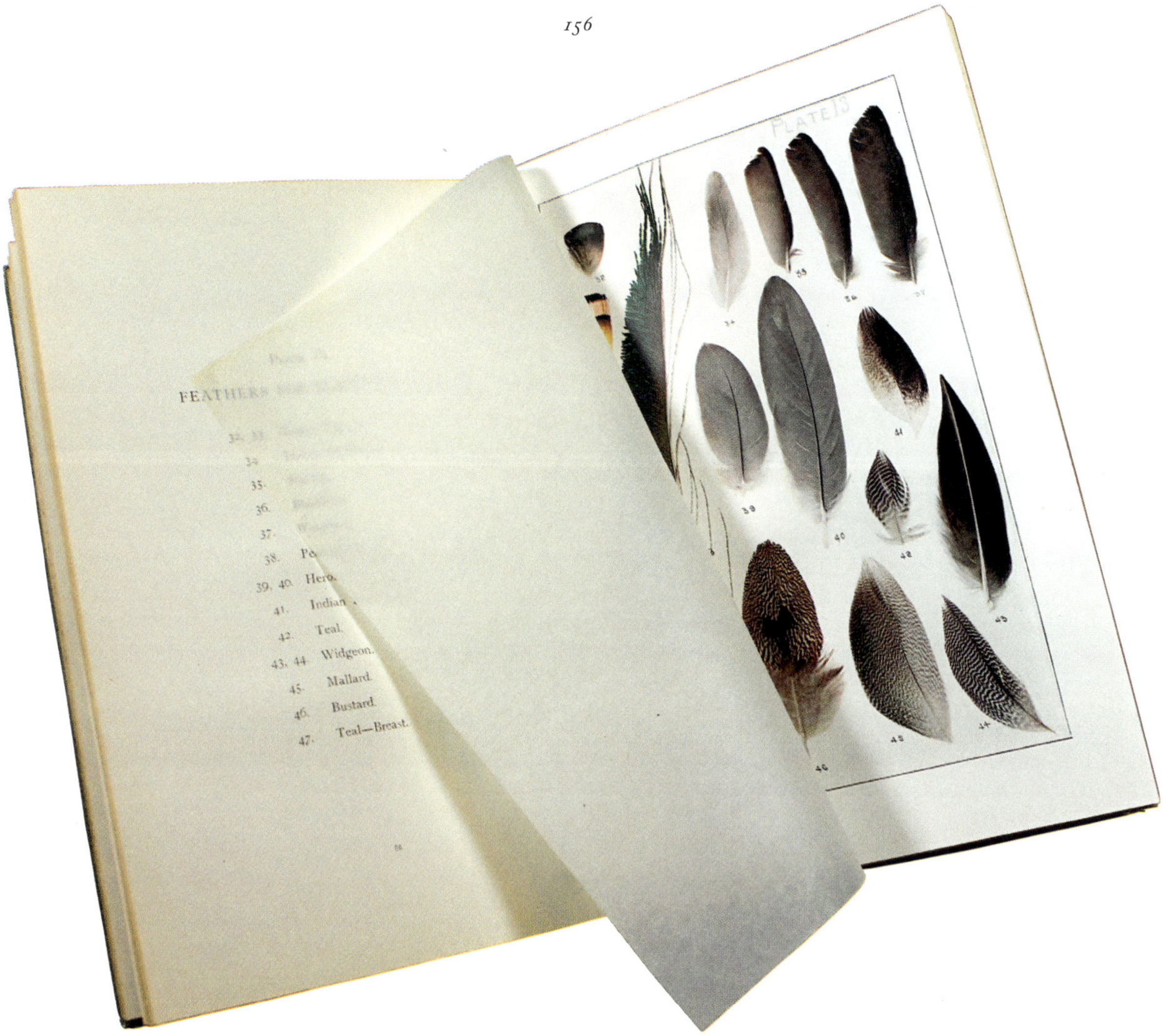

78

WEST, LEONARD. *The Natural Trout Fly and Its Imitation*. ST. HELENS: LEONARD WEST, [1912]. [SH 541 W46 1912] 23.0 CM X 15.0 CM

This title is an angler's entomology featuring natural streamside insects and methods for their imitation. The introduction details the major orders and families of interest to the angler with notes on the anatomy and classification of each. West branches out from the traditional "EPT" (Ephemeroptera, Plecoptera, and Trichoptera) to detail other aquatic insects

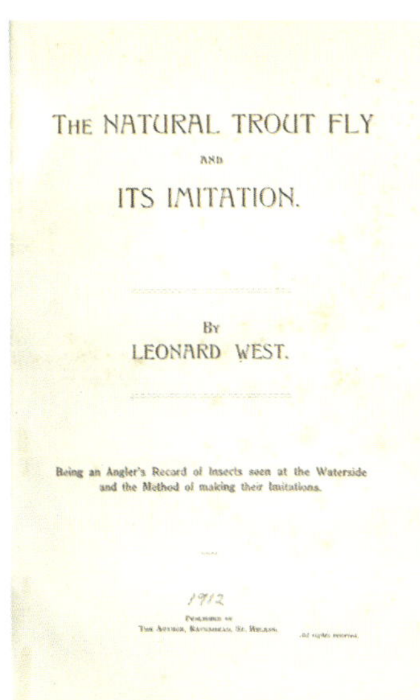

THE NATURAL TROUT FLY

AND

ITS IMITATION.

BY

LEONARD WEST.

Being an Angler's Record of Insects seen at the Waterside and the Method of making their Imitations.

1912

commonly consumed by trout, including beetles, true bugs, and true flies. Several excellent colour plates—drawn by the author—illustrate the stream insects next to their imitations. There is a tipped in letter on the front free endpaper signed by West and presenting the book to its recipient.

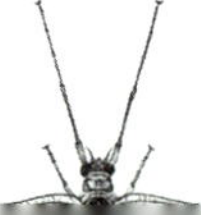

79

QUACKENBOS, JOHN D[UNCAN]. *Geological Ancestors of the Brook Trout: And Recent Saibling Forms from Which It Evolved.* NEW YORK: TOBIAS A. WRIGHT, 1916. [QL 618.2 Q33 1916] 21.4 CM X 15.9 CM NO. 265 OF 300

The phylogeny of the chars has long been a challenge for taxonomists. This title was printed for The Anglers' Club of New York and attempts to classify several species and subspecies of salmon and trout. Quackenbos was a physician, and the book is an interesting mix of scientific and angling content with attractive colour plates of subspecies of east coast chars and a phylogenetic tree.

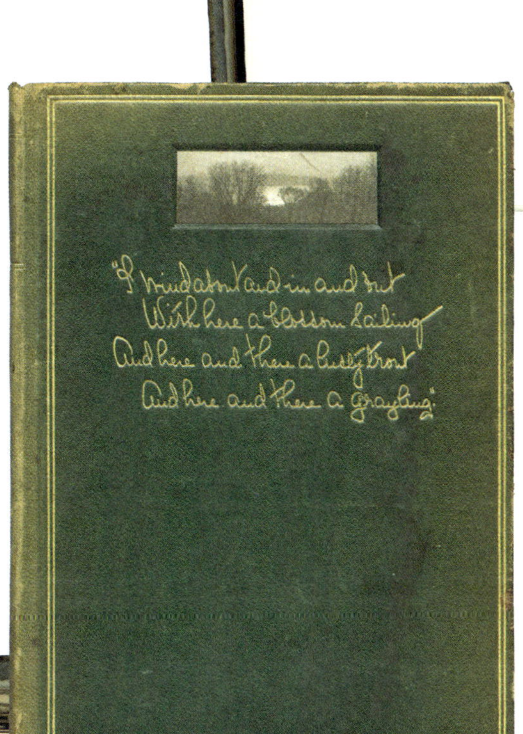

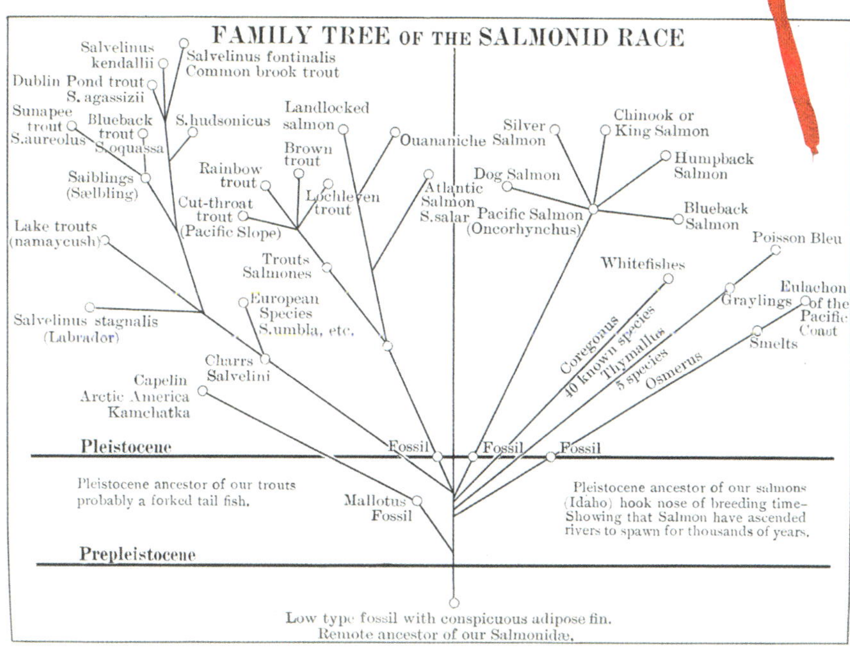

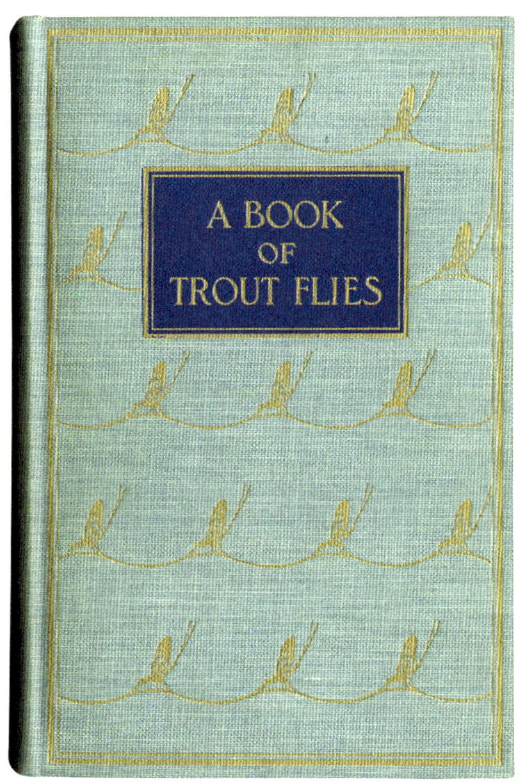

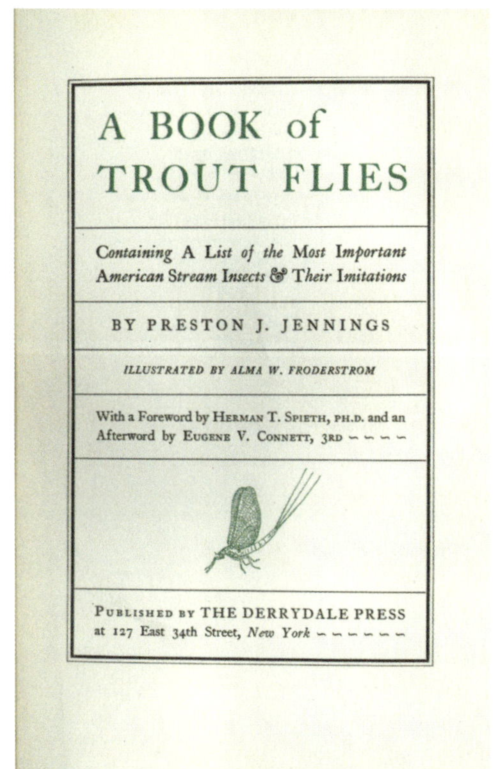
A BOOK of
TROUT FLIES

Containing A List *of the* Most Important
American Stream Insects & Their Imitations

BY PRESTON J. JENNINGS

ILLUSTRATED BY ALMA W. FRODERSTROM

With a Foreword by HERMAN T. SPIETH, PH.D. and an
Afterword by EUGENE V. CONNETT, 3RD

PUBLISHED BY THE DERRYDALE PRESS
at 127 East 34th Street, *New York*

80

JENNINGS, PRESTON J. *A Book of Trout Flies: Containing a List of the Most Important American Stream Insects and Their Imitations.* NEW YORK: DERRYDALE PRESS, 1935.
[SH 451 J46 1935] 24.6 CM X 16.5 CM
NO. 692 OF 850

Jennings did for American stream insects what Ronalds (item 74) did for British stream insects, and in doing so, answered Gill's (item 22) call for an American angler's entomology. Jennings bridged the "inexact and colourful English of fly-fishing tradition and the precise and rigid Latin of entomology" (Gingrich 278) and provided detailed observations of insect biology and behaviour. Unfortunately for Jennings, he did not live to see the book's lasting popularity. Nick Lyons reissued the title with a new introduction by Ernest Schwiebert, and it quickly went through several printings (Gingrich 280).

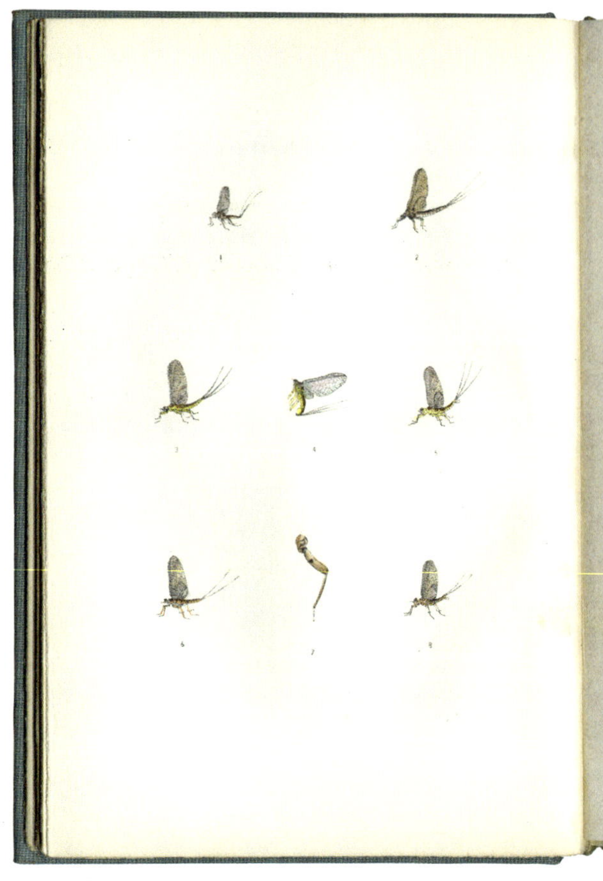

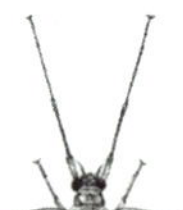

81

FLICK, ART. *Streamside Guide to Naturals and Their Imitations.* NEW YORK: G.P. PUTNAM'S SONS, 1947. [SH 451 F55 1947] 17.7 CM X 11.0 CM

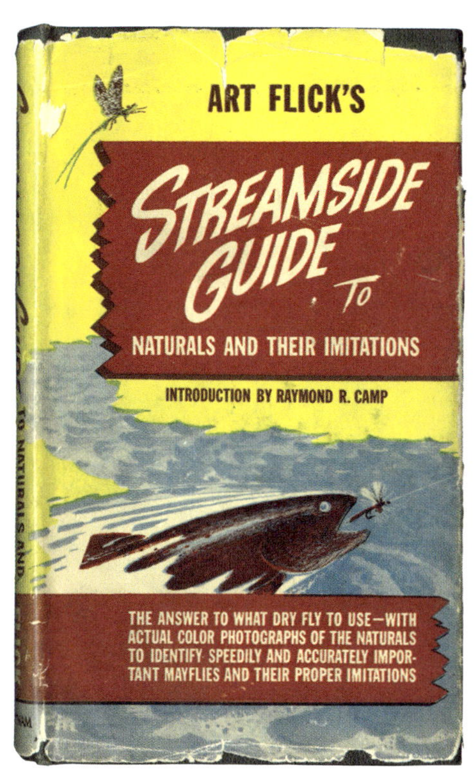

This title is an example of a modern angler's entomology that Gingrich describes as "one of the most valuable and useful pocket books a fly fisher can have" (315). The book typically saw heavy use, and the first edition in a dust jacket is relatively scarce.

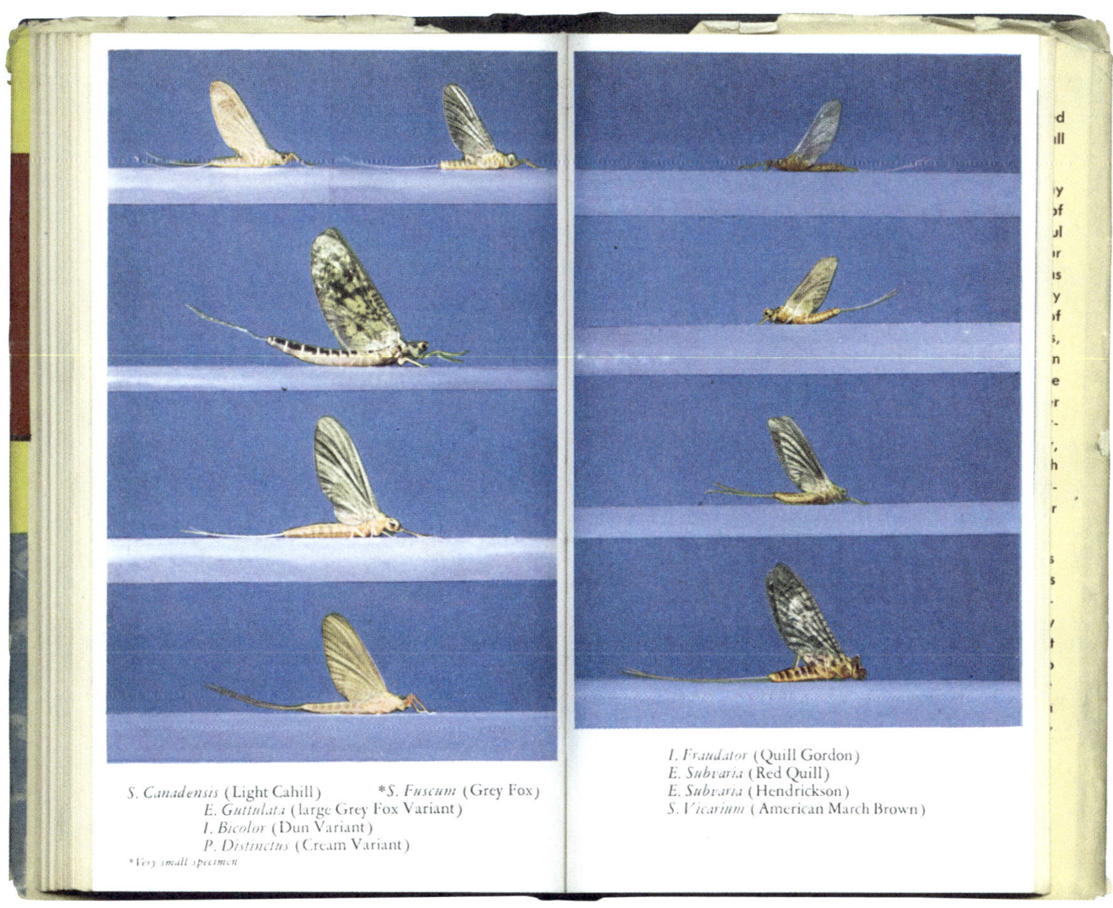

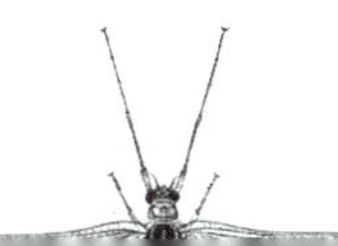

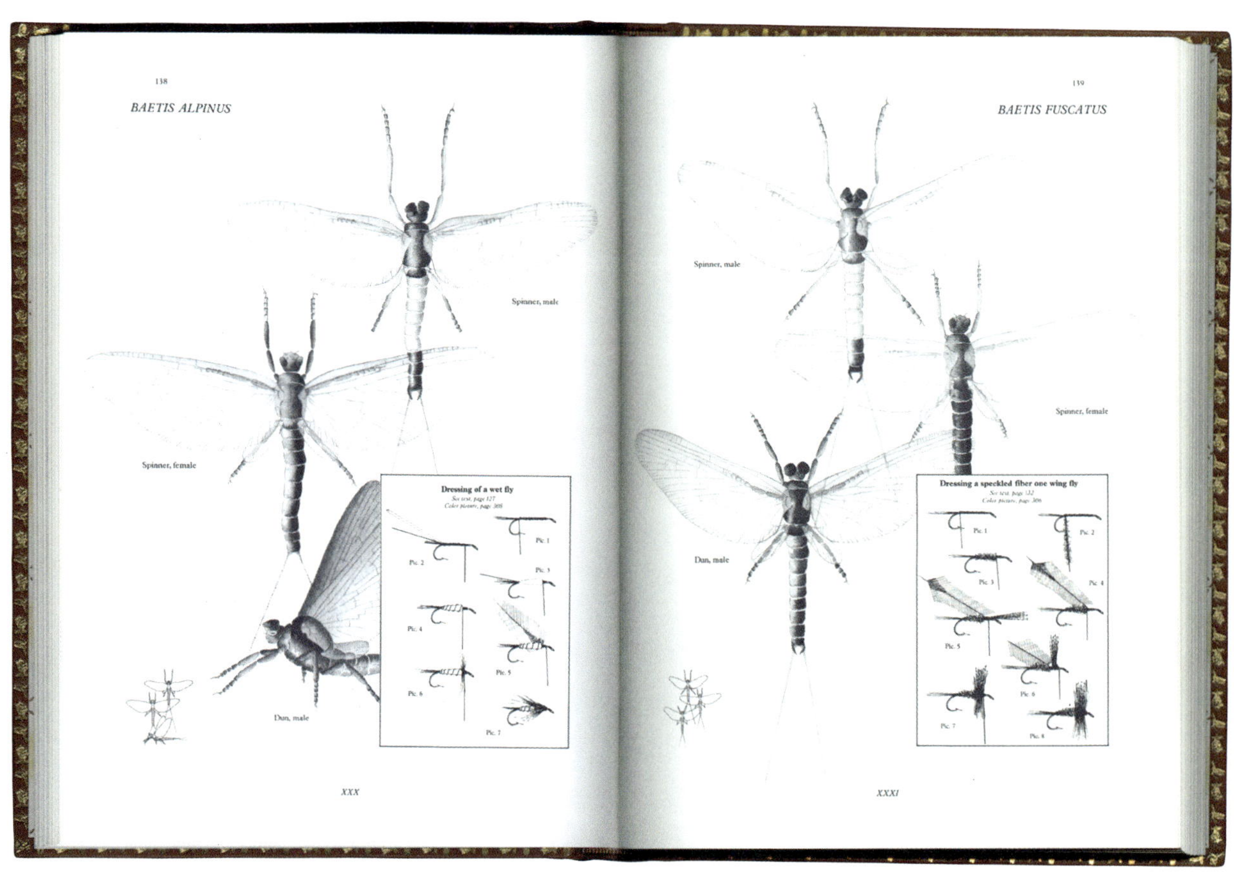

82

GAIDY, CHARLES. *Ephemeras: "Mayflies": Naturals and Artificials.* NEW YORK: EDICOM, 1986.
[SH 451 G35 1986 FOLIO] 33.9 CM X 25.4 CM | NO. 155 OF 300 COPIES

A limited edition dedicated to just one family of aquatic insects, the Ephemeroptera. The book delves deeply into entomological terminology, which is an absolute requirement to distinguish between different genera and species of mayflies.

The book also includes colour photographs of flies and incredibly-detailed line drawings of individual species of mayflies. Each species is accompanied with tying instructions. A beautiful lithograph of three mayflies was issued with this limited edition.

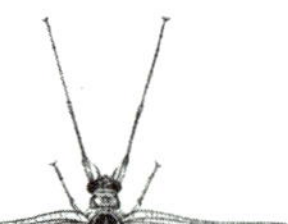

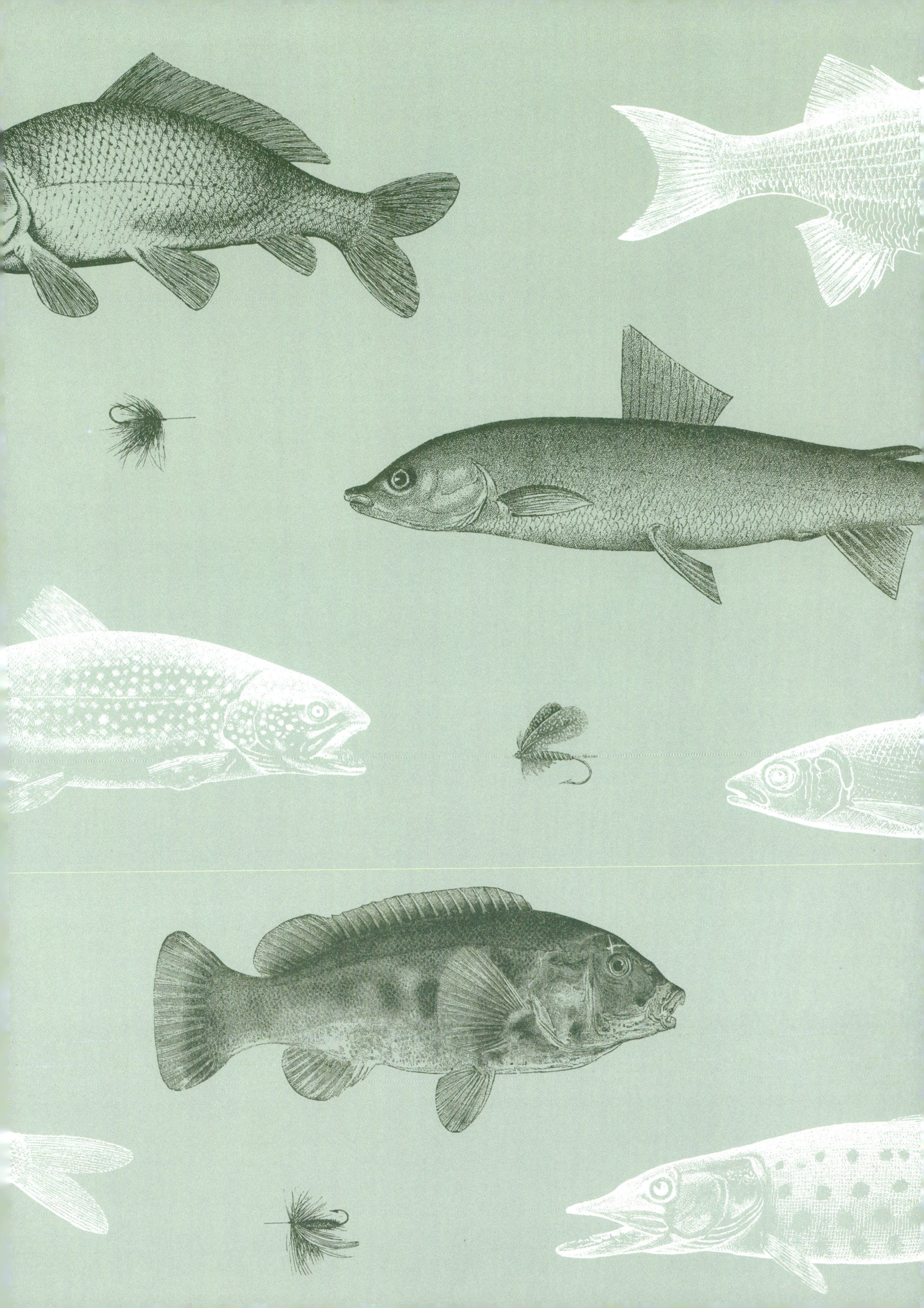

TROUT.

Minnow Tackle.
May Fly.
Moth Fly.
Green Drake.
Red brown Fly.
Pal mer.
J. Scott sculp.

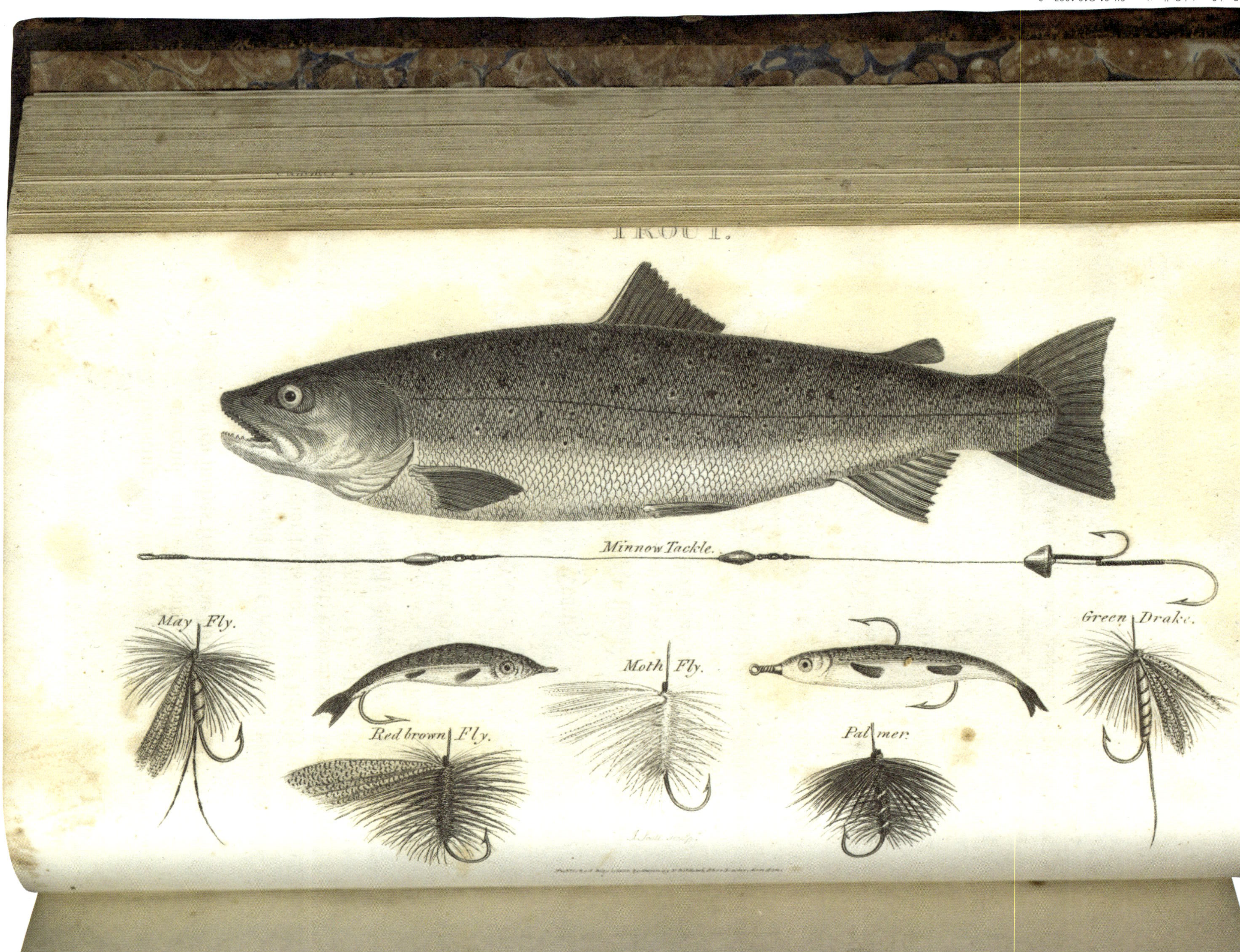

WORKS CITED

Badham, Richard. *Prose Halieutics or Ancient and Modern Fish Tattle.* London: John W. Parker and Son, 1854.

Connett, Eugene V., III. "Some Random Notes on the Derrydale Press." *The Princeton University Chronicle.* XVIII.1 (Autumn 1956): 11-14. Princeton University Library. 6 February 2018. libweb5.princeton.edu/visual_materials/pulc/pulc_v_18_n_1.pdf.

The Ford Historical Society. *Thomas Chubb's Fish Rod Factory.* 5 February 2018. www.thetfordhistoricalsociety.org/Chubb.html.

Gingrich, Arnold. *The Fishing in Print.* New York: Winchester Press, 1974.

Haig-Brown, Roderick. *On Making a Library.* Vancouver: Black Stone Press, 2004.

Hills, John Waller. *A Summer on the Test.* London: Philip Allan & Co., [1924].

Kaufman, William. "The Lore and Lure of Trout Fishing." Review of *Trout* by Ernest Schwiebert. *Washington Post.* 4 February 1979. 5 February 2018. www.washingtonpost.com/archive/entertainment/books/1979/02/04/the-lore-and-lure-of-trout-fishing/ab5ad992-dfe8-4014-b77b-dd12e4a42bf5/?utm_term=.ba7fec7b0c84.

Keeling, Arn. "'A Dynamic, Not a Static Conception': The Conservation Thought of Roderick Haig-Brown." *Pacific Historical Review.* 71.2 (May 2002): 239-268. 1 March 2018. DOI: 10.1525/phr.2002.71.2.239.

Lawson, Carol. "He Fishes. She Paints. The Twain Meet." *New York Times.* 1 January 1997. 7 February 2018. www.nytimes.com/1997/01/01/garden/he-fishes-she-paints-the-twain-meet.html.

Ledlie, David B. "Dean Sage Part II – The First Trip." *The American Fly Fisher.* 3.2 (Spring 1976): 16-19. 6 February 2018. amff.wpengine.com/wp-content/uploads/2016/01/1976-Vol03-No2web.pdf.

Ledlie, David B. "Dean Sage Part IV – The Ristigouche and Its Salmon Fishing and The Angling Library of Dean Sage." *The American Fly Fisher.* 4.1 (Winter 1977): 25-28. 6 February 2018. http://amff.wpengine.com/wp-content/uploads/2016/01/1977-Vol04-No1web.pdf).

Lothian, W.F. *A Brief History of Canada's National Parks.* N.p.: Minister of the Environment Minister and Minister of Supply and Services Canada, 1987.

Marston, R.B. *Walton and Some Earlier Writers on Fish and Fishing.* London: Elliot Stock, 1894.

Martin, Darrell. *The Fly-Fisher's Craft: The Art and History.* New York: Skyhorse Publishing, 2016.

Schurr, Ruth. "Izaak Walton's complete Compleat Angler." *The Times Literary Supplement.* 26 Feb 2014. 9 February 2018. www.the-tls.co.uk/articles/public/izaak-waltons-complete-compleat-angler/.

Schwantes, Carlos A. "Tourists in Wonderland: Early Railroad Tourism in the Pacific Northwest." *Columbia Magazine.* 7.4 (Winter 1993-94). 2 February 2018. www.washingtonhistory.org/files/library/tourists-in-wonderland.pdf.

Westwood, Thomas. *The Chronicle of The "Compleat Angler" of Izaak Walton and Charles Cotton. Being a Bibliographical Record of Its Various Phases and Mutations. A New Edition with Some Notes and Additions by Thomas Satchell.* London: W Satchell, 1883.

Westwood, Thomas. *The Chronicle of The 'Compleat Angler' of Izaak Walton and Charles Cotton. Being a Bibliographical Record of Its Various Phases and Mutations.* London: Willis and Sotheran, 1864.

Westwood, Thomas, et al. *Bibliotheca Piscatoria. A Catalogue of Books on Angling, the Fisheries and Fish Culture, by T. Westwood & T. Satchell. 1883. And the Supplement to Bibliotheca Piscatoria by R. B. Marston 1901.* Mansfield Centre, CT: Martino Publishing, n.d.

Wetzel, Charles. *American Fishing Books. A Bibliography from the Earlier Times up to 1948 Together with a History of Angling and Angling Literature in America. 1950.* Mansfield Centre, CT: Martino Publishing, n.d.

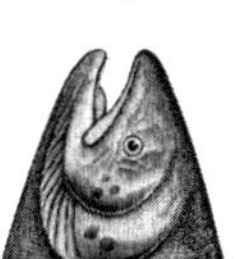

ABOUT THE AUTHOR

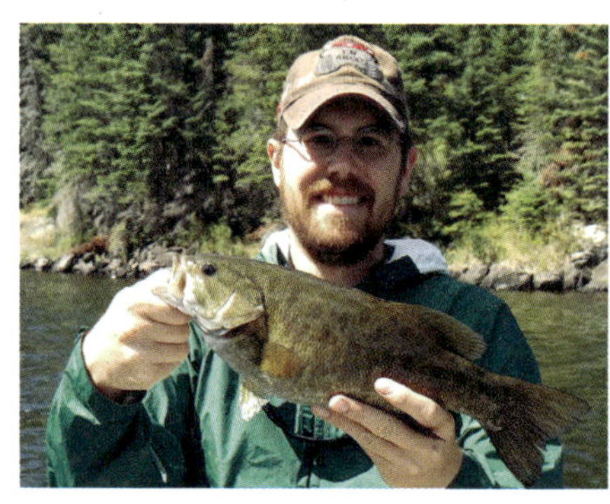

JUSTIN HANISCH is a biologist with the Government of Alberta and an avid collector of antiquarian books on the natural and social history of fish. Born in Michigan and naturalized in Canada, Justin received his MSc and PhD in aquatic ecology at the University of Alberta. In 2011, Justin won the second National Book Collecting Contest for Canadians under the age of 30 and was subsequently invited by the Peel library to curate an online exhibition of his collection. Justin's passions are split between science and books; his passion for books lead him to a brief "sabbatical" from his PhD to work as a cataloguer at a well-known antiquarian bookstore in Calgary. Outside of the office, Justin enjoys fishing, backcountry adventures with his partner Brianne and cockapoo Aurora, and scouring sources for old books on fish.

ABOUT THE COLLECTOR

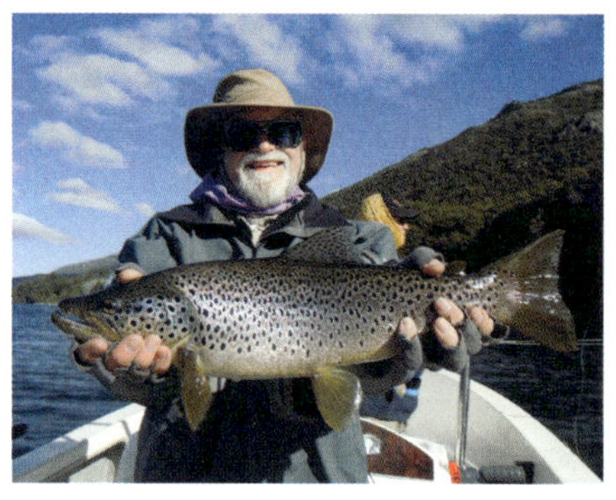

BRUCE DANCIK is an avid fly fisher and outdoorsman. He spent most of his career at the University of Alberta where he taught woody plants and tree improvement courses, supervised over 50 graduate students and post-doctoral fellows, and conducted research in forest genetics and ecology. He published nearly 100 papers in the fields of genecology, forest genetics, and ecology and is known for his expertise in scientific publishing. For 26 years he was the Editor-in-Chief of Canadian Science Publishing, the largest scientific publisher in Canada. A Fellow of the Royal Society of Canada, he still enjoys reading science-related papers as well as angling literature, which he has collected for over 60 years. He is happiest when fishing or surrounded by the books he loves, and he can often be found in the natural history or angling section of both new and used bookstores or fishing in western Canada for cutthroat, brown, and rainbow trout; the Upsalquitch in New Brunswick for Atlantic salmon; or northern Patagonia for brown, rainbow, and brook trout. His passions include photography, music, fly fishing, reading widely, and trekking about and observing the natural world around him.

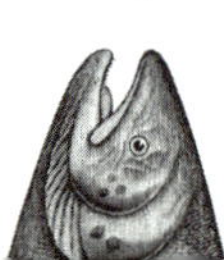

ABOUT THE BRUCE P. DANCIK COLLECTION OF ANGLING BOOKS

THE BRUCE P. DANCIK COLLECTION OF ANGLING BOOKS consists of more than 3,000 volumes and an equal number of ephemeral publications. Rare and limited edition books in the Dancik Collection are housed in Bruce Peel Special Collections, while less valuable books are dispersed among other University of Alberta Libraries. Many books held in the Peel library are titles of extreme rarity, often illustrated with woodcuts, copper or steel engravings, chromolithographs, and photoengravings.

Beyond documenting the history and practice of angling, the collection is a significant research resource for freshwater biologists, limnologists, and ichthyologists, and for the study of ecology and wildlife resource management. The Dancik Collection was donated to the library over a period of several years by Bruce Dancik, and some further book acquisitions were made possible with funds generously contributed by Brenda Laishley and other donors.

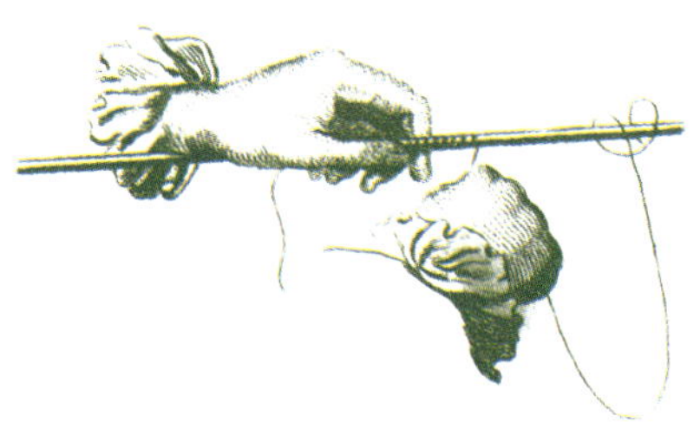

About the Angling Ephemera

IN ADDITION to the thousands of angling books that he has donated to the Peel library over the years, Bruce Dancik also donated a wide range of fishing-related ephemera in 2015. This donation features materials in a wide range of formats, including brochures, maps, photographs, photo albums, magazine clippings, catalogues, typed speeches, menus, and anglers' association membership books. Of particular interest is a charming photo album containing six original silver prints from 1935 gifted by J. Hughes-Parry, a British journalist and the author of *Fishing Fantasy: A Salmon Fisherman's Notebook* (1949), to his friend Charles V. Hancock, Literary Editor of *Birmingham Post*. Items in this collection were produced in North America, the United Kingdom, or Australia. Most of the material is from the mid-twentieth century, but can be dated as early as 1909 and as late as 2000. Researchers can use the digital finding aid that is available through the Peel library's website (https://bpsc.library.ualberta.ca/) to navigate the collection and request access to particular items.

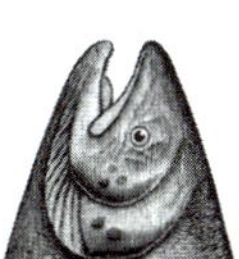

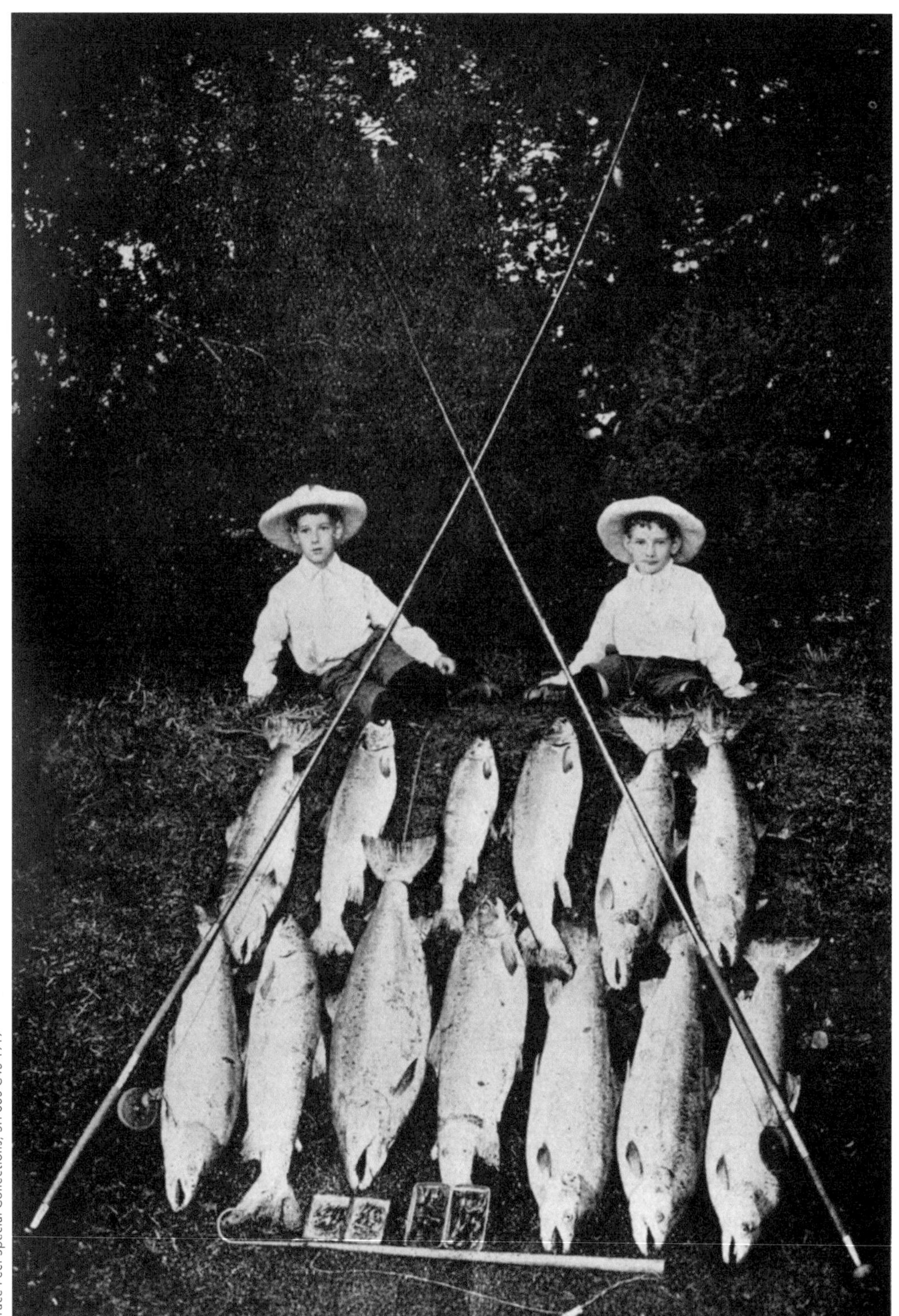

ACKNOWLEDGEMENTS

THANK YOU to Robert Desmarais for inviting me to curate this exhibition and write this catalogue. I feel humbled and privileged by the opportunity, and Robert's encouragement and enthusiasm have made working with the Peel library a true pleasure. Thanks, also, to Bruce Dancik for sharing his collection and his passion for books and angling. Both Bruce and his partner Brenda Laishley generously invited me into their beautiful home to talk books and fishing, and it is a true pleasure to discuss a book collection with its collector. Cheryl Cundell's keen eye has improved this catalogue greatly, and I am fortunate to have her as an editor for the text. Linda Quirk, Jeff Papineau, Kevin Zak, and the staff of the Peel library helped me to make the most of each research visit to the library. Kevin Zak provided his considerable talents in taking the photographs for this catalogue and in designing the exhibition itself. Lara Minja's layout and design work for the exhibition catalogue exceeded all my expectations. Jeff Papineau provided digital scans and Michaela Stang provided bibliographic descriptions of each of the items. I owe an immense thank you to my parents, Mark and Sheila Hanisch, and my brother, Brandon Hanisch, for encouraging my love of books and collecting at an early age. And finally thank you to Brianne Lunn for supporting my bibliomania and work on this exhibition and catalogue.

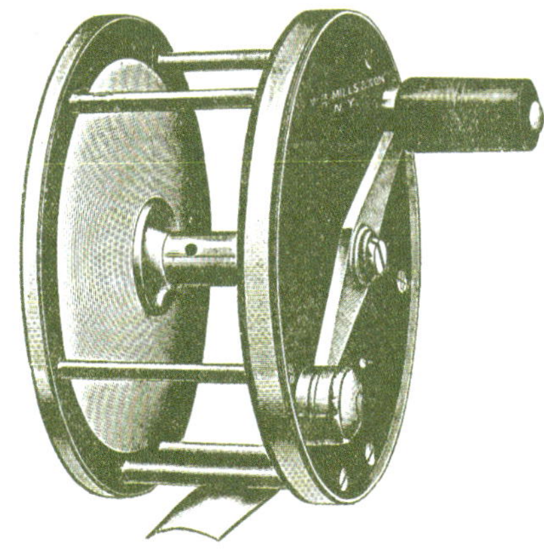

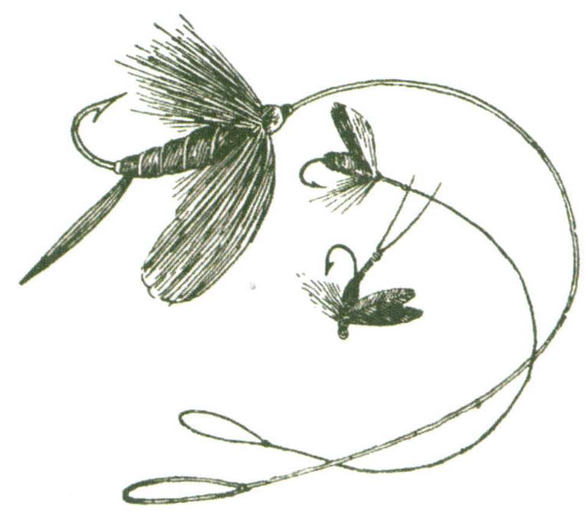

THIS CATALOGUE WAS PRINTED in a hardcover edition of 400 copies with a special limited edition of 25 copies, each one of which contains a fly that was hand tied by Bruce P. Dancik. Copies of the special edition are signed and numbered, and they are available for sale exclusively through Bruce Peel Special Collections.

The jacket and cover illustration is a reproduction of a colour lithograph picturing an October Grayling that Thomas Even Pritt created for his *The Book of the Grayling: Being a Description of the Fish, and the Art of Angling for Him: As Practised Chiefly in the Midlands and the North of England* (1888), published by Goodall and Suddick of Leeds (item 20 in the exhibition, call number SH 691 G7 P75 1888). The call number associated with the image facing the table of contents is SH 461 J7 1902 V.1.

The main body text is set in Adobe Caslon Pro regular, italic, and small caps, with titles, subtitles, and headers set in Lulo.

Printed on 80 lb Rolland Opaque White text by Friesen's in Altona, Manitoba.

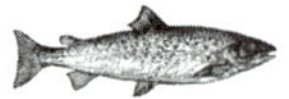